BANKING LAW

WALLACE AND McNEIL'S
BANKING LAW

TENTH EDITION

by
DONALD B. CASKIE, M.A., LL.B., W.S., A.I.B.(Scot)

Solicitor,
Partner, W. & J. Burness, W.S., Edinburgh,
formerly Law Secretary, Clydesdale Bank PLC

W. GREEN/Sweet & Maxwell
Law Publishers
EDINBURGH
1991

FIRST EDITION 1894
SECOND EDITION 1899
THIRD EDITION 1906
FOURTH EDITION 1913
FIFTH EDITION 1923
SIXTH EDITION 1927
SEVENTH EDITION 1933
EIGHTH EDITION 1949
   ,,   ,, ... REPRINTED 1950
NINTH EDITION 1986
TENTH EDITION 1991

ISBN 0 414 00967 3

Printed in Great Britain

PREFACE TO TENTH EDITION

The first edition of Wallace and McNeil's *Banking Law* was published in 1894. Now, almost one hundred years later, a tenth edition is being published. Although the gap between this edition and the ninth is much shorter than between the ninth and eighth editions (which was thirty-seven years) there have nevertheless been a number of important developments in banking law which have made a new edition desirable. There is a new Banking Act; the Financial Services Act 1986 has impacted on the banks and their customers; there has been further legislation in the area of company law; the Office of the Banking Ombudsman has come into existence; and the banks have had to take steps to deal with the problems of drug-trafficking and money-laundering. In Scotland legislation has dealt with diligence against earnings, civil evidence and charities, to take three examples. There have been several important cases concerning receivership, retention of title and companies, as well as a number of others which have clarified other aspects of banking law. This new edition has also provided the opportunity to cite as references the Acts which consolidated the changes to companies and insolvency legislation which appeared in the last edition.

In preparing this edition I am grateful to my former colleagues in the Clydesdale Bank who have kept me informed about changes in banking practice which I might otherwise have overlooked since my return to private practice. They are not however responsible for any errors or omissions. Responsibility for these is mine alone.

I have endeavoured to state the law as at 31 January 1991, on the assumption that all of the relevant sections of the Companies Act 1989 are in force.

D.B.C.

May 1991.

CONTENTS

TABLE OF CASES

TABLE OF STATUTES

SUBORDINATE LEGISLATION

PART I

THE GENERAL RELATIONSHIP BETWEEN A BANK AND ITS CUSTOMER

"Banks are not charitable institutions. . ." *National Westminster Bank plc* v. *Morgan* [1983] 3 All E.R. 85 at p. 91, *per* Dunn L.J.

CHAPTER 1

BANKER AND CUSTOMER

Banking in Scotland has no legal history prior to 1695. In that year, an Act of the Scots Parliament incorporated the Bank of Scotland as a joint stock bank with the exclusive privilege of banking for twenty-one years. By 1845, there were eighteen Scottish banks issuing notes but as a result of failures and amalgamations there were only three such banks in existence when the Banking Act was passed in 1979. This Act has since been largely repealed and replaced by the Banking Act 1987. Although this Act now regulates banks and banking business the answer to the question "What is a bank?" is still significant because the terms "bank", "banker" and "banking business" appear in a number of statutes without being adequately defined.[1] In law what constitutes the business of banking was confirmed in *United Dominions Trust Ltd.* v. *Kirkwood*.[2] In this case the characteristics of banking were described as the conduct of current and deposit accounts and the payment and collection of cheques for customers.[3]

Banking Act 1987

The Act sets out the legal basis for the Bank of England's supervision and regulation of the United Kingdom banking system. One important effect of the Act is to eliminate the distinction under previous legislation between recognised banks and licensed deposit-taking institutions. Both become "authorised institutions" subject to a single set of rules and regulations. Section 8 provides that any institution making an application for authorisation shall accompany its application with a statement setting out the nature and scale of the deposit-taking business which the applicant intends to carry out, any plans for the future development of that business and particulars of the applicant's arrangements for the management of the business. The Bank may only grant an application if it is satisfied that the criteria specified in Schedule 3 to the Act are fulfilled with respect to the applicant. The minimum criteria for authorisation set out in the Schedule are that the directors and managers of the institution must be fit and proper persons, that the business be directed by at least two individuals and that in the case of an institution incorporated in the United Kingdom the directors include such number, if any, of directors without executive responsibility for the management of the business as the Bank considers appropriate. The institution must conduct its business

---

[1] The relevant statutes were considered in *United Dominions Trust Ltd.* v. *Kirkwood* [1966] 2 Q.B. 431 at p. 432.

[2] [1966] 2 Q.B. 431.

[3] Only a banker is entitled to the protection of the Bills of Exchange Act 1882 and the Cheques Act 1957.

in a prudent manner and will not be regarded as doing so unless it maintains net assets which together with other financial resources available to it are considered appropriate by the Bank and are of an amount which is commensurate with the nature and scale of the institution's operations and of an amount and nature sufficient to safeguard the interests of its depositors. The business of the institution must be carried on with integrity and the professional skills appropriate to the nature and scale of its activities. At the time when authorisation is granted the institution must have net assets amounting to not less than £1m, "net assets" in relation to a body corporate meaning its paid-up capital and reserves. In terms of section 6 a business is a deposit-taking business for the purposes of the Act if in the course of the business money received by way of deposit is lent to others or any other activity of the business is financed, wholly or to any material extent, out of the capital of or the interest on money received by way of deposit.

The Act gives the Bank power to revoke or restrict an authorisation (sections 11 and 12) and also entitles it by virtue of section 19 to give an institution directions when giving it notice that the Bank proposes to revoke its authorisation. These directions shall be such as appear to the Bank to be desirable in the interests of the institution's depositors. Section 21 gives the Bank power to object to controllers of authorised institutions, a controller being a person who wishes to become a minority, majority or principal shareholder controller or an indirect controller of an authorised institution incorporated in the United Kingdom. As an extension of this power, by virtue of section 24 the Bank is entitled to serve a written notice of objection on someone who is an existing shareholder controller if it appears to the Bank that he is no longer a fit and proper person to be such a controller of an authorised institution. The Act contains corresponding provisions regarding rights of appeal and the Bank's supervisory functions are backed up by penalties.

Section 32 permits the Treasury after consultation with the Bank and the Building Societies Commission to make regulations for regulating the issue, form and content of deposit advertisements, that is, any advertisement containing an invitation to make a deposit or information which is intended to lead directly or indirectly to the making of a deposit. Section 38 provides that an authorised institution shall make a report to the Bank if it has entered into a transaction or transactions relating to any one person as a result of which it is exposed to the risk of incurring losses in excess of 10 per cent of its available capital resources or it proposes to enter into a transaction or transactions relating to any one person which either alone or together with a previous transaction or transactions, would result in its being exposed to the risk of incurring losses in excess of 25 per cent of those resources. The Bank has wide powers of inspection and these are backed up by section 46 which requires an authorised institution to give notice to the Bank if the institution proposes to remove an auditor before the expiration of his term of office or if a person ceases to be an auditor otherwise than in consequence of an ordinary resolution replacing an auditor at the expiration of his term of office with a different auditor. An auditor has himself an obligation to give notice to the Bank of these events, and section 47 provides that no duty to which he may be subject shall be regarded as contravened by reason of his communicating in good faith to the Bank, whether or not in response to a request made by it, any information or opinion on a matter to which section 47 applies and which is relevant to any function of the Bank under the Act. The section applies to any matter of which the auditor becomes aware in his capacity as auditor and which relates to the business or affairs of the institution or any associated body.

Part II of the Act sets out a deposit protection scheme and a Deposit Protection Fund to which all authorised institutions are liable to contribute. Compensation payments to depositors may be made out of the Fund by virtue of section 58 to each depositor who has a protected deposit with that institution in an amount equal to three-quarters of this protected deposit. Section 60 provides that a depositor's protected deposit is the total liability of the institution to him immediately before the time when it becomes insolvent, limited to a maximum of £20,000 in respect of the principal amounts of and accrued interest on sterling deposits made with United Kingdom offices of the institution.

Part III deals with banking names and descriptions. By virtue of section 67 no person carrying on any business in the United Kingdom shall use any name which indicates or may be understood to indicate that he is a bank or banker or is carrying on a banking business unless he is an authorised institution to which the section applies. Authorised institutions covered by this section are companies incorporated in the United Kingdom which have an issued share capital in respect of which the amount paid up is not less than £5m or undistributable reserves of not less than that sum or such undistributed reserves of an amount which together with the amount paid up in respect of this issued share capital equals not less than £5m. The National Savings Bank is exempted from section 67, as are the Bank itself and a number of other central and investment banks.

Girobank

The Post Office has powers to provide banking services arising from section 7(1)(b) of the Post Office Act 1969 (as substituted by s. 58(1) of the British Telecommunications Act 1981). Between 3 October 1985 and 2 July 1990 it did so through a wholly-owned subsidiary, Girobank plc. Girobank plc was granted recognition as a bank for the purposes of the Banking Act 1979 and is now authorised under the Banking Act 1987. On 2 July 1990 the Post Office sold its shares in Girobank plc to the Alliance & Leicester Building Society. Girobank plc is thus at present in the unique position of being both authorised under the Banking Act 1987 and, as a subsidiary of a building society, subject to constraints under the Building Societies Act 1986. Girobank services continue to be available at post offices. Girobank offers a wide range of banking services to personal customers, clubs and societies, sole traders, partnerships, companies, local and public authorities and Government Departments. As a building society subsidiary it cannot lend to any customer unsecured on land an amount greater than that prescribed under building societies legislation (£10,000 at present). However, it has arrangements with a number of financial institutions for the provision of lending facilities to its corporate customers. Deposits to an account can be made either at a post office or sent by post to the Girobank Centre, depending on the nature of the item being deposited. Girobank cheques are regarded as cheques in law and can be cashed at post offices subject to restrictions on the frequency and amount of encashments. The terms and conditions under which accounts are conducted are contained in services booklets which can be obtained from Girobank plc, Bootle, Merseyside, GIR OAA. Girobank accounts will be treated as arrested in Scotland when the arrestment is served at its office in Scotland.

National Savings Bank

Various enactments relating to the National Savings Bank were consolidated in the National Savings Bank Act 1971. The National Savings Bank Regulations 1972 made under section 2(1) of the Act regulate its accounts.[4] A deposit with the National Savings Bank may be made either as an ordinary deposit or as an investment deposit (s. 3(1)). Ordinary accounts may be opened by anyone aged 7 or over (Regs. 5(1) and (20)). For a child under 7, a relative or friend may open the account but normally no withdrawals may be made until the child reaches the age of 7 and can authorise them personally (Regs. 6 and 25). Accounts may also be opened by two or more persons jointly and one or more persons in trust for another person but clubs, associations and similar organisations may no longer open new accounts (Regs 8 to 12). The limit for deposits in an ordinary account is fixed from time to time but societies and other organisations which handle large funds may apply for authority to exceed the limit. Investment accounts may be opened in the same way as ordinary accounts and the maximum balance that may be kept in an investment account is again fixed from time to time. Interest on deposits may be credited to accounts in excess of the limit.

The manner and frequency of withdrawals depends on the type of account and the amount being withdrawn. The first £70 of interest on an ordinary account in the name of an individual is exempt from United Kingdom income tax at all rates. This concession applies to both husband and wife, *i.e.* up to £140 on a joint account or up to £70 each on individual accounts. Interest on investment accounts is taxable but tax is not deducted at source. Money payable by the Crown to any person on account of a deposit in the National Savings Bank can now be arrested.[5]

---

[4] S.I. 1972 No. 764 (as amended).

[5] Crown Proceedings Act 1947, s. 46 as amended by the Law Reform (Misc. Prov.) (Scotland) Act 1985, s. 49. In England, such a deposit may be attached by a judgment creditor. See *Brooks Associates Inc.* v. *Basu* [1983] 2 W.L.R. 141.

On the death of a depositor, up to £5,000 may currently be repaid without the necessity for a confirmation to be produced.[6]

The customer

Although the law of banking, strictly speaking, deals with the relationship between banker and customer Scots law has not attempted to define a customer. If banking other than for the purpose of authorisation under the Banking Act 1987 is described as the conduct of current and deposit accounts and the payment and collection of cheques for customers[7] then an important criterion for defining a customer must be that there exists an account with a bank through which transactions are passed. Accordingly, it has been held that a person was not a customer of a bank although the bank had for some years been in the habit of paying him cash for cheques and subsequently collecting the amounts.[8] But the relationship would now seem to begin as soon as an account is opened and the first cheque is paid in and accepted by the banker for collection.[9] It has also been held that the relationship of banker and customer existed between the parties even before the account was opened from the time when the bank accepted instructions to collect money from a building society, where there was the likelihood that an account would be opened by the bank for the person who had given the instructions, as in fact it was shortly afterwards.[10]

---

[6] National Savings Bank (Amendment) (No. 2) Regulations 1984 (S.I. 1984 No. 602).
[7] *United Dominions Trust Ltd.* v. *Kirkwood* [1966] 2 Q.B. 431.
[8] *Great Western Ry.* v. *London and County Banking Co. Ltd.* [1901] A.C. 414; see also *Matthews* v. *Brown & Co.* (1894) 10 T.L.R. 386.
[9] *Commissioners of Taxation* v. *English, Scottish and Australian Bank* [1920] A.C. 683.
[10] *Woods* v. *Martins Bank Ltd.* [1959] 1 Q.B. 55.

CHAPTER 2

CONTRACT BETWEEN BANKER AND CUSTOMER

General terms

A banker is under no legal obligation to open an account with any member of the public who applies to him and he is at liberty to choose the persons with whom he does business. In opening an account, a banker is not normally under an obligation to inquire into the commercial propriety of the business for which the account has been opened and he does not expose himself to a charge of dishonesty because, for example, he provides the banking facilities to a business which is being conducted in breach of fiduciary duties owed by employees to employers.[1] Banks and other financial institutions have however been issued with Guidance Notes (whose application has the support of the Bank of England) to prevent "money laundering", a phrase covering all procedures to change the identity of illegally obtained money so that it appears to have originated from a legitimate source. These call for banks to establish satisfactorily the identity of their customer at the time when the relationship is established. In the absence of an introduction from a known and respected source, positive identification should be obtained from documents such as a "full" passport, Armed Forces identity card, signed known employer identity card bearing a photograph and signature or full U.K. driving licence. Other, easily obtainable, identification documents should not be accepted as the sole means of identification. The prospective customer's name and permanent address should be verified by referring to the Voters' Roll, the local telephone directory, a credit reference agency or requesting sight of a recent utility or community charge bill. If necessary a bank should approach another financial institution to verify identity and that institution should respond positively. Particular care should be taken when dealing with accounts opened by post. In the case of corporate customers, the usual documents should be obtained and in the event of doubt, a search made at Companies House.

The relationship between banker and customer, once the account has been opened, is one of contract. For ordinary current account operations, the contract is rarely written[2] but invariably the customer is asked to sign an opening account or mandate form which contains a request for the opening of an account and an instruction to the banker to honour to the debit of that account all cheques or orders signed by the customer or

---

[1] *Sybron Corpn.* v. *Barclays Bank PLC* [1984] 3 W.L.R. 1055.
[2] A Code of Practice in the process of being drafted by the banks is expected to set out the principal terms and conditions of the contract.

on his behalf. For the most part, the other terms of the contract are implied but expression has been given to them in a number of judgments.

For many years the relationship was defined as one of debtor and creditor with the added obligation on the part of the banker to honour his customer's cheques provided there were sufficient funds available to meet them.[3] There is no fiduciary relationship between a banker and a customer in respect of money paid into a bank. In the leading case of *Joachimson* v. *Swiss Bank Corporation*[4] the relationship was described as follows:

> "The bank undertakes to receive money and to collect bills for its customer's account. The proceeds so received are not to be held in trust for the customer, but the bank borrows the proceeds and undertakes to repay them. The promise to repay is to repay at the branch of the bank where the account is kept and during banking hours. It includes a promise to repay any part of the amount due, against the written order of the customer addressed to the bank at the branch, and as such written orders may be outstanding in the ordinary course of business for two or three days, it is a term of the contract that the bank will not cease to do business with the customer except upon reasonable notice. The customer on his part undertakes to exercise reasonable care in executing his written orders so as not to mislead the bank or to facilitate forgery. I think it is necessarily a term of such contract that the bank is not liable to pay the customer the full amount of his balance until he demands payment from the bank at the branch at which the current account is kept. Whether he must demand it in writing it is not necessary now to determine."

The customer accordingly has the right to repayment of the money which he has deposited with the banker. If the funds are held on current account he is entitled to payment on demand. Where the money is lodged on deposit receipt or in a savings account, the banker's obligation is to return to the customer an equivalent sum of money on demand, with the appropriate interest. If the funds are held in any other type of account the money is repayable on a fixed date or on notice. Repayment can only be demanded by the customer at the branch of the bank where the account is kept and not at any other branch[5] and he is only entitled to demand repayment during normal banking hours.[6] Derived from the right to repayment on demand is the right of the customer to draw cheques up to the amount of the funds standing to his credit on current account or the limit of an agreed overdraft, since a cheque is in essence simply a written order from a customer to his banker to pay money on demand. The banker's obligation to repay a sum standing at the credit of a customer on

---

[3] *Foley* v. *Hill* (1848) 2 H.L.Cas. 28.
[4] [1921] 3 K.B. 110 at p. 127.
[5] *Clare & Co.* v. *Dresdner Bank* [1915] 2 K.B. 576; *Bank of Scotland* v. *Seitz*, 1990 S.L.T. 584.
[6] *Baines* v. *National Provincial Bank* (1927) 96 L.K.J.B. 801.

current account is extinguished by the long negative prescriptive period of 20 years unless a relevant claim has been made or the existence of the obligation has been relevantly acknowledged by him during that period.[7]

Banking hours

In the matter of when he opens for business the banker owes a duty to his customers and not to the general public. He may close his doors when he chooses but failure to give notice to his customers if he has led them to believe that he will be open for business will be regarded as a breach of his contract with them. Bank holidays in Scotland are now regulated by the Banking and Financial Dealings Act 1971. Section 1(1) provides that the days listed in Schedule 1 to the Act shall be bank holidays in Scotland. Subsection (3) also provides that by Royal Proclamation any day may be declared to be a bank holiday either locally or nationally. It is now customary for Boxing Day and the last Monday in May to be bank holidays in Scotland in addition to those specified in Schedule 1. The combined effect of the provisions of the Act is to provide for two bank holidays at Christmas and two at New Year, so arranged that none of them falls on a Saturday or Sunday, with in addition Good Friday, the first Monday in May, the last Monday in May and the first Monday in August. Section 1(4) provides that no person shall be compellable to make any payment or to do any act on a bank holiday which he would not be compellable to make or do on Christmas Day or Good Friday and where apart from this subsection he would be compellable on a bank holiday, he will be deemed to have complied with his obligation if he makes the payment or does the act on the next day on which he is compellable. Section 3 made Saturday a non-business day for the purposes of section 92 of the Bills of Exchange Act 1882 and abolished days of grace as provided for in section 14(1) of that Act. The Treasury is also given powers by statutory instrument laid before Parliament to suspend financial dealings if it is in the national interest and to declare a day to be a non-business day for the purpose of enactments relating to bills of exchange and promissory notes. The order may direct that no person carrying on the business of a banker shall in the course of that business effect any transaction of such a kind as may be specified in the order (s. 2).

Similarly, in the matter of banking hours the duty owed by the banker is to his customers and not to the public. The significance of the hours during which he opens for business lies in the rights of his customers in relation to cheques which they have issued and the right of bankers to protection under the Bills of Exchange Act 1882 and the Cheques Act 1957. Payment of cheques outwith business hours is not in the ordinary course of business and can put the banker at risk. Failure to observe the rule that payment of a cheque should be made during the bank's advertised hours for conducting business or within a reasonable business

---

[7] Prescription and Limitation (Scotland) Act 1973, s. 7. *Cf. Macdonald* v. *North of Scotland Bank*, 1942 S.C. 369.

margin of the advertised time for closing might enable a customer to establish that he had been deprived of the opportunity to countermand payment of a cheque.[8]

Banker's duty to his customer's cheques

As previously stated, a banker is bound to honour his customer's cheque if presented to him during banking hours and he has funds belonging to his customer sufficient to meet it. Wrongful dishonour of a cheque is a breach of contract and the customer is entitled to damages; but these will be nominal unless the customer is in business and his credit has been damaged[9] or he can prove actual loss.[10] He will not be liable in damages to the payee, to whom he has no obligation. A banker is not entitled to retain the money of his customer against a claim in respect of which there is no more than a presumption of liability and to dishonour his customer's cheque in consequence.[11] A banker who has been in the habit of taking up his customer's bills and permitting his customer to overdraw on his current account without making reference to the advances made to meet these bills, is not entitled without express notice to his customer, suddenly to debit the current account with such advances if the result is to exhaust the funds standing to his customer's credit and to lead to the dishonour of the customer's cheques.[12] No action will lie against the banker, however, for dishonouring cheques where his customer's funds have been exhausted by the payment of bills accepted by the customer and made payable at the bank, as the acceptance of such bills is sufficient authority to the banker to pay the amounts due under them.[13]

The name or heading of an account opened in a customer's name is sufficient notice to the banker of the nature of the account. An account opened in the name of "A B, executor of C D" is notice to the bank that any money lodged by A B for the credit of that account is not his unrestricted property and falls to be distinguished, and treated differently, from any moneys lodged either in his individual name or, for example, as "trustee of E F". Where however an account is opened and instructions given that money is to be drawn out in a certain way and payments are made in that way, the banker is free from further claims in respect of that money, no matter under what heading the account may have been opened.[14] In order to justify a banker refusing to meet the demand of a customer occupying a fiduciary position and drawing a cheque in that capacity, there must be some misapplication or other form

---

[8] *Baines* v. *National Provincial Bank* (1927) 96 L.K.J.B. 801.

[9] *King* v. *British Linen Co.* (1899) 1 F. 928.

[10] *Gibbons* v. *Westminster Bank* [1939] 2 K.B. 882.

[11] *Paul & Thain* v. *Royal Bank of Scotland* (1869) 7 M. 361; *Ireland* v. *North of Scotland Banking Co.* (1880) 8 R. 215; *King* v. *British Linen Co.* (1899) 1 F. 928. See also *Kirkwood* v. *Clydesdale Bank*, 1908 S.C. 20 at p. 25.

[12] *Cumming* v. *Shand* (1860) 29 L.J. Ex. 129; *Garnett* v. *McKewan* (1872) L.R. 8 Ex. 10.

[13] *Kymer* v. *Laurie* (1849) 18 L.J.Q.B. 218.

[14] *Struthers Patent Diamond Rock Pulverising Co.* v. *Clydesdale Bank* (1886) 13 R. 434.

of breach of trust intended by the customer and proof that the banker is aware of such intention. If it can be shown that the banker is to derive personal advantage from the transaction, that circumstance, above all others, will most readily support an allegation that he was a party to the breach of trust. A banker may not, therefore, honour a cheque which to his knowledge or reasonable belief is drawn in breach of trust and for his benefit, as for example, where an executor draws a cheque on an executry account in payment of a debt due by himself to the bank.[15] If however a cheque so drawn is not for the banker's own benefit, he is not bound to inquire whether the cheque has been drawn in breach of trust or not and he will be discharged by the signature of the party who lodged the money.[16]

An overdraft constitutes the lending of money and a banker is not obliged to let his customer overdraw his account unless he has agreed to do so or such an agreement can be inferred from the course of business between them.[17] If the banker has funds belonging to his customer but insufficient in amount to meet a cheque drawn on the account, presentation of the cheque operates in Scotland, but not in England, as an assignation of the funds available in the hands of the banker to meet it.[18] In such cases the practice is to return the cheque with a marking "Insufficient funds" and to place the amount standing at the credit of the customer in a separate account bearing reference to the cheque. If the presenter of the cheque offers to deliver it up with a receipt endorsed on the back for the sum which has been attached, he is entitled to payment of this sum. When several cheques come in through the same clearing or by the same post and there are insufficient funds to meet them all, the banker in Scotland cannot select from the cheques sufficient to exhaust the creditor balance and return the others. He must return all the cheques marked "Refer to drawer" and place the whole creditor balance in a separate account bearing reference to these particular cheques.

Overdrafts

If a banker has permitted his customer to overdraw his account with or without security, his having done so in the past does not preclude his refusing to continue to do so in the future. The banker may, without assigning any reason, intimate that he is not willing to allow any further overdrafts on the account and may call upon the customer and his sureties, if any, to make immediate provision for the liquidation of the

---

[15] *Gray* v. *Johnston* (1868) L.R. 3 E. & I. App.Cas. 1.

[16] *Ireland* v. *North of Scotland Banking Co.* (1880) 8 R. 215; *Struthers Patent Diamond Rock Pulverising Co.* v. *Clydesdale Bank* (1886) 13 R. 434. See also *Lipkin Gorman* v. *Karpnale Ltd., The Times*, November 19, 1988.

[17] *Brooks & Co.* v. *Blackburn Benefit Society* (1884) 9 App.Cas 857 at p. 864; *Cumming* v. *Shand* (1860) 5 H. & N. 95.

[18] *British Linen Co.* v. *Carruthers* (1883) 10 R. 923; Bills of Exchange Act 1882, s. 53(2). If payment has been countermanded the banker is treated as having no funds available for payment: 1882 Act, s. 75A.

debt.[19] An overdraft is repayable on demand and the forms of security documents are drawn accordingly. If a demand is made, it does not mean that the customer is bound to pay the money in the very next instant of time. He must be given a reasonable time to implement the mechanics of payment by, for example, delivering a cheque by return or transferring the funds from one bank account to another, but he is not entitled to time to raise the money if it is not at hand.[20] Where a customer has been allowed to overdraw against security, the banker is under no obligation to continue facilities until the security is exhausted, and where no special period has been stipulated for he may at any time refuse to cash his customer's cheques and call for repayment. This rule is, however, modified to the extent that the banker must not act so as unduly to prejudice his customer and if the customer has in the past been allowed to overdraw his account the banker is liable in damages if in similar circumstances with the same customer without reasonable notice[21] he dishonours a cheque drawn in the belief that the facility was available.[22] In *Barnes* v. *Williams and Glyn's Bank Ltd.*[23] the rule was expressed in the following terms:

"There is an obligation upon the bank to honour cheques drawn within the agreed limit of an overdraft facility and presented before any demand for repayment or notice to terminate a facility has been given. That obligation, however, does not by itself require any period of notice beyond the simple demand. The bank may, by the contract, be required to honour cheques drawn within the agreed facility before the demand for repayment or notice to terminate but still be free to require payment by the customer of any sums previously lent, which will be increased by any further cheques which the bank must honour."

The drawing of a cheque or the accepting of a bill payable at the bank, when the drawer knows that he has not provided funds in his account to meet it, may be taken as a request for an overdraft. By section 74(1) of the Consumer Credit Act 1974 (as amended) an agreement to allow a debtor to overdraw a current account is currently exempt from Part V of the Act. Joint drawers of a cheque are, in the absence of an arrangement to the contrary, only liable *pro rata* for the amount at the debit of the joint account[24] but to obviate any question as regards liability it is the general practice of banks to take from all parties to a joint account a mandate instructing operations and defining the liability for overdrafts as joint and

---

[19] *Johnston* v. *Commercial Bank of Scotland* (1858) 20 D. 790; *Ritchie* v. *Clydesdale Bank* (1886) 13 R. 866.

[20] *Toms* v. *Wilson* (1863) 4 B. & S. 442 at p. 453; applied in *R.A. Cripps & Son Ltd.* v. *Wickenden* [1973] 2 All E.R. 606; *Bank of Baroda* v. *Panessar* [1986] 3 All E.R. 751.

[21] *Johnston* v. *Commercial Bank of Scotland* (1858) 20 D. 790; *Smith* v. *Hughes* (1871) L.R. 6 Q.B. 597; *Buckingham* v. *London and Midland Bank* (1895) 12 T.L.R. 70.

[22] *Forman* v. *Bank of England* (1902) 18 T.L.R. 339.

[23] (1981) Com.L.R. 205.

[24] *Coats* v. *Union Bank of Scotland*, 1929 S.C. (H.L.) 114.

several. The customer has no right to draw cheques against a deposit account but where a customer draws a cheque on his current account when there are insufficient funds in that account to meet it, the banker may pay it and rely on his right of set-off against the deposit account.

Interest

There is no common law right to charge or recover simple interest on an overdraft but the claim can be supported on the ground of the universal custom of bankers or on the basis of implied agreement or of a course of dealing.[25] Interest is chargeable as from the date of the respective debits to the account, that is, the date of payment in each case and not as from the date of the cheques. Unless on a final settlement of accounts, as for example on the closing of an account, a banker may not without prior notice to his customer debit interest at any time other than his usual date for debiting interest. It is now the practice to debit customers' accounts quarterly at dates corresponding to the particular bank's quarterly and annual balances.

The question of whether the sum debited for interest remains interest throughout the account, for which the obligant under a guarantee would be liable under the clause in the obligation to pay interest on the sums advanced from the date or dates of advance until payment, was considered in *Reddie* v. *Williamson*[26] and the decision has been followed and approved in a series of cases since.[27] In that case the court held that at the half-yearly balances, or otherwise as may be arranged with the customer, the interest accrued during the period is added to the principal sum due whereupon the interest loses its character as such and is in the same position as if a cheque for the amount had been passed on the account by the holder. Although the point was raised in connection with a cash-credit bond, the rule as to the accumulation of interest with principal applies to all current accounts. "The privilege of a banker to balance the account at the end of the year and accumulate the interest with the principal is founded on this plain ground of equity, that the interest should then be paid, and because it is not paid the debtor becomes thenceforth debtor in the amount as a principal sum itself bearing interest."[28] Nevertheless, the bank is not bound to, and indeed should not, accumulate interest with principal on an account after the customer has become insolvent, whether by his estates being sequestrated, by compounding with his creditors or by granting a trust deed for their behoof. In the event of insolvency the bank is entitled (assuming interest has not been applied) to go back to the (quarterly) balance immediately preceding the event and to charge interest from that date.[29] If court action

---

[25] Paget, *Law of Banking* (9th ed.), p. 116.
[26] (1863) 1 M. 228.
[27] *Gilmour* v. *Bank of Scotland* (1880) 7 R. 734; *Commercial Bank of Scotland* v. *Pattison's Trs.* (1891) 18 R. 476.
[28] *Reddie* v. *Williamson* (1863) 1 M. 228 at p. 237.
[29] *Gilmour* v. *Bank of Scotland* (1880) 7 R. 734.

is taken to recover the amount of an overdraft, the court will grant a decree for payment to include the agreed rate of interest rather than the legal rate[30] and cannot refuse to do so *ex proprio motu* on the ground that the rate is penal.[31]

By section 37 of the Pupils Protection Act 1849 every bank in Scotland with which any money has been lodged by any judicial factor, tutor or curator or under authority of any court in Scotland, whether on deposit receipt or current account or otherwise, is required at least once in every year to accumulate the interest with the principal sum so that both thereafter bear interest together as principal. Although the Act does not, in its general scope, embrace any other class of officers of court than those acting for pupils, absent persons and persons under mental incapacity (for whose benefit the legislation was enacted) the section quoted has a more extensive application and seems to apply to all moneys lodged under authority of any court in Scotland or with reference to any proceedings in any court in Scotland.

Banker's duty to his customer's acceptances

In the absence of any special stipulation to the contrary, an agreement on the part of a banker to pay his customer's acceptances when they fall due imports on the one hand an undertaking on the part of the customer to furnish or repay to the banker the funds required to meet such obligations, and on the other hand an undertaking on the part of the banker to apply the money provided by the customer, or advanced on his account, in such a manner as to extinguish the liability created by the customer's acceptances. The duty of identifying the person to whom payment is made with the payee whose name is on the bill devolves upon the banker and if he pays the wrong person, even in good faith and in circumstances which might have misled the customer himself or anyone of ordinary prudence, he cannot take credit for any such payment in a question with his customer since no payment made by him, which leaves the liability of his customer as acceptor undischarged, can be debited to the latter. The only person who can give a valid discharge for such a payment is a holder in due course.

The acceptance by the customer of a bill payable at his bank is equivalent to an order to pay the amount of the bill to the person who can give a valid discharge for it, and the banker is bound to obey if he has funds of his customer in his hands.[32] The customer as acceptor, however, is entitled prior to the maturity of the bill to instruct the banker not to pay it and the banker must obey this instruction. If the bill is duly presented, presentment operates as an intimated assignation of money in the banker's hands available for its payment, and in such circumstances the banker should follow the same procedure as in the case of a cheque which

---

[30] *Bank of Scotland* v. *Davis*, 1980 S.L.T. 2.
[31] *United Dominions Trust Ltd.* v. *McDowell*, 1984 S.L.T. (Sh. Ct.) 10.
[32] *British Linen Co.* v. *Rainey's Trs.* (1885) 12 R. 825; *Robarts* v. *Tucker* (1851) 16 Q.B. 560.

has been returned unpaid through lack of funds.[33] While a banker is protected who pays a cheque in good faith and without negligence upon an indorsement which subsequently turns out to have been forged, he has no such protection in the case of bills unless there are circumstances which prevent the customer from setting up the forgery, such as a direction from him to the banker to pay the bill without reference to the genuineness of the indorsement, or an admission, actual or implied, as to its genuineness. Since a bank has no better means of ascertaining the genuineness of an indorsement in the case of a bill than it has in the case of a cheque, the banker should, in order to avoid the responsibility of deciding the genuineness of an indorsement, require his customer to domicile his bills at the branch where his account is kept and to retire them by cheques drawn upon his account there.[34]

The Bills of Exchange Act 1882, section 75 provides in the case of cheques that the banker's authority to pay them does not cease until notice of the customer's death has actually reached him. No such provision is made in the case of bills, from which it might be inferred that the banker's authority to pay them ceases at the date of the customer's death. If this is so, a banker who has paid a customer's acceptance after death but before notice of the fact has reached him, must look to the representatives of his deceased customer for reimbursement on the ground either (1) that by paying the bill he has become the holder in due course or (2) that he has done so on behalf of the representatives and so made them the holders of the bill. He cannot, however, without the representatives' consent debit the deceased's account with the amount of the acceptance.[35]

Banks as investment advisers

In so far as they provide investment services, banks are regulated by the Financial Services Act 1986. Most banks are members of the Investment Management Regulatory Organisation ("IMRO"). Its Rules, in addition to dealing with such matters as advertising, unsolicited calls, published recommendations and research, regulate the conduct of business by its members. Rule 1 of Chapter III imposes the obligation to "Know your Customer", and a member may not perform any investment service for a customer unless it has taken reasonable steps to ascertain from the customer such facts about his personal and financial circumstances as may be expected to be relevant for the proper performance of the particular investment service. However, this Rule does not apply to a transaction effected with a person who is an execution-only customer or if the service is performed for a person whom the member reasonably believes to be a business investor, an experienced investor or a pro-

---

[33] Bills of Exchange Act 1882, s. 53(2). See p. 12.
[34] See *Robarts* v. *Tucker* (1851) 16 Q.B. 560.
[35] See *Rogerson* v. *Ladbroke* (1882) 1 Bing. 93; *Newell* v. *National Provincial Bank of England* (1876) 1 C.P.D. 496.

fessional investor. An execution-only customer is a customer, who, in relation to a particular transaction, can reasonably be assumed by the employee of the member who deals with him regarding that transaction not to be relying on the member to advise him on, or to exercise any judgment of his about, the merits of or the suitability for him of that transaction. The same Rule obliges the member to ensure that in the course of carrying on any investment business there is in effect a customer agreement which is appropriate to the type of customer the member believes him to be. An execution-only customer is an exception to Rule 1.03, as is a customer whose requirements at the relevant time are limited to transactions in a life policy or units in a unit trust. There are also a number of other exceptions to this Rule. Rule 2 of Chapter IV deals with Best Advice, and in recommending or effecting any transaction a member must have reasonable grounds for believing that the recommendation or transaction is suitable for that customer having regard to the information required under the "Know your Customer" Rules. These Conduct of Business Rules also cover such matters as record keeping and the disclosure of remuneration. In addition, the member must disclose whether or not as advisers on life assurance, personal pensions and/or unit trust products they are representatives of a particular company or independent. This disclosure, along with certain other information, must be included in a Buyer's Guide which the member must give or send to the customer not earlier than six months before the member endeavours to have a person enter into an agreement relating to such investments.

Rule 12 of the General Rules deals with company representatives, *i.e.* employees of members, and imposes on the member the obligation to establish and maintain procedures for ensuring that each company representative does not procure or endeavour to procure a person to enter into an investment transaction if the company representative is not competent to advise on that transaction or to assess its suitability for investors. In addition, the member must ensure that each company representative complies with the requirements of Rule 16 of Chapter IV which deals with the conduct of company representatives in the area of personal visits and conversations. A record must be maintained of the names of the company representatives of the member in accordance with Chapter VI of the Rules. Rule 7.01 of this Chapter calls for the record to indicate (a) the categories of transactions which the person named is competent to advise on, and to assess the suitability of, for customers; and (b) the nature of that person's training, experience and formal qualifications (if any) on the basis of which he is judged to be so competent.

Legal tender

A banker, like any other creditor, in the absence of any agreement to the contrary, is entitled to insist on payment in legal tender.[36] Under the

---

[36] *Smith* v. *Mercer* (1815) 6 Taunt. 76; *Wilkinson* v. *Johnson* (1824) 3 B. & C. 428; *Glasgow Pavilion Ltd.* v. *Motherwell* (1903) 6 F. 116 at p. 119.

Coinage Act 1971 gold coins are legal tender to any amount; coins of cupro-nickel or silver of denominations exceeding 10p up to £10 but otherwise only up to £5; and coins of bronze up to 20p (s. 2(1) (as amended by the Currency Act 1983)). Coins of nickel brass of the denomination of £1 are legal tender up to any amount.[37] By the Currency and Bank Notes Act 1954 the Bank of England is empowered to issue bank notes of such denominations as the Treasury may approve (s. 1(1)). Bank notes issued by a bank of issue in Scotland are not legal tender even in Scotland. A cheque, if accepted, is conditional payment. The condition is resolutive so that the debt is extinguished but revived if the cheque is dishonoured.[38] If payment is made in any unusual or unbusinesslike manner, any loss by theft or fraud will fall upon the debtor.[39]

Appropriation of payments

A customer has the right to appropriate in any manner he pleases a payment made by him[40] and the banker who accepts such payment without objection to the way in which it is directed to be applied is under an obligation to see that his customer's instructions are carried out. Accordingly, a customer who has overdrawn his account is at liberty to appropriate a payment to meet a bill[41] or where he is indebted to the bank on two separate accounts he may appropriate the payment towards the liquidation, either in whole or in part, of either account and that whether the accounts are of the same nature or not. Where a customer has a current account and a loan account under an arrangement that the two accounts must be kept separate and distinct, the effect of the arrangement is that payments to the credit of the current account are appropriated to that account and cannot be treated as in reduction of the loan account.[42] Again, if there is only one debt, with arrears of interest, and the debtor ascribes his payment to part payment of the principal, the creditor is not bound to accept the appropriation but if he keeps the money he must apply it as instructed.[43] The appropriation must be made at the time of payment.

Appropriation of a payment need not necessarily be express as it may be inferred from circumstances, such as the customer's conduct at the time when payment is made, the nature of the debt, the source or nature of the payment and the position of the debtor. Where the debtor is requested to clear off a liability, a general payment by him without specific appropriation will be inferred to have been made in payment of

---

[37] Royal Proclamation of 20 April 1983 pursuant to s. 3 of the 1971 Act (as amended).
[38] *Leggat Bros.* v. *Gray*, 1908 S.C. 67; *Bolt & Nut Co. (Tipton)* v. *Rowlands Nicholls & Co.* [1964] 2 Q.B. 10.
[39] *Robb* v. *Gow* (1905) 8 F. 90; *Mitchell Henry* v. *Norwich, etc., Assurance Co.* [1918] 2 K.B. 67.
[40] *Deeley* v. *Lloyds Bank Ltd.* [1912] A.C. 756 at p. 783. See also *Siebe Gorman & Co. Ltd.* v. *Barclays Bank Ltd.* [1979] 2 Lloyd's Rep. 142.
[41] *Greenhalgh* v. *Union Bank of Manchester* [1924] 2 K.B. 153.
[42] *Bradford Old Bank* v. *Sutcliffe* [1918] 2 K.B. 833.
[43] *Wilson's Tr.* v. *Watson & Co.* (1900) 2 F. 761.

the particular debt in respect of which the application was made.[44] So interest is presumed to be paid before principal,[45] and money paid is presumed to be in discharge of a customer's own debts rather than of those for which he is liable in a fiduciary capacity. The proceeds of the realisation of a security are presumed to be applied in extinction of the debt secured.[46] Where the security applies to several debts, the creditor may appropriate the proceeds of the security towards liquidation of such of the debts, and in such proportions as he thinks fit.[47]

Unappropriated payments

In the absence of any special instructions from his customer or previous agreement with him, a banker may appropriate money paid to him by his customer as he thinks fit[48] and such appropriation becomes irrevocable whenever the fact is communicated by the banker to the customer.[49] When a debtor pays money on account to his creditor and makes no appropriation to particular items, the creditor has the right of appropriation and may exercise this right up to the very last moment; the application of the money is governed not by any rigid rule of law but by the intention of the creditor, whether it be expressed, implied, or presumed.[50] A creditor may appropriate money received from his debtor in discharge of a debt which has prescribed[51] or of a recent debt in preference to one of long standing. He may ascribe the money to an unsecured debt, leaving a secured debt unpaid in a question not only with the debtor but also with a cautioner[52] or with holders of security rights in subjects conveyed in security.[53] He may also ascribe the money towards payment of interest which is due, leaving the principal unpaid[54] and is entitled to ascribe indefinite payments to a debt which does not bear interest rather than a debt which does.[55] The debt to which the money is appropriated must be liquid and not contingent and the banker is not entitled to appropriate a payment made by a customer *qua* executor or trustee in liquidation of a debt due by him, for example, as an individual, and vice versa.

The rule in Clayton's Case

The general rule for an ordinary banking current account where special

---

[44] *Peters* v. *Anderson* (1814) 5 Taunt. 596.
[45] *Bower* v. *Marris* (1841) Cr. & Ph. 351; *Thompson* v. *Hudson* (1874) L.R. 10 Eq. 497; *Re Warrant Finance Co.* (1869) L.R. 5 Ch. App. 86.
[46] *Brett* v. *Marsh* (1687) 1 Vern. 468; *Young* v. *English* (1843) 7 Beav. 10; *Pearl* v. *Deacon* (1857) 24 Beav. 186.
[47] *ex p. Dickin* (1884) L.R. 20 Eq. 767.
[48] *Jackson* v. *Nicoll* (1870) 8 M. 408.
[49] *Simson* v. *Ingham* (1823) B. & C. 65; *Mills* v. *Fowkes* (1839) 1 Bing. N.C. 455.
[50] *Cory Bros* v. *Owners of the "Mecca"* [1897] A.C. 286; *Hay & Co.* v. *Torbet*, 1908 S.C. 781. But see Consumer Credit Act 1974, s. 81 in relation to regulated agreements covered by that Act.
[51] *Good* v. *Smith* (1779) Mor. 6816; but see *Couper* v. *Young* (1849) 12 D. 190 (prescribed bill).
[52] *Anderson* v. *North of Scotland Bank*, 1909 2 S.L.T. 262.
[53] *Mackenzie* v. *Gordon* (1837) 6 S. 311; affd. (1839) McL. & R. 117.
[54] *Scott* v. *Sandeman* (1849) 11 D. 405.
[55] *Bremner* v. *Mabon* (1837) 6 S. 213.

appropriation has not been made either by the customer or by the banker is as laid down in *Clayton's Case*,[56] namely, that the earlier items of the account are presumed to be discharged before the latter, the appropriation taking place by the very act of setting the two items against one another. In other words, the first item on the credit side is presumed to discharge or reduce *pro tanto* the first item on the debit side and the sum first paid in is presumed to be the first drawn out. The practical effect of this rule is illustrated in *Christie* v. *Royal Bank of Scotland*.[57] In this case a partner granted a bond and disposition in security to cover advances made to his firm. When he died the firm's current account was overdrawn but the bank allowed it to continue to be operated without a break. On the subsequent bankruptcy of the firm it was held that the bank could not apply the security because (1) the balance due by the firm to the bank on bankruptcy consisted of debits made after the death of the partner who had granted the security and (2) the overdrawn balance at the date of his death had been repaid by subsequent credits to the account.

To prevent the operation of the rule in *Clayton's Case* it is necessary for the account to be broken. Where a bank is the creditor in a standard security and receives notice of the creation of a subsequent security over the same subjects or of the subsequent assignation or conveyance of these subjects, the preference in ranking of the bank's security is restricted to security for present advances and any future advances which the bank may be required to make under the contract to which the security relates, together with interest.[58] Again, where a bank is the holder of a floating charge and receives intimation in writing of the subsequent registration of another floating charge over the same property, the preference in ranking of the first floating charge is similarly restricted.[59] In both cases, if the account is not broken the preference in ranking of the security will be lost if the sum representing present advances is repaid by subsequent credits to the account. Similarly, when a bank receives notice either that a guarantor intends to withdraw from the obligation which he has undertaken or that he has died, operations on the guaranteed account should be stopped. If payments-in continue to be made in either case the rule in *Clayton's Case* will apply to the effect that these will reduce *pro tanto* the debt secured under the guarantee.[60] In all of these situations a new account should be opened for future operations and this account should be kept in credit while fresh security arrangements are made.

The rule in *Clayton's Case* does not apply where there is no account current between the parties nor where from an account rendered or other circumstances it appears that the creditor intended not to make any appropriation but to reserve the right.[61] It has also been decided in

---

[56] *Devaynes* v. *Noble (Clayton's Case)* (1816) 1 Mer. 608; *Cuthill* v. *Strachan* (1894) 21 R. 549.
[57] (1839) 1 D. 745; affd. (1841) 2 Rob. 118.
[58] Conveyancing and Feudal Reform (Scotland) Act 1970. s. 13(1).
[59] Companies Act 1985, s. 464(5).
[60] *Buchanan* v. *Main* (1900) 3 F. 215; *London and County Banking Co.* v. *Terry* (1884) 25 Ch.D. 692.
[61] *Cory Bros.* v. *Owners of the "Mecca"* [1897] A.C. 286; *Hay & Co.* v. *Torbet*, 1908 S.C. 781.

England that where a trustee or other person entrusted with money in a fiduciary capacity pays such money into his own private account and inmixes it with his own money, and afterwards draws out sums by cheques in the ordinary manner, the rule will not apply for he is presumed to draw out his own money in preference to the trust money. In the event of his death or absconding, the person for whom he held the money is entitled to a preferable claim for any money in the banker's hands.[62] In Scotland it has been decided that if a trustee pays trust money into a bank to the account of himself and not in any way earmarked to the trust, and also has private money of his own in the same account, the court will endeavour to disentangle the account by separating the trust money from the private money and award the former specifically to the trust beneficiaries.[63]

Lien

A banker has at common law a general lien or right of retention over all unappropriated negotiable instruments belonging to and deposited with him as banker by a customer for the general balance due by such customer on his banking transactions. The lien covers all negotiable instruments which have been lodged by the customer with the banker for the purpose of collecting the proceeds and crediting the customer's account therewith. In England the lien is more extensive and applies to all unappropriated securities in the hands of a banker, whether negotiable or not.[64]

The generally accepted interpretation of the term "negotiable instrument" is an instrument where the property is acquired by anyone taking it *bona fide* and for value, notwithstanding any defect of title in the person from whom he took it. It follows that an instrument cannot be negotiable unless the true owner is in a position to transfer the contract or engagement therein by simple delivery of the instrument without any other legal formality. Thus bills of exchange indorsed in blank or payable to bearer, promissory notes, exchequer bills,[65] coupons and bearer bonds of foreign governments,[66] and cheques[67] have been held to be proper subjects of lien. A banker has no right of lien in Scotland over registered share certificates in name of his customer, these being merely representative of property vested in the customer. Where however shares are transferred into the name of a bank or its nominee and the transfer is duly registered in the books of the company, the banker is not bound to retransfer the shares unless and until the whole obligations of the customer are satisfied.[68] This rule holds good although the *ex facie* absolute title has

---

[62] *Knatchbull* v. *Hallett* (1880) L.R. 13 Ch.D. 696.

[63] *Jopp* v. *Johnston's Tr.* (1904) 6 F. 1028; see also *Hayman & Son* v. *Thomson McLintock* (1906) 13 S.L.T. 863 and *Macadam* v. *Martin's Trs.* (1872) 11 M. 33.

[64] *Re London & Globe Finance Corp.* [1902] 2 Ch. 416.

[65] *Brandao* v. *Barnett* (1846) 12 Cl. & Fin. 787.

[66] *Jones* v. *Peppercorne* (1858) 28 L.J. Ch. 138; *Wylde* v. *Bradford* (1863) 33 L.J. Ch. 51.

[67] *Scott and Others* v. *Franklin* (1812) 15 East 428. See also *Jeffreys* v. *Agra and Masterman's Bank* (1866) L.R. 2 Eq. 674 and *Currie* v. *Misa* (1876) 1 App.Cas. 554.

[68] *Hamilton* v. *Western Bank* (1856) 19 D. 152.

been qualified by a back letter or other agreement declaring that it has been granted in security of a particular debt unless it is stated that the securities are to be held for that debt alone and no other.

A banker has a general lien over all bills lodged by a customer for collection[69] and not specifically appropriated and to entitle the customer to demand the return of any bill he must have paid the whole balance due by him. However, the banker has no right of lien over bills which he knows do not belong to his customer[70] nor over bills deposited with him simply for safe custody[71] nor over bills handed to him to be discounted but which he has refused to discount[72] since until the bill is discounted the banker holds it as a deposit[73] and as soon as he discounts it he becomes its owner and as such is entitled to sue upon it.[74] An averment that a bill has been indorsed to a banker for discount and not by way of security can only be proved by the writ or oath of the banker.[75] Bills handed to a banker before they are due are prima facie the property of the person handing them in and therefore subject to the banker's right of lien.[76] But bills handed to a banker on a date long prior to their falling due and as a fund of credit against which advances on other and smaller bills were made during their currency, have been held to become the property of the banker in respect that full value for them had been given by way of advances.[77] Where the lien covers bills lodged for collection the banker is bound to negotiate them and is entitled to apply the proceeds in payment or reduction of any sum due to him by the person who lodged the bills. Where a firm consisting of two or more partners has an account with a bank and the individual partners have also accounts with the same bank, on the ground that every partner of a firm is liable to the full extent of his means for the firm's debts it is thought, although there is no express decision on the point, that in Scotland—it is otherwise in England[78]—a banker has a lien over the deposits or securities of a partner, so far as not specifically appropriated, for the general balance due by the firm.

To enable a banker in Scotland to exercise his right of lien over the property of a customer the following matters are essential. The property of the customer should actually be in the banker's possession and such possession must have been legitimately obtained. Accordingly, there is no right of lien over securities left with a banker by mistake or accident,[79] nor over securities contained in a box, the key of which is retained in the

---

[69] As to the ranking of such bills in a liquidation, see *Clydesdale Bank Ltd.* v. *Liqr. of James Allan, Senior & Son Ltd.*, 1926 S.C. 235.

[70] *Dunlop's Trs.* v. *Clydesdale Bank Ltd.* (1893) 20 R. 59.

[71] *Leese* v. *Martin* (1873) L.R. 17 Eq. 224.

[72] *Borthwick* v. *Bremner* (1833) 12 S. 121.

[73] *ex p. Twogood* (1812) 19 Ves. 231.

[74] *Carstairs* v. *Bates* (1812) 3 Camp. 301; *Attwood* v. *Crowdie* (1816) 1 Stark. 483.

[75] *Glen* v. *National Bank of Scotland* (1849) 12 D. 353.

[76] *Giles* v. *Perkins* (1807) 9 East. 12.

[77] *Glen* v. *National Bank of Scotland* (1849) 12 D. 353; *Patten* v. *Royal Bank of Scotland* (1853) 15 D. 617.

[78] *Watts* v. *Christie* (1849) 11 Beav. 546.

[79] *Lucas* v. *Dorrien* (1816) 7 Taunt. 279.

customer's possession.[80] The right of lien ceases with loss of possession.[81] It is essential that the property over which the right of lien is sought to be exercised should belong to the customer,[82] or that the bank have reasonable grounds for assuming that it belongs to him. The general rule is that in dealing with a negotiable instrument the person in possession of it may be treated as having authority to deal with it (in the absence of any knowledge to the contrary).[83] However, the property over which the right of lien is sought to be exercised must not have been deposited with the banker for a specific purpose and one inconsistent with such right. There is, however, a presumption that the possession of securities belonging to a customer who is indebted to a bank gives the bank a general right of lien over such securities and to overcome that presumption the conditions on which the securities are deposited must be clear and specific.[84] Again, possession of the property must have been obtained by the banker in his capacity as a banker and not, for example, as a depositary or custodier. The fact of a banker charging remuneration for such services would be prima facie evidence that the performance of the act for which such remuneration is accepted is one which does not fall properly within the scope of his business as a banker.[85] Again, the customer must be indebted to the bank. Where the customer has more than one bank account or where he has accounts at various branches, the right of lien cannot arise unless the general balance on all accounts in his name taken together is against the customer.[86] A banker with whom a customer opens several accounts has a lien on them all, except where there is a special agreement to keep them separate.[87] Where a customer is neither bankrupt nor *vergens ad inopiam*, the banker's lien does not, in the absence of special agreement, extend to debts which have not become prestable. Thus a banker has no right in such circumstances to retain a sum of money at a customer's credit on current account as security for a bill under discount which has not yet become due.[88]

In Scotland a banker is not entitled, without the consent of his customer, to sell or to make over to a third party the subjects of lien, even although he may have assigned his debt to such third party. All he can do is retain these until his claim is settled.[89]

---

[80] *Leese* v. *Martin* (1873) L.R. 17 Eq. 224.

[81] *Lloyds Bank Ltd.* v. *Swiss Bankverein* (1913) 29 T.L.R. 219.

[82] *Farrar & Rooth* v. *N. B. Banking Co.* (1850) 12 D. 1190; *Attwood & Others* v. *Kinnear & Son* (1832) 10 S. 817.

[83] *London Joint Stock Bank* v. *Simmons* [1892] A.C. 201; *Mitchell* v. *Heys & Son* (1894) 21 R. 600; *Brandao* v. *Barnett* (1846) 12 Cl. & F. 787; *Wookey* v. *Pole* (1820) 4 B. & Ald. 1.

[84] *Robertson's Tr.* v. *Royal Bank of Scotland* (1893) 20 R. 12; *Alston's Tr.* v. *Royal Bank of Scotland* (1893) 20 R. 887.

[85] *Brandao* v. *Barnett* (1846) 12 Cl. & F. 787.

[86] See *European Bank, Re Agra Bank Claim* (1872) 8 Ch. App. 41; *Garnett* v. *McKewan* (1872) L.R. 8 Exch. 10.

[87] *Greenwood Teale* v. *William Williams, Brown & Co.* (1894) 11 T.L.R. 56. On the distinction between lien and set-off, see *Halesowen Presswork and Assemblies Ltd.* v. *Westminster Bank Ltd.* [1970] 3 All E.R. 473 at p. 477.

[88] *Paul & Thain* v. *Royal Bank of Scotland* (1869) 7 M. 361; *King* v. *British Linen Co.* (1899) 1 F. 920.

[89] *Robertson's Tr.* v. *Royal Bank of Scotland* (1886) 14 R. (H.L.) 1.

Compensation or set-off

Where one person who is under an obligation to another has as against that other a right of the same nature, so that each has an independent obligation to the other, the respective obligations are said to compensate one another so that if equal in amount both are extinguished and if not equal, the larger debt is extinguished *pro tanto*. However, where the relationship between banker and customer is a single one, albeit embodied in a number of accounts, this gives rise instead to an accounting situation, in which the existence and amount of one party's liability to the other can only be ascertained by discovering the ultimate balance of their mutual dealings.[90] Accordingly, where several bank accounts are opened by one customer under various headings, with the object of keeping the sums paid into the respective accounts separate and distinct, the various accounts may be treated by the banker as one, so far as the relation of debtor and creditor between banker and customer is concerned, so that a debit balance in one account may be set against a credit balance in another.[91] The banker has the right to combine accounts in this manner whenever he wishes and to set off one account against the other, unless he has made some agreement, express or implied, to keep them separate.[92]

The right of compensation, properly so called, that is, to set one independent obligation against another, is founded on the Compensation Act 1592 (c. 141) which provides that any liquid debt instantly verified by writ or oath of the party pleading it shall be admitted by all judges by way of exception or defence where it is proponed before the granting of decree. The rules which govern the operation of compensation are as follows:

(1) Compensation does not operate *ipso jure*. It must be pleaded by way of defence and the plea must be sustained.

(2) The obligation in respect of which compensation is pleaded as a defence must be of the same nature and description as that sued on, and there must have been no specific appropriation.[93]

(3) The debt must be due at the time when the plea is set up. Thus a contingent or conditional debt cannot be pleaded against one due so that a banker cannot without notice set off a balance on current account against an amount contingently due on bills[94] or outstanding on a loan account unless the loan is repayable on demand or repayment has been demanded.[95] Again, a debt contracted subsequent to bankruptcy cannot be pleaded against one incurred prior to that event.[96] The general rule

---

[90] *Halesowen Presswork & Assemblies Ltd.* v. *Westminster Bank Ltd.* [1970] 3 All E.R. 473 at p. 488.

[91] *Kirkwood* v. *Clydesdale Bank Ltd.*, 1908 S.C. 20.

[92] *Re E. J. Morel (1934) Ltd.* [1961] 1 All E.R. 716: *Halesowen Presswork and Assemblies Ltd.* v. *Westminster Bank Ltd.* [1972] 1 All E.R. 641.

[93] *Middlemas* v. *Gibson*, 1910 S.C. 577; *Mycroft, Petr.*, 1983 S.L.T. 342. See also *Smith* v. *Lord Advocate (No. 2)*, 1981 S.L.T. 19 (Government's right of set-off).

[94] *Jeffreys* v. *Agra and Masterman's Bank* (1866) L.R. 2 Ex. 674; *Baker* v. *Lloyds Bank Ltd* [1920] 2 K.B. 322.

[95] *Buckingham & Co.* v. *London and Midland Bank Ltd.* (1895) 12 T.L.R. 70; *Bradford Old Bank Ltd.* v. *Sutcliffe* [1918] 2 K.B. 833; *Re E. J. Morel (1934) Ltd.* [1962] Ch. 21.

[96] *Taylor's Tr.* v. *Paul* (1888) 15 R. 313.

applies, however, only where both parties are solvent; if one is bankrupt, the other may plead compensation in respect of a debt not yet due.

(4) The debt, besides being actually exigible, must be liquid or fixed in amount, or capable of being immediately made liquid.[97]

(5) There must be *concursus debiti et crediti* or, in other words, the parties must occupy the positions of debtor and creditor to one another respectively in the same capacity and at the same time. A person sued for a private debt is not entitled to plead compensation in respect of a debt due to him in a representative capacity.[98] Thus, where an agent as such and on behalf of a principal, whether disclosed or not, has dealings with a third party, that party is not entitled to set off against a claim by the principal in respect of such dealings a debt due by the agent as an individual.[99] Further, compensation cannot be pleaded by an agent against a claim for money paid to him by his principal.[1] Similarly, if a bank is aware that a customer holds funds in an account in a fiduciary capacity, it is not entitled to set off that sum against an overdraft allowed to the customer on another account[2] but where a customer of a bank was indebted to the bank at the date of his death and his executors in administering his estate opened an account in their names as executors into which was paid a sum practically equal to that due by the deceased customer, the bank on the sequestration of the deceased debtor's estate was held entitled to set off the one sum against the other.[3] A banker who has granted a deposit receipt payable to either of two persons cannot refuse payment to one of them by pleading compensation in respect of a debt due by the other.[4]

(6) In partnership where a firm sues for a debt, the debtor cannot set off against such a claim a debt due to him by one of the partners of the firm as an individual because there is no *concursus*.[5] The firm, not the individual partner, is the creditor in the debt sued for but the firm is not the debtor in the debt which it is proposed to set off. Accordingly, a bank cannot set off against a claim by a firm for repayment of a sum standing to their credit in its books a debt due to it by an individual partner in his own name. However, if a claim is made by a bank against a firm, the bank can set off this claim against a demand for payment of a credit balance due by it to an individual partner on the basis that the partners are personally liable *singuli in solidum* for the firm's debts.[6]

(7) The *concursus debiti et crediti* must take place at or prior to the time

---

[97] *Edwards* v. *Adam* (1821) 1 S. 27. See also *Johnston* v. *Robertson* (1861) 23 D. 646 and *Munro* v. *McDonald's Exrs.* (1866) 4 M. 687.

[98] *Stewart* v. *Stewart* (1869) 7 M. 366.

[99] *Lavaggie* v. *Pirie & Sons* (1872) 10 M. 312; *Matthews* v. *Auld & Guild* (1874) 1 R. 1224. On the question of set-off in the case of a company in receivership, see *Myles J. Callaghan Ltd.* v. *City of Glasgow D.C.*, 1988 S.L.T. 227.

[1] *Campbell* v. *Little* (1823) 2 S. 484.

[2] *United Rentals Ltd.* v. *Clydesdale & North of Scotland Bank Ltd.*, 1963 S.L.T. (Sh. Ct.) 41. A banker may otherwise combine accounts unless there is an agreement that they be kept separate. See p. 24.

[3] *Alexander's Exr.* v. *Mackersy* (1905) 8 F. 198.

[4] *Anderson* v. *North of Scotland Bank Ltd.* (1901) 4 F. 49.

[5] *Morrison* v. *Hunter* (1822) 2 S. 68.

[6] *Mitchell* v. *Canal Basin Foundry Co.* (1869) 7 M. 480; *Thomson* v. *Stevenson* (1855) 17 D. 739.

when either of the parties becomes bankrupt. There can be no compensation between debts incurred by a person before his bankruptcy and liabilities incurred to the trustee as representing the bankrupt's creditors.[7]

(8) Compensation is not pleadable by a depositary against a depositor.[8]

(9) Compensation cannot be pleaded in respect of a debt acquired *mala fide* in order to gain an undue advantage or under circumstances in which, if the plea was sustained, the diligence of third parties would be defeated. Thus the debtor of a deceased person cannot plead compensation in respect of a debt acquired subsequent to the date of his creditor's death. Similarly, when payment of a debt is demanded by a trustee in bankruptcy and the defence is compensation, it can only be pleaded on the basis that the *concursus debiti et crediti* arose before bankruptcy. This precludes the acquisition by a debtor to a bankrupt estate of claims against the bankrupt and a plea of compensation founded on such claims,[9] as well as a plea founded on subsequent transactions with the bankrupt.[10]

(10) Compensation may be pleaded not only by the principal but by anyone who has an interest as, for example, a cautioner.

(11) Compensation cannot be pleaded subsequent to decree unless the decree is reduced.

Customer's right to secrecy

It is an implied term of a banker's contract with his customer that he shall not disclose any details relating to the account of the customer except in certain circumstances. The qualifications of the contractual duty of secrecy were laid down by the Court of Appeal in England in *Tournier* v. *National Provincial and Union Bank of England*.[11] In his judgment Bankes L.J. said:

> "On principle I think that the qualifications can be classified under four heads: (a) where disclosure is under compulsion by law; (b) where there is a duty to the public to disclose; (c) where the interests of the bank require disclosure; (d) where the disclosure is made by the express or implied consent of the customer."

In the course of the judgments in the Court of Appeal it was stated that information gained during the currency of the account remains confidential unless released in circumstances bringing the case within one of the above classes of qualifications. The duty of non-disclosure is not confined to information derived from the customer or his account, but includes information obtained by the banker in his character as such. The implied

---

[7] *Asphaltic Limestone Co.* v. *Corporation of Glasgow*, 1907 S.C. 463.
[8] Bell, *Prin.*, § 574; *Mycroft, Petr.*, 1983 S.L.T. 342.
[9] Bell, *Comm.*, II, 123; *Cauvin* v. *Robertson* (1783) Mor. 2581.
[10] *Hannay & Son's Tr.* v. *Armstrong Brothers* (1875) 2 R. 399; affd. (1877) 4 R. (H.L.) 43.
[11] [1924] 1 K.B. 461.

legal duty does not apply to knowledge which the bank acquires before the relation of banker and customer was in contemplation or after it has ceased.

The duty of confidentiality between banker and customer is subject to, and overridden by, the duty of any party to a contract to comply with the law of the land. If it is the duty, whether at common law or under statute, of a party to a contract to disclose in defined circumstances confidential information, then he must do so and any express term of the contract to the contrary would be illegal and void. In the case of banker and customer, the duty of confidentiality is subject to the overriding duty of the banker at common law to disclose and answer questions as to his customer's affairs when he is asked to give evidence about them in the witness box in a court of law. Accordingly, if a banker is to give evidence in court about his customer's affairs he must be formally cited as a witness. Nevertheless, it is the practice of the Scottish banks to provide without further formality if requested a statement restricted to the effect that no account is held in the name of a person who is the subject of police inquiries or confirmation that the answer on a cheque "Account closed" was correct.

Bankers' Books Evidence Act 1879

In criminal proceedings when production of bank books, or of any entries in them, is called for a copy of any entry in a banker's book is entitled to be received as prima facie evidence of the existence of such entry and of the matters, transactions and accounts therein recorded (s. 3). Section 9 of the 1879 Act has been superseded by a new section 9 set out in Schedule 6 to the Banking Act 1979 and is in the following terms (as further amended):

> **"Interpretation of 'bank', 'banker' and 'bankers' books'**
> **9**—(1) In this Act the expressions 'bank' and 'banker' mean—
>   (*a*) an institution authorised under the Banking Act 1987 or a municipal bank within the meaning of that Act;
>   (*b*) a building society within the meaning of the Building Societies Act 1986;
>   (*c*) the National Savings Bank; and
>   (*d*) the Post Office, in the exercise of its powers to provide banking services.
> (2) Expressions in this Act relating to 'bankers' books' include ledgers, day books, cash books, account books and other records used in the ordinary business of the bank, whether those records are in written form or are kept on microfilm, magnetic tape or any other form of mechanical or electronic data retrieval mechanism."

It has been held that an entry in a banker's book includes any form of permanent record by means made available by modern technology including microfilm.[12] Letters contained in a bank correspondence file are not included in the definition[13] nor are cleared cheques and paying-in slips.[14]

An order under section 7 of the Act may be sought by any party to a legal proceeding[15] with or without summoning the bank and must be served on the bank three clear days before it is to be obeyed, unless the court otherwise directs. In criminal proceedings the procurator-fiscal applies to the sheriff for an order under section 7. The application cannot be presented before criminal proceedings have become proceedings in court.[16] Further, the application should only be granted provided that it is not oppressive, is limited in time and not used for ulterior motives.[17] Also, there ought to be no disclosure of entries in the account made prior to the period covered by a criminal charge as this could not be said to cast light on the offences charged.[18] In ordinary civil litigation an order under section 7 is normally only made in respect of a party to the litigation. In criminal cases an order can be made against a non-party but the jurisdiction of the court to make such an order should be exercised with "great caution".[19] There is no obligation on a bank to disclose to a customer an order granted to the police allowing them to inspect an account.[20]

Section 6(3) of the Civil Evidence (Scotland) Act 1988 provides that sections 3 to 5 of the 1879 Act do not apply to civil proceedings. In their place section 5 of the Act provides that unless the court otherwise directs, a document may in such proceedings be taken to form part of the records of a business if it is certified as such by an officer of the business and it may be received in evidence without being spoken to by a witness. Further, by section 6 a copy of a document, purporting to be authenticated by a person responsible for the making of the copy shall, unless the court otherwise directs, be deemed a true copy and treated for evidential purposes as if it were the document itself.

Disclosure in other circumstances

There appears to be no reported case where a banker has thought himself under a duty to the public to disclose but he has such a duty if he suspects that his bank is holding funds derived from drug trafficking. Disclosure in such circumstances is not treated as a breach of his duty not

---

[12] *Barker* v. *Wilson* [1980] 2 All E.R. 81.
[13] *R.* v. *Dadson, The Times*, 10 March 1983. In Scotland, the procurator-fiscal has at common law power to search under warrant and can use this power to obtain items not capable of recovery under the 1879 Act. See *MacNeill, Complainer*, 1984 S.L.T. 157.
[14] *Williams* v. *Williams* [1987] 3 W.L.R. 790.
[15] "Legal proceedings" include proceedings before any body exercising disciplinary functions in relation to solicitors (Solicitors Act 1974, s. 86).
[16] *Carmichael* v. *Sexton*, 1986 S.L.T. 16 at p. 17H.
[17] *Owen* v. *Sambrook* [1981] Crim.L.R. 329. In England, the police may obtain an injunction restraining an accused person from withdrawing from a bank account money which is said to represent the proceeds of cheques which he has forged: *Chief Constable of Kent* v. *V.* [1983] 1 Q.B. 34.
[18] *Owen* v. *Sambrook* [1981] Crim.L.R. 329.
[19] *R.* v. *Grossman* [1981] Crim.L.R. 396.
[20] *Barclays Bank PLC* v. *Taylor* [1989] 1 W.L.R. 1066.

to disclose his customer's affairs.[21] There is however no general duty to give information to the police about a customer suspected of a crime, but a bank might disclose to the police the time and place of use of a customer's cash card if it was believed that the customer was in personal danger when the card was used. When a bank sues to recover money advanced to a customer it is entitled to disclose in the writ the amount of the customer's debt. Even in this situation, however, no more should be disclosed than is strictly necessary to establish the point at issue.

Authorised disclosure

A banker may disclose information when he is expressly authorised by his customer to do so. An example of express consent is where a customer advises his banker that his name has been given as a referee and asks him to reply to a particular inquiry when it is received. Similarly, customers in trade and commerce authorise disclosure indirectly when they expressly provide their banker's name for a reference. They know that an inquiry will follow and it is clearly their intention that their banker should reply. In many cases, however, a customer may be unaware that his banker has received and replied to an inquiry concerning his credit-worthiness since it is not the general practice of bankers to advise their customers that such inquiries have been received. Replies are usually sent to the bank of the inquirer and given on the basis that the bank has the implied consent of its customer to the provision of the information. The banks rely on the judgment in *Tournier* v. *National Provincial and Union Bank of England*[22] to support the view that the giving of a reference is not a breach of the banker-customer relationship. However, doubt has been cast on this explanation of the legal position but no final judicial pronouncement on the position in law of a banker who provides a reference on the basis of the implied consent of his customer has been made. Information when it is given is usually accompanied by an intimation that it is given in confidence, for the private use of the other bank, and without responsibility on the part of the bank providing the information or its officials. Such a disclaimer of responsibility was successful in protecting the bank in *Hedley Byrne & Co. Ltd.* v. *Heller & Partners Ltd.*[23] but the position is now affected by the Unfair Contract Terms Act 1977. It is not yet certain how far the Act bears on bankers' references but it would seem that the question of whether or not the term of any agreement between the banker and his customer, or of any notice given by the banker, intended to relieve him from responsibility will actually relieve the banker from liability, will depend upon whether any such term or notice satisfies the requirement of reasonableness.[24]

In answering questions as to the financial position of their customers or

---

[21] Criminal Justice (Scotland) Act, 1987, s. 43. See also Prevention of Terrorism (Temporary Provisions) Act 1989, s. 11.
[22] [1924] 1 K.B. 461.
[23] [1964] A.C. 465.
[24] See ss. 2 and 3 of the Act; also Paget, *Law of Banking* (9th ed.), p. 159.

their ability to meet certain obligations care has to be exercised. When a banker is asked for a reference he is not bound to make inquiries outside as to the solvency or otherwise of his customer nor is he bound to do more than answer honestly, in the light of what he knows from the books and accounts before him, the question he is asked. It should be noted that if the representations or statements made by a banker are of the nature of or amount to a guarantee or warranty, they must in order to render his bank liable in damages to the person to whom he furnishes such information, be in writing and subscribed by the bank or by its express authority.[25] While a branch manager will bind his bank by any act which falls within the scope of his authority in the conduct of his banking business he has no implied authority to bind the bank by granting guarantees or making such representations and assurances as amount to guarantees and involve the bank in liability. Although in answering questions as to a customer's financial position he is acting within the scope of his delegated authority and in accordance with general custom, any answer which a branch manager may make can only bind the bank if it be truthful and not such as would involve practically a guarantee, since the granting of a guarantee is generally speaking *ultra vires* his position as a branch manager.[26] A doubt has been expressed as to whether or not section 6 of the Mercantile Law Amendment Act 1856, requiring guarantees or representations to be made in writing, applies to representations made by a branch manager to an intending guarantor of the account of a customer.[27]

The Hedley Byrne decision

Prior to the decision in *Hedley Byrne & Co. Ltd.* v. *Heller & Partners Ltd.*[28] it was the law that when an inquiry was made by one banker of another who stood in no special relation to him, there was no duty in the absence of special circumstances from which a contract to be careful could be inferred excepting that of common honesty.[29] In this case however the facts were that through their bankers the plaintiffs made inquiry of the defendant bank as to the financial stability of one of their customers and acting on the answer which they received they incurred liabilities which resulted in a loss. The House of Lords held that there may be a special relationship between two parties deriving neither from contract nor from fiduciary responsibility which will give rise to a duty to take care in giving a reference but that in the simple case involving a banker's reference no such relationship arises and in any event a bank could safeguard itself by giving the information without responsibility. However, the relationship between banker and customer can become the

---

[25] Mercantile Law Amendment (Scotland) Act 1856, s. 6.
[26] See *British Bank of the Middle East* v. *Sun Life Assurance Co. of Canada (U.K.) Ltd.* (1983) Com.L.R. 187; also *U.B.A.F. Ltd.* v. *European American Banking Corporation* [1984] 2 All E.R. 226.
[27] *Royal Bank of Scotland Ltd.* v. *Greenshields*, 1914 S.C. 259.
[28] [1964] A.C. 465.
[29] *Robinson* v. *National Bank of Scotland*, 1916 S.C. (H.L.) 154.

sort of relationship which gives rise to a responsibility on the part of the banker towards a customer who acts upon his information or advice and so creates for the banker a duty of care towards the customer. An instance of the "special relationship" was the case in which a branch manager in answering a customer's request for an advance told him that he (the manager) would have to get head office approval but that he had no doubt such approval would be given. The customer acted on this opinion, the advance was not approved and he suffered loss. The bank was liable since the manager was not obliged to predict the outcome of the application but having done so he was under a duty to take reasonable care since he knew that his prediction would be relied on.[30] Similarly, where a customer was negligently advised that a bank mortgage of an "all moneys" type was similar to a building society mortgage for a limited amount, the bank was liable in damages.[31]

A customer's duties to his banker

A customer undertakes to exercise reasonable care in drawing his cheques so as not to mislead his banker or facilitate forgery. This undertaking is illustrated by the decision of the House of Lords in *London Joint Stock Bank Ltd.* v. *Macmillan and Arthur.*[32] A clerk in the employment of customers of a bank presented to one of the partners for signature a cheque drawn in favour of the firm or bearer. There was no sum in words in the space provided for writing but the figure "2" had been inserted in the space for figures. The partner signed the cheque and the clerk subsequently added the words "One hundred and twenty pounds" in the space for words, and inserted the figures "1" and "0" respectively on either side of the figure "2", space having been left to allow for the insertion of these figures. The clerk presented the cheque for payment at the firm's bank and obtained payment of £120. He absconded and the firm declined to recognise the debit for this amount but the court held that the account had been properly debited. In their judgment the House of Lords declared:

> "It is beyond dispute that the customer is bound to exercise reasonable care in drawing the cheque to prevent the banker being misled. If he draws the cheque in a manner which facilitates fraud, he is guilty of a breach of duty as between himself and the banker and he will be responsible for any loss sustained by the banker as a natural and direct consequence of this breach of duty."[33]

The application of this rule was unsuccessfully invoked in a later case where the drawers of a cheque had not drawn a line after the payee's

---

[30] *Box* v. *Midland Bank Ltd.* [1979] 2 Lloyd's Rep. 391. See also *Lloyds Bank Ltd.* v. *Bundy* [1978] Q.B. 326; *National Westminster Bank PLC* v. *Morgan* [1985] 2 W.L.R. 588.
[31] *Cornish* v. *Midland Bank plc* [1985] 3 All E.R. 513.
[32] [1918] A.C. 777.
[33] *per* Lord Finlay L.C., at p. 789.

name and so had enabled a fraud to be committed. The drawers were successful in an action against the bank on the ground that the cheque had been fraudulently altered in a material particular, the Court of Appeal rejecting the argument that the drawers had been negligent on the ground that it was not at that time a "usual precaution" to draw lines before or after the payee's name.[34]

A customer also has a duty to inform his banker if he discovers that cheques purporting to have been signed by him have been forged.[35] In England, a failure to disclose may give the bank the right to set up an estoppel.[36] In Scotland, where a banker pays a cheque, the signature to which has been forged or adhibited without the drawer's authority, he will be liable to the drawer for the amount unless the circumstances have been such as to preclude the drawer from setting up the forgery or want of authority. In *Orr and Barber* v. *Union Bank of Scotland*[37] the position was stated as follows:

> "The principle is a sound one, that where a customer's neglect of due precaution has caused his bankers to make a payment on a forged order, he shall not set up against them the invalidity of a document which he has induced them to act on as genuine."[38]

The customer may by his conduct be precluded from setting up the forgery if, for example, he has kept silent or otherwise led the bank to believe in the genuineness of his signature and as a result the bank has lost some opportunity of recovering on the cheque, which, had the forgery been known, it might have used.[39] Such delay in disclosing the forgery would effect a sufficient alteration in the bank's position to preclude the drawer of the cheque from setting up the forgery. However, where a customer was first informed by the accredited agent of a bank, who requested his silence, that certain entries debited against his account were in respect of cheques forged by one of the bank's servants, it was held that the customer, in complying with this request honestly and with a view to what he believed to be the bank's interest, had not inflicted a legal wrong upon the bank and that he was not prevented from founding on the forgery.[40] But where intimation was given to the drawer of a bill bearing his signature that it had been presented for payment and an agent, acting on his instructions, called on the banker and after examining the bill did not deny but rather by implication admitted that the signature was

---

[34] *Slingsby and Others* v. *District Bank Ltd.* [1932] 1 K.B. 544.

[35] *Greenwood* v. *Martin's Bank Ltd.* [1933] A.C. 51.

[36] *Greenwood* v. *Martin's Bank Ltd.*, *supra*; *Brown* v. *Westminster Bank Ltd.* [1964] 2 Lloyd's Rep. 187.

[37] (1854) 1 Macq. 513.

[38] *per* Lord Cranworth, at p. 523.

[39] This type of case has to be distinguished from the case of a non-customer who receives intimation from a bank that a bill bearing his signature is in the bank's hands for payment and ignores the intimation. See *Mackenzie* v. *British Linen Co.* (1881) 8 R. (H.L.) 8 and the cases therein referred to.

[40] *Ogilvie* v. *West Australian Mortgage and Agency Corp. Ltd.* [1896] A.C. 257.

genuine, the drawer was precluded from setting up the forgery.[41] However, although a customer has a duty to exercise reasonable care in drawing his cheques and to notify the bank of any forgery of which he becomes aware, unless otherwise agreed he does not owe a duty to the bank in contract or in delict either to take precautions to prevent forged cheques being presented to his bank for payment, or to check his periodic bank statements so as to be able to notify the bank of any items debited to his account which have not been authorised by him.[42]

Office of the Banking Ombudsman

The main object of the Office of the Banking Ombudsman is to receive unresolved complaints about the provision of banking services to individuals and facilitate their settlement. A bank is treated as providing banking services to an individual if it is an executor of the estate of a deceased person and the individual is a beneficiary or if it has the benefit of a guarantee or security granted by the individual to secure facilities granted to another individual. The service is provided free as far as the individual is concerned.

The Ombudsman may request a bank named in a complaint to provide any information relating to the subject-matter of the complaint which is in its possession. Any information supplied may be treated as confidential if this is requested. The Ombudsman is not bound by any legal rule of evidence. At any time that a complaint is under consideration by him he may seek to promote a settlement or withdrawal of the complaint by agreement between the applicant and the bank involved. In the absence of agreement he may make a recommendation for settlement or withdrawal of the complaint after giving both parties at least one month's notice of his intention to make a recommendation. If the Ombudsman has made a recommendation which, within one month after it is made, has been accepted by the applicant but not by the bank, he may make an award against the bank comprising a sum of money not exceeding £100,000. The award shall state that, if within one month after its issue the applicant agrees to accept it in full and final settlement of the complaint, the award shall be binding on him and (in accordance with its undertaking to the Office) the bank against whom it is made. In making any recommendation or award the Ombudsman must observe any applicable rule of law or relevant judicial authority and have regard to general principles of good banking practice and any relevant code of practice applicable to the subject-matter of the complaint. He is not bound by any previous decision made by him or by any predecessor in his office.

The powers of the Ombudsman are limited in that he cannot consider a complaint (a) to the extent that it relates to a bank's commercial judgment about lending or security, but this does not prevent him from

---

[41] *Brown* v. *British Linen Co.* (1863) 1 M. 793; *Wilson's Trs.* v. *Bank of England*, House of Lords, 16 July 1926 (not reported).

[42] *Tai Hing Cotton Mill Ltd.* v. *Liu Chong Hing Bank Ltd.* [1985] 2 All E.R. 947.

considering complaints about maladministration in such matters; (b) to the extent that the complaint relates to a bank's general interest rate policies; (c) to the extent that the complaint relates to (i) any decision taken by a bank in accordance with a discretion exercisable by it under any will or trust or (ii) any lack of consultation with beneficiaries before exercising any such discretion, but this does not exclude complaints about maladministration in dealing with wills or trusts; (d) if the complaint relates to banking services provided to an employee of the bank; (e) if it appears to him that it is more appropriate that the complaint be dealt with by a court or under some other independent procedure; (f) if it appears to him that the amount which the applicant has claimed or could claim in respect of the subject-matter of the complaint exceeds £100,000; or (g) the subject-matter of the complaint falls within the jurisdiction of any procedure established under the Financial Services Act 1986. The Ombudsman can only consider a complaint made to him if he is satisfied that the senior management of the bank involved have had the opportunity to consider the complaint but the applicant has not accepted any conditions of settlement offered by the bank and deadlock has been reached. Any complaint must be made to him not later than six months after the bank has informed the complainant that deadlock has been reached and informed him also of the existence of the Ombudsman and of the six months limit. The act or omission giving rise to the complaint must have occurred not more than six months before the applicant first made the complaint in writing to the bank involved.

At any time before the Ombudsman has made an award a bank may give him a notice in writing (a) stating that in the opinion of the bank the complaint involves an issue which may have important consequences for the business of the bank or banks generally or an important point of law and (b) undertaking that if within six months after the Ombudsman's receipt of the notice either the applicant or the bank institutes court proceedings against the other in respect of the complaint, the bank will pay the applicant's costs and expenses of the proceedings at first instance and any subsequent appeal proceedings commenced by the bank. When he receives such a notice the Ombudsman must cease to consider the complaint and inform the applicant accordingly.

CHAPTER 3

DETERMINATION OF CONTRACT

Since the relationship between banker and customer is contractual, like any other such relationship it may be terminated by mutual agreement. In practice, however, the ending of the relationship is usually the unilateral act of one party.

Closure of account by customer

The balance standing to the credit of a customer on a current or deposit account is repayable on demand by the customer. Accordingly, if he wishes to close the account he simply requires to demand payment of the balance due, less accrued bank charges. The banker should however ascertain that the intention is to close the account rather than simply withdraw the credit balance. If a customer wishes to close his current account when it is overdrawn then he may do so by repaying the overdraft plus any outstanding interest and charges. In either case, the customer should make provision for any cheques which he has issued but which have not been presented for payment by the time the account is closed. If this is not done, the banker is entitled to dishonour such a cheque with the answer "Account closed".

Closure of account by banker

One of the terms of the contract between banker and customer is that the banker will not cease to do business with the customer "except upon reasonable notice".[1] The period of notice must be long enough to enable the customer, having regard to the circumstances which have led the banker to seek to have the account closed, to make alternative arrangements. A month's notice may not be adequate if the circumstances demand that it should be longer.[2] Where the account is overdrawn a banker may be entitled to demand repayment of an overdraft without necessarily being entitled to close the account at the same time. It would always be open to the customer to repay the overdraft and subsequently pay in cash to meet further cheques which he had issued.[3] The banker is only entitled to withdraw banking facilities after giving sufficient notice to the customer to enable him to make other arrangements. When the account has been closed, either by the bank or by the customer, the relationship of banker and customer is ended. The banker nevertheless

---

[1] *Joachimson* v. *Swiss Bank Corporation* [1921] 3 K.B. 110 at p. 127.
[2] *Prosperity Ltd.* v. *Lloyds Bank Ltd.* (1923) 39 T.L.R. 372.
[3] On this subject, see *Barnes* v. *Williams and Glyn's Bank Ltd.* (1981) Com.L.R. 205.

remains under a duty of secrecy so far as his former customer's affairs are concerned.[4]

Death of customer

The duty and authority of a banker to pay a cheque drawn on him by his customer are determined by notice of the customer's death.[5] The person who then gives the banker a valid discharge for the payment of any sum standing to the credit of the account of the deceased customer is the deceased's executor.[6] If the deceased left no will, the appointment is made by the sheriff of the county in which the deceased died domiciled. An executor thus appointed is called an executor-dative in distinction to an executor-nominate, i.e. one named by the deceased in his testamentary disposition. In both cases the title of the executor is completed by confirmation granted by the sheriff of the county in which the deceased died domiciled. The effect of confirmation is to give a title to the executor to administer the estate of the deceased. As a matter of practice, banks do on occasion release funds in the accounts of deceased customers to the persons who appear to be entitled either under the will of a customer or according to the laws of intestacy without insisting that confirmation is taken out. A discharge and indemnity is taken from the person or persons receiving the money.

Section 75 of the Bills of Exchange Act 1882 provides in the case of cheques that the banker's authority to pay them does not cease until notice of the customer's death has actually reached him. The section does not indicate what constitutes notice. When a cheque has to be returned unpaid by reason of the customer's death, the correct answer on the cheque is "Drawer deceased". It is thought that in the case of payments made under standing order, the banker's authority is similarly not determined until actual notice of the customer's death is received. If a deceased customer is indebted to a bank a claim should be intimated against his estate. An executor cannot however be compelled to pay away any part of the estate until six months after the date of death since until that period has elapsed it cannot be known for certain how many creditors there are with claims against the estate of the deceased.[7]

Mental incapacity of customer

Persons who are insane cannot contract and their seeming contracts are void. Such a person therefore cannot open a bank account. The effect of supervening insanity in the case of an existing customer is less well defined. It has been held that temporary insanity did not put an end to the contract between agent and principal and the agent was entitled to charge

---

[4] See *Tournier* v. *National Provincial and Union Bank of England* [1924] 1 K.B. 461.
[5] Bills of Exchange Act 1882, s. 75(2).
[6] *Cf.* the position of the National Savings Bank in this connection. See p. 7.
[7] This is the effect of the Act of Sederunt of 28 February 1662. See also *Taylor & Ferguson* v. *Glass's Trs.*, 1912 S.C. 165.

for work done while his principal was insane.[8] Again, where a party who subsequently became insane had granted a mandate he remained liable on business contracts entered into by the mandatary until the insanity was made public.[9] Where a person becomes incapable of managing his own affairs then it is normal for the court on the petition of a relative or some other person, supported by two medical certificates, to appoint a curator bonis to the incapax. Such an appointment terminates the authority of an incapax customer.[10] It is then the duty of the curator to manage the estate and he is entitled to uplift any sum standing to the credit of the incapax on production of a certified copy of the interlocutor appointing him.

Drunkenness may produce incapacity to consent and therefore incapacity to contract if it reaches a stage at which a person no longer knows what he is doing but if such a person is merely under the influence of drink without being completely intoxicated any contract which he enters into will generally not be reduced on this ground. An obligation undertaken in a state of intoxication is voidable but even in cases of intoxication amounting to complete incapacity it would appear that a party cannot be relieved from his contract unless he repudiates as soon as he recovers his senses and realises what he has done.[11]

Sequestration

The Bankruptcy (Scotland) Act 1985 makes provision for the sequestration of the estate of an individual debtor, a partnership (including a limited partnership), a trust and an unincorporated body (ss. 5 and 6). In all questions under the Act the date of sequestration is either the date on which sequestration is awarded, if the petition is presented by the debtor, or in any other case, the date on which the court grants warrant for the citation of the debtor (s. 12(4)). The act and warrant of confirmation in favour of the permanent trustee vests in him, as at the date of sequestration, all property of the debtor (s. 31) and subject to section 32(9) no dealing of the debtor with such property is of any effect in a question with the permanent trustee (s. 32(8)). Accordingly, sequestration terminates the banker's authority to pay cheques drawn on him by the debtor unless the cheques have been drawn in the ordinary course of business between him and the debtor and the banker was unaware of the sequestration and had no reason to believe that his customer's estate had been sequestrated or was the subject of sequestration proceedings (s. 32(9)(b)(iii)).[12] Consequently, on learning that a petition has been presented to sequestrate a customer, a banker should forthwith cease to honour his cheques. Operations on the account should only be resumed once the petition has actually been dismissed since another creditor may have himself sisted in place of the petitioning creditor and follow out the

---

[8] *Wink* v. *Mortimer* (1849) 11 D. 995.
[9] *Pollok* v. *Paterson*, 10 December 1811, F.C.
[10] *Mitchell & Baxter* v. *Cheyne* (1891) 19 R. 324.
[11] *Pollok* v. *Burns* (1875) 2 R. 497.
[12] See *Minhas's Tr.* v. *Bank of Scotland*, 1990 S.L.T. 23.

proceedings should the latter withdraw his petition (s. 5(8)). Any credit balance in the account should in due course be paid to the permanent trustee on production of his act and warrant. If the account is overdrawn, the permanent trustee is entitled to recover sums lodged on the date of sequestration.[13]

There is nothing in the 1985 Act to prevent an undischarged bankrupt from continuing or entering into any trade or business,[14] although he may not act as a director of a limited company or be concerned in its management except by leave of the court by which he was made bankrupt.[15] The bankrupt is entitled to obtain employment and retain for himself the money which he earns from this employment except to the extent that the sheriff, on the application of the permanent trustee, determines that his income exceeds what is required to maintain him and his family (s. 32(1) and (2)). It follows therefore that a bankrupt may open a bank account in connection with a business or simply to enable him conveniently to arrange for payment of his living expenses. He may not however obtain credit of £250—the currently prescribed amount—or more without disclosing that he is an undischarged bankrupt (s. 67(9)).

It is also competent for the affairs of an insolvent debtor to be wound up by a voluntary arrangement such as a trust deed for behoof of creditors. The trustee acting under such a deed obtains a specific right of property in the estate conveyed to him by the insolvent. He is accordingly entitled to uplift any credit balance on an account belonging to the insolvent on exhibiting the trust deed in his favour or an extract registered copy of it.

Voluntary winding up

A voluntary winding up of an incorporated company is usually initiated by the company either resolving by special resolution to wind up its affairs—the result is a members' voluntary winding up—or by extraordinary resolution resolving that it cannot, by reason of its liabilities, continue its business and that it is advisable to wind up—a creditors' voluntary winding up (Insolvency Act 1986, s. 84). Whether the winding up is a members' voluntary winding up or a creditors' voluntary winding up it is deemed to commence at the time of the passing of the resolution for voluntary winding up (s. 84). As soon as the banker learns of the passing of the resolution, the mandate for operations on the company's account should be regarded as determined and no further cheques should be paid. If the account of the company is overdrawn then as soon as he receives notification that a meeting of creditors is to be held under section 98 of the Insolvency Act 1986 he is justified in not paying further cheques drawn on the company's account even although the company is not yet in liquidation since payment would simply benefit other creditors at the expense of

---

[13] *Cook's Tr., Petr.*, 1985 S.L.T. 33.
[14] Bell, *Comm.*, II, 434.
[15] Company Directors Disqualification Act 1986, s. 11.

the bank. An exception may be made in the case of a request to pay a cheque drawn for wages since sums advanced for this purpose are entitled to a preferential ranking in the subsequent winding up (Insolvency Act 1986, s. 386 and Sched. 6). Nevertheless, the stipulation should be made that the bank's position must not deteriorate as a result of paying such a cheque and to prevent an increase in the overdraft a lodgment would have to be made to the account. Where the account is in credit the banker is not justified in refusing to honour cheques simply because a meeting of creditors under section 98 of the Insolvency Act 1986 has been advertised. Similarly, there is no bar against the collection of cheques payable to the company—certainly where the account is in credit. Where the account is overdrawn, then unless the cheques are lodged by the company for collection in the ordinary course of business and without collusion between the bank and the company there is the danger that the resultant reduction in the overdraft will be regarded as an unfair preference.[16]

Compulsory winding up

A winding up by the court, usually called compulsory winding up, is initiated by a petition to the court. A company may be wound up by the court if the company is unable to pay its debts or the court is of opinion that it is just and equitable that the company be wound up (Insolvency Act 1986, s. 122(1)(f) and (g)).[17] In both cases the winding up commences at the time of presentation of the petition to the court (s. 129). Operations on the company's account should be stopped immediately. They should only be resumed once the petition has actually been dismissed since any other creditor may have himself sisted in place of the petitioning creditor and follow out the proceedings should the petitioning creditor withdraw his petition.[18]

The time of presentation is important since section 127 provides that any disposition of the company's property after the commencement of the winding up is void unless the court orders otherwise. In *Re Gray's Inn Construction Co. Ltd.*[19] a petition was presented to wind up the company on 3 August 1972. The company's bank, without obtaining a validating order from the court, allowed the company to continue operating its account until 9 October 1972 when a compulsory winding-up order was made by the court. The Court of Appeal held that (1) payments into the account during the period from 3 August to 9 October constituted dispositions of the company's property within section 227 of the Companies Act 1948 (now section 127 of the Insolvency Act 1986) and all payments out of the account, and not merely the excess over payments in, during the same period likewise constituted dispositions of the company's

---

[16] On this subject see *Nordic Travel Ltd.* v. *Scotprint Ltd.*, 1980 S.L.T. 189 and the earlier cases reviewed therein.

[17] s. 122 also lists a number of other grounds on which the petition to wind up may be based.

[18] See *Hepburn & Ross* v. *Tritonia Ltd.*, 1951 S.L.T. (Sh. Ct.) 6; Rules of Court 1965, rule 218C; A.S. Sheriff Court Company Insolvency Rules 1986, rule 21.

[19] [1980] 1 All E.R. 814; see also *Re McGuinness Bros. (U.K.)* (1987) 3 B.C.C. 571.

property; (2) the court's discretion under section 227 should be exercised in the context of the liquidation provisions of the 1948 Act and the court should not, in exercising that discretion, validate any transaction which would result in a pre-liquidation creditor being paid in full at the expense of other creditors who would only receive dividends, unless to do so would benefit the unsecured creditors as a whole. The view was expressed by the court that where it is in the interests of the general body of all creditors of a company which is in the course of being wound up that the company be permitted to continue trading, the court's proper course is to freeze the company's bank account as at the date of presentation of the winding-up petition by discontinuing all further dealings on the existing account as from that date and requiring all subsequent dealings to be on a new and separate account. The Court of Appeal did not deal specifically with payments in cash to the company and it might be possible for a bank still to argue that cheques drawn by the company and presented for payment at the bank counter by one of the company's officials are simply payments to the company of its own money and not dispositions within section 127. There is however no need for any bank to run a risk in this respect since it cannot be compelled to continue an account without the protection of a validating order.

Where the court is asked to wind up a company on the ground that it is just and equitable that it should be wound up it may be common ground between the parties in dispute that the company is solvent and a going concern. Nevertheless, to enable the company's bank to honour the company's cheques it is still necessary for a validating order to be made. If the company is continuing to trade then the order sought is usually one to enable it to sell goods for the time being constituting part of its stock-in-trade in the ordinary course of its business and to pay all debts due or becoming due in the ordinary and proper course of that business. Without such an order, the bank is just as much at risk as in a winding-up situation resulting from the company's inability to pay its debts.

When a winding-up order has been made by the court, the liquidator has a duty to take into his custody or under his control all the property to which the company is entitled (s. 144). He is accordingly entitled to uplift any credit balance on a bank account subject to any claim of the bank by way of set-off or otherwise.

Receivership

The holder of a floating charge over all or any part of the property of a company may appoint a receiver of such part of the property of the company as is subject to the charge (Insolvency Act 1986, s. 51(1)). Additionally, the court, on the application of the holder of such a floating charge, may appoint a receiver (s. 51(2)). Where a receiver is appointed by the holder of the floating charge he is regarded as having been appointed on the day and at the time at which he received the deed of appointment (s. 53(6)). In a court appointment, he is regarded as having been appointed on the date of his appointment (s. 54(5)). Once appointed, the receiver has power to take possession of, collect and get in the property of the company which has been attached by the floating charge by virtue of which he was appointed (s. 55 and Sched. 2). On the appointment of a receiver therefore the bank account of the company should be frozen. If it is in credit, then the receiver has power to uplift this balance subject to the right of the bank to exercise any claim on the money by way of set-off or otherwise. As proof of his appointment, the receiver will be able to produce either his deed of appointment (or a duly certified copy thereof) or a certified copy interlocutor from the court in the case of a court appointment.

Administration order

Section 8 of the Insolvency Act 1986 makes provision for the making of an administration order by the court. During the period for which the order is in force, the affairs, business and property of the company are managed by an administrator appointed for the purpose. An application for an order may be made either by the company or by a creditor. Once a petition has been presented for an order, no steps may be taken to enforce any security over the company's property or carry out any diligence except with the leave of the court (Insolvency Act 1986, s. 10). Once the administration order has been made, the administrator has a duty to take into his custody or under his control all the property to which the company is entitled (Insolvency Act 1986, s. 17). Accordingly, as soon as a banker learns that a petition has been presented for an administration order operations on the company's bank account should be stopped. If the account is in credit, the administrator is entitled to uplift the balance on production of a certified copy of the interlocutor making the administration order.

CHAPTER 4

SPECIAL CUSTOMERS

Married women

With the passing of the Married Women's Property (Scotland) Act 1920 came to an end the long era of subjection, in a legal sense, of married women to their husbands. A married woman, if of full age, is capable of entering into contracts and incurring obligations as if she were unmarried, and her husband is not liable in respect of any contract she may enter into or obligation she may incur on her own behalf.[1] Moreover, any money or estate of a wife lent or intrusted by her to her husband or inmixed with his funds is, on his bankruptcy, no longer treated as an asset of the husband.[2]

Firms and partners

The law relating to partnership is regulated by the Partnership Act 1890.[3] Partnership is defined in section 1(1) as the relation which subsists between persons carrying on a business (and that includes every trade, occupation or profession (s. 45)) in common with a view to profit. Companies registered under the Companies Acts or incorporated by Act of Parliament or Royal Charter are declared not to be partnerships within the meaning of the Act. Societies, clubs and other organisations not conducted with a view to profit are not partnerships. Persons who have entered into partnership are for the purposes of the Act called collectively a firm and the name under which the business is carried on is called the firm name (s. 4(1)). By section 716 of the Companies Act 1985 no partnership may consist of more than 20 persons if formed for the purpose of carrying on a business. However, this does not restrict the formation of professional partnerships. Any number is now permitted in the case of a firm practising as solicitors or (subject to each partner being qualified in terms of section 389 of the 1985 Act) accountants or members of a recognised stock exchange.[4] Regulations made under section 716(3) of the 1985 Act have authorised unrestricted partnerships in the case of patent agents, surveyors, auctioneers, estate agents, valuers, chartered engineers, building designers and loss adjusters, subject in each case to a prescribed proportion of members of the firm being members of the appropriate professional body.

---

[1] Its provisions are effectively restated in s. 24 of the Family Law (Scotland) Act 1985.

[2] Bankruptcy (Scotland) Act 1985, s. 75(2).

[3] Common law otherwise prevails except so far as inconsistent with the express provisions of the Act (s. 46).

[4] Companies Act 1985, s. 716(2).

In determining whether a partnership does or does not exist section 2 of the 1890 Act provides that regard shall be had to the following rules. (1) Joint tenancy, tenancy in common, joint property, common property or part ownership, does not of itself create a partnership as to anything owned, whether the tenants or owners do or do not share any profits made by the use of the property.[5] (2) The sharing of gross returns does not of itself create a partnership, whether the persons sharing such returns have or have not a joint or common right or interest in any property from which the returns are derived. (3) The receipt by a person of a share of the profits of a business is prima facie evidence that he is a partner in the business but the receipt of such a share, or of a payment contingent on or varying with the profits of a business, does not of itself make him a partner in the business; though a contract that a person shall receive a fixed sum "out of the profits" of a business is equivalent to a contract that he shall receive a "share of the profits".[6] In particular, (a) the receipt by a person of a debt or other liquidated amount by instalments or otherwise out of the accruing profits of a business does not make him a partner in the business or liable as such; (b) a contract for the remuneration of a servant or agent of a person engaged in a business by a share of the profits of the business does not of itself make the servant or agent a partner in the business or liable as such; (c) a person being the widow or child of a deceased partner and receiving by way of annuity a portion of the profits made in the business in which the deceased was a partner, is not by reason only of such receipt a partner in the business; (d) the advance of money by way of loan to a person engaged or about to engage in any business, on a contract with that person that the lender shall receive a rate of interest varying with the profits or shall receive a share of the profits arising from carrying on the business, does not of itself make the lender a partner with the person or persons carrying on the business or liable as such, provided that the contract is in writing and signed by all of the parties; (e) a person receiving by way of annuity or otherwise a portion of the profits of a business in consideration of the sale by him of the goodwill of the business is not by reason only of such receipt a partner in the business.

These rules are based on the supposition that each set of circumstances occurs in isolation. They provide that any such set of circumstances shall not "of itself" be conclusive in determining the existence or otherwise of a partnership. The same facts, in association with other facts, may nevertheless be important elements in deciding whether there is a partnership or not.[7] The main rule at common law is that regard must be paid to the real agreement and true intention of the parties as appearing from the whole facts of the case and if the agreement is not in writing the agreement and intention must be ascertained from the words and conduct of the parties.[8] A person may be barred by his personal actings from

---

[5] *Glasgow Heritable Trust* v. *Inland Revenue*, 1954 S.L.T. 97.
[6] *Re Young* [1896] 2 Q.B. 484.
[7] *Stewart* v. *Buchanan* (1903) 6 F. 15 at p. 22.
[8] *Badley* v. *Consolidated Bank* (1888) 38 Ch.D. 238.

pleading that he is not a partner in a firm for everyone who represents himself, or knowingly allows himself to be represented, as a partner in a particular firm is liable as a partner to anyone who has, on the faith of such representation, given credit to the firm (s. 14(1)). Where, however, after a partner's death the partnership business is carried on in the old firm name the continued use of that name or of the deceased partner's name as part of it, does not of itself render his estate liable for any partnership debts incurred after his death (s. 14(2)).

Firm a separate person

It is a distinctive feature of the law of Scotland that a partnership or firm is deemed in law to be a person distinct from the individual partners and capable of entering into obligations and contracts and of holding moveable property in its own distinctive name and for its own benefit. As a consequence, the funds of a partnership belong to itself (and not to the partners as joint owners) and debts due by the firm must, in the first instance, be constituted against the firm itself and not against the individual partners, although they are ultimately liable *singuli in solidum* for the debts of the partnership due to third parties. In addition, the firm may stand in the relation of debtor and creditor to any of its partners and may sue and be sued by them. A firm may be sequestrated while the individual partners remain solvent and creditors may arrest in the hands of a firm moneys due to an individual partner.

Joint and several liability of partners

Every partner in a firm is liable jointly with the other partners, and in Scotland severally also, for all debts and obligations of the firm incurred while he is a partner; and after his death his estate is also severally liable for such debts and obligations so far as they remain unsatisfied, but subject in England and Northern Ireland to the prior payment of his separate debts (s. 9). A person who is admitted as a partner into an existing firm is not, without a special stipulation to that effect, liable for any debts contracted prior to his becoming a partner (s. 17(1)). Where a person deals with a firm after a change in its constitution he is entitled to treat all apparent members of the old firm as being still members until he has notice of the change (s. 36(1)). The estate of a partner who dies, or who becomes bankrupt, or of a partner who, not having been known to the person dealing with the firm to have been a partner, retires from the firm, is not liable for partnership debts contracted after the date of the death, bankruptcy or retirement respectively (s. 36(3)). After the dissolution of a partnership, the authority of each partner to bind the firm and the other rights and obligations of the partners, continues, so far as may be necessary, for the purpose of winding up the affairs of the partnership and completing transactions begun but unfinished at the date of dissolution (s. 38).[9] With regard to persons who had dealings with a firm prior to the retiral of a partner, it is only necessary to show that such persons actually had notice of the fact of retiral. Intimation in the *London* or *Edinburgh Gazette* or in a newspaper is sufficient if it can be shown that the customer of the firm actually saw it or had it brought to his notice. Intimation by circular, a change in the name of the firm displayed on its premises, general knowledge as to the change of name, an alteration in the manner of signing cheques, are each sufficient provided it can be shown that the creditor was aware of the fact.

Powers and liabilities of partners

Every partner is an agent of the firm and his other partners for the purpose of the business of the partnership; and the acts of every partner who does any act for carrying on, in the usual way, business of the nature carried on by the firm of which he is a partner, binds the firm and his co-partners, unless the partner so acting has, in fact, no authority to act for the firm in the particular matter and the person with whom he is dealing either knows this or does not know or believe him to be a partner (s. 5). The rules which regulate the relations between a firm and persons dealing with it are governed by law and cannot be modified by any agreement made among the partners themselves. From the fact that each partner is the agent of the firm it follows that an admission or representation made by any partner concerning the partnership affairs in the ordinary course of its business is evidence against the firm (s. 15) and notice to a partner who habitually acts in the partnership business of any matter relating to partnership affairs operates as notice to the firm, except in the case of a fraud on the firm committed by that partner (s. 16). A partner of a trading firm has ostensible authority on behalf of his firm to enter into a composition contract with a debtor[10] and to purchase goods of the type dealt in by the firm,[11] but not in the normal case to undertake a cautionary obligation.[12]

Each partner has an implied power to borrow money or to overdraw on the credit of the firm, provided that the borrowing of money is necessary or incidental to the business of the firm, as in the case of an ordinary trading firm.[13] Where a partner has such an implied authority a bank is not bound to inquire as to how the money is to be applied.[14] The power to borrow money implies the power to pledge the firm's personal property in security of an advance.[15] If the business of the partnership is not of such a nature as to require the granting of bills, no partner has an implied

---

[9] In *Dickson* v. *National Bank of Scotland*, 1917 S.C.(H.L.) 50 it was held that a partner of a firm who, eight years after the dissolution of the firm, indorsed a deposit receipt payable to the firm, had authority to do so.

[10] *Mains & McGlashan* v. *Black* (1895) 22 R. 329.

[11] *Logy* v. *Durham* (1697) Mor. 14566.

[12] *Shiell's Trs.* v. *Scottish Property Investment Co. Bldg. Socy.* (1884) 12 R. (H.L.) 14.

[13] *Bryan* v. *Butters* (1892) 19 R. 490.

[14] *Ibid.*

[15] *ex p. Bonbonus* (1803) 8 Ves. 540.

authority to draw or indorse bills in the firm name.[16] For example, the drawing and indorsing of bills does not fall within the implied power of a partner of a firm of solicitors[17] nor does the borrowing of money by him on behalf of his firm.[18]

Where one partner pledges the credit of the firm for a purpose apparently not connected with the firm's ordinary course of business the firm is not bound unless such partner is in fact specially authorised by the other partners (s. 7).[19] Accordingly, a person who has dealings with a partner in matters outwith the scope of his firm's business or in matters purely personal to that partner, cannot subsequently bind the firm. In *Paterson Brothers* v. *Gladstone*[20] a partner in a building firm who had no authority to sign bills on behalf of the firm adhibited the firm's signature to promissory notes in favour of a moneylender. He used the money for his own purposes and it was held that the firm was not liable for payment since the transaction had not been in the course of the firm's business and the moneylender had discounted the notes in suspicious circumstances, without inquiry. Similarly, a partner cannot pledge his firm's goods or credit for his private debt.[21] Where there is an agreement between the partners that the power of one or more of them shall be restricted no act done in contravention of the agreement is binding on the firm as regards persons having notice of it (s. 8).

Where one partner acting within the scope of his apparent authority receives the money or property of a third person and misapplies it, or where a firm in the course of its business receives money or property of a third person and this is misapplied by one or more of the partners while it is in the custody of the firm, the firm is liable to make good the loss (s. 11). The liability of the partners is joint and several (s. 12). A firm is not responsible for the wrongful act of a partner if the wrongful act is not connected with, or is outwith the scope of, the partnership business nor is the firm responsible if one of the partners, while acting as a trustee, improperly employs trust money, though this money may be followed and recovered from the firm if still in its possession or under its control (s. 13).

Changes in constitution of firms

A partner who retires from a firm does not thereby cease to be liable for partnership debts or obligations incurred before his retirement (s. 17(2)). No agreement with his partners can free him—even if he leaves enough money to pay the partnership debts and takes a bond from his partners that they will do so he remains liable unless the debts are in fact paid.[22] However, payment of a debt by one partner releases all the others from

---

[16] *Backhouse* v. *Charlton* (1878) 8 Ch.D. 444.
[17] *Forster* v. *Mackreth* (1867) L.R. 2 Exch. 163.
[18] *Plumer* v. *Gregory* (1874) L.R. 18 Eq. 621.
[19] *Clydesdale Bank Ltd.* v. *Continental Chocolate Co.* (1917) (not reported).
[20] (1891) 18 R. 403.
[21] *Walker* v. *Smith* (1906) 8 F. 619.
[22] *Walker* v. *Davidson* (1821) 1 S. 21; *Milliken* v. *Love* (1803) Hume 754.

liability and a payment by the new firm discharges the old firm. Similarly, the release of one partner from a partnership debt releases all the others, subject to the rules of sequestration where such rules apply. A retiring partner may be discharged from any existing liabilities by an agreement to that effect between himself and the members of the firm as newly constituted and the creditors, and this agreement may be either express, or inferred as a fact from the course of dealing between the creditors and the firm as newly constituted (s. 17(3)). A creditor, by treating the continuing partners as his debtors, does not necessarily discharge a retiring partner but he will be held as having done so by adopting the continuing partners as his debtors.[23] Where a partner dies, a creditor who is aware of the fact does not release that partner's estate simply by continuing to deal with the firm as before unless there is evidence that he has shown an intention to abandon his right of recourse against the deceased partner's estate.

A person who is admitted as a partner into an existing firm does not thereby become liable to the creditors of the firm for anything done before he became a partner (s. 17(1)). By the admission of another partner into a firm a new firm is constituted but the partners of a firm which has contracted a trade or other debt cannot free themselves of the obligation to pay that debt by the mere act of entering into a new partnership with a third person.[24] So, if at the time of the assumption of a partner, the old firm is indebted to a bank, the bank is entitled on the bankruptcy of the firm subsequent to the admission of the new partner to rank on the estates of the new firm and of the old partners, even although no operations by the new firm have taken place on the account.[25] It is settled law that when the whole assets of a going concern are handed over to a new partnership and the business is continued on the same footing as before, the presumption is that the liabilities are taken over with the assets.[26] Where, however, a partner assumed into a business contributes to the capital of the business a sum of money, while the other partners contribute merely their respective shares in the concern, it is possible that special circumstances would require to be proved in order to render the new partner liable for obligations incurred prior to the change.[27]

Any partner may, if he choose, assign either absolutely or in security his own share in a firm to a third party, so long as this does not interfere with the conduct of the partnership or the rights and interests of the respective partners.[28] The assignation does not entitle the assignee to interfere in the management of the partnership and he is only entitled to receive the share of profits to which the assigning partner would otherwise have been entitled (s. 31(1)). Where the assignation has been

---

[23] *Pearston v. Wilson* (1859) 19 D. 197.
[24] *Ridgway v. Brock* (1831) 10 S. 105.
[25] *Miller v. Thorburn* (1861) 23 D. 659; *Heddle's Exrx. v. Marwick & Hourston's Tr.* (1888) 15 R. 698.
[26] *Thomson & Balfour v. Boag & Son*, 1936 S.C. 2.
[27] *Stephen's Tr. v. Macdougall & Co.'s Tr.* (1889) 16 R. 779; *Heddle's Exrx. v. Marwick & Hourston's Tr.*, supra; *Thomson & Balfour v. Boag & Son*, supra.
[28] *Cassels v. Stewart* (1879) 6 R. 936; (1881) 8 R. (H.L.) 1.

granted simply as a security, the assignee, although entitled to a share in the profits of the business, is not personally liable for any of the firm's debts.[29]

Dissolution of partnership

Subject to any agreement between the partners, a partnership is dissolved (a) if entered into for a fixed term, by the expiration of that term; (b) if entered into for a single adventure or undertaking, by the termination of that adventure or undertaking; (c) if entered into for an undefined time, by any partner giving notice to the others of his intention to dissolve the partnership (s. 32). Subject to any agreement between the partners, every partnership is dissolved as regards all the partners by the death or bankruptcy of any partner (s. 33(1)) and a partnership may, at the option of the partners, be dissolved if any partner suffers his share of the partnership property to be charged under the Act for his separate debt (s. 33(2)). On the application of a partner, the court may grant a decree of dissolution of partnership (a) when any partner becomes insane; (b) when any partner other than the partner suing, becomes permanently incapable of performing his part of the partnership contract; (c) when any partner other than the partner suing, has been guilty of such conduct as in the opinion of the court, having regard to the nature of the business, is calculated to affect prejudicially the carrying on of the business; (d) when any partner, other than the partner suing, wilfully or persistently commits a breach of the partnership agreement or otherwise so conducts himself in matters relating to the partnership business as to make it unreasonably practicable for the other partners to carry on the business in partnership with him; (e) when the business can only be carried on at a loss; or (f) when circumstances have arisen which in the opinion of the court render it just and equitable that the partnership be dissolved (s. 35).

Firm as customer of a bank

Whenever a partner signs the name of his firm in connection with transactions relating to the ordinary business of the firm, such signature is sufficient to bind the firm and all the partners (s. 6). Any partner has a prima facie authority to draw on the firm bank account in the firm name and implied authority to bind the firm by cheque,[30] as long as it is not postdated.[31] Where an account is opened in the name of a firm, a bank is, in the absence of special agreement, bound only to honour cheques signed with that name.[32] On the death of one partner in a firm having an account at a bank, the surviving partner or partners may continue to operate it.[33] Where a partner of a firm opens an account in his own name,

---

[29] *Hardie* v. *Cameron* (1879) 19 S.L.R. 833; Act, s. 2(3).
[30] *Backhouse* v. *Charlton* (1878) 8 Ch.D. 444.
[31] *Forster* v. *Mackreth* (1867) L.R. 2 Ex. 163.
[32] *Ibid.*
[33] *Backhouse* v. *Charlton*, *supra.*

he may prove that in doing so he was acting not on his own behalf, but as the agent of his firm.[34] It then follows that if it is known to the banker to be a partnership account, all the partners are entitled to sue the banker for dishonouring a cheque drawn on the bank by one partner for partnership purposes.[35] The mere existence of a trade partnership does not, however, imply that a partner has power to open an account in his own name for behoof of the firm so as to make his co-partners liable for any debit balance.[36] In such a case a mandate, or alternatively, a guarantee should be taken binding the firm and partners jointly and severally.

While a bank is bound to honour the cheque of any partner of a firm drawn on an account in name of the firm and signed in the firm name, they are not bound to honour a cheque drawn by anyone purporting to be a partner but not known to the bank as such and with whose signature they are not acquainted.[37] Where a bank has accounts in the name of a firm, each partner having the right to draw cheques, and also in name of the individual partners, it is not the duty of the bank to inquire into the propriety of any transfer of funds which may be made to and from the different accounts.[38] Any partner of a firm may intimate that cheques on the firm's account are not to be honoured unless he signs and effect must be given to this intimation. A partner has authority also to countermand payment of a cheque drawn in the firm name by another partner.[39] One partner, however, has no authority to authorise an employee of the firm or other third party to operate on the partnership account. The mandate to operate should be signed by all of the partners.

On the death or bankruptcy of a partner, no notice of any kind is required to free his representatives of liability for debts contracted subsequent to such event—each is a public fact. If it is the bank's intention to hold a retiring partner, or the representatives of a deceased partner, liable for the obligations due as at the date of retiral or death of that partner, the bank must, on receiving notice of the retiral or the death of the partner, stop operations on the account. If this is not done and operations are allowed to continue, the rule of *Clayton's Case* will apply.[40] If the retiring or deceased partner has pledged security for the firm's obligations, he or his representatives are entitled to call on the bank to reconvey the security subjects in the event of subsequent payments into the account being sufficient to extinguish the balance outstanding at the date of retiral or death, as the case may be.[41]

---

[34] *Cooke* v. *Seeley* (1848) 2 Ex. 746.
[35] *Ibid.*
[36] *Alliance Bank Ltd.* v. *Kearsley* (1871) L.R. 6 C.P. 433.
[37] *Cooke* v. *Seeley, supra.*
[38] *Backhouse* v. *Charlton* (1878) 8 Ch.D. 444.
[39] *Gaunt* v. *Taylor* (1843) 2 Hare 413.
[40] *Devaynes* v. *Noble (Clayton's Case)* (1816) 1 Mer. 572; see also *Deeley* v. *Lloyd's Bank* (1912) 29 T.L.R. 1.
[41] *Christie* v. *Royal Bank of Scotland* (1839) 1 D. 745; affd. (1841) 2 Rob.App. 118.

Limited partnerships

The Limited Partnerships Act 1907 has a misleading title for a condition precedent to any benefit to be derived from the statute in that there must be in the firm one or more persons, called general partners, who incur full liability. Subject to the provisions of the 1907 Act, the Partnership Act 1890 and the rules of equity and common law applicable to partnerships, except so far as they are inconsistent with the express provisions of the last-mentioned Act, apply to limited partnerships (1907 Act, s. 7).

A limited partnership is bound by the restrictions on the number of its partners in the same way as an ordinary partnership since in the relevant statutory provisions the word "partnership" is used without qualification. It must "consist of one or more persons, called general partners, who shall be liable for all debts and obligations of the firm, and one or more persons to be called limited partners, who shall at the time of entering into such partnership contribute thereto a sum or sums as capital or property valued at a stated amount, and who shall not be liable for the debts or obligations of the firm beyond the amount so contributed" (s.4(2)). In the case of limited partnerships, the word "limited" does not form part of the firm name and those trading with the partnership are not put upon inquiry and made aware that there is a limitation to the liability of some of the partners. The registration of a limited partnership is effected by sending to the Registrar of Companies a statement signed by the partners containing the particulars of registration prescribed by section 8. If the statement is not registered the partnership is deemed to be a general partnership and every limited partner is deemed to be a general partner (s. 5).

A limited partner under the Act labours under certain disabilities. For instance, he cannot during the continuance of the partnership draw out or receive back any part of his contribution and if he does so he still remains liable for the debts and obligations of the firm up to the amount drawn out or received back (s. 4(3)). Again, he has no power to take part in the management of the partnership business nor to bind the firm. He may, however, at any time inspect the books of the firm and consult with the partners about the partnership business; but if he takes part in the management of the partnership business (what degree of management is not specified) he is liable for all the debts and obligations of the firm incurred while he takes part in the management as though he were a general partner (s. 6(1)). Further, subject to any agreement between the partners, any difference arising as to ordinary matters connected with the partnership business may be decided by a majority of the general partners. A limited partner may, with the consent of the general partners, assign his share in the partnership. The other partners are not entitled to dissolve the partnership by reason of any limited partner suffering his share to be charged for his separate debt and a person may be introduced as a partner without the consent of the existing limited partner. A limited partner is not entitled to dissolve the partnership by notice (s. 6(5)).

Business names

The provisions of the Business Names Act 1985 apply to persons who have a place of business in Great Britain and who carry on business in Great Britain under a name which in the case of a partnership does not consist of the surnames or corporate names of all the partners, or in the case of an individual does not consist of that individual's name, or in the case of a limited company does not consist of its corporate name (s. 1(1)). Persons subject to section 1 may not give the impression of any connection with H.M. Government or a local authority or include any word or expression prohibited by regulation without the written approval of the Secretary of State (s. 2(1)). A person to whom the provisions of the Act apply must (1) except for partnerships of more than 20 persons, state legibly on all business letters, orders to suppliers and similar documents issued in the course of business: (a) in the case of a partnership, the name of each partner; (b) in the case of an individual, his name; (c) in the case of a limited company, its corporate name; and (d) for each person named, an address in Great Britain at which service of documents relating to the business will be effective (s. 4(1)(a)); (2) in any business premises to which customers or suppliers have access, display prominently a notice containing the names and addresses referred to in (1) in a place where it may easily be read (s. 4(1)(b)); and (3) supply in writing the names and addresses referred to in (1) to any person with whom anything is discussed in the course of business and who asks for such details (s. 4(2)).

In the case of a partnership consisting of more than 20 persons there is an exemption from listing all the names and addresses of the partners provided that a list of their names is kept at the firm's principal place of business (s. 4(3)). To take advantage of this exemption, the firm's stationery must state the address of the partnership's principal place of business and indicate that the list of the partners' names is open to inspection there (s. 4(3)(b)).

The civil remedy provided for a breach of these regulations is that legal proceedings brought by any person to enforce a right under a contract made in the course of a business may be dismissed if that person was in breach of the disclosure requirements. The defender, however, has to show that he in turn has been unable to pursue a claim against that person arising out of the same contract because of the failure to disclose or that he has suffered financial loss in connection with the contract because of the failure (s. 5).

Factors, agents and mandataries

There are various kinds of agency. A factor is an agent who buys or sells for his principal on commission and is intrusted with the possession, management and disposal of his principal's property. A broker, like a factor, is an agent who buys or sells for his principal but is not intrusted with the custody of his principal's property. A factor cannot bind his principal without a specific mandate to do so or possession of his principal's goods. A mandatary is one who, properly speaking, acts for another gratuitously and is in consequence responsible to his principal in a lesser degree than a paid agent.

The relation of principal and agent is a personal one and generally speaking an agent has no power to delegate his authority. Agency may be either general or special. In the former case the agent undertakes the management of his principal's affairs, either entirely or of some particular branch, according to the usage of trade in that business. In the latter, the agent's authority is limited to the performance of a particular act or class of acts, or the conduct of a particular business transaction.

General agency

A general agent has power to bind his principal by any act which properly comes within the scope of his authority and is sanctioned by the usage of trade. A general agent, even if he has special instructions from his principal as to the particular course he has to follow in the conduct of the business, will nevertheless effectually bind his principal for any act done in the course of that business, though contrary to his special instructions, provided that the person with whom he deals was unaware of the restrictions imposed on him and that the acts were done in accordance with the usual powers entrusted to an agent and with the usage of the particular trade. This rule applies even to the case of a wrongful or fraudulent act on the part of the agent, committed by him for purposes of his own, provided that the third party has acted with due caution. Even if the principal is not liable on the contract, he is liable in damages. In such circumstances, where one of two innocent parties must suffer, the law holds that the loss must fall on him who has given occasion for the commission of the act by which the loss has arisen.[42] Without express authority, however, he has no implied power to borrow money on his principal's credit,[43] but he will bind his principal if the money so borrowed has been applied for the benefit of his principal and not of himself.[44] An agent, though not authorised to draw cheques in the name of his principal and even where there is a stipulation that he is not to do so,[45] can still bind his principal, provided the drawing and indorsing of cheques is incidental to the business of the agency intrusted to him and the person with whom he deals has no notice of the limitation of the agent's authority.[46] It is probably the law that if an agent is placed in apparent control and management of a business, his undisclosed principal is liable on all

---

[42] *Lloyd* v. *Grace, Smith & Co.* [1912] A.C. 716.
[43] *Sinclair, Moorhead & Co.* v. *Wallace & Co.* (1880) 7 R. 874.
[44] *Reid* v. *Rigby & Co.* [1894] 2 Q.B. 40; *Clydesdale Bank* v. *Paul* (1877) 4 R. 626. See also *Commercial Bank of Scotland* v. *Biggar,* 1958 S.L.T. (Notes) 46 (borrowing by solicitor on behalf of client).
[45] *Edmunds* v. *Bushell & Jones* (1865) L.R. 1 Q.B. 97.
[46] *Howard* v. *Bailey* (1795) 2 H.Bl. 618; *Davidson* v. *Stanley* (1841) 2 Man. & G. 721.

contracts which fall within the ordinary scope of that business, even although he has given instructions to the agent not to enter into the particular contracts and the other party has contracted with the agent in the belief that he was a principal.[47] The manager of a business, however, has no power to borrow on the credit of moneys due to his principal.[48]

Special agency

The powers of a special agent are confined to the particular act or class of acts authorised by the principal. A banker dealing with such an agent should take care to see that all actings by him are specifically authorised and should insist on production of his warrant, whether it be a power of attorney or a simple mandate. In the former case if the original deed is not to be delivered a registered extract should be exhibited or a certified copy delivered. In the case of a simple mandate, this should be delivered as a matter of course. An authority to draw on behalf of another does not necessarily imply an authority to indorse on his behalf but, where a person has been in the habit of drawing cheques on his principal's behalf and has on occasion been authorised to indorse cheques and receive payment of them, a presumption may be created that such a person has a general authority to indorse on behalf of his principal.[49] Where power is conferred on an agent to operate on a current account, this power will be held as extending only to operations on the account while it is in credit and no power is implied either to overdraw the account[50] or accept or indorse bills or indorse deposit receipts. Further, a special agent entitled to operate on a current account has no authority, after exhausting that account, to transfer the amount standing at his principal's credit on deposit receipt to the current account in order that he may make further drawings on it. A special agent has no implied authority to do, and cannot bind his principal by, any act unless specific authority has been delegated to him. Accordingly, a solicitor intrusted with the custody of a deposit receipt and in the habit of uplifting the interest due upon it has no authority to uplift the principal.[51] Again, an agent who is instructed to receive payment in cash and who accepts the debtor's cheque, will render himself liable for the amount of the debt if the cheque is subsequently dishonoured.[52]

Termination of agency

Agency may be terminated by notice, written or verbal, or by implication. Recall of the agency by the principal terminates its existence as between the agent and third parties from the time when they become aware of it. The death or bankruptcy of the principal operates as a recall

---

[47] *Hogarth* v. *Wherley* (1875) L.R. 10 C.P. 630.
[48] *Ross, Skolfield & Co.* v. *State Steamship Co.* (1875) 3 R. 134. However, acquiescence by the principal can amount to a mandate. See *Swinbourne & Co.* v. *Western Bank* (1856) 18 D. 1025.
[49] *Prescott* v. *Flinn* (1832) 9 Bing. 9.
[50] *Jacobs* v. *Morris* [1902] 1 Ch. 816.
[51] *Forbes' Exr.* v. *Western Bank* (1854) 16 D. 807.
[52] *Papé* v. *Westacott* [1893] 1 Q.B. 272.

of the agent's authority but transactions entered into by the agent in good faith before he becomes aware of the fact or has had reasonable time to learn of it are valid and binding on the principal or his representatives. Insanity of the principal does not however appear to operate as a recall of the agent's authority, at least until the person dealing with the agent is put in *mala fide* by becoming aware of the insanity.[53] A banker who himself becomes aware of any of these facts should not, of course, honour any further cheques drawn by the agent.

The agency may also be terminated by (1) lapse of time, as when an agent has been appointed for a particular period; (2) the appointment of another agent in place of the first one appointed and due intimation thereof; and (3) the need for an agent ceasing to exist, as on the return of a principal from abroad or his restoration to health, where the agent has been appointed to act during his absence or illness. In such cases a banker who deals with an agent in *bona fide* ignorance of the termination of the agency will be protected. Where a principal places money in a bank on the terms that a known agent should draw on it, he retains the power, if he rightly determines the agency, to require the bank to return the undrawn balance to him.[54]

Investment advisers

The Financial Services Act 1986 established a new regulatory régime for firms and individuals engaged in investment business. The Securities and Investment Board ("SIB"), which exercises powers delegated to it by the Secretary of State for Trade and Industry, in turn operates in the main through Self-Regulatory Organisations ("SROs") and Recognised Professional Bodies ("RPBs"). It is an essential feature of investor protection that a person conducting investment business treats any money, investments or other property of his clients as belonging to such clients. Under section 55 of the Act the SIB may make regulations with respect to the holding of clients' money on trust and the establishment and operation of segregated clients' accounts and it has done so. The Financial Services (Clients' Money) Regulations 1987 require that all clients' money held by a firm in the course of investment business carried on in Scotland is held by the firm as agents (reg. 2.2(1)(*a*)) in a clients' bank account maintained at an approved bank (reg. 3.1(1)). Investors must be paid interest on their accounts unless there is an agreement to the contrary (reg. 2.3). On opening a clients' bank account, the firm must give written notice to the bank concerned (a) that all money in the account is held by the firm as agent and that the bank is not entitled to combine the account with any other account or to exercise any right of set-off and (b) requiring the bank to acknowledge in writing that it accepts the terms of the notice (reg. 3.1(4)). The provisions of the

---

[53] *Pollock* v. *Paterson*, 10 December 1811, F.C.; *Wink* v. *Mortimer* (1849) 11 D. 995; *Drew* v. *Nunn* (1879) L.R. 4 Q.B.D. 661.
[54] *Société Coloniale Anversoise and Others* v. *London and Brazilian Bank Ltd.* (1911) 28 T.L.R. 44.

regulations as to the duties of a firm holding clients' money have effect in place of the corresponding duties which would be owed by a person holding clients' money as agent under common law (reg. 2.2(5)).

The rules do not necessarily apply to members of SROs or RPBs in relation to investment business which they regulate (s. 48(1)), since these bodies set rules for their members which provide investor protection equivalent to that provided by the SIB rules. The rules of The Securities Associations ("TSAs") which govern stockbrokers provide for money held by a firm in the course of investment business carried on in Scotland to be held by the firm as agent upon the terms and for the purposes set out in the SIB regulations already referred to (TSA, CH.III.r.100.02). The Rules of the Financial Intermediaries, Managers and Brokers Regulatory Organisation ("FIMBRA") provide for the same regulations to have effect as part of the FIMBRA Rules (rule 14.4.2). Life assurance intermediaries who describe themselves as insurance "brokers" are required to register with the Insurance Brokers Registration Council and to comply in addition with its rules on separate insurance broking accounts under the terms of the Insurance Brokers (Registration) Act 1977. Section 138(2) of the Financial Services Act 1986 provides that rules made pursuant to sections 10 to 12 of the 1977 Act must take proper account of any provisions applicable to registered insurance brokers under the 1986 Act.

A stockbroker, as a broker, is not entitled without his client's consent to pledge the securities of his client but the fact that a broker is, by implication from a general course of business or actually to the bank's knowledge, acting on behalf of a client, does not amount to a limitation of the broker's authority as to the amount of advances to be obtained on the pledge of any particular security. Even if a broker borrows without any authority from his client an amount larger than he was authorised to borrow, his client as the true owner of the stock which has been pledged will nevertheless be bound by his acts to the extent of the sums advanced by the bank on express contracts of loan.[55] While it is settled that a stockbroker may pledge the securities of his client without his authority, or even against his express instructions, so as to give the bank a valid title to retain them against the specific advances made on their security, it is also equally settled that to enable the bank to do so it must have acted in *bona fide* and with reasonable caution.[56]

Where a stockbroker places the proceeds of a sale of shares to the credit of his own account and that account is overdrawn, it appears that the bank is entitled, without inquiry, and even in the full knowledge that the money so paid in is the proceeds of a sale of stock, to retain the money and apply it in reduction of the overdraft. If, however, the bank has

---

[55] *National Bank of Scotland* v. *Dickie's Tr.* (1895) 22 R. 740.
[56] *London Joint Stock Bank* v. *Simmons* [1892] A.C. 201. See also *Earl of Sheffield* v. *London Joint Stock Bank* (1888) L.R. 13 A.C. 333.

actual knowledge that money paid into a broker's account is paid in fraudulently, it cannot plead a right to retain the money.[57]

Insurance brokers

The Insurance Brokers (Registration) Act 1977 established the Insurance Brokers Registration Council with powers *inter alia* to set up a system of registration for practising brokers and to make rules governing the conduct of insurance broking business. The Insurance Brokers Registration Council (Accounts and Business Requirements) Rules Approval Order 1979[58] governs the manner in which the bank accounts of registered brokers are to be maintained. One or more separate bank accounts have to be maintained with approved banks for each trading name under which insurance business is carried on and the name of the broking firm or company must be incorporated in each account title. In addition, each account must be designated "Insurance Broking Account" and money standing to the credit of such an account must be used solely for the purpose of the Rules (rule 6(1)). In particular, when such an account is opened the bank must confirm in writing that it will not be entitled to any charge, encumbrance, lien, right of set-off, compensation or retention against money standing to the credit of the account except in certain circumstances (rule 6(2)). The purpose of the insurance broking account is to isolate all receipts and payments arising directly from the insurance broking business and accordingly brokers are required to pay into the account money received from all sources relating to insurance transactions in connection with insurance broking business. Additionally, no other account may be used for payment to an insured or an insurance company of money due under insurance transactions of any kind in connection with insurance broking business (rule 6(3) and (4)).

Insurance brokers are however entitled under the Rules to use credit balances from an insurance broking account to purchase "approved short-term assets" which must be in the name of the broker and again designated "Insurance Broking Account" (rule 6(6)). Approved short-term assets include deposit receipts and deposit accounts with banks. No advance, whether by way of loan, overdraft or otherwise, may be obtained by a practising insurance broker for any purpose relating to the insurance broking account except on a bank account with an approved bank in circumstances which do not give rise to a breach of the requirements of rule 8 (rule 6(7)(i)(a)). Loans, which must be of a temporary nature, may be made available to brokers only in respect of payments due by them under insurance transactions in connection with the insurance broking business. Short-term assets may be charged as security for these advances, as well as other assets not subject to the rules (rule 6(7)(i)(c)). It should be noted that these Rules apply only to brokers registered with the Insurance Brokers Registration Council; they do not affect Lloyds

---

[57] *Dunlop's Trs.* v. *Clydesdale Bank* (1893) 20 R. (H.L.) 59.
[58] S.I. 1979 No. 489.

Insurance Brokers who are governed by regulations laid down by the Committee of Lloyds.

Solicitors

The Solicitors (Scotland) Act 1980 empowers the Council of the Law Society of Scotland to make rules as to *inter alia* the opening and keeping by solicitors of accounts and deposits at banks for money not belonging to them and received by them in the course of their practice (s. 35(1)(*a*)). The Solicitors (Scotland) Accounts Rules 1989 provide that every solicitor shall (a) ensure that at all times the sum at the credit of his client account shall not be less than the total of the clients' money held by him and (b) pay into his client account without delay any sum of money exceeding £50 held for or received from or on behalf of a client (rule 4). A "client account" means a bank account in the name of the solicitor in the title of which the word "client", "trustee", "trust" or other fiduciary term appears (rule 2). In respect of such an account, a bank has no right of set-off as against any other liability of the solicitor to it (s. 61(3)). Where a solicitor holds money for a client and, having regard to the amount of the money and the length of time for which it is likely to be held, it is reasonable that interest should be earned for the client, the solicitor is obliged to place such money in a separate interest-bearing client account in the title of which the client's name is specified and to account to the client for any interest earned thereon (rule 13). Without prejudice to the generality of this provision it is reasonable that interest should be earned for a client from the date on which a solicitor receives for the client a sum of money not less than £500 which at the time of its receipt is unlikely within two months thereafter to be either wholly disbursed or reduced by payments to a sum less than £500.

Where the Council of the Law Society of Scotland is satisfied that a sole solicitor is incapacitated by illness or accident to such an extent that he cannot operate on his client account, the right to operate the account vests in the Council if no other arrangements acceptable to the Council have been made (s. 46). Similar provisions are made to deal with a sole solicitor who has died and with solicitors who have been struck off or suspended from practice (s. 45).

There is no accepted rule of law that a solicitor opening an account in his own name for a named client is personally responsible for any debit balance that may become due on the account.[59] Authority to a solicitor to open and operate a current account does not automatically include authority to overdraw but if such authority is granted by the client it need not be written.[60] In such a case, the bank ought to direct the attention of the client to the fact that the account is overdrawn. Even if the solicitor has no authority to overdraw the account, on the principle of recompense

---

[59] *Royal Bank of Scotland* v. *Skinner*, 1931 S.L.T. 382.
[60] *Ibid.*

his client will be liable for any overdraft (including interest) to the extent that he has benefited.[61] A solicitor cannot obtain overdraft facilities in his own name for a client unless (1) he gives the bank details of the client and the arrangements for repayment and (2) he has no personal liability for repayment of the facilities (rule 8).

Clubs, associations, etc.

Where an account is opened in the name of a club, association or other unincorporated body, to be operated on by certain named officials, so long as the bank conforms to the instructions received it is free from responsibility in connection with operations on it. Such an authority, however, does not confer power to borrow since an unincorporated association has, unlike a partnership, no legal personality and cannot incur legal liability. The general rule is that liability for a club debt attaches to the persons who are to be taken to have accepted responsibility for the transaction, or in the case of committee members and office bearers by their knowledge of the transaction.[62] Before any overdraft is allowed on such an account the constitution of the body should be examined to ascertain whether or not there is a power to borrow and, if required, grant security over its property. If there is no such power, the rules should be altered in the manner provided for by the constitution. The rules should also spell out how the power is to be exercised. Since an unincorporated association can now be sequestrated,[63] bankruptcy need not be constituted either against the individual members or those members who are appointed to represent it. To establish personal liability, a guarantee or guarantees should be obtained from members or officials as individuals.

Charities

The Law Reform (Miscellaneous Provisions) (Scotland) Act 1990 made new provision for charities in Scotland and it applies to "recognised bodies". A recognised body is one recognised by the Inland Revenue for the purposes of relief under section 505 of the Income and Corporation Taxes Act 1988 and which is established under the law of Scotland or managed or controlled wholly or mainly in or from Scotland. Such a body may describe itself as "a Scottish Charity" (s. 1). The Act imposes on charities the duty to keep accounting records (s. 4) and to prepare annual amounts and a report (s. 5). Someone who has been convicted of an offence involving dishonesty, is an undischarged bankrupt, has been removed from the management of a charity under section 7 of the Act or is subject to a disqualification order under the Company Directors Disqualification Act 1986, is disqualified from being concerned in the

---

[61] *Commercial Bank of Scotland* v. *Biggar*, 1958 S.L.T. (Notes) 46.
[62] *Cromarty Leasing Ltd.* v. *Turnbull*, 1988 S.L.T. (Sh.Ct.) 62.
[63] Bankruptcy (Scotland) Act 1985, s. 6(1)(c).

management of a charity (s. 8). Where the bank account of a charity is dormant and the balance does not exceed £5,000, then the Scottish charities nominee is empowered to transfer the balance to another recognised body unless there is still someone concerned in the management of the charity or other circumstances make it inappropriate to make the transfer (s. 12(3)). Where the balance exceeds £5,000 (or section 12(3) in general does not apply), the Lord Advocate may appoint new trustees or apply to the Court of Session for the appointment of an interim judicial factor or, as an alternative to the foregoing, apply subsection (3) as if the balance was less than £5,000 and neither paragraph (*a*) nor (*b*) of that subsection applied. The receipt of the nominee when an account is closed is a full and valid discharge to the bank holding the account (s. 12(7)).

Tutors and curators

The office of tutor relates to the guardianship of pupils, that is, of children until they reach in the case of boys the age of fourteen, and in the case of girls the age of twelve; and the office of curator to minors, that is, children from the above ages until they respectively attain the age of eighteen. Between the two offices there is a marked distinction. A tutor has control over both the person and property of the pupil, whereas a curator has control only over the property of the minor. A tutor acts on his own responsibility without any consent on the part of the pupil, who during the period of pupillarity is absolutely incapable of entering into any contract. A curator, on the other hand, acts along with the minor, by whom the obligation is undertaken with consent of the curator. Where a minor has a curator his consent is necessary to his every act except, for example, where he enters into a contract of apprenticeship. Where he has none the law, as gathered from various decisions of the courts, is thus stated in *Jack* v. *North British Railway*[64]: "Where minors have no curators they may act by themselves, and payments made to them by their debtors will be valid and effectual. But the Court of Session will not, in every instance, compel a debtor to pay to a minor who has no curators, at least without his giving security to keep the debtor indemnified, thus indirectly compelling the minor, where this appears to be necessary for his own protection, to have curators appointed to him".

Contracts entered into by a pupil or a minor are voidable at his instance during the *quadriennium utile*—the name given to the period of four years immediately following his attaining majority—on proof of his minority and enorm lesion. Enorm lesion is presumed in the case of a gift by the minor, of a cautionary obligation entered into by him[65] and even in a personal bond for borrowed money, unless it is proved that the money was expended for the actual benefit of the minor.[66] If a minor ratifies the transaction after attaining majority, in the knowledge of his right to

---

[64] (1886) 14 R. 263.
[65] *Macmichael* v. *Barbour* (1840) 3 D. 279.
[66] *Harkness* v. *Graham* (1833) 11 S. 760; *Ferguson* v. *Yuill* (1835) 13 S. 886.

challenge, the contract is binding on him.[67] It is proper to mention, also, that if a minor engages in business, his curator's consent is not required to his dealings and a mercantile obligation is as binding on him as if entered into after the attainment of majority.[68] Similarly, if the minor falsely represented himself as major and was reasonably believed to be such, he is not entitled to restitution.[69]

To those who are unable to manage their own affairs, such as persons incapacitated by reason of senility or mental disorder, the Court of Session or the appropriate sheriff court may, on the application supported by two medical certificates of the next of kin or any near relation, appoint a judicial factor or curator bonis to act for such persons. A local authority or the Mental Welfare Commission may also in appropriate cases petition for the appointment of a curator bonis. When a curator bonis has been appointed to a person of unsound mind, that person is incapacitated from dealing with his own estate.[70] The curator bonis is usually, although not necessarily, a chartered accountant and he is under the supervision of the Accountant of Court. Before entering upon his duties he must find caution for his intromissions. Before permitting the curator to operate on the bank account of the ward the banker is entitled to see his authority in the form of an extract of his act and warrant. Under section 94 of the Mental Health (Scotland) Act 1984 hospital boards of management have limited powers to receive and hold money and valuables on behalf of any person detained under that Act. Currently, they may hold up to £3,000. The consent of the Mental Welfare Commission is required for larger sums.

Executors and trustees

Where an account is opened in the names of the executors of a deceased person, if there are only two executors, cheques on the account must be signed by both. If there are more than two, the signatures of a majority are sufficient. A banker is under no obligation to ascertain more than the fact that executors have a prima facie title. Executors nominate, that is acting under a will, have, unless precluded by the terms and purposes of the will, power to borrow on the security of the estate in the same manner as trustees under section 4 of the Trusts (Scotland) Act 1921 (as amended). Generally speaking, borrowing will only be of a temporary nature as, for example, to meet inheritance tax pending the issue of confirmation and the ingathering of the estate. Such borrowing is usually by way of overdraft from a bank, instructed by a minute from the executors. In the case of executors-dative, who are appointed by the court and require to find caution for their actings, the consent of the cautioner and, possibly, even of the beneficiaries on the estate, might be

---

[67] *Henry* v. *Scott* (1892) 19 R. 545.
[68] Ersk., I, vii, 38; Bell, *Prin.*, § 2100. See *McFeetridge* v. *Stewarts & Lloyds,* 1913 S.C. 773.
[69] Ersk., I, vii, 36; *Kennedy* v. *Weir* (1665) Mor. 11658.
[70] *Mitchell & Baxter* v. *Cheyne* (1891) 19 R. 324.

required for any general borrowing. But where this is simply to meet inheritance tax, etc., a bank will be guided largely by its own knowledge of, and reliance on, the executors personally and/or their solicitors and again an appropriate minute will require to be obtained.

As regards trustees, their powers and duties are regulated primarily by the trust deed under which they act but, where not at variance with the terms and purposes of the trust, trustees are given full power under section 4 of the Trusts (Scotland) Act 1921 (as amended) to borrow money on the security of the trust estate, heritable as well as moveable. The trust nature of such an account should be clearly shown in the bank's books and where cheques are not to be signed by at least a majority and quorum of the trustees (assuming this is in accord with the trust deed), operations should be instructed by a minute containing, if necessary, power to overdraw. If trustees borrow in the course of administering the trust estate, they are personally liable unless it has been agreed with the bank that the trust estate alone is to be liable.[71] Similarly, if trustees continue the truster's business or enter into a new one, they are personally liable to trade creditors.[72]

Incorporated companies

The Companies Act 1985 (since amended by the Companies Act 1989) consolidated the bulk of the previous Companies Acts. While it governs all registered companies all companies are not incorporated under it. By far the largest number of companies are incorporated under the earlier Companies Acts and although a company can still be incorporated by Royal Charter or by a private Act of Parliament such companies are quite exceptional. A public company means a company limited by shares or limited by guarantee having a share capital, being a company (a) whose memorandum states that it is to be a public company and (b) which has been registered or re-registered as a public company (s. 1(3)). "Private company" means a company that is not a public company (s. 1(3)). The minimum number of persons who may form a public company is now two instead of seven as formerly (s. 1(1)). The name of a public company must in all cases end with the words "public limited company" and must not be preceded by the word "limited" (s. 25(1)). A company whose registered office is in Wales may use the Welsh language equivalent. (There is no provision for a company registered in Scotland to use the Gaelic language equivalent.) It is also permissible to use the abbreviation "p.l.c." or its Welsh equivalent. Public companies must have an allotted capital of not less than the authorised minimum, fixed at present at £50,000 (s. 118(1)), all of which must be issued but need only be one-quarter paid-up; any share premium must be fully paid-up (s. 101(1)). Companies limited by guarantee and having a share capital may continue in existence but no

---

[71] *Gordon* v. *Campbell* (1842) 1 Bell's App. 428.
[72] *Ford & Sons* v. *Stephenson* (1886) 16 R. 24.

such companies may be created in future (s. 1(4)). The Act provides no specific definition of a private company, this being the residual category of companies which are not public companies. All companies whose names end merely with the word "limited" are taken to be private companies. Private companies must not offer shares or debentures to the public either directly or indirectly (s. 81). A private company is not required to restrict the transferability of its shares but if it does not do so it may be difficult to determine whether or not an offer of shares is in breach of the prohibition on offers to the public.

There are a relatively small number of private unlimited companies which have been registered under the Companies Acts in this form. An unlimited company is defined as "a company not having any limit on the liability of its members" (s. 1(2)(c)). Although the liability of the members of an unlimited company is unlimited, their position is fundamentally different from the partners of a partnership, whose obligation for partnership debts is also unlimited. If the creditors of an unlimited company cannot obtain payment from the company, they may petition the court for a winding-up order; the liquidator will then ask the members to contribute to the payment of the company's debts and the costs of the winding up and their liability to do so is unlimited. The name of the company need not incorporate "limited" or "public limited company" at the end. The articles of association of an unlimited company must be registered and a banker dealing with an unlimited company will be guided by its memorandum and articles of association, which must conform to Table E as now prescribed by statutory instrument.

Execution of documents

When a company is incorporated a separate legal entity comes into existence, acting through its representatives and agents. The company contracts through those parties authorised to act on its behalf whether their authority is express or implied. Section 72 of the Law Reform (Miscellaneous Provisions) (Scotland) Act 1990 introduced a new section 36B into the 1985 Act dealing with the execution of documents. Its provisions apply to documents which are governed and construed in accordance with the law of Scotland and executed by companies whether or not such companies are themselves incorporated in Scotland. Subsection (2) provides that a document is validly executed by a company if it is signed on behalf of the company by a director or the secretary or by a person authorised by the company to sign the document. In the case of bills of exchange (including cheques) the signatory should expressly state that he is signing "on behalf of" the company. However, for the purposes of the law relating to the authentication of documents, a document is validly executed if it is subscribed on behalf of the company by (a) two directors; (b) a director and the secretary; or (c) two persons authorised to subscribe the document. The subscription need not be attested by witnesses and the document need not be sealed (s. 36B(3)). A document executed in this fashion is a probative document (s. 36B(4)).

Bills of exchange (including cheques) or promissory notes may be drawn, accepted or indorsed in the name of the company by any person acting under its authority (s. 37). A document or proceeding merely requiring authentication by a company may be signed by a director, secretary or other authorised officer of the company and need not be under its common seal (s. 41). A company no longer has to have a common seal (s. 36B(5)).

Directors and other officers

Every company must have at least one director. A private company need only have one director unless the articles of association provide otherwise (s. 282(3)). A public company unless registered before 1929 must have at least two directors (s. 282(1)). Every company must have a secretary and the sole director cannot also be the secretary nor can an act requiring the authority of two officers of the company be done on the authority of one person holding the offices of both director and secretary (ss. 283 and 284). The Act requires the secretary of a public company to have certain qualifications. He must be a member of one of the legal or accountancy professions or a chartered secretary or be someone who, in the opinion of the directors, is capable of discharging the functions of company secretary (s. 286). In principle, no person can be appointed a director of a public company if at the time of his appointment he has attained the age of 70 (s. 293(2)). The Company Directors Disqualification Act 1986 provides that an undischarged bankrupt cannot act as a director or take part in the management of a company except with the leave of the court which adjudged him bankrupt (s. 11). In addition, the same Act provides that the following persons may be subject to disqualification orders by the court: (1) persons convicted of an offence in connection with the management or the liquidation or receivership of a company; (2) persons persistently in default in connection with the delivering to the Registrar of Companies of documents required by the Companies Act; and (3) in the course of a winding up, persons guilty of an offence under section 458 (fraudulent trading) or otherwise guilty of breach of duty as an officer, liquidator or receiver or manager of a company. Disqualification orders may cover a period of up to five years in the case of (2) but otherwise up to 15 years (ss. 2, 3 and 4). Further, by section 5 of the Act, a person who has been a director of an insolvent company and whose conduct demonstrates that he is unfit to be concerned in the management of a company can be disqualified for a minimum period of two years.

Certificate of incorporation

This certificate, issued by the Registrar of Companies, is conclusive evidence that the statutory requirements in connection with the incorporation of the company have been complied with (s. 13(7)). A private company can commence business immediately this certificate is granted and accordingly operations on its bank account, including borrowing, can begin whenever the original certificate has been exhibited to the bank. In the case of a newly formed public company, before the banker can permit operations on the bank account, he must also see the certificate from the Registrar entitling the company to commence business (s. 117). Prior to this, the banker may permit payments into the company's account but he cannot allow withdrawals with the exception of allotment money repaid to applicants. There is no requirement for the approval of the Department of Trade to be obtained for the adoption or the change of a company's name. The burden of choosing a legally admissible name rests on the incorporators of the company. When a company has changed its name, the Registrar issues a new certificate of incorporation, showing the new name of the company. The date of issue of the certificate of incorporation on change of name is the effective date of the name change (s. 28(6)) and from this date the company must use the new name on all letters, documents, deeds and on its seal. Certain companies formed for the purpose of promoting art, science, religion, charity or any similar object may dispense with the use of the word "limited" in their name. The responsibility for complying with the statutory requirements for such exemption now rests on those who seek to obtain it and they do so by making a statutory declaration in the prescribed form (s. 30(4)). It should be noted that the memorandum and articles of association of such a company must require its profits or other income to be applied in promoting its objects and they must prohibit the payment of dividends or the distribution of its assets to its members.[73]

Memorandum and articles of association

Information regarding the powers and objects of a company is contained in its memorandum of association. The arrangements regarding the internal management of the company are contained in the articles of association. It is essential that a copy of a company's memorandum and articles of association be in the possession of its bankers. The memorandum of association can be altered by special resolution but only to the extent permitted by the Act (s. 4). The articles of association on the other hand can be altered or amended by special resolution without restriction (s. 9). Companies limited by shares are not obliged to have their own articles of association although this is essential in the case of a company limited by guarantee or an unlimited company (s. 7). The Companies (Tables A to F) Regulations 1985[74] contain a set of regulations for the management of a company limited by shares known as Table A. They may be adopted in whole or in part by any company. It is usually necessary therefore when referring to a company's arrangements for internal management to read the company's articles of association in conjunction with Table A. If articles are not registered—and in the case of a company limited by shares there is no obligation to register articles—

---

[73] Where a company is a charity, this must be clearly stated. See p. 70.
[74] S.I. 1985 No. 805.

Table A in the form in which it is in force at the date of registration will constitute its articles (s. 8). In the case of a company limited by shares formed after the passing of the 1985 Act, the regulations contained in Table A as prescribed, so far as not excluded or modified, apply to the company (s. 8(2)). It should be noted however that companies incorporated prior to the passing of the 1985 Act are regulated by the regulations contained in the version of Table A contained in the particular Act under which they were incorporated. It is however open to such companies by special resolution to adopt Table A as now prescribed.

OBJECTS CLAUSE AND ULTRA VIRES DOCTRINE. The objects clause which is contained in the company's memorandum of association defines the capacity of the company to act as a legal person and a company cannot act beyond the powers (*i.e. ultra vires*) defined in this clause. A transaction which is *ultra vires* the company is void and is incapable of ratification by the unanimous consent of all the shareholders.[75] A general meeting may alter and extend the objects of the company but such an alteration can have no retrospective effect. In this connection it should be noted that section 3A of the 1985 Act provides that where a company's memorandum states that the object of the company is to carry on business as a general commercial company, then the object of the company is to carry on any trade or business whatsoever with power to do everything incidental or conducive to the carrying on of any trade or business. It is thought however that such a one-line objects clause gives a company only those powers which are incidental or conducive to the trade or business actually carried on by the company.

In *Rolled Steel Products (Holdings) Ltd.* v. *British Steel Corporation*[76] the law was stated as follows: (1) The legal personality of a company exists only for the purpose of its incorporation as defined in the objects clause. It does not, however, follow that any act is beyond its capacity unless expressly authorised by its objects clause. Any company is treated as having implied powers to do any act which is reasonably incidental to the attainment or pursuit of any of its express objects, unless such act is expressly prohibited by the memorandum. (2) The question of whether or not a clause in a memorandum contains a separate independent object of the company is purely one of construction of that memorandum. Full force must be given, so far as possible, to any provision which directs that each sub-clause shall be construed independently of the other sub-clauses. A sub-clause must be treated as containing a substantive object unless either (a) the subject-matter of this sub-clause is by its nature incapable of constituting a substantive object or (b) the wording of the memorandum shows expressly or by implication that the sub-clause was intended to constitute an ancillary power only. (3) Nevertheless, if a particular act (such as the giving of a guarantee and the granting of a floating charge in support of it) is of a category which, on the true

---

[75] *Thomson* v. *J. Barke & Co. (Caterers) Ltd.*, 1975 S.L.T. 67 at p. 71.

[76] [1985] 2 W.L.R. 908. The facts which gave rise to the case occurred prior to the enactment of s. 9(1) of the European Communities Act 1972 (later re-enacted as s. 35(1) of the Companies Act 1985).

construction of the company's memorandum, is capable of being performed as reasonably incidental to the attainment of its objects it will not be rendered *ultra vires* the company merely because in a particular instance its directors, in performing the act in its name, are in truth doing so for purposes other than those set out in its memorandum; and a statement in the memorandum that a power is exercisable "for the purposes of the company" will ordinarily be construed as imposing a limit on the directors' authority rather than on the company's capacity. (4) A company holds out its directors as having ostensible authority to bind the company to any transaction which falls within the powers expressly or impliedly conferred on it by its memorandum of association and unless he is put on notice to the contrary, a person dealing in good faith with a company which is carrying on an *intra vires* business is entitled to assume that its directors are probably exercising such powers for the purposes of the company as set out in its memorandum. (5) If however a person dealing with the company is on notice that the directors are exercising their relevant power for purposes other than the purposes of the company, he cannot rely on the ostensible authority of the directors and, on the ordinary principles of agency, cannot hold the company to the transaction.[77]

The *ultra vires* rule has been modified by section 108 of the 1989 Act which substituted a new section 35 in the 1985 Act. The new section 35(1) enacts that a company's capacity is not limited by its memorandum by providing that the validity of an act done by a company shall not be called into question on the ground of lack of capacity by reason of anything in the company's memorandum. This section goes on to provide that a member of a company may nevertheless bring proceedings to restrain the doing of an act which but for subsection (1) would be beyond the company's capacity (s. 35(2)). It still remains the duty of directors to observe any limitations on their powers flowing from the company's memorandum and any action by the directors which but for subsection (1) would be beyond the company's capacity may only be ratified by the company by special resolution (s. 35(3)). The operation of new section 35 is restricted by a new section 322A which makes invalid transactions involving directors if the board of directors, in connection with the transaction, exceeds any limitation on their powers under the company's constitution.

BORROWING POWERS. It is to the company's own act of incorporation that one must look in the first instance to ascertain its power to borrow. If the objects and powers specified in its memorandum include an express power to borrow, the banker need look no further, provided of course that the power is exercised in relation to one of the authorised objects of the company.[78] If the memorandum of association contains no reference

---

[77] *Ibid.* at pp. 946 and 947.
[78] *Re Introductions Ltd.* [1968] 2 All E.R. 1221; affd. *sub nom. Introductions Ltd.* v. *National Provincial Bank Ltd.* [1970] Ch. 199.

to borrowing, clearly the power is not there—with this qualification, that an implied power to borrow arises whenever the objects are such that a power to borrow may fairly be regarded as incidental to these objects. A company incorporated for the purpose of trading has an implied power to borrow money up to a reasonable amount for its requirements.[79] A banker is not bound to do more than acquaint himself with the constitution of the company as contained in its memorandum and articles of association; and if he finds no prohibition but a power to borrow subject, for example, to this being confirmed by a resolution of the company, he is entitled to assume, if it so appears on the face of a document authorising borrowing, that such resolution has been duly and properly arrived at. This is the rule laid down in *Royal British Bank* v. *Turquand*.[80] This rule has been reinforced by section 711A of the 1985 Act which provides that a person shall not be taken to have notice of any matter merely because of its being disclosed in any document kept by the Registrar of Companies (and thus available for inspection).[81] A company which is not authorised by its memorandum of association to borrow and which is not a company formed for the purpose of trading, has no power to overdraw its bank account, either with or without security. Consequently, a banker who lends to such a company by way of overdraft is not a creditor of the company, though where he has taken security he may hold it for repayment of so much of the money advanced as has been applied in payment of the company's debts, but the burden of proving that the money has been so applied rests on him.[82] Action by the directors which but for section 35(1) would be beyond the company's capacity may only be ratified by the company by special resolution. A company which has no power by its memorandum to borrow can acquire such a power by altering its objects in the manner provided by section 4 of the 1985 Act. Such an alteration, however, cannot be retrospective in effect and the alteration should be made in the prescribed manner before borrowing is permitted. Where a power to borrow is contained in the memorandum of association, it is usually coupled with a power to grant security for repayment by way of mortgage, standard security or other form of charge. Additionally, it is competent under the law of Scotland for a company to grant a floating charge for the purpose of securing any debt or obligation (including a cautionary obligation).[83]

EXERCISE OF BORROWING POWERS. If a company has power to borrow, or if this should be incidental to the conduct of its business, the articles of association will usually authorise the directors to exercise the company's borrowing powers. It is however not uncommon for the articles to provide that without the sanction of the company in general meeting the

---

[79] *General Auction Estate and Monetary Co.* v. *Smith* [1891] 3 Ch. 342.
[80] (1856) 6 E. & B. 332.
[81] This section does not affect the operation of s. 416 of the same Act (deemed notice of charges).
[82] *Brooks & Co.* v. *Blackburn Benefit Society* (1884) 9 App.Cas. 857.
[83] Companies Act 1985, s. 462.

directors shall not borrow more than a specified amount.[84] Nevertheless, if a bank genuinely believes and acts upon the information furnished to it by the company or its recognised officials, it will be protected. The bank need not inquire into the "indoor management" of the company and may rely on the maxim *omnia praesumuntur rite ac solemniter esse acta, i.e.* is entitled to assume that all is being done regularly.[85] On the other hand, if there are circumstances of which the bank ought to be aware nullifying, or limiting, the authority of the directors they will not be protected since the rule in *Turquand's* case cannot be relied on where the bank has been put on inquiry but has nevertheless acted in contravention of the company's true mandate to it.[86]

A new section 35A, also inserted into the 1985 Act by section 108 of the 1989 Act, deals with the power of directors to bind the company and provides that in relation to a person dealing with a company in good faith, the power of the board of directors to bind the company or authorise others to do so, is deemed to be free of any limitation under the company's constitution (s. 35A(1)). For this purpose a person is not regarded as acting in bad faith by reason only of his knowing that an act is beyond the powers of the directors under the company's constitution, and he is presumed to have acted in good faith unless the contrary is proved (s. 35A(2)). Once again a member of the company is given the right to bring proceedings to restrain the directors from doing an act which is beyond their powers (s. 35A(4)). Similarly, any liability incurred by the directors by reason of their exceeding their powers is not affected. Once again, the operation of this section is restricted by section 322A. Finally, section 35B provides that a party to a transaction with a company has no duty to inquire as to whether it is permitted by the company's memorandum or as to any limitation on the powers of the directors to bind the company or authorise others to do so.

If the loan is *ultra vires* and the banker cannot avail himself of the protection of section 35 he may nevertheless have certain rights against the company in respect of the money which he has lent to it. He may stand in the shoes of any creditor of the company whose debt has been paid by the company out of money which the directors have purported to borrow in excess of their powers.[87]

LIABILITY OF DIRECTORS. If the directors assume an authority which they do not possess to borrow money or grant a guarantee, or if they act under a misapprehension, however honest, as to the extent of their power or authority to do so and induce a person to deal with or lend money to the company on the faith of such assumed or exceeded authority, they will render themselves personally liable for any loss which may accrue.[88] It

---

[84] See, for example, Article 79 of Table A of the Companies Act 1948.

[85] *Mahoney* v. *East Holyford Mining Co.* (1875) L.R. 7 H.L. 869 at p. 898.

[86] *B. Liggett (Liverpool) Ltd.* v. *Barclays Bank Ltd.* [1928] 1 K.B. 48; see also *Rolled Steel Products (Holdings) Ltd.* v. *British Steel Corporation* [1985] 2 W.L.R. 908.

[87] See, for example, *Brooks & Co.* v. *Blackburn Benefit Society* (1884) 9 App.Cas. 857; *Sinclair* v. *Brougham* [1914] A.C. 398; also *A. L. Underwood Ltd.* v. *Bank of Liverpool* (1924) 1 K.B. 775 at p. 794.

[88] *Beattie* v. *Lord Ebury* (1874) L.R. 7 Ch. 777.

makes no difference to the liability of the directors in such a situation that they did not know they were exceeding their powers.[89] The mis-representation must, however, be one of fact and not of law. Accordingly, the directors of a company possessing power to borrow with the consent of a general meeting of shareholders, but not otherwise, render themselves personally liable if they obtain a loan on the representation that they have obtained authority for it when as a matter of fact they have not.[90]

The terms of section 35A(1) of the 1985 Act have reduced the practical effect of this liability. If a lender enters into a transaction "in good faith" for the purposes of this section the transaction in consequence will be binding on the company. Only if the company is insolvent will a lender seek to bring home liability to the directors. However, the section does not affect any liability incurred by the directors by reason of them exceeding their powers (s. 35A(5)). Where directors personally guarantee the repayment of borrowing by a company which is *ultra vires* the company and undertake to pay those sums which the company as principal debtor has promised to pay, whether the company is lawfully bound to repay them or not, they will be liable since the matter is one of construction of the guarantee.[91]

POWER TO GRANT GUARANTEES. Before accepting a guarantee by a limited company, a banker must satisfy himself that a clear and unqualified power to grant such an obligation is given by or can be read into the company's memorandum of association. In *Rolled Steel Products (Holdings) Ltd.* v. *British Steel Corporation*[92] the plaintiff company's memorandum of association empowering the company to lend money and give guarantees was found not to contain an independent object but merely a power ancillary to the objects of the company to be exercised when expedient in furtherance of those objects. On this footing it was held that a transaction which involved the granting of a guarantee and a debenture and which had been entered into in furtherance of a purpose which was not authorised by the memorandum of association could nevertheless not be described as being *ultra vires* the company, since the granting of the guarantee and debentures were, on the face of them, capable of falling within the company's objects. However, it was held that the transaction was beyond the authority of the directors, because the guarantee and debenture were entered into in furtherance of purposes not authorised by the memorandum, the court deciding that an independent board of directors would not have decided that it was in the plaintiff company's interests to enter into the transaction. It was held to amount to a gratuitous disposition on the part of the plaintiff company which could not be justified as being for its purposes or in its interests. Since the defendants had notice that the directors were exercising the relevant

---

[89] *Weeks* v. *Propert* (1873) L.R. 8 C.P. 427.
[90] *Beattie* v. *Lord Ebury* (1874) L.R. 7 Ch. 777.
[91] *Heald* v. *O'Connor* [1971] 2 All E.R. 1105.
[92] [1985] 2 W.L.R. 908.

powers for purposes other than the purposes of the plaintiff company, the plaintiff company was entitled to have the guarantee set aside and the sum paid under it repaid with interest.

Authority to sign bills and cheques

As regards companies formed under the Companies Acts, the form in which a bill or note is to be executed so as to bind the company is regulated by section 37 of the 1985 Act, which provides that a bill of exchange or promissory note shall be deemed to have been made, accepted or indorsed on behalf of the company, if made, accepted or indorsed in name of or by or on behalf or on account of the company by any person acting under its authority. Cheques are not included by name, nor does the word "drawn" occur, but on the principle that the greater includes the less or, alternatively, that a cheque is a bill of exchange payable on demand, they are to be regarded as covered by the section. The authority must be in express terms. Nevertheless, a bank is not necessarily liable if it pays cheques bearing only one signature when the mandate for operations on the account requires two if there is evidence that the company has ratified the payments.[93] The section requires that the person signing should do so "by or on behalf of an account of" the company. In one case, two directors signed a cheque as drawers, adding after their subscriptions the word "director". The place for the signature of the secretary was left blank. The cheque was issued in favour of A. The name of the company was printed near the top of the cheque but did not appear elsewhere. In an action by A against the two directors as individuals, it was held that they were personally liable for the amount of the cheque, on the ground that in signing the cheque they did not indicate that they did so on behalf of the company even although they added words to show their representative capacity.[94] On the other hand, if on the face of the cheque it appears that the directors sign only for and on behalf of the company, they are not personally liable should the cheque not be met.[95]

Section 37 of the 1985 Act should be read along with section 349 of the same Act which provides that the name of the company must appear on all bills, promissory notes, indorsements, cheques and orders for money or goods which purport to be signed on behalf of the company. (Where a company is a charity, and its name does not include "charity" or "charitable", the fact that it is a charity must similarly appear.)[96] Where this is not done, any person who has signed or authorised to be signed on behalf of the company any such instrument is personally liable to the holder of the instrument for its amount unless it is duly paid by the company. The

---

[93] *London Intercontinental Trust Ltd.* v. *Barclays Bank Ltd.* [1980] 1 Lloyd's Rep. 241.
[94] *Landes* v. *Bradwell* (1909) 25 T.L.R. 478. See also *Brebner* v. *Hamilton*, 1925 S.C. 643.
[95] *E. Will Finance Co.* v. *Cowan* (1962) 78 Sh.Ct.Rep. 196; *Bondina Ltd.* v. *Rollaway Shower Blinds Ltd.* [1986] 1 All E.R. 564.
[96] Companies Act 1989, s. 112(6).

terms of section 349 require strict compliance.[97] Where an ampersand was omitted from the company's name on a company cheque, the signing directors were liable under section 349(4)[98] and the omission of the word "Ltd." in the drawing of a cheque made the signatory similarly liable.[99] An abbreviation of the company's name where there is no possibility of confusion is permitted. Thus "Ltd." for "Limited"[1] and "Co." for "Company"[2] are acceptable, but the abbreviation of, for example, "Michael" to "M." is not.[3]

Loans to directors

Generally speaking, it is prohibited for a company to make a loan to a director. No company, public or private, may make a loan to a director of the company or of its holdings company or enter into a guarantee or provide any security in connection with a loan made by a third party to such a director, unless the amount of the loan does not exceed £5,000 (ss. 330(2) and 334). No public company nor a company which is part of a group containing a public company (a "relevant company" (s. 331(6)) may make a loan to a person connected with such a director or provide a guarantee or security in respect of a loan made by another person to a connected person (s. 330(3)). "Connected persons" are defined by section 346 of the Act and include a director's spouse and infant children, a company with which he is associated, a trustee of a trust in which any of the foregoing are beneficiaries and a partner of the director or of any person connected with him. The prohibition on loans and the giving of guarantees is relaxed in the case of companies whose ordinary business includes lending money (s. 338) provided that the loan or guarantee is effected in the ordinary course of the company's business and the amount of the transaction is not greater, nor the terms more favourable, than it would be reasonable to expect the company to offer to a third party of the same financial standing (s. 338(3)). The amount of the loan however must not exceed £100,000 but recognised banks are not restricted in the amount they can lend to directors for any purpose on ordinary commercial terms (s. 338(4)). The consequences of a contravention of section 330 of the Act are as follows. The company has a civil remedy and is entitled to have the transaction set aside, where this is feasible, and to be reimbursed for any loss which it has suffered (s. 341). In addition, it is a criminal offence for directors of a relevant company to authorise prohibited loans and appropriate penalties are laid down (s. 342).

Financial assistance for the acquisition of a company's own shares

Section 151 of the Act now closely defines the rule that a company

---

[97] *Scottish & Newcastle Breweries Ltd.* v. *Blair,* 1967 S.L.T. 72.
[98] *Hendon* v. *Adelman and Others, The Times,* 16 June 1973.
[99] *British Airways Board* v. *Parrish* [1979] 2 Lloyd's Rep. 361.
[1] *F. Stacey & Co. Ltd.* v. *Wallis* [1912] 28 T.L.R. 209.
[2] *Banque de l'Indochine et de Suez* v. *Euroseas Group Finance Co. Ltd.* [1981] 3 All E.R. 198.
[3] *Durham Fancy Goods Ltd.* v. *Michael Jackson (Fancy Goods) Ltd.* [1968] 2 Q.B. 839.

should not give financial assistance for the acquisition of shares in itself or in its holding company. Subject to certain conditions private companies are not prohibited from giving such financial assistance and provided these conditions are met, a bank can now take security from a company in connection with the acquisition of the company's shares by a third party. Although the basic prohibition has been retained it applies in a different manner according to the timing of the financial assistance relative to the share acquisition. Again, the prohibition does not apply if the giving of the financial assistance does not have as its principal purpose the acquisition of the company's shares or is merely an incidental part of some larger purpose of the company, provided the assistance is given in good faith in the interests of the company (s. 153(1)).

All companies may provide assistance in the form of distributions by way of lawful dividend or distributions made in the course of winding up (s. 153(3)(*a*)). Further, there are exceptions to the prohibition in the case of the lending of money by a company in the ordinary course of its business (s. 153(4)(*a*)) or the provision of money for the acquisition of fully paid shares in accordance with an employees' share scheme (s. 153(4)(*b*)). There is in addition a specific relaxation of the rule in the case of private companies. Section 151 provides that so long as a private company has net assets which are not reduced by providing financial assistance or, to the extent that they are reduced, the financial assistance is provided out of distributable profits, it will not be illegal for that company to give financial assistance for the acquisition of its shares or shares in another private company of which it is a subsidiary.[4]

The rule in Victor's case

The rule in *Victors Ltd.* v. *Lingard*[5] is generally taken to refer to the general equitable rule that a director may not vote at board meetings on matters in which he has a personal and possibly conflicting interest. If he has such an interest in a guarantee and floating charge which it is proposed be granted by the company, it is possible neither will be duly executed if he fails to declare his interest.[6] For the purpose of the rule, a director will be so interested even if he has not yet signed a guarantee in favour of the company's bank but it is contemplated by him and the bank that he will do so in the near future. The rule may be expressly reflected in the articles of association but is frequently made subject to exceptions or excluded altogether. Where Article 94 of Table A has been adopted by the company a director is not entitled to vote on any resolution in which he has, directly or indirectly, an interest or duty which is material and which conflicts or may conflict with the interests of the company. He may vote if his interest arises out of a resolution relating to the giving of a security by the company to a third party, such as the company's bank, in

---

[4] *Brady* v. *Brady* [1988] 2 W.L.R. 1308.
[5] [1927] 1 Ch. 323.
[6] See, for example, *Rolled Steel Products (Holdings) Ltd.* v. *British Steel Corporation* [1985] 2 W.L.R. 908.

respect of an obligation which the director has personally guaranteed or secured. If a quorum of disinterested directors is not available, a resolution of the members of the company in general meeting is required to permit interested directors to vote.

Building societies

The Building Societies Act 1986 contains the statutory provisions regulating building societies and all societies incorporated under previous enactments are now deemed to be incorporated under this Act. By section 7, a society may (a) raise funds by the issue of shares to members, or (b) borrow money and receive deposits for the purposes of the society, provided that its liabilities in respect of its non-retail funds and deposits (that is, transferable instruments and qualifying time deposits as defined in subsection (19) and deposits from trustees for corporate bodies, friendly societies, charities and pension schemes) shall not exceed 20 per cent (subject to variation by statutory instrument) of its total liabilities in respect of shares and deposits. Under section 8, the amount of principal and interest on deposits must not exceed 50 per cent of the aggregate of that amount and the amount of the principal and interest on shares of the society. Sections 10 to 23 contain greatly increased powers for societies to engage in activities which will produce assets (usually in the form of debts owed to societies) while sections 34 and 35 give them power to provide financial services (including banking) or services relating to land. It should be noted that many of the powers must be specifically adopted and are not available to all societies, and to discover which powers a society has adopted reference must be made to the memorandum adopted by the society in terms of paragraph 2 of Schedule 2 (or Schedule 20) and kept in the public file maintained pursuant to section 106.

A society cannot borrow for any purpose inconsistent with its adopted powers but if a society's liabilities in respect of its non-retail funds and deposits exceeds the limit in force, this fact does not affect the validity of transactions carried out in excess of that limit (s. 7(18)).

Local authorities

The Local Government (Scotland) Act 1973 completely reorganised local authorities in Scotland. The whole country, apart from Orkney, Shetland and the Western Isles, is now divided into local government areas known as Regions. In each Region there are local government areas known as Districts. Orkney, Shetland and the Western Isles are each all-purpose local government areas known as Islands Areas. Every authority has a council consisting of a chairman and councillors.

Schedule 3 to the Local Government (Scotland) Act 1975 sets out the purposes for which local authorities in Scotland may borrow money. The main purpose of borrowing has to be to finance capital expenditure but short-term loans can be raised to finance temporary shortfalls in revenue receivable within the financial year to provide working capital. In this connection, a local authority may borrow by way of a temporary loan or overdraft from a bank or otherwise any sums which they may temporarily require for the purpose of defraying expenses pending the receipt of revenues receivable by them in respect of the year in which those expenses are chargeable (para. 3(*a*)). They may borrow in a similar manner for the purpose of the raising of a loan in the exercise of any statutory borrowing power (para. 3(*b*)). A local authority may also borrow by the issue of bills, payable within 12 months from the date of issue, provided that the aggregate amount outstanding on such bills does not exceed 20 per cent of the authority's gross income from the rates and the community charges (para. 6).

All money borrowed under any statutory borrowing power by a local authority is secured upon the whole funds, rates and revenues of the authority and all money borrowed by whatever method is deemed to have the same charge and security and to rank *pari passu* (para. 8(1)). The interest for the time being payable in respect of money borrowed by a local authority is the first charge on the rates and revenues comprising the security for the money (para. 8(2)). A person lending money to a local authority is not bound to inquire whether the borrowing of the money is legal or regular or whether the money raised was properly applied and is not prejudiced by any illegality or irregularity or by the misapplication or non-application of any of the money (para. 26). If at any time any sum due by way of principal or interest on any security created by a local authority remains unpaid for a period of two months after demand in writing, the person entitled to payment, provided he is the holder of a security to the amount of not less than £1,000, may present a petition to the Court of Session for the appointment of a judicial factor (para. 20(1)). If appointed, the judicial factor is entitled to exercise all the powers of the local authority in the matter of levying rates and community charges and collecting and recovering sums due to the authority together with such other powers and duties as the court shall think fit to give him (para. 20(2)).

When opening an account for a local authority, a certified excerpt from a minute of a meeting of the council should be obtained authorising the opening of the account, the operations on it and, where applicable, the limit of borrowing. The excerpt minute must be from a meeting of the council and not from a meeting of the finance committee. The bank should also be provided with a certificate from the authority stating that the borrowing is within the authorised statutory limit and that the consent of the Secretary of State has been obtained and showing the total amounts of money borrowed by the local authority for capital purposes and the periods to maturity of the loans outstanding.

CHAPTER 5

MISCELLANEOUS BANKING SERVICES

In addition to the payment and collection of cheques, bankers provide their customers with a number of other banking services.

Cheque cards and credit cards

A cheque card is a document issued by a bank which, typically, guarantees to third parties the payment of one cheque only not exceeding £50 in any single transaction within the United Kingdom provided the cheque (a) is signed in the presence of the payee and the signature corresponds with that on the card; (b) is drawn on one of the bank's cheque forms bearing the code number shown on the card and dated before the expiry date of the card; and (c) has the card number written on the back by the payee. The terms of the agreement which the customer enters into with the bank at the time when the card is issued preclude the customer from countermanding payment of any cheque which the payee has received in reliance upon the bank's guarantee given by the use of the card. Further, the bank may debit to the customer's account any cheque issued in conjunction with the card notwithstanding that the cheque may bear technical irregularities. The customer also undertakes not to create any indebtedness by the use of the card except with the previous agreement of the bank.[1] A cheque card is not considered to be a credit-token for the purposes of section 14 of the Consumer Credit Act 1974 and accordingly the agreement under which the cheque card is issued is not a credit-token agreement within section 14(1)(b). It is uncertain whether the agreement is a regulated consumer credit agreement for the purposes of the Act. Example 21 in Schedule 2, Part II to the Act suggests that it is an unrestricted-use debtor-creditor agreement by virtue of section 13(c) but this is considered doubtful.

In addition to cheque cards, banks now issue cash cards which in conjunction with a personal identification number allow the customer to withdraw cash from machines outwith normal banking hours. The terms of the agreement for the issue of such cards require the customer to keep the personal identification number secret and normally authorise the bank to debit the customer's account with the amounts of all withdrawals effected by means of the card except for any transactions effected after the bank has received notice that the card has been lost, mislaid or stolen. Although the customer undertakes not to create any indebtedness by the use of the card unless that indebtedness has been previously agreed by the bank, it is nevertheless thought that the agreement for its issue is a credit-

---

[1] See *R.* v. *Charles* [1977] A.C. 177 (dishonest use of a cheque card).

token agreement for the purposes of section 14 of the 1974 Act whether or not an overdraft is available. Further it is considered that an overdraft used in connection with such a card may still constitute a debtor-creditor-supplier agreement in terms of the Act even if the card is not a credit-token.

Distinct from cheque cards and cash cards are credit cards which are designed to be used in conjunction with a credit limit advised to the customer when his card is issued. (A charge card has no credit limit and because the card holder is required to settle in full his account with the card issuer when it is rendered the agreement for its use is treated as an exempt agreement under the 1974 Act.) A credit card is regarded as a credit-token and the credit-token agreement entered into by the customer when it is issued is a regulated agreement for the purposes of the 1974 Act. It is a debtor-creditor-supplier agreement and regarded as an unrestricted-use credit agreement in terms of section 12(c). It is an offence to give a person a credit-token if he has not asked for it (s. 51). If the debtor under the credit-token agreement, i.e. the holder of the card, has in relation to a transaction financed by the agreement, any claim against the supplier in respect of a misrepresentation or breach of contract, he has a similar claim against the creditor who, along with the supplier, is jointly and severally liable to him (s. 75).[2] The liability of the creditor for breaches by the supplier does not apply to a claim under a non-commercial agreement nor to any single item with a cash price not exceeding £100 or more than £30,000 (s. 75(3)).[3] The card holder is liable to the creditor to the extent of £50 for any loss to the creditor arising from misuse of the card after it has been lost or stolen (s. 84(1))[4] but this provision does not apply to any use of the card after the creditor has been given oral or written notice that it has been lost or stolen or is for any other reason liable to misuse (s. 84(3)).[5] In the absence of terms in the agreement to the contrary, payment by means of a credit card does not constitute conditional payment only (as does payment by cheque) and the use of the card in payment of the purchase price of goods and services is not conditional on the card issuer honouring his agreement with the supplier.[6]

Standing orders and direct debits

Payments may be made by banks on behalf of customers by means of standing orders. A standing order is a written order given by a customer to his bank to make a series of payments on his behalf. These payments are of a fixed amount and are due at fixed intervals. The mandate to the banker is to pay the standing order on its due date (or the first business

---

[2] See *United Dominions Trust Ltd.* v. *Taylor*, 1980 S.L.T. (Sh. Ct.) 28.
[3] Consumer Credit (Increase of Monetary Limits) Order 1983 (S.I. 1983 No. 1878).
[4] Consumer Credit (Increase of Monetary Limits) Order 1983 (S.I. 1983 No. 1571).
[5] See *R.* v. *Lambie* [1981] 2 All E.R. 776 (dishonest use of a credit card).
[6] *Re Charge Card Services Ltd.* [1988] 3 W.L.R. 1311.

day thereafter) subject to funds being available. If there are insufficient funds to enable the payment to be made on the due date the banker has no obligation to monitor the account thereafter with a view to making the payment when there are sufficient funds available.[7]

An alternative method of transferring funds is for the creditor who is due to receive the payment to use the service known as direct debiting. By this system, the payee or creditor claims the payment from his debtor's bank and initiates the entry in the debtor's bank account. The system may be used for fixed amounts due at fixed intervals or for varying amounts due at varying intervals. Before a company or other organisation is allowed to use the system it is required to execute an indemnity addressed to all the English and Scottish clearing banks. By the terms of this indemnity the creditor agrees to keep each bank indemnified against all claims arising directly or indirectly from the debiting of the customer's account. If a debit cannot be paid by a bank because of lack of funds it is returned unpaid.

Bank as custodier

Banks frequently have deposited with them for safe custody locked boxes or sealed parcels containing jewellery, deeds and securities of various kinds. In the case of locked boxes, the depositor retains the key of the box in his possession. The usual practice is for the bank to issue a receipt for the box or parcel with the description "Contents unknown to the bank" since the bank will not agree or verify the contents. The bank usually undertakes to use reasonable care to safeguard items deposited but will not accept liability for any loss or damage to them however caused.[8] In the absence of an express undertaking, when no payment is made by the depositor for this service, the banker is a gratuitous depositary. When he acts gratuitously, the banker is not bound to exercise more than ordinary care; and the negligence for which alone he becomes responsible is the want of such care as an ordinarily prudent man of business would take of property of a similar description belonging to himself.[9] The bank is not responsible for any loss arising as a result of theft from boxes or parcels deposited with it for safe custody committed by a member of staff unless the act could be said to have been done within the scope of the member of staff's authority. Where a fraud has been committed in the course of, and within the scope of, the duties entrusted to the member of staff involved, the bank is answerable for his conduct.[10] More care is required from the banker when he charges a commission.[11] The profit derived from keeping his customer's banking account is not,

---

[7] *Whitehead* v. *National Westminster Bank Ltd., The Times,* 9 June 1982.

[8] A disclaimer in such terms may be affected by the Unfair Contract Terms Act 1977. See p. 80.

[9] *Giblin* v. *McMullen* (1868) L.R. 2 P.C. 317, disapproved in *Port Swettenham Authority* v. *T. W. Wu & Co.* [1979] A.C. 580; *Langtry* v. *Union Bank of London* (1896) 1 Legal Decisions Affecting Bankers 229. See also *Wilson* v. *Orr* (1879) 7 R. 266.

[10] *Lloyd* v. *Grace, Smith & Co.* [1912] A.C. 716; *Morris* v. *C. W. Martin & Sons Ltd.* [1966] 1 Q.B. 716.

[11] *Re United Service Co., Johnstone's Claim* (1870) 6 Ch. App. 212.

however, sufficient to constitute the banker an onerous custodier.[12] Property deposited with a banker for safe custody must be returned to the person who deposited it and the banker cannot take notice of claims made by other persons to that property.[13]

As a general rule, a banker has no right of retention or lien over articles of value or securities, whether negotiable or not, deposited with him for safe custody. The mere fact that a banker grants an acknowledgment of the receipt of negotiable instruments "for safe custody", unqualified by any expression indicating that the deposit is for safe custody only or exclusively, does not necessarily exclude the banker's right to retain such documents in security for a general balance due to him by the depositor, if there are circumstances which show that the deposit, although ostensibly one for safe custody, was essentially and actually in security of an overdraft.[14]

At some offices, banks let safe deposit boxes to customers and others, again on condition that the bank is not responsible for loss or damage to the contents. The contents, if valuable, should be insured by the hirer of the box.

Banker as surety

In recent years banks have been called upon to provide bonds and guarantees in connection with contracts undertaken by their customers, both at home and abroad. There are two basic types—default bonds and demand guarantees. A default bond is regarded as a conditional undertaking obliging the guarantor to make good any loss suffered by the buyer as a result of the failure of the seller to complete the contract in accordance with its terms and conditions. Before the guarantor pays, there must be an unremedied breach of contract by the seller and the buyer must prove his loss.[15] Demand guarantees on the other hand entitle a buyer to payment on demand without proof of loss through breach of contract or other default. Such guarantees are either guarantees payable "on first demand" or provision is made for the guarantees to be payable on demand provided that stated conditions acceptable to both parties and contained in the guarantees are met. For such guarantees to be in an acceptable form from a bank's point of view the maximum amount of the bank's liability should be stated or be capable of being readily established from the terms of the document. Similarly, the maximum duration of the bank's liability should be fixed or be capable of being determined by reasonable notice. The terms should require the bank to pay on the simple demand of the beneficiary or on production of some clearly stated piece of evidence.

If a demand guarantee is called, the bank must pay the amount of the

---

[12] *Giblin* v. *McMullen* (1868) L.R. 2 P.C. 317.
[13] *Leese* v. *Martin* (1873) L.R. 17 Eq. 224.
[14] *Robertson's Tr.* v. *Royal Bank of Scotland* (1890) 18 R. 12.
[15] *Royal Bank of Scotland plc* v. *Dinwoodie*, 1987 S.L.T. 82.

guarantee forthwith whether or not the seller is in default under the contract. A bank has no duty imposed on it to inquire whether or not the seller has failed to fulfil his obligations under the contract and is in no way concerned with any contractual dispute which might have arisen between the buyer and the seller.[16] Only the contracting parties are bound by the terms of the basic contract; the commitments of the guarantor and the seller are independent.[17] Only in exceptional cases will the courts interfere with the machinery of irrevocable obligations assumed by banks[18] and the only possible exception would be in a case where the bank had notice of clear fraud on the part of the buyer.[19] The position of the seller is that he has virtually no power to prevent payment by a bank under a "first demand" guarantee and he will ultimately become liable for this payment himself because of the counter-indemnity required from him by the bank when it agreed to undertake the obligation for him. (He has a further difficulty in some foreign countries where buyers insist on demand guarantees which are open-ended, *i.e.* have no definite expiry date or one that is nebulous.)

If a guarantee has an expiry date, claims may nevertheless be intimated after that date if on the true construction of its terms the obligation of the guarantor is to indemnify, not at the date when the loss has been quantified and intimated, but at the date when the seller failed to carry out his obligations to the buyer if this failure occurred prior to the date of expiry of the guarantee.[20]

Consumer Credit Act 1974

The Consumer Credit Act was passed in 1974 but some of its provisions have not yet been implemented and are unlikely to be implemented in the future. The final set of regulations to be made under the Act came into force on 20 May 1985 and after that date so much of the Act as is likely to be implemented will be in force. A licence is required for carrying on a consumer credit business (Part III of the Act) and although the Act does not apply to all banking activities, banks nevertheless hold licences to cover such activities as credit brokerage, debt adjusting, debt counselling and debt collecting.

The upper limit, below which an advance is regulated, was originally £5,000 (s. 8(2)) but this was increased to £15,000 as from 20 May 1985. A regulated agreement is any personal credit agreement in terms of which a creditor provides credit of £15,000 or less to an individual (s. 8(3)). The term "individual" includes all non-corporate debtors, such as individuals, sole traders, partnerships, executors, trustees, clubs, societies and

---

[16] *R. D. Harbottle (Mercantile) Ltd.* v. *National Westminster Bank Ltd.* [1977] 2 All E.R. 862.
[17] *Howe Richardson Scale Co. Ltd.* v. *Polimex-Cekop and National Westminster Bank Ltd.* [1978] 1 Lloyd's Rep. 161.
[18] *R. D. Harbottle (Mercantile) Ltd.* v. *National Westminster Bank Ltd., supra.*
[19] *Edward Owen Engineering Ltd.* v. *Barclays Bank International* [1978] 1 All E.R. 976 *Cf. United City Merchants (Investments) Ltd.* v. *Royal Bank of Canada* [1981] 3 All E.R. 142.
[20] *National House-Building Council* v. *Fraser* [1983] 1 All E.R. 1090.

associations (s. 8(1)). All regulated agreements except in the case of overdrafts must be in the prescribed form (s. 60(1)) and certain procedures have to be followed to enter into a regulated agreement (ss. 61 to 65). Special procedures also apply where an agreement is to be secured on land (except in the case of an agreement for the purchase of the land (s. 58)) or where the agreement is signed away from business premises (s. 67). A statutory cooling-off period may apply if an agreement is cancellable (s. 68).

Both the total charge for credit and the annual percentage rate of interest must be shown in the agreement together with details of the security, if any, being taken by the creditor. If an agreement does not comply with the relevant regulations, it is enforceable only on the order of the court (s. 127). Other regulations spell out the procedures to be followed to bring an agreement to an end (s. 98) either under the borrower's statutory right under the Act to repay early (s. 94) or on default by him (s. 87). There are statutory formulae for calculating the rebates payable to borrowers who have repaid their loans in advance (s. 95) and regulations provide for the occasions on which and the form in which borrowers are entitled to information about the state of their account (s. 97).

By virtue of Determinations made by the Director General of Fair Trading under the Act dated 3 November 1983 agreements enabling a debtor to overdraw on a current account (as defined in s. 10) are exempt from Part V of the Act with the result that the forms to be used and procedures to be followed when entering into a regulated agreement do not apply to such an agreement, as in certain circumstances are agreements relating to advances made to cover statutory payments arising on death.

Unfair Contract Terms Act 1977

This Act has yet to be considered judicially in a banking context but it is of importance to banks since it may call into question the effectiveness of provisions in contracts which have the object of excluding or restricting a bank's liability for breach of duty arising in the course of its business. Such a term will have no effect if it was not fair and reasonable to incorporate the term in the contract (s. 16(1)). In determining whether it was fair and reasonable to incorporate a term in a contract, regard shall be had only to "the circumstances which were, or ought reasonably to have been, known to or in the contemplation of the parties to the contract at the time the contract was made" (s. 24(1)). "Guidelines" for the application of the reasonableness test are set out in Schedule 2 to the Act. The onus of proving that it was fair and reasonable to incorporate a term in a contract lies on the party so contending (s. 24(4)).

PART II

BILLS OF EXCHANGE, CHEQUES AND PROMISSORY NOTES

"It is not to be expected that the officials of banks should also be amateur detectives." *Lloyds Bank Ltd.* v. *Chartered Bank of India, Australia and China* [1929] 1 K.B. 40 at p. 73, *per* Sankey L.J.

CHAPTER 6

BILLS OF EXCHANGE

Where a document involving a personal obligation to pay money is assigned, the general rule is that the assignation must be completed by intimation to the debtor and the title of the assignee remains subject to any defect which affected the title of the assignor. Some documents used in commerce are recognised by the courts as being exempt from this rule. These documents are known as negotiable instruments and any document which evidences a debt and (1) is transferable by simple delivery and (2) confers on a *bona fide* holder for value a valid right to the obligation which it embodies is a negotiable instrument. Examples of negotiable instruments are bank notes, bills of exchange, cheques, promissory notes, dividend warrants and share warrants payable to bearer. The law relating to bills of exchange, cheques—including dividend warrants and drafts drawn by one branch of a bank on another—and promissory notes is now governed by the Bills of Exchange Act 1882 as modified by the Cheques Act 1957.[1]

Essentials

A bill of exchange is an unconditional order in writing addressed by one person to another signed by the person giving it, requiring the person to whom it is addressed to pay on demand, or at a fixed or determinable future time, a sum certain in money to, or to the order of, a specified person, or to bearer (s. 3(1)). An instrument which does not comply with these conditions or which orders any act to be done in addition to the payment of money, is not a bill of exchange. A writing defective in any of these essentials may be capable, however, of being made a bill of exchange and in any case can always be used as a document of debt even although it is not entitled to the privileges of a bill.[2] A bill is not invalid by reason (a) that it is not dated (though it is irregular to issue such a bill); (b) that it does not specify the value given or that any value was given; or (c) that it does not specify the place where it is drawn or the place where it is payable (s. 3(4)). The Act distinguishes between inland and foreign bills but the distinction is important only as regards the necessity for protest (ss. 4 and 51). Bills of exchange are probative though not holograph nor granted *in re mercatoria*. They are however generally used *in re mercatoria* and as privileged writings are sufficiently authenticated by the

---

[1] In Part II, references to sections are to sections of the Bills of Exchange Act 1882 unless otherwise stated. See *Lewis* v. *Clay* (1897) 14 T.L.R. 149 at p. 150, as to the manner in which the Act is to be interpreted.

[2] *Brice* v. *Bannister* (1878) L.R. 3 Q.B.D. 569; *Lawson's Exrs.* v. *Watson* (1907) 9 F. 1353.

signature of the grantor. They prove their dates without witnesses and the designations of the drawer and acceptor are not essential.

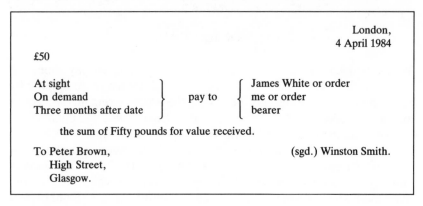

London,
4 April 1984

£50

At sight
On demand   }   pay to   {   James White or order
me or order
Three months after date   bearer

the sum of Fifty pounds for value received.

To Peter Brown,   (sgd.) Winston Smith.
    High Street,
    Glasgow.

Terms

(1) Drawer is the person who draws the bill, *i.e.* gives the order (Smith). (2) Drawee is the person on whom the bill is drawn, *i.e.* to whom the order is given (Brown). (3) Acceptor is the drawee when he has acknowledged his liability to the drawer by signing his name, with or without the word "Accepted" (Brown, after he has accepted the bill (s. 17(1))). (4) Payee may be the drawer (*i.e.* me) or someone else mentioned in the bill (White) or bearer. (5) Bearer is the person in possession of a bill or note payable to bearer (s. 2). (6) Indorser is the holder of a bill payable to order who indorses it, *i.e.* writes on the back of it his signature, with or without the name of a transferee, in order to put it in a proper state for transfer by delivery. (7) Indorsee is the person to whom the bill is specifically assigned by having his name written on the back of the bill by holder, who is then the indorser, *e.g.* White writes on the back of the bill "Pay to Thomas Gray or his order. James White." Gray is the indorsee. (8) Issue means the first delivery of a bill or note complete in form, to a person who takes it as a holder (s. 2), *e.g.* delivery by Smith to White, or retention by Smith as being himself payee, or delivery by him to bearer. (9) Negotiation means the transfer of a bill from one person to another in such a manner as to constitute the trans-feree the holder of the bill (s. 31(1)), *e.g.* indorsement by White to Gray. (10) Holder means the payee or indorsee of a bill or note who is in possession of it, or the bearer (s. 2), *e.g.* White, or Gray, or a bearer. (11) Holder in due course is included in the term holder and means a holder who gets an unassailable title to the bill, because certain conditions are satisfied (s. 29). (12) Maturity is the time at which payment of the bill may be demanded by the holder, *e.g.* at sight, on demand, or three months after date. After maturity it is overdue and loses its negotiable character. It can still be transferred but not so as to give an unassailable title to the transferee. (13) Dishonour by non-acceptance is the refusal of the drawee (Brown) to accept the bill on presentment to him for acceptance prior to

maturity (s. 43). (14) Dishonour by non-payment is the refusal or failure of the drawee or acceptor (Brown) to pay the bill at maturity on due presentment when presentment is necessary or his failure to pay when presentment is not necessary, is not made and the bill is overdue (s. 47(1)).

Drawee

The order contained in a bill of exchange must be an order in writing, signed by the person giving it, that is, the drawer. The order must be addressed to another person. This means that the drawee must be named or otherwise indicated with reasonable certainty (s. 6(1)), as, for example, by his official title. A bill may be addressed to two or more drawees whether they are partners or not, but not alternatively or in succession (s.6(2)).

Payee

Where a bill is not payable to bearer, the payee must be named or otherwise indicated with reasonable certainty (though not necessarily by means of a full description) (s. 7(1)).[3] An instrument which, when issued, does not contain the payee's name may, if a space has been left for the purpose, be converted into a bill by the person in possession of it filling in a name (s. 20). A bill may be made payable to two or more payees jointly or it may be made payable in the alternative to one of two or one or some of several payees or to the holder of an office for the time being (s. 7(2)). Where the payee is a fictitious or non-existent person, the bill may be treated as payable to bearer (s.7(3)). This includes not only the case where the payee is actually non-existent but also the case where the name of an existing person is inserted by the drawer without any intention that that person should receive the money or have any connection with the bill.[4] Even the fact that the drawer was induced by fraud to draw the bill in favour of a person whom he believed to exist, but who was actually non-existent, is immaterial in a question with a *bona fide* holder for value.[5]

Negotiability

When a bill contains words prohibiting transfer, or indicating an intention that it shall not be transferable, it is valid as between the parties to it but is not negotiable (s. 8(1)). The prohibition should be clear and unequivocal as, for example, where a bill is payable "to the order of C only" and is further crossed "Not negotiable".[6]

---

[3] Ersk., III, ii. 26; *McCubbin* v. *Stephen* (1856) 18 D. 1224.
[4] *Vagliano Bros.* v. *Bank of England* (1889) 23 Q.B.D. 243; revsd. *sub nom. Bank of England* v. *Vagliano Bros.* [1891] A.C. 107.
[5] *Clutton* v. *Attenborough* [1897] A.C. 90.
[6] *Hibernian Bank Ltd.* v. *Gysin & Hanson* [1939] 1 K.B. 483. A special statutory meaning is attached to this expression on a crossed cheque. See s. 81 of the 1882 Act.

Sum payable

The sum payable by a bill is a sum certain within the meaning of the Act although it is required to be paid (a) with interest provided the amount of interest payable is "certain" or ascertainable by numerical calculation from information contained in the bill itself[7]; (b) by stated instalments[8]; or (c) by stated instalments with a provision that upon default in payment of any one instalment the whole sum shall become due and payable (s. 9(1)).[9] Where the sum payable is expressed in words and also in figures and there is a discrepancy between the two, the sum denoted by the words is the amount payable (s. 9(20)).[10] The figures may be looked at to explain an ambiguity in the words[11] but they are not an essential or operative part of a bill. A drawer who leaves a blank for the words, while filling in the sum in figures, may on account of his negligence be liable to the holder for the amount filled up in the vacant space,[12] though generally he may prove that the bill as issued did not contain the words, which consequently amount to an unauthorised alteration.[13] Where a bill is expressed to be payable with interest, unless the instrument otherwise provides interest runs from the date of the bill[14] and if the bill is undated from the date of its issue.[15]

Time of payment

A bill is payable on demand (1) which is expressed to be payable on demand or at sight or on presentation or (2) in which no time for payment is expressed (s. 10(1)). A bill is payable at a determinable future time within the meaning of the Act which is expressed to be payable (1) at a fixed period after date or sight or (2) on or at a fixed period after the occurrence of a specified event which is certain to happen, even though the time of happening is uncertain (s. 11) (such as "one year after my death" or "two months after demand in writing").[16] The words "on or before 31 December 1956" have been held to create an uncertainty and a contingency in the time of payment.[17] Where a bill expressed to be payable at a fixed period after date is issued undated or where the acceptance of a bill payable at a fixed period after sight is undated, any holder may insert the true date of issue or acceptance and the bill is payable accordingly (s. 12). Where the holder in good faith and by mistake inserts a wrong date and in every case where a wrong date is

---

[7] *Morgan* v. *Morgan* (1866) 4 M. 321; *Tennent* v. *Crawford* (1878) 5 R. 435; *Vallance* v. *Forbes* (1879) 6 R. 1099; *Lamberton* v. *Aitken* (1899) 2 F. 189.
[8] See *McFarlane* v. *Johnstone* (1864) 2 M. 1210.
[9] *Carlon* v. *Kenealy* (1843) 12 M. & W. 374.
[10] *Saunderson* v. *Piper* (1839) 5 Bing. N.C. 425; *Garrard* v. *Lewis* (1882) 10 Q.B.D. 30.
[11] *Gordon* v. *Sloss* (1848) 10 D. 1129.
[12] *London Joint Stock Bank* v. *Macmillan and Arthur* [1918] A.C. 777.
[13] See ss. 64 and 100.
[14] See ss. 12, 13(2) and 20; *Doman* v. *Dibdin* (1826) R. & M. 381.
[15] See s. 100.
[16] *Roffey* v. *Greenwell* (1839) 10 A. & E. 222; *Price* v. *Taylor* (1860) 5 H. & N. 540.
[17] *Williamson* v. *Rider* [1963] 1 Q.B. 89.

inserted, if the bill subsequently comes into the hands of a holder in due course the bill is not avoided but operates and is payable as if the date so inserted had been the true date.[18] Where a bill or an acceptance or any indorsement on a bill is dated that date shall, unless the contrary is proved, be deemed to be the true date of the drawing, acceptance or indorsement, as the case may be (s. 13).[19] A bill is not invalid by reason only that it is antedated or post-dated or dated on a Sunday.

Computation of time of payment

Where a bill is not payable on demand the day on which it falls due is determined in accordance with the provisions of section 14 of the Act as amended by the Banking and Financial Dealings Act 1971, section 3(2). Such a bill is due and payable in all cases on the last day of the time of payment as fixed by the bill or, if that is a non-business day, on the succeeding business day (s. 14(1)). Where a bill is payable at a fixed period after date or after the happening of a specified event, the time of payment is determined by excluding the day from which the time is to begin to run and by including the day of payment (s. 14(2)). Where a bill is payable at a fixed period after sight, the time begins to run from the date of the acceptance if the bill be accepted, and from the date of noting or protest if the bill be noted or protested for non-acceptance, or for non-delivery (s. 14(3)). The term "month" in a bill means calendar month (s. 14(4)). There are no longer any days of grace.

Limitation of liability

The drawer of a bill and any indorser may insert in the bill an express stipulation (1) negativing or limiting his own liability to the holder; (2) waiving as regards himself some or all of the holder's duties (s. 16). The addition to the signature of a drawer or indorser of the words "Pay D or order without recourse to me", or "Pay D or order at his own risk", while negativing or limiting the drawer's or indorser's liability, leaves the holder with recourse against any other party to the bill whose liability is not so qualified.[20]

Acceptance

The acceptance of a bill (that is, acceptance completed by delivery or notification) is the signification by the drawee of his assent to the order of the drawer (s. 17(1)). Save in the cases provided for by sections 65 to 68 of the Act and the special case provided for by section 349 of the Companies Act 1985[21] no one can become a party to a bill as an acceptor who is not a proper drawee, or, in other words, an addressee.[22] Where a bill is

---

[18] See s. 20, which is limited by s. 12.
[19] See also ss. 21 and 100.
[20] See *Castrique* v. *Buttigieg* (1855) 10 Moo. P.C. 94 at pp. 110–112 and 117.
[21] See, for example, *Scottish & Newcastle Breweries Ltd.* v. *Blair*, 1967 S.L.T. 72.
[22] *Walker's Trs.* v. *McKinlay* (1880) 7 R. (H.L.) 85.

addressed to B, and C accepts it, C is not liable as an acceptor.[23] But where a bill is addressed to a firm and one of the partners accepts in his individual name he alone is liable.[24] An acceptance is invalid unless it complies with the following conditions. It must be written on the bill and signed by the drawee. The mere signature of the drawee without additional words is sufficient. The drawee's signature is necessary and the word "Accepted" without his signature does not constitute a valid acceptance. The acceptance must be on the bill itself and not on a copy but it may be written on the back of the bill.[25] A bill may be accepted before it has been signed by the drawer or while it is otherwise incomplete (s. 18(1))[26]; and even when it is overdue[27] or after it has been dishonoured by a previous refusal to accept or by non-payment (s. 18(2)).

An acceptance can be general or qualified (s. 19). A general acceptance assents without qualification to the order of the drawer (and binds the acceptor to pay the sum for which the bill is drawn to the person named in the bill and his indorsers, on the date and at the place stated in the bill, or if no place is stated, then at the place of business or residence of the drawee). In the case of a qualified acceptance, to avail the acceptor in question with a holder in due course, the qualification must appear *ex facie* the bill and be in such unmistakable terms that any person taking the bill could not, if he acted reasonably, fail to perceive that the acceptance was subject to an express qualification.[28]

The holder of the bill may refuse to take a qualified acceptance and treat the bill as dishonoured by non-acceptance (s. 44). An acceptance is qualified which is (1) conditional, that is to say, makes payment by the acceptor dependent on the fulfilment of a stated condition. Such an acceptance does not warrant the use of the summary diligence, since the fulfilment of the condition must be a matter of proof; (2) partial, that is to say, an acceptance to pay part only of the amount for which the bill is drawn; or (3) local, that is to say, an acceptance to pay only at a particular specified place (though such an acceptance is general unless it expressly states that the bill is to be paid there only and not elsewhere). An acceptance may also be qualified as to time[29] or it may be by one or more of the drawees but not by all (s. 19(2)).

Inchoate bill

Where a simple signature on a blank piece of paper is delivered by the signer in order that it may be converted into a bill it operates as a *prima facie* authority to fill it up as a complete bill for any amount, using the signature for that of the drawer or the acceptor or an indorser and in like

[23] *Davis* v. *Clark* (1844) 6 Q.B. 16.
[24] *Owen* v. *Von Uster* (1880) 10 C.B. 318.
[25] *Walker's Trs.* v. *McKinlay* (1880) 7 R. (H.L.) 85.
[26] See s. 20.
[27] See ss. 14, 45(1) and (2).
[28] *Meyer* v. *Decroix, Verley & Co.* [1891] A.C. 520.
[29] *Russell* v. *Phillips* (1850) 14 Q.B. 891.

manner when a bill, assuming it bears the signature of the drawer or maker, is wanting in any material particular, the person in possession of it has a *prima facie* authority to fill up the omission in any way he thinks fit (s. 20(1)). The signature on the bill and his possession of it is proof of the holder's authority to fill it up as a complete bill but the person who signed the blank paper may prove, by parole or other evidence, that the bill has not been filled up in accordance with his instructions.[30] Where a bill is admitted or proved to have been signed while inchoate or incomplete, the onus is on the holder to prove that it was delivered for the purpose of being converted into a bill. In order that a signature on blank paper, or a bill which is wanting in a material particular, may be enforceable against any person who became a party to it prior to its completion, it must be filled up within a reasonable time and strictly in accordance with the authority given.[31] Reasonable time for this purpose is a question of fact which varies according to circumstances and is reckoned from the date of delivery by the signer of the blank paper or incomplete bill (s. 20(2)).[32] If any such instrument after completion is negotiated to a holder in due course, it is valid and effectual for all purposes in his hands and he may enforce it as if it had been filled up within a reasonable time and strictly in accordance with the authority given. A holder, even with knowledge sufficient to deprive him of his own rights under the bill, may nevertheless transfer it to another who is not a party to any irregularity so as to invest the transferee with all the rights of a holder in due course.[33]

Delivery

Every contract on a bill, whether it be that of the drawer, the acceptor or the indorser, is incomplete and revocable until delivery of the instrument, *i.e.* the transfer of possession, actual or constructive, from one person to another (s. 21)[34] but where an acceptance is written on a bill and the drawee gives notice to the person entitled to the bill that he has accepted it, the acceptance then becomes complete and irrevocable. As between immediate parties and as regards a remote party other than a holder in due course, the delivery in order to be effectual must be made either by or under the authority of the party drawing, accepting or indorsing, as the case may be. Delivery may be shown to have been conditional or for a special purpose only and not for the purpose of transferring the property in the bill (s. 20(2)).[35] Where a bill is no longer in the possession of a party who has signed it as drawer, acceptor or indorser, a valid and unconditional delivery by him is presumed unless the contrary is proved but if the bill is in the hands of a holder in due

---

[30] See s. 100; and *Lyon* v. *Butter* (1841) 4 D. 178; *Anderson* v. *Lorimer* (1857) 20 D. 74; *Jackson* v. *McIver* (1875) 2 R. 882; *Walkins Bros. Ltd.* v. *Lamb and Robertson* (1901) 17 T.L.R. 777.

[31] See *Anderson* v. *Sommerville, Murray & Co.* (1898) 1 F. 90.

[32] *McLean* v. *McEwan & Son* (1899) 1 F. 381.

[33] See s. 29(3); *Garrard* v. *Lewis* (1882) 10 Q.B.D. 30.

[34] See s. 2; and *Miller* v. *Miller* (1874) 1 R. 1107; *Martini & Co.* v. *Steel and Craig* (1878) 6 R. 342.

[35] *Castrique* v. *Buttigieg* (1855) 10 Moo. P.C. 94.

course, a valid delivery of the bill by all prior parties, so as to make them liable to him, is conclusively presumed (s. 21(2)).

Signatures of parties

Capacity to incur liability as a party to a bill is co-extensive with capacity to contract (s. 22). No person can be liable as a drawer, indorser or acceptor of a bill who has not signed it as such and no person can be liable on a bill except in one or other of these three capacities (s. 23). Where a person signs a bill in a trade or assumed name he is liable as if he had signed it in his own name (s. 23(1)). The signature of the name of a firm is equivalent to the signature by the person so signing of the names of all persons liable as partners in that firm (s. 23(2)). Such signature renders action or diligence competent against all the partners of the firm.[36] Where a signature is common to an individual and a firm of which the individual is a member, there is a presumption that the bill was given for the firm and is binding on it, at least where the individual carries on no business separate from that of the firm of which he is a partner. A partner signing a bill in connection with the winding up of the affairs of a dissolved firm will bind the former partners.[37] Where a partner who is precluded from signing the firm's name to bills or notes does so outwith the course of the firm's business and the proceeds are applied for his own pecuniary benefit, the circumstances being such as to awaken suspicion in the mind of a reasonably careful man, the loss will not fall on the other partners who are ignorant of the transaction and who obtained no benefit from it.[38]

Forged or unauthorised signatures

Subject to the provisions of the Act, where a signature on a bill is forged or placed thereon without the authority of the person whose signature it purports to be, the forged or unauthorised signature is wholly inoperative and no right to retain the bill or to give a discharge or to enforce payment against any party to it can be acquired through or under that signature, unless the party against whom it is sought to retain or enforce payment of the bill is precluded from setting up the forgery or want of authority (s. 24). Nothing however in section 24 affects the ratification of an unauthorised signature which is not a forgery.[39] When a person asserts that the signature on a bill has not been adhibited by him or with his authority, the onus of proving the genuineness of the signature lies upon the person who seeks to enforce payment under it.[40] He may however be barred by his conduct or by his negligence or delay in taking action after becoming aware of the forgery from denying the genuineness

---

[36] *Drew* v. *Lumsden* (1865) 3 M. 384.
[37] *Dickson* v. *National Bank of Scotland*, 1971 S.C. (H.L.) 50.
[38] *Paterson Bros.* v. *Gladstone* (1891) 18 R. 403.
[39] *British Linen Co.* v. *Cowan* (1906) 8 F. 704. A forged signature may however be adopted: *Mackenzie* v. *British Linen Co.* (1881) 8 R. (H.L.) 8.
[40] *British Linen Co.* v. *Cowan, supra.*

of his signature.[41] The mere fact, however, that a person whose signature has been forged does not answer letters addressed to him regarding the bill does not of itself preclude his afterwards setting up the forgery. Mere silence on his part will not infer adoption of the signature so as to render him liable.[42] It is immaterial that the holder had no notice of the forgery or want of authority and no one can be a holder in due course who derives his title through a forged indorsement.

If a person, by false pretences, induces another to draw a bill in favour of a third party, who takes it in good faith and for value, the innocent third party, being the original payee, is not a holder in due course and cannot enforce payment.[43]

Procuration signatures

A signature by procuration operates as a notice that the agent has only a limited authority to sign and the principal is only bound by such signature if the agent in so signing was acting within the actual limits of his authority (s. 25).[44] Where an agent accepts or indorses "per procuration", the taker of the bill or note which has been so accepted or indorsed is given notice that it has been accepted or indorsed by a person having limited power for special purposes, and a warning to see that the bill is being used for the special purposes to which the procurator had a right to apply it.[45] A person signing as procurator for another must sign "per procuration" or show in some other way that he is signing merely as an agent, otherwise he does not bind his principal,[46] and if the principal is not liable the agent may be, and if he signs without authority will be, held bound as principal. Where a person signs a bill as a drawer, indorser or acceptor, and adds words to his signature indicating that he signs for or on behalf of a principal, or in a representative character, he is not personally liable but the mere addition to his signature of words describing him as an agent or as filling a representative character, as, for example, that of a director,[47] trustee[48] or executor[49] does not exempt him from personal liability (s. 26(1)). The signatures of officials or directors adhibited "on behalf of" a company do not bind such individuals personally.[50]

Valuable consideration and holder for value

Valuable consideration for a bill may be constituted by (1) any consideration sufficient to support a simple contract or (2) any antecedent

[41] *Brook* v. *Hook* (1871) L.R. 6 Ex. 89. See also *Arnold* v. *Cheque Bank* (1846) 1 C.P.D. 585; *Greenwood* v. *Martins Bank* [1933] A.C. 51.
[42] *British Linen Co.* v. *Cowan* (1906) 8 F. 704.
[43] *Jones* v. *Waring & Gillow* [1926] A.C. 670; *Williams* v. *Williams*, 1980 S.L.T. (Sh.Ct.) 55.
[44] *Reid* v. *Rigby & Co.* [1984] 2 Q.B. 40.
[45] See, for example, *Edmunds* v. *Bushell and Jones* (1865) L.R. 1 Q.B. 97; *Swinburne & Co.* v. *Western Bank* (1856) 18 D. 1025.
[46] *North British Bank* v. *Ayrshire Iron Co.* (1853) 15 D. 782.
[47] *Landes* v. *Bradwell* (1909) 25 T.L.R. 478.
[48] *Brown* v. *Sutherland* (1875) 2 R. 615.
[49] *Eaton, Hammond & Sons* v. *McGregor's Exrs.* (1837) 15 S. 1012.
[50] Companies Act 1985, s. 37.

debt or liability. Such a debt is deemed valuable consideration whether
the debt is payable on demand or at a future time (s. 27(1)). In Scotland,
to render a bill valid it does not require to have been granted for value[51]
nor do the words "for value received" require to form part of it, whether
value has been received or not. But the lack of value (non-onerosity) may
be pleaded in evidence when a bill is challenged on other grounds, such as
illegality, fraud or failure of the consideration.[52] In the cases following the
plea that the bill had been granted for no valuable consideration might be
a relevant defence which, if proved, would preclude an original party and
even a holder, but not a holder in due course, from enforcing it: (1) where
the bill has been signed without intention to grant an obligation, as, for
example, where it has been obtained by fraud or force and fear; (2) where
the consideration has failed, as where the bill has been given for a special
purpose which cannot be carried out or to be used on the occurrence of an
event which does not happen or in payment of goods which are not
delivered; (3) where it is an accommodation bill; (4) where it is given for
an immoral or illegal consideration or one which the law does not
recognise,[53] or under such circumstances as to make the transaction
iniquitous and tantamount to a fraud; or (5) where the bill is reducible by
the grantor's creditors. Where value has at any time been given for a bill,
the holder is deemed to be a holder for value as regards the acceptor and
all parties to the bill who became parties prior to such time (s. 29(2)).
Where the holder of a bill has a lien on it, arising either from contract or
by implication of law, he is deemed to be a holder for value to the extent
of the sum for which he has a lien (s. 29(3)).[54]

Accommodation bill or party

An accommodation party to a bill is a person who has signed a bill as
drawer, acceptor or indorser without receiving value and for the purpose
of lending his name to some other person (s. 28(1)). In effect an accommodation bill is one in which the acceptor, that is, the principal debtor *ex
facie* the bill, is in substance a surety for some other person who may or
may not be a party to the bill. It is the duty of a drawer or indorser for
whose accommodation a bill is accepted to provide funds to meet the bill
at maturity and consequently such a party cannot, as a rule, avail himself
of want of due presentment for payment, notice of dishonour or protest.
An accommodation party is liable on the bill to a holder for value and it is
immaterial whether, when the holder for value took the bill, he knew
such party to be an accommodation party (s. 28(2)). The ordinary rule
that payment or satisfaction by the drawer to the holder does not
discharge the holder's claim against the acceptor, does not apply when
the bill has been accepted for the accommodation of the drawer.

---

[51] *Law* v. *Humphreys* (1876) 3 R. 1192.
[52] Bell, *Prin.*, § 333.
[53] In this connection, see Consumer Credit Act 1974, s. 123.
[54] See banker's lien at p. 21.

Holder in due course

A holder in due course is a holder who has taken a bill, complete and regular on the face of it, under the following conditions, namely, (1) that he became the holder of it before it was overdue and without notice that it had been previously dishonoured, if such was the fact and (2) that he took the bill in good faith and for value and that at the time the bill was negotiated to him he had no notice of any defect in the title of the person who negotiated it (s. 29(1)).[55] But if *ex facie* of the bill a warning is conveyed, the holder, however honest, cannot acquire a better title to it than the person from whom he took it had. Notice in this context does not necessarily imply formal notice but either knowledge of the facts or a suspicion of something wrong combined with a wilful disregard of the means of knowledge.[56] No one can be a holder in due course of a bill the signature to which has been forged or adhibited without authority.[57] In particular, the title of a person who negotiates a bill is defective within the meaning of the Act if he obtained the bill or its acceptance by fraud,[58] duress, force and fear,[59] or other unlawful means, or for an illegal consideration,[60] or when he negotiates it in breach of faith,[61] or under such circumstances as amount to fraud (s. 29(2)). A person whose title is defective is to be distinguished from one who has no title at all and can give none, such as a person taking title to a bill through a forged indorsement.[62] A holder, whether for value or not, who derives his title to a bill through a holder in due course and who is not himself a party to any fraud or illegality affecting it, has all the rights of that holder in due course as regards the acceptor and all parties to the bill prior to that holder (s. 29(3)).[63] Every holder of a bill is *prima facie* deemed to be a holder in due course; but if in an action on a bill it is admitted or proved that the acceptance, issue or subsequent negotiation of the bill is affected with fraud, duress, or force and fear, or illegality, the burden of proof is shifted unless and until the holder proves that, subsequent to the alleged fraud or illegality, value has in good faith been given for the bill (s. 30(2)).

Negotiation of bills

A bill is negotiated when it is transferred from one person to another in such a manner as to constitute the transferee the holder of the bill. The delivery of unindorsed bills to a person is not negotiation of them except

---

[55] See ss. 90 and 27; also Consumer Credit Act 1974, s. 125; also *Jones* v. *Gordon* (1877) 2 App.Cas. 616.

[56] *Raphael* v. *Bank of England* (1885) 17 C.B. 1616 at p. 174; *McLean* v. *Clydesdale Bank* (1883) 11 R. (H.L.) 1; see also *Baker* v. *Barclays Bank* [1955] 2 All E.R. 571.

[57] See s. 24.

[58] *Smith* v. *Bank of Scotland* (1829) 7 S. 244; *Couston* v. *Miller* (1862) 24 D. 607; *Home* v. *Hardy* (1842) 4 D. 1184.

[59] *Gelot* v. *Stewart* (1870) 8 M. 649.

[60] See, for example, Consumer Credit Act 1974, s. 125.

[61] *Thomson* v. *McLauchlin* (1823) 2 S. 497.

[62] See s. 24.

[63] See, for example, *May* v. *Chapman* (1847) 16 M. & W. 355.

that a bill payable to bearer is negotiated by delivery. A bill payable to order is negotiated by the indorsement of the holder completed by delivery (s. 31). Where any person is under an obligation to indorse a bill in a representative capacity, he may indorse it in such terms as to negative personal liability (s. 31(5)).[64]

Section 32 provides that an indorsement in order to operate as a negotiation must be written on the bill itself and be signed by the indorser. The simple signature of the indorser, even on the face of the bill,[65] without additional words is sufficient. It may be in pencil. The fact that a person writes his name on the back of a bill and hands it to another does not necessarily constitute him an indorser[66] though it may render him liable as a guarantor.[67] The indorsement must be an indorsement of the entire bill (s. 32(2)). A partial indorsement, that is an indorsement which purports to transfer to the indorsee a part only of the amount payable or which purports to transfer the bill to two or more indorsees severally does not operate as a negotiation of the bill.[68] There would seem to be nothing, however, to prevent the holder after obtaining a payment to account from indorsing the bill *quoad* the balance. Where a bill is payable to the order of two or more payees or indorsees who are not partners all must indorse, unless the one indorsing has authority to indorse for the others (s. 32(3)). Where the payee or indorsee is wrongly designated or his name is mis-spelt, he may indorse the bill as therein described, adding, if he think fit, his proper signature (s. 32(4)). If the proper signature is not added, summary diligence is incompetent in Scotland. An indorsement may be made in blank or special. It may also contain terms making it restrictive (s. 32(6)) but where a bill purports to be indorsed conditionally, the condition may be disregarded by the payer and payment to the indorsee is valid whether the condition has been fulfilled or not (s. 33).

An indorsement in blank specifies no indorsee and a bill so indorsed becomes payable to bearer (s. 31(1)). A special indorsement specifies the person to whom or to whose order the bill is to be payable. "Pay to A B", "Pay to A B or order" or "Pay to A B's order" are special indorsements (s. 34(2)). An indorsement is restrictive which prohibits the further negotiation of the bill or which expresses that it is a mere authority to deal with the bill as thereby directed and not a transfer of the ownership of it, as, for example, if a bill is indorsed "Pay D only", or "Pay D for the account of X" or "Pay D or order for collection" (s. 35). A restrictive indorsement gives the indorsee the right to receive payment of the bill and to sue any party that the indorser could have sued but gives him no power to transfer his rights as indorsee unless it expressly authorises him to do so.

---

[64] See ss. 16(1) and 26.
[65] *Young* v. *Glover* (1857) 3 Jur. (N.S.) Q.B. 637.
[66] *Westacott* v. *Smalley* (1885) 1 C. & E. 529.
[67] *Stagg, Mantle & Co.* v. *Brodrick* (1895) 12 T.L.R. 12.
[68] See ss. 7(2) and 34(3); *Heilbut* v. *Nevill* (1869) L.R. 4 C.P. 354.

Where a bill is negotiable in its origin it continues to be negotiable until it has been restrictively indorsed or discharged by payment or otherwise (s. 36(1)). When an overdue bill is negotiated it can only be negotiated subject to any defect of title affecting it at its maturity and thereafter no one who takes it can acquire or give a better title than that which the person from whom he took it had (s. 36(2)). A bill of exchange payable on demand is ordinarily given with a view to present payment. The reasonable time allowed for presentment will necessarily vary with the circumstances. In the case of a cheque—which is a bill of exchange payable on demand, drawn on a banker—the period is short. Bills of exchange payable on demand are perhaps not on the same footing as cheques but, save in exceptional circumstances, it is outwith the ordinary course of business to hold up such documents for any protracted period.[69] A bill payable on demand is deemed to be overdue when it appears on the face of it to have been in circulation for an unreasonable length of time, something which is a question of fact (s. 36(3)). Where a bill which is not overdue has been dishonoured, any person who takes it with notice of the dishonour takes it subject to any defect of title attaching to it at the time of dishonour (s. 36(5)) but the rights of a holder in due course are not affected. A bill known to be dishonoured is thus on the same footing as one overdue.

Rights and powers of a holder

The rights and powers of a holder of a bill are set out in section 38. He is entitled to raise an action on the bill in his own name against any or all of the parties liable on it unless it can be shown that he holds the bill adversely to the interests of the true owner. He may also proceed with summary diligence or claim in a multiplepoinding[70] or found on the bill as a ground of compensation. Where he is a holder in due course, he holds the bill free from any defect of title of prior parties, as well as from mere personal defences available to prior parties among themselves and may enforce payment against all parties liable on the bill (s. 38(3)).[71] Where his title is defective (as, for example, if he has obtained the bill by fraud or other unlawful means including violence) if he negotiates the bill to a holder in due course, that holder obtains a good and complete title to the bill. Further, if he obtains payment of the bill, the person who pays him in due course gets a valid discharge for it. A defective title has to be distinguished from a complete lack of title. A person claiming under a forgery, for example, has no title.[72] In this context the right to negotiate a bill, which is an incident of ownership, is not to be confused with the power to negotiate it, which is an incident of apparent ownership.

---

[69] See, for example, *Easdale Slate Quarries Co. Ltd.* v. *Reid*, 1910 2 S.L.T. 295.
[70] *Agnew* v. *Whyte* (1899) 1 F. 1026.
[71] See, for example, *Barclays Bank Ltd.* v. *Astley Industrial Trust Ltd.* [1970] 1 All E.R. 719.
[72] See Chalmers, *Bills of Exchange* (13th ed.) at p. 127 for a commentary on the holder's rights of action acquired by negotiation.

Presentment for acceptance

Where a bill is payable after sight presentment for acceptance is necessary in order to fix the maturity of the instrument (s. 39(1)). An acceptor ought to date his acceptance but the lack of the date does not affect the maturity of the bill. It is competent for the holder to insert the true date. Where a bill expressly stipulates that it shall be presented for acceptance or where a bill is drawn payable elsewhere than at the residence or place of business of the drawee, it must be presented for acceptance before it can be presented for payment (s. 39(2)). In no other case is presentment for acceptance necessary in order to render liable any party to the bill. Where the holder of a bill drawn payable elsewhere than at the place of business or residence of the drawee has not time with the exercise of reasonable diligence (which varies according to circumstances[73]) to present the bill for acceptance before presenting it for payment on the day it falls due, the delay caused by presenting the bill for acceptance before presenting it for payment is excused and does not, as in the ordinary case, discharge the drawer and indorsers (s. 39(4)). When a bill payable after sight is negotiated the holder must either present it for acceptance or negotiate it within a reasonable time. If he does not do so, the drawer and all indorsers prior to that holder are discharged (s. 40).

Rules for presentment for acceptance

By section 41, a bill is duly presented for acceptance when it is presented in accordance with the following rules. (1) The presentment must be made by or on behalf of the holder to the drawee or to some person authorised to accept or refuse acceptance on his behalf, at a reasonable hour (that is, during business or bank hours, in the case of a merchant or banker[74]) on a business day[75] and before the bill is overdue. Where a bill is drawn on a company incorporated under the Companies Acts, presentment must be made to a person authorised by the company to accept bills.[76] (2) Where a bill is addressed to two or more drawees who are not partners, presentment must be made to them all unless one has authority to accept for all, in which case presentment may be made to him only. A bill addressed to several drawees, acceptance of which is refused by one, need not be presented to the others since such an acceptance is qualified and the taking of it, without the express or implied consent of the drawer and indorsers, would discharge them.[77] (3) Where the drawee is dead, presentment may be made to his personal representatives and where he is bankrupt, to him or to his trustee. Where authorised by agreement or usage, a presentment through the post office is sufficient.

Presentment in accordance with these rules is excused and a bill may be treated as dishonoured by non-acceptance (1) where the drawee is dead,

---

Gladwell v. Turner (1870) L.R. 5 Ex. 59.

[74] Neilson v. Leighton (1843) 6 D. 622.

[75] See s. 92, as amended by the Banking and Financial Dealings Act 1971, ss. 3(1) and 4(4).

[76] Companies Act 1985, s. 37.

[77] See ss. 19(2)(e) and 44(1).

or bankrupt, or is a fictitious person, or a person not having capacity to contract by bill; (2) where, after the exercise of reasonable diligence, presentment cannot be effected; (3) where, although the presentment has been irregular, acceptance has been refused on some other ground (as, for example, where the bill has been presented on a non-business day or after hours and refused on the ground of lack of funds) (s. 41(2)). The fact that the holder has reason to believe that the bill on presentment will be dishonoured does not excuse presentment (s. 41(3)). Presentment for acceptance differs from presentment for payment in that it should be personal while presentment for payment should be local and be made where the money is. The distinction may be material in deciding whether or not the holder has used reasonable diligence in presenting.

When a bill is duly presented for acceptance and is not accepted within the customary time, the person presenting it must treat it as dishonoured by non-acceptance. If he does not, the holder loses his right of recourse against the drawer and indorsers (s. 42). The drawee may require that the bill be left with him for acceptance and he is entitled to retain it for the customary period, usually 24 hours, but this varies according to the custom of the place of presentment. On the lapse of this time, however, he must deliver it, accepted or not accepted,[78] and in the latter event it must be noted for non-acceptance or otherwise treated as dishonoured. A bill is dishonoured by non-acceptance when it is duly presented for acceptance and such an acceptance as is prescribed by the Act is refused or cannot be obtained, or when presentment for acceptance is excused and the bill is not accepted (s. 43(1)). Subject to the provisions of the Act,[79] when a bill is dishonoured by non-acceptance an immediate right of recourse against the drawer and indorsers accrues to the holder and no presentment for payment is necessary (s. 43(2)). Notice of dishonour must, however, be given and the bill protested where necessary to complete the holder's cause of action.[80] The holder of a bill may refuse to take a qualified acceptance and if he does not obtain an unqualified acceptance may treat the bill as dishonoured by non-acceptance (s. 44(1)) but when the drawer or indorser of a bill receives notice of a qualified acceptance and does not within a reasonable time (which depends on the circumstances of each particular case) express his dissent to the holder, he is deemed to have assented to it (s. 44(3)).

Presentment for payment

Subject to the provisions of the Act,[81] a bill must be duly presented for payment. Presentment for payment implies a demand for payment.[82] If it is not so presented it would seem that the drawer and indorsers are

---

[78] *Bank of Van Diemen's Land* v. *Bank of Victoria* (1871) L.R. 3 P.C. 526 at pp. 542 and 543.
[79] See ss. 16, 22, 40, 48 to 51, 64 and 65.
[80] *Castrique* v. *Bernaso* (1844) 6 Q.B. 498.
[81] See ss. 39(4), 43, 44, 46, and 67.
[82] *Bartsch* v. *Poole & Co.* (1895) 23 R. 328.

discharged, not only of all liability on the bill itself but of the debt for which the bill was granted,[83] at least if they have suffered damage by the delay.[84]

Rules for presentment for payment

A bill is duly presented for payment which is presented in accordance with the rules set out in section 45. When the bill is not payable on demand, presentment must be made on the date it falls due. Where the bill is payable on demand, then presentment must be made within a reasonable time after its issue in order to render the drawer liable, and within a reasonable time after its indorsement in order to render the indorser liable. In determining what is a reasonable time, regard has to be had to the nature of the bill, the usage of trade with regard to similar bills and the facts of the particular case. Presentment must be made by the holder[85] or by some person authorised to receive payment on his behalf, at a reasonable hour on a business day at the proper place, either to the person designated by the bill as payer (that is, either the drawee or acceptor, or, if the bill is payable elsewhere than at the drawee's residence or place of business, the person with whom it is domiciled[86]) or to some person authorised to pay or refuse payment on his behalf, if with the exercise of reasonable diligence such person can be found there. The reasonableness of the hour depends on circumstances. If a bill is domiciled at a bank it must be presented during banking hours; if at a trader's place of business, then within business hours; if at a dwelling-house, presentment at any time until bedtime would probably be sufficient.[87] Presentment is not excused because of the acceptor's or drawee's bankruptcy,[88] and presentment must be made to the bankrupt and not to his trustee. In the case of a company being wound up, presentment should be made to the liquidator.

Where a place of payment is specified in the bill, a bill is presented at the "proper place" in terms of section 45(4) when the bill is presented there. If the acceptor has accepted it payable at his bankers, the bill must be presented at the bank.[89] Where no place is specified but the address of the drawee or acceptor is given in the bill, the bill should be presented there. If no address is given, the bill should be presented at the drawee's or acceptor's place of business, if known and if not, at his ordinary residence, if known. In any other case, the bill should be presented to the drawee or acceptor wherever he can be found or at his last known place of business or residence. Where a bill is presented at the proper place and after the exercise of reasonable diligence no person authorised to pay or

---

[83] *Peacock* v. *Purssell* (1863) 32 L.J.C.P. 266.
[84] The acceptor, however, is liable without the necessity of being charged for payment. See s. 52; *Gordon* v. *Kerr* (1898) 25 R. 570.
[85] See s. 24.
[86] Presentment to an acceptor personally of a bill payable at his bankers is unnecessary.
[87] *Wilkins* v. *Jadis* (1831) 2 B. & D. 188.
[88] *Esdaile* v. *Sowerby* (1809) 11 East. 114 at p. 117.
[89] *Saul* v. *Jones* (1858) 28 L.J. Q.B. 37.

refuse payment can be found there, no further presentment to the drawee or acceptor is required (s. 45(5)). Where a bill is drawn upon or accepted by two or more persons who are not partners and no place of payment is specified, presentment must be made to all of them. A refusal to pay on the part of one does not, as in the case of presentment for acceptance, dispense with presentment to the others (s. 45(6)).

Delay in making presentment for payment is excused when the delay is caused by circumstances beyond the control of the holder, such as his sudden illness or death,[90] and not imputable to his default, misconduct or negligence (s. 46(1)). Presentment for payment is dispensed with (1) where after the exercise of reasonable diligence presentment as required by the Act cannot be effected; but the fact that the holder has reason to believe that the bill will on presentment be dishonoured does not dispense with the necessity of presentment[91] nor does the fact of the acceptor's bankruptcy[92]; and (2) where the drawee is a fictitious person or he waives presentment or it is excused (s. 46(2)).

A bill is dishonoured by non-payment (1) when it is duly presented for payment and payment is refused or cannot be obtained or (2) when presentment is excused and the bill is overdue and unpaid (s. 47(1)). Since the acceptor has the whole of the day on which the bill falls due for payment in which to pay the bill, the holder has no right of action against him until the expiry of that day although he is entitled at any time on that day to give notice of dishonour to the drawer and indorsees.[93]

Notice of dishonour

When a bill has been dishonoured by non-acceptance or by non-payment notice of dishonour (that is, formal notification) must be given to the drawer and each indorser and, subject to the provisions of section 48 of the Act, any drawer or indorser to whom such notice is not given is discharged. This is the case even although the omission to give notice has caused them no injury. In order to be valid and effectual notice of dishonour must be given in accordance with the rules contained in section 49. The notice must be given by or on behalf of the holder, or by or on behalf of an indorser, who at the time of giving it is himself liable on the bill. Where the notice is given by the holder, it enures for the benefit of all subsequent holders and all prior indorsers, who have a right of recourse against the party to whom it is given. Where notice is given by an indorser, it enures for the benefit of the holder and all indorsers subsequent to the party to whom notice is given. The notice may be given in writing or by personal communication and may be in any terms which sufficiently identify the bill (as by specifying its date, sum and the parties to it) and intimate that the bill has been dishonoured by non-acceptance

---

[90] *Rothschild* v. *Currie* (1841) 1 Q.B. 47.
[91] *Keith* v. *Burke* (1885) 1 C. & E. 551.
[92] *Sands* v. *Clarke* (1849) 19 L.J.C.P. 84.
[93] *Kennedy* v. *Thomas* [1894] 2 Q.B. 759.

or non-payment, as the case may be. The fact of the bill having been noted or protested and that recourse is claimed against the party to whom the notice is given, should be intimated. The onus of proving notice is on the holder.[94] The return of a dishonoured bill to the drawer or indorser is, in point of form, deemed a sufficient notice of dishonour (s. 49(6)). A misdescription of the bill (as, for example, where the notice transposes the names of the drawer and acceptor[95]) or generally any misdescription which could not mislead the person to whom notice is given does not vitiate the notice unless the party to whom notice is given is in fact misled.

Where notice of dishonour is required to be given to any person, it may be given either to him or to his agent. Verbal notice given to his solicitor is insufficient[96] but notice, written or verbal, to a merchant's clerk given at his place of business is sufficient.[97] Where the drawer or indorser is dead and the party giving notice knows it, the notice must be given to a personal representative, if there is one and he can be found. Notice sent to a drawer or indorser in ignorance of his death is thought to be sufficient. Where the drawer or indorser is bankrupt, notice may be given either to the party himself or to his trustee. Where there are two or more drawers or indorsers who are not partners, notice must be given to each of them unless one of them has authority to receive such notice for the others.

The notice must be given as soon as the bill is dishonoured and must be given within a reasonable time thereafter.[98] In the absence of special circumstances, notice is not deemed to have been given within a reasonable time unless (1) where the person giving and the person to receive the notice reside in the same place, the notice is given or sent off in time to reach the latter on the day after the dishonour of the bill or (2) where the person giving and the person to receive notice reside in different places, the notice is sent off on the day after the dishonour of the bill (if there is a post at a convenient hour on that day and if there is no such post on that day, then by the next post thereafter). Non-business days are excluded in both cases.[99] Where a bill when dishonoured is in the hands of an agent, he may either himself give notice to the parties liable on the bill or he may give notice to his principal. If he gives notice to his principal, he must do so within the same time as if he were the holder, and the principal, upon receipt of such notice, has himself the same time for giving notice as if the agent had been an independent holder.[1] Where a notice of dishonour is duly addressed and posted, the sender is deemed to have given due notice

---

[94] *Grayson* v. *Smith*, 3 A. & E. 499.

[95] *Mellersh* v. *Rippen* (1852) 7 Ex. 578.

[96] *Crosse* v. *Smith* (1813) 1 M. & S. 545.

[97] *Viale* v. *Michael* (1874) 30 L.T. 453.

[98] *Hirschfield* v. *Smith* (1866) L.R. 1 C.P. 340; *Gladwell* v. *Turner* (1870) L.R. 5 Ex. 61.

[99] See s. 92, as amended by the Banking and Financial Dealings Act 1971, ss. 3(1) and 4(4); also *Fielding & Co.* v. *Corry* [1898] 1 Q.B. 268.

[1] *Lombard Banking Ltd.* v. *Central Garage and Engineering Co. Ltd.* [1963] 1 Q.B. 220; *Yeoman Credit* v. *Gregory* [1963] 1 W.L.R. 343. Where presentment has been made through a banker that may be a "special circumstance" justifying the holder in waiting for the return of the dishonoured bill before giving notice.

of dishonour notwithstanding any miscarriage by the post office. If a holder does not know the address of an indorser, he is entitled to time to make inquiries.[2]

Delay in giving notice of dishonour is excused where the delay is caused by circumstances beyond the control of the party giving notice and not imputable to his default, misconduct or negligence (s. 50(1)). Notice of dishonour is dispensed with when, after the exercise of reasonable diligence, notice as required by the Act cannot be given to, or does not reach, the drawer or indorser sought to be charged or when it is waived, expressly or impliedly (s. 50(2)).[3] As regards the drawer, it may be dispensed with in the following cases, namely (1) where the drawer and drawee are the same person; (2) where the drawee is a fictitious person or a person not having capacity to contract; (3) where the drawer is the person to whom the bill is presented for payment; (4) where the drawee or acceptor is, as between himself and the drawer, under no obligation to accept or pay the bill or (5) where the drawer has countermanded payment (s. 50(2)(c)). As regards the indorser, it may be dispensed with in the following cases, namely (1) where the drawee is a fictitious person or a person not having capacity to contract and the indorser was aware of the fact at the time he indorsed the bill; (2) where the indorser is the person to whom the bill is presented for payment or (3) where the bill was accepted or made for his accommodation (s. 50(2)(d)).

Noting and protest

Where an inland bill has been dishonoured it may, if the holder thinks fit, be noted for non-acceptance or non-payment, as the case may be; but it is not necessary to note or protest any such bill in order to preserve recourse against the drawer or indorser (s. 51). It is, however, advisable in most cases to have bills noted if only to preserve evidence of their due presentment and noting is necessary to warrant summary diligence in the case of a bill drawn payable after sight in order to fix the date of maturity.[4] The noting consists of a marking put on the bill by a notary public recording the presentment of the bill for acceptance or payment and its dishonour. The following is the usual memorandum of noting put upon bills:— "4/4/84 pnp. C.D., N.P." or "4/4/84 pnac. C.D., N.P." ("pnp" standing for protest for non-payment and "pnac" protest for non-acceptance). Although the extended protest must be signed by the notary he need not be in attendance when the bill is presented. He is warranted in making the protest on the report of his clerk or other trustworthy person. Nor is it necessary that the witnesses referred to in the protest should see the presentment. They do not require to sign the protest as witnesses. If the protest bears that the bill was protested on a date

---

[2] *Baldwin* v. *Richardson* (1823) 1 B. & C. 245.
[3] *Cf.* s. 46(2) and *Cairns' Trs.* v. *Brown* (1836) 14 S. 999; *Allhusen & Sons* v. *Mitchell & Co.* (1870) 8 M. 600; see also *Campbell* v. *Ratten* (1833) 12 S. 269; *Cordery* v. *Colville* (1863) 32 L.J.C.P. 210.
[4] See s. 14(3).

different from that shown in the notary's marking on the bill itself, diligence thereon is inept. Where a payment to account of a bill has been made after noting, the protest may be subsequently extended and summary diligence proceeded with for any balance due under the bill.

Where a foreign bill, appearing on the face of it to be such, has been dishonoured by non-acceptance, it must be duly protested for non-acceptance, and where such a bill which has not been previously dishonoured by non-acceptance is dishonoured by non-payment, it must be duly protested for non-payment. If it is not so protested, the drawer and indorsers are discharged. Where a bill does not appear on the face of it to be a foreign bill, protest in case of dishonour is unnecessary (s. 51(2)).

A bill which has been protested for non-acceptance may be subsequently protested for non-payment (s. 51(3)). When a bill is noted or protested it may be noted on the day of its dishonour and must be noted not later than the next succeeding business day. When a bill has been duly noted, the protest may be subsequently extended as of the date of the noting (s. 51(4)).[5] Where the acceptor of a bill becomes bankrupt or insolvent or suspends payment before it matures, the holder may cause the bill to be protested for better security against the drawer and indorsers (s. 51(5)). No right of recourse however accrues to him until the date of maturity. A bill in such circumstances may be accepted *supra* protest.[6] In Scotland, if during the currency of a bill a party liable thereon is considered to be *vergens ad inopiam* (*i.e.* approaching insolvency) the holder may use diligence to prevent the obligant's property being disposed of. In such cases a warrant for diligence is granted only on an averment that the obligant is *vergens*.

A bill must be protested at the place where it is dishonoured[7] provided that when a bill is presented through the post office and returned by post dishonoured, it may be protested at the place to which it is returned, and on the day of its return if received during business hours. If not received during business hours, it may be protested not later than the next business day. When a bill drawn payable at the place of business or residence of some person other than the drawee has been dishonoured by non-acceptance, it must be protested for non-payment at the place where it is expressed to be payable and no further presentment for payment to, or demand on, the drawee is necessary (s. 51(6)).

A protest must contain a copy of the bill, must be signed by the notary making it and must specify (1) the person at whose request the bill is protested and (2) the place and date of protest, the cause or reason for protesting the bill, the demand made and the answer given, if any, or the fact that the drawee or acceptor could not be found (s. 51(7)). Where a bill provides that payment is to be made at the drawer's office, it is an undertaking on the part of the acceptor that he will attend there on the

---

[5] See *McPherson* v. *Wright* (1885) 12 R. 942.
[6] See s. 65(1).
[7] As to places where there is no notary, see s. 94.

day specified and pay the bill, and if he fails to do so the bill must be protested on the grounds that the acceptor could not be found and not that, the bill having been presented and there being no funds to meet it, payment was refused.[8] Where a bill is lost or destroyed, or is wrongly detained from the person entitled to hold it, the protest may be made on a copy or written particulars thereof (s. 51(8)). Protest is dispensed with by any circumstance which would dispense with notice of dishonour. Delay in noting or protesting is excused when the delay is caused by circumstances beyond the control of the holder and not imputable to his default, misconduct or negligence. (The want of a notary does not excuse delay in noting or protesting.[9])

Duties of holder to drawee or acceptor

When a bill is accepted generally, presentment for payment is not necessary in order to render the acceptor liable (s. 52(1)) for, at common law, he is bound to seek out his creditor and pay him. Presentment, protest and notice of dishonour are necessary only to preserve the holder's recourse against the drawer and indorsers, so that each in turn may be in a position to enforce without delay his recourse against those liable to him. It is competent, as between the holder and acceptor, to present a bill and proceed with summary diligence at any time within six months after its maturity.[10] When by the terms of a qualified acceptance, presentment for payment is required (as where the acceptor makes presentment a condition precedent of his liability) the acceptor, in the absence of an express stipulation to that effect, is not discharged by the omission to present the bill for payment on the day that it matures (s. 52(2)).[11] In order to render the acceptor of a bill liable it is not necessary to protest it or that notice of dishonour be given to him (s. 52(3)). Where the holder of a bill presents it for payment, he must exhibit the bill to the person from whom he demands payment and when a bill is paid, the holder must forthwith deliver it up to the party paying it. Where the payment is partial, the amount should be noted on the bill but the holder is not bound to deliver it except against payment in full (s. 52(4)).

Bill as an intimated assignation

Subject to section 75A of the Act, in Scotland, though not in England, where the drawee of a bill has in his hands funds available for its payment, the bill operates as an assignment of the sum for which it is drawn in favour of the holder from the time when the bill is presented to the drawee (s. 53(2)). In an action against the drawee the bill is founded on as an assignation and not solely as a bill, the holder's right to recover being dependent on the existence of a debt due by the drawee to the drawer and

[8] *Bartsch* v. *Poole & Co.* (1895) 23 R. 329.
[9] See ss. 93 and 94.
[10] *McNeil & Son* v. *Innes, Chambers & Co.*, 1917 S.C. 540.
[11] *Smith* v. *Vertue* (1860) L.J.C.P. 59.

on the validity of the assignation of that debt to him. A bill granted for valuable consideration cannot (unlike a cheque) be countermanded by the drawer and if the drawee refuses to pay, the holder's remedy is to raise an action of multiplepoinding. The acceptance of a bill payable at a bank is authority to the banker to pay the bill and it is the banker's duty (in the sense of legal obligation) to his customer, the acceptor, to act on the authority and pay accordingly. But while the authority proceeds from the customer, to whom the banker owes a primary duty, a legal relationship is also created between the banker and the holder of the bill whose rights must be kept in view.[12] Where a banker has funds in his hands but insufficient to meet the bill, the practice is to transfer the amount standing at the credit of the customer to a suspense account earmarked against the bill and to retain the amount until the matter is arranged between the parties or judicially settled. Bills are preferable according to their respective dates of presentment to the drawee.

Liability of acceptor

The acceptor of a bill by accepting it engages that he will pay it according to the tenor of his acceptance (s. 54(1)). He is precluded from denying to a holder in due course (1) the existence of the drawer, the genuineness of his signature and his capacity and authority to draw the bill; (2) in the case of a bill payable to the drawer's order, the then capacity of the drawer to indorse but not the genuineness or validity of his indorsement and (3) in the case of a bill payable to the order of a third person, the existence of the payee and his then capacity to indorse, but not the genuineness or validity of his indorsement. The acceptor, therefore, may refuse to pay on the ground that the payee's signature is forged.[13] Where a bill accepted by two persons jointly is at maturity paid by one of them it is competent in a claim for relief by the person who has paid the bill against the other acceptor to prove by parole the true nature of the transaction between the acceptors and their reciprocal obligations.[14]

Liability of drawer

The drawer of a bill by drawing it engages that on due presentment it will be accepted and paid according to its tenor and that if it is dishonoured he will compensate the holder or any indorser who is compelled to pay it, provided that the requisite proceedings on dishonour have been duly taken; and he is precluded from denying to a holder in due course the existence of the payee and his then capacity to indorse (s. 55(1)).

---

[12] See *British Linen Co.* v. *Rainey's Trs.* (1885) 12 R. 825 at p. 831.
[13] See *London and River Plate Bank* v. *Bank of Liverpool* [1896] 1 Q.B. 7 (acceptor cannot recover money paid on an indorsement which subsequently turned out to have been forged).
[14] *Crosbie* v. *Crosbie's Trs.* (1900) 3 F. 83.

Liability of indorsers

The indorser of a bill by indorsing it engages that on due presentment it will be accepted and paid according to its tenor and that if it is dishonoured he will compensate the holder or a subsequent indorser who is compelled to pay it, provided that the requisite proceedings on dishonour have been taken. He is precluded from denying to a holder in due course the genuineness and regularity in all respects of the drawer's signature and all previous indorsements and also from denying to his immediate or a subsequent indorsee that the bill was at the time of his indorsement a valid and subsisting bill and that he had a good title to it (s. 55(2)). The indorser of a bill is in the nature of a new drawer in his relationship with the holder and the liabilities *inter se* of successive indorsers of a bill must, in the absence of evidence to the contrary, be determined according to the ordinary principles of the law merchant whereby a prior indorser must indemnify a subsequent one. But it is competent to refer to the whole circumstances attendant upon the making, issue and transfer of a bill for the purpose of ascertaining the true relation to each other of the signing parties, either as makers or indorsers.[15]

Where a person signs a bill otherwise than as a drawer or acceptor, he thereby incurs the liabilities of an indorser to a holder in due course (s. 56). To this quasi-indorsement, which in continental countries would be termed an "aval" (an antiquated term signifying underwriting), attach consequences comparable with those which follow an indorsement by the holder. The liability of a person who subscribes a bill *per aval* is that of an indorser and is limited to those who succeed him so that he incurs no liability to the drawer[16]; nor has he any right of recourse against the drawer unless he has signed on the drawer's behalf.

Measure of damages

Where a bill is dishonoured, the measure of damages, which are deemed to be liquidated damages and for which the parties to a bill are respectively liable, is specified in section 57 of the Act.

Payment in due course

A bill is discharged by payment in due course by or on behalf of the drawee or acceptor. "Payment in due course" means payment made at or after the maturity of the bill to the holder (or to his authorised agent) in good faith and without notice that his title to the bill is defective (s. 59(1)). Payment by a banker to a private individual is complete when the money is laid on the counter.[17] When a bill is paid by the drawer or an indorser it is not discharged (s. 59(2)). A bill may also be discharged by confusion when the acceptor of a bill becomes the holder of it at or after

---

[15] See, for example, *Macdonald* v. *Whitfield* (1883) L.R. 8 App.Cas. 733.

[16] *Walker's Trs.* v. *McKinlay* (1880) 7 R. (H.L.) 85.

[17] *Chambers* v. *Miller* (1862) 32 L.J.C.P. 30.

its maturity in his own right (s. 61),[18] by renunciation when the holder of a bill at or after its maturity absolutely and unconditionally renounces his rights against the acceptor (s. 62),[19] by cancellation when a bill is intentionally cancelled by the holder and the cancellation is apparent on the bill (s. 63)[20] and by alteration where a bill or acceptance is materially altered without the assent of all the parties liable on the bill (s. 64). A bill is not however avoided as against the party who has himself authorised the alteration and subsequent indorsers, provided that where a bill has been materially altered but the alteration is not apparent and the bill is in the hands of a holder in due course, such holder may avail himself of the bill as if it had not been altered and may enforce payment of it according to its original tenor (s. 64(1)). An alteration is "apparent" when it is such as would be noticed by an intending holder who scrutinised the instrument with reasonable care.[21] The following alterations are material, namely, any alteration of the date, the sum payable, the time of payment, the place of payment, and where the bill has been accepted generally, the addition of a place of payment without the acceptor's consent (s. 64(2)). A mere correction is not a material alteration nor is the addition of words which do not alter the effect of the bill as issued.[22]

Holder's right to duplicate bill

Where a bill has been lost or accidentally destroyed before it is overdue the person who was the holder of it may apply to the drawer to give him another bill of the same tenor, giving security to the drawer, if required, to indemnify him in case the bill alleged to have been lost is found again (s. 69).[23] If the drawer refuses to give a duplicate bill, he may be compelled to do so. In a question with the finder of the bill, the person in right of it has a good action for recovery of the instrument but if it is in the possession of a holder in due course no right of action for recovery against such a holder exists. However, the person in right of the bill can recover from the finder whatever value he has received for it.

In an action upon a bill (or even on the debt contained in it) the court may order that the loss (or destruction) of the instrument need not be set up, provided an indemnity is given to the satisfaction of the court against the claims of any other person upon the instrument in question (s. 70). Notwithstanding the loss of a bill, the holder is bound to take all steps incumbent on him. Presentment for payment may be excused or dispensed with in certain cases but the loss of the bill will not excuse delay in giving notice of dishonour nor of protesting when necessary.[24]

---

[18] *Nash* v. *De Freville* [1900] 2 Q.B. 72.
[19] *Crawford* v. *Muir* (1873) 1 R. 91; 2 R. (H.L.) 148.
[20] *Yglesias* v. *River Plate Bank* (1877) 3 C.P.D. 60; *Bank of Scotland* v. *Dominion Bank* (1889) 16 R. 1081; (1891) 18 R. (H.L.) 21.
[21] *Woollatt* v. *Stanley* (1928) 138 L.T. 620.
[22] *Speirs & Knox* v. *Semple* (1901) 9 S.L.T. 153.
[23] As to bills in a set, see s. 71.
[24] See ss. 46(1), (2) and 51.

Good faith

A thing is deemed to be done in good faith within the meaning of the Act where it is in fact done honestly, whether it is done negligently or not (s. 90).[25] But if the facts show that the holder must have had a suspicion that something was wrong and he refrained from inquiry lest his suspicions should be confirmed, the court would regard that as dishonesty.[26] If a person has in his possession the means of knowing that a bill for which he is asked to give value has been stolen or otherwise fraudulently obtained and wilfully disregards these, he is not acting in good faith.

Computation of time

Where by the Act the time limited for doing any act or thing is less than three days, in reckoning time non-business days are excluded. Non-business days in Scotland, for the purposes of the Act, mean (a) Saturday, Sunday, Good Friday, and Christmas Day; (b) a bank holiday under the Banking and Financial Dealings Act 1971; (c) a day appointed by Royal Proclamation as a public fast or thanksgiving day; and (d) a day declared by an order under section 2 of the 1971 Act to be a non-business day.[27] Any other day is a business day.

Summary diligence

Section 98 provides that nothing in the Act shall alter the law and practice in Scotland in regard to summary diligence. In order to warrant summary diligence as between the holder of a bill and the drawer and indorsers, the bill must be presented on its due date and timeously noted. Summary diligence is, however, competent as against the acceptor if the bill is presented and noted within a period of six months from its due date.[28] The protest of a bill or note made by a notary may be registered within six months after the date of the bill in the event of non-acceptance and within six months after its maturity in the event of non-payment, or within six months of the date of presentation for payment in the case of bills payable on demand,[29] in the Books of Council and Session or in the Sheriff Court Books within the jurisdiction of which the person charged resides.[30] An extract of the registered protest containing a warrant to charge the obligant to pay the sum in the bill with interest and expenses, within six days if resident in Scotland and fourteen days if resident furth of Scotland, may then be obtained. Although a bill may be accepted payable in England where there is no such diligence, summary diligence on protest of a bill is competent against any party liable on the instrument and domiciled in Scotland.

---

[25] *Swan* v. *North British Australasian Co.* (1863) 2 H. & C. 184.
[26] *Jones* v. *Gordon* (1877) 2 App.Cas. 616 at p. 629.
[27] See p. 10.
[28] *McNeill & Son* v. *Innes, Chambers & Co.*, 1917 S.C. 540.
[29] *Bou* v. *Lord Rollo* (1850) 12 D. 1310.
[30] *Sutherland* v. *Gunn* (1854) 16 D. 339.

Summary diligence is competent at the instance of any holder whose title is in order *ex facie* of the bill.[31] If a bill is indorsed after protest, the protest may be assigned to the indorsee to the effect of enabling him to use or proceed with diligence already begun on it. Summary diligence is competent in the case of an accepted bill against any party liable on it, provided due notice of dishonour has been given to him and, in the case of an unaccepted bill, against the drawer and prior indorsers but not the drawee,[32] even although he may have funds in his hands sufficient to meet it. Where a firm is the drawer, diligence is competent against any member of the firm although his name does not appear on the bill.[33]

Diligence is competent on a bill signed on behalf of the acceptor by a notary, law agent or justice of the peace in the presence of two witnesses; but not on one signed by the party's initials or by mark; nor on an undated bill or one lacking in any material particular; nor on one irregular in form or *ex facie* vitiated or altered; nor on a bill accepted conditionally; nor on a lost bill, or one past due and torn up; nor on an imperfect bill not completed; nor on a bill on which an ordinary action is pending in court. Summary diligence is not competent on any bill of exchange or promissory note granted to a creditor under a regulated consumer credit agreement in discharge or security of any sum payable by the debtor or surety in relation to such an agreement.[34] Summary diligence may be competent on a householder's certificate of protest under section 94 but a contrary view has been expressed.[35]

The charge must conform strictly to its warrant and be executed against the party or parties named in the protest. The debtor, if he feels aggrieved, may crave the court for a suspension of a charge or threatened charge on a bill but unless the bill appears *ex facie* vitiated he must, as a condition of having the note passed to try the question, find caution or consign the sum in the bill.

Parole evidence

In any judicial proceedings in Scotland any fact relating to a bill, cheque or promissory note which is relevant to any question of liability thereon may be proved by parole evidence (meaning proof by the evidence of witnesses) (s. 100). Nevertheless, it is provided that the Act shall not in any way affect the existing law and practice whereby the party who is, according to the tenor of any bill of exchange, cheque or promissory note, debtor to the holder in the amount thereof, may be required as a condition of obtaining a sist of diligence or suspension of a charge or threatened charge, to make such consignation or to find such caution as the court before whom the cause is depending may require.

Section 100 can apply only to cases where the alleged liability is rested

---

[31] *Fraser* v. *Bannerman* (1853) 15 D. 756.
[32] See s. 54.
[33] *Wallace* v. *Plock* (1841) 3 D. 1047.
[34] Consumer Credit Act 1974, s. 125.
[35] *Sommerville* v. *Aaronson* (1898) 25 R. 524.

exclusively upon a bill. The introduction of parole evidence should be only for the purpose of showing the true position of the parties and can have no application to cases where a bill is used purely as a method of carrying into effect a written contract. Where bills are granted for the purpose of working out such a contract with the result that the actual terms on which the bills are to be drawn and accepted are not to be gathered solely from the bills themselves but rather from the agreement which is carried into execution by their being accepted, it is contrary to well settled rules of evidence to allow the terms of the agreement to be altered or enlarged by parole evidence. In such a case, therefore, it is not a relevant defence on the part of the acceptor to offer to prove by parole evidence that at the time the bills were accepted there was an agreement other than the written agreement which was the foundation of the obligation.[36]

Section 100 has given rise to differences of opinion in court and no authoritative decision as to its exact meaning has yet been pronounced.[37] The net result of the various decisions appears to be that as between the parties to a bill who stood in the relation of debtor and creditor respectively as regards the original (as opposed to the ultimate) liability on the bill, it is competent for the debtor to prove by parole evidence any agreement with the creditor which shows or tends to show that the liability *ex facie* of the document was modified or altered. However, it appears to be incompetent by such proof to prove (1) as between the original parties to the bill that the debtor was relieved of his ultimate liability to the creditor and (2) as between the acceptor or the drawer and an indorsee (except an indorsee who was a party to the agreement sought to be proved by parole) any modification or alteration whatever of the liability of the acceptor or drawer to such indorsee or a holder in due course. In other words, an acceptor cannot prove by parole evidence any agreement between himself and the drawer which entirely negatives his liability on the instrument; nor as between himself and a third party into whose hands the bill has onerously come, can he prove by parole evidence any agreement by which his liability *ex facie* of the bill is in any way modified or altered unless such third party shall have been cognisant of and a party to the agreement at the time when the bill was accepted. To put it broadly, the section makes it competent to prove what could not at common law be proved by parole evidence, namely, the true relations to each other of the parties to a bill. In other words, it is possible to prove by parole evidence that the indebtedness which *ex facie* of the bill is upon the acceptor is in certain cases not really upon him at all. The section has however nothing to do with the general rule of law that a written agreement cannot be altered or varied by parole evidence and it has also been

---

[36] *Stagg & Robson, Ltd.* v. *Stirling*, 1908 S.C. 675 at p. 680.
[37] See, for example, *National Bank of Australasia* v. *Turnbull & Co.* (1891) 18 R. 692; *Vianni & Co.* v. *Gunn & Co.* (1904) 6 F. 989; *Manchester and Liverpool Bank Co.* v. *Ferguson & Co.* (1905) 7 F. 865; *Stagg & Robson, Ltd.* v. *Stirling*, 1908 S.C. 675; *Thompson* v. *Jolly Carter Inns Ltd.*, 1972 S.C. 215.

decided that the section under discussion does not make parole proof of payment of a bill competent.[38]

Prescription

By the Prescription and Limitation (Scotland) Act 1973 any obligation under a bill of exchange or promissory note is extinguished by the short negative prescriptive period of five years.[39] The *terminus a quo* is the date when the obligation became enforceable.[40] The effect of prescription is to extinguish the bill or note as a document of debt but not to extinguish the original debt itself which may then be proved by writing subsequent in date to the running of the prescription or by reference both of the constitution of the debt and the resting-owing to the debtor's oath.[41] In order to prove the resting-owing of the debt in a bill or note which has prescribed, it is not necessary to prove that the debt existed prior to the granting of the bill or note, and if it is in the hands of a creditor it is available as an adminicle of evidence to prove the debt and that it is resting-owing. Payment of interest on a prescribed bill or debt after the period of prescription has run has frequently been sustained as proof of the existence of the debt and its resting-owing.[42]

Stamp duty

By virtue of the Finance Act 1970, bills of exchange are exempt from stamp duty.[43]

---

[38] *Stagg & Robson, Ltd.* v. *Stirling*, 1908 S.C. 675; *Nicol's Trs.* v. *Sutherland*, 1951 S.C.(H.L.) 21.
[39] s. 6 and Sched. 1, para. 1(e).
[40] s. 6(3).
[41] *Easton* v. *Hinshaw* (1873) 1 R. 23; *McBain's Exr.* v. *McBain's Exr.*, 1930 S.C.(H.L.) 72.
[42] *Campbell's Trs.* v. *Hudson's Exr.* (1895) 22 R. 943.
[43] s. 32 and Sched. 7.

CHAPTER 7

CHEQUES

Since a cheque is a bill of exchange the provisions of the Bills of Exchange Act 1882 apply generally to cheques but they are specially dealt with in sections 73 to 82 of the Act, as amended by the Cheques Act 1957.

Definition

Sections 3(1) and 73 of the 1882 Act define a cheque as a bill of exchange drawn on a banker payable on demand. In other words, it is an unconditional order in writing, addressed to a banker, signed by the person giving it, requiring the banker to pay on demand a sum certain in money to or to the order of a specified person or to bearer. Cheques differ from bills of exchange payable on demand in that they are not intended to be and are not in fact accepted by the banker on whom they are drawn. Also, they are granted not as a continuing obligation but for more or less immediate payment and may therefore become "stale" or overdue sooner than a bill. The drawer of a cheque is not discharged by undue delay in presentment unless he has been prejudiced by the delay and the banker, who is the drawee, is not liable for having paid on a forged or unauthorised indorsement. Cheques may also be countermanded after issue.

Essentials

A cheque must be in writing. It does not require to be drawn on paper specially appropriated to its use and it is sufficient if a person draws his cheque on a sheet of notepaper. In practice however banks insist that cheques be drawn on the special cheque forms which they provide which bear magnetic ink characters designed to be read by computers.[1] Cheques need not be drawn in ink and may be drawn in pencil but because of the ease with which such a cheque can be altered the bank on which it is drawn is entitled to return it unpaid with the answer "Drawer's instructions require confirmation in ink".

A cheque need not be dated and it is not invalid by reason only that it is post-dated, ante-dated, or dated on a Sunday. However, a banker is not entitled to cash a cheque prior to the date on which it purports to be drawn and if he does the payment is made at his own risk. It would appear that a post-dated cheque may be validly negotiated for value prior to the date it bears.[2] An unauthorised alteration in the date of a cheque will

---

[1] In this connection, see *Burnett* v. *Westminster Bank Ltd.* [1966] 1 Q.B. 742.
[2] *Royal Bank of Scotland* v. *Tottenham* [1894] 2 Q.B. 715.

invalidate it and a person taking such a cheque even without negligence and in ignorance of the alteration cannot recover from the drawer.[3]

A cheque must contain an unconditional order to pay. An order to pay money on condition that the payee complete a receipt form indorsed on or attached to the cheque has been held not to be unconditional and therefore not a cheque within the meaning of the Act.[4] In all such cases where a bank agrees to a customer's request to have such a receipt indorsed on the cheque it is the practice to stipulate for an indemnity from the customer. If however the order relating to completion of the receipt is addressed not to the banker upon whom the cheque is drawn but to the payee, the cheque may be accepted as unconditional.[5]

A cheque must be drawn on a banker, that is, addressed by name to a person or body of persons, whether incorporated or not, carrying on the business of bankers. Drafts drawn by one branch of a bank on another branch or on the head office of the same bank are not cheques drawn on a banker because the head office and all the branches are considered to be one institution and the drawer and drawee of a cheque must be distinct parties. The holder of such an instrument may treat it, at his option, either as a bill of exchange or a promissory note (s. 5(2)).

A cheque must be signed by the drawer. The signature is usually, though not necessarily, adhibited in the lower right-hand corner of the cheque form. The signature must be that of the person in whose name the account is kept or of someone authorised by him to sign that name or the signature of a person who has authority, as agreed between the banker and his customer, to operate on the account. When a customer's signature differs from that with which the banker is familiar, the banker is under no obligation to pay the cheque even on satisfactory evidence of the authenticity of the signature. Signature does not, however, necessarily mean subscription. It is sufficient if the customer's instructions are adequately authenticated and a cheque which is holograph of the drawer and which contains his name is sufficient authority to the banker to honour the cheque. The signature may be in pencil[6] but for obvious reasons a banker is entitled to have his customer confirm his instructions in ink. Large companies and other businesses may make use of cheque forms to which are adhibited printed facsimile signatures or which may even have the "signature" printed on the form by a computer along with the date, amount, etc. Banks require an indemnity from such customers since it is a matter of debate whether or not such instruments are valid cheques and whether or not the purported drawers can be held liable on them.

A cheque must be payable on demand. A cheque is payable on demand

[3] *Vance* v. *Lowther* (1876) 1 Ex.D. 176.
[4] *Capital and Counties Bank Ltd.* v. *Gordon* [1903] A.C. 240 at p. 252; *Bavins, Junr. & Sims* v. *London and South Western Bank Ltd.* [1900] 1 Q.B. 270. Such an instrument would however fall within the terms of the Cheques Act 1957, ss. 1(2)(a), 4(2)(b) and 5.
[5] *Nathan* v. *Ogdens Ltd.* (1905) L.T. 126.
[6] *Geary* v. *Physic* (1826) 5 B. & C. 234.

when it is expressed to be so payable or when it is drawn payable at sight or on presentation or when no time for payment is expressed (s. 10(1)).

A cheque must be an order to pay a sum certain in money. The sum payable may be expressed in words or figures or both and where there is a discrepancy between the two the sum denoted by the words is the sum payable (s. 9(2)). In practice, such cheques are returned unpaid with the answer "Words and figures differ". If, however, the amount in figures is the smaller amount, some banks will pay that amount in cases where the discrepancy is not large.

A cheque must be made payable to a specified person or to bearer. A cheque may be made payable (1) "to bearer", "to myself or bearer" or "to A B or bearer". In the last two cases it is regarded as payable to bearer, the name of the payee being disregarded. Such a cheque is negotiated by delivery without indorsement but it may be indorsed by A B, or any subsequent holder; (2) "to myself", "to myself or order" or "to . . . order", in which case it is payable to the order of the drawer and requires his indorsement. The expression "to . . . order" is to be construed as meaning "to my order"[7] but it has been questioned whether a cheque payable "to . . . or order" is a valid document so long as the blank is not filled up.[8] A document in the form of a cheque payable "to Cash or order" has been held not to be a cheque within the meaning of the 1882 Act[9] but it is a valid order for the payment of money and falls within the provisions of the Cheques Act 1957.[10] A bank paying such a cheque to an employee or agent of the drawer gets a good discharge[11]; (3) "to A B", "to A B or order" or "to the order of A B", in which cases the cheque is payable to A B and is negotiated by his indorsement completed by delivery. Where the indorsement is blank (s. 34) it is payable to bearer; (4) "to A B and C D or order". A cheque payable to two or more persons jointly must be indorsed by all to render it negotiable. A cheque payable to two or more persons jointly and severally is payable to, and is negotiated by the indorsement of, any one of them; (5) "to A B or C D or order". A cheque payable in the alternative to one of two persons is negotiable by the indorsement of either of them (s. 7(2)); (6) to the holder of an office for the time being, such as the secretary, treasurer, cashier, president, etc., of the A B company, association, club, etc., or to such person or his order, or to the order of such person. Cheques so drawn are payable to the holder of the office for the time being (s. 8(1)) but cheques payable simply to the holder of the office for the time being without the addition of the words "or order", in so far as they contain words prohibiting transfer or indicating an intention that they should not be transferable, are not negotiable by the indorsement of the payee.

---

[7] *Chamberlain* v. *Young* [1893] 2 Q.B. 206.
[8] *Henderson, Sons & Co. Ltd.* v. *Wallace and Pennell* (1902) 5 F. 166.
[9] *North and South Insurance Corporation Ltd.* v. *National Provincial Bank Ltd.* [1936] 1 K.B. 328; *Cole* v. *Milsome* [1951] 1 All E.R. 311; *Orbit Mining & Trading Co. Ltd.* v. *Westminster Bank Ltd.* [1962] 3 All E.R. 565.
[10] ss. 1(2)(*a*), 4(2)(*b*) and 5.
[11] *North and South Insurance Corporation Ltd.* v. *National Provincial Bank Ltd.* [1963] 1 K.B. 328.

Where a cheque is payable to the holder of an office for the time being, or to his order, it may be negotiated by the indorsement of the payee. The indorsement should bear the signature of the holder of the office and should be expressed to be signed by him as representing his office (s. 31(5)); (7) "to A (or, to A only) for the account of B", or "to A or order for collection" or "to A or for order for my use" are each restrictive directions and prohibit the negotiation of a cheque. A banker paying an indorsee of such a cheque has notice that the payee has power to deal with it only in a specified way and he would be liable to the drawer in repetition of the amount in the event of the indorsee misapplying it; (8) to a fictitious or non-existing person. A cheque drawn to the order of such a person may be treated as payable to bearer (s. 7(3)), even although the drawer believes and intends the cheque to be payable to the order of a real person. The fact that the drawer was induced by fraud to draw the cheque in favour of a person whom he believed to exist but who was actually non-existent, is immaterial in a question with a *bona fide* holder for value.[12] In dealing with such cheques, the paying banker is protected by section 60 of the 1882 Act. The collecting banker is protected by section 4 of the Cheques Act 1957 and need only concern himself with section 7(3) of the 1882 Act if he took such a cheque as holder for value.

Crossed cheques

Crossed cheques came into use when persons drawing cheques adopted the practice of marking their cheques with the name of the payee's banker (a special crossing) or if they did not know where the payee banked, they merely wrote "& Co." on the face of the cheque (a general crossing) with the object of ensuring that such cheques would only be paid through a banker. In time the crossing came to be recognised by bankers as a direction to pay only to a banker. The practice eventually received statutory recognition and now the law relating to crossed cheques is to be found in sections 78 to 82 of the 1882 Act, the provisions of section 82 however having been repealed and re-enacted in the Cheques Act 1957.

Where a cheque bears across its face an addition of (1) the words "and company" or any abbreviation thereof between two parallel transverse lines, either with or without the words "Not negotiable", or (2) two parallel transverse lines simply, either with or without the words "Not negotiable", that addition constitutes a crossing and the cheque is crossed generally (s. 76(1)). Where a cheque bears across its face an addition of the name of a banker, either with or without the words "Not negotiable", that addition constitutes a crossing and the cheque is crossed specially to that banker (s. 76(2)). The crossing, including the words "Not negotiable", is a material part of the cheque and cannot lawfully be obliterated or, save as authorised by the Act, added to or altered (s. 78). A cheque may be crossed generally or specially by the drawer (s. 77(1)). Where a

---

[12] *Clutton* v. *Attenborough & Son* [1897] A.C. 90.

cheque is uncrossed, the holder may cross it generally or specially (s. 77(2)) and where a cheque is crossed generally, the holder may cross it specially (s. 77(3)). Where a cheque is crossed generally or specially, the holder may add the words "Not negotiable" (s. 77(4)). Where a cheque is crossed specially the banker to whom it is crossed may again cross it specially to another banker for collection (s. 77(5)). Where an uncrossed cheque or a cheque crossed generally is sent to a banker for collection, he may cross it specially to himself (s. 77(6)).

By crossing a cheque generally a direction is given to the banker on whom it is drawn that if he is to escape liability for negligence he must pay the cheque only to another banker (s. 80); and to the holder, an intimation that he can receive payment only through a banker. Section 80 places the paying banker, provided he pays in good faith and without negligence, in the same position as if he had paid the true owner of the cheque. If he disregards the crossing he is negligent so that if he pays a cheque to a thief or a finder, or upon a forged or unauthorised indorsement, in disregard of a general or special crossing, he is liable to the true owner if that true owner can prove that he has suffered loss by the cheque having been so paid.[13] If the drawer of the cheque suffers loss as a result of payment to someone who was not entitled, the banker cannot debit his account, not only because he was negligent but also because he paid in breach of his mandate. By crossing a cheque specially a direction is given to the banker on whom it is drawn to pay only to the banker with whose name the cheque is crossed or to his agent for collection, being a banker. The banker on whom is drawn a cheque crossed specially to more than one banker, except where the second special crossing is to a banker for collection, is bound to refuse payment of it (s. 79(1)).

"Not negotiable" crossing

In addition to the crossing on a cheque, the drawer or holder may add the words "Not negotiable" (s. 76). Such words are not to be taken as implying any limitation in the transferability of the cheque but a person who takes a crossed cheque bearing on it the words "Not negotiable" has not, and cannot give, a better title to the cheque than that of the person from whom he took it (s. 81). If a cheque is obtained from a drawer by fraud—as in the case where an employee induces his employer to draw a cheque in favour of a fictitious person or where the payee himself obtains a cheque by fraud or false pretences—and it is subsequently indorsed to an innocent third party who gives value for it, then if the cheque is an open one or even if it is crossed generally or specially, the innocent third party may be able to enforce payment against the drawer. If however the cheque is crossed "Not negotiable" the third party cannot obtain any better title to the cheque than the payee had—which in the examples was none at all—and so the drawer will not be liable to the third party. The object of the addition of the words is to give protection to the true owner

---

[13] *Smith* v. *Union Bank of London* (1875) 1 Q.B.D. 31; *Bobbett* v. *Pinkett* (1876) 1 Ex.D. 368.

of the cheque by preserving his rights against any subsequent holder. A cheque crossed "Not negotiable" imposes on the banker no liability other than that attaching to crossed cheques generally. A collecting banker is not put upon inquiry even if the cheque is placed in his hands for collection by someone other than the named payee.[14] It is now considered that the words "Not negotiable" appearing on an uncrossed cheque have no statutory effect on their own.

Addition of words "Account payee"

There exists a practice of adding to an ordinary crossing words such as "Account payee" or "Account of A B". These words have no statutory significance and do not restrict the transferability of a crossed cheque payable to order or to bearer.[15] Such crossings, however, are not without legal significance. The words are held to be a direction to the collecting banker that the account of the payee should be credited with the proceeds of the cheque when received—a direction which he disregards at his peril. If a collecting banker credits the account of another person with the proceeds of a cheque crossed in this manner, he may be liable for any ensuing loss since he has not collected the proceeds of such a cheque "without negligence" and in consequence has lost the protection of section 4 of the Cheques Act 1957.[16] The duty imposed on the collecting bank by the crossing is to ensure that the payee is not defrauded; it does not extend to protect the drawer against the payee's fraud nor does it prevent the cheque's negotiation.[17]

Indorsement

Unless a cheque contains words prohibiting transfer the holder of a cheque may negotiate it to another person. A cheque is negotiated when it is transferred from one person to another in such a manner as to constitute the transferee the holder of the cheque (s. 31(1)). A cheque payable to bearer is negotiated by delivery alone (s. 31(2)) whereas a cheque payable to order is negotiated by the indorsement of the holder completed by delivery (s. 31(3)). The effect of indorsement is to entitle the indorsee to sue the indorser and any prior holder. Since the passing of the Cheques Act in 1957 indorsement has largely been dispensed with. Paying and collecting bankers are, in certain circumstances, not liable if they pay or collect cheques on which there is no, or an irregular indorsement.[18] Banks no longer require a payee to indorse a cheque to the banker on whom it is drawn, except in the case of a cheque cashed at the counter. This indorsement is not such as to subject the payee to any liability, being looked on rather as an acknowledgment of payment.

An indorsement proper may be defined as the signature on a cheque,

---

[14] See Paget, *Law of Banking* (9th ed.) at p. 209.
[15] *National Bank* v. *Silke* [1891] 1 Q.B. 435.
[16] *House Property Co. of London* v. *London, County and Westminster Bank* (1915) 84 L.J.K.B. 1846.
[17] *Kenton* v. *Barclays Bank Ltd.*, Chorley and Smart, *Leading Cases* (6th ed.), p. 186.
[18] See ss. 1(1) and 4(3) of the 1957 Act; also *Westminster Bank Ltd.* v. *Zang* [1966] A.C. 182 at p. 218.

usually written on the back, of the holder, followed by delivery of the cheque. By signing the cheque in this manner, the holder of a cheque payable to his order negotiates it to another person who takes it as the next holder. It must be an indorsement of the entire cheque. An indorsement which purports to transfer a part only of the amount payable or to transfer the cheque to two or more indorsees severally does not operate as a negotiation of the cheque (s. 32(2)). An indorsement may be either in blank or special (s. 34) and may be restrictive (s. 35).

A cheque is payable to bearer which is expressed to be so payable or on which the only or last indorsement is an indorsement in blank. Such a cheque is negotiable by delivery without indorsement and may be passed from hand to hand like a bank note. A cheque drawn payable to bearer, so long as it purports to be so payable, cannot be specially indorsed by the payee or any subsequent holder so as to be payable to the order of the indorsee, although the payee of such a cheque is entitled to substitute the word "order" for the word "bearer" in the body of the cheque and so to change the cheque from one payable to bearer to one payable to order.

One of the requisites of a valid indorsement is that it must be written on the cheque itself and be signed by the indorser or his duly authorised agent (ss. 32(1) and 91(1)). A signature by procuration operates as notice that the agent has only a limited authority to sign and the principal is only bound by such signature if the agent in signing was acting within the actual limits of his authority (s. 25). Where a cheque is payable to the order of two or more payees or indorsees who are not partners all must indorse, unless the one indorsing has authority to indorse for the others (s. 32(3)). As far as partners are concerned, section 5 of the Partnership Act 1890 provides that every partner is an agent of the firm and his other partners for the purpose of the business of the partnership. One partner may therefore indorse cheques which are payable to the partnership. Where in a cheque payable to order the payee or indorsee is wrongly designated or his name is misspelt, he may indorse the cheque in the manner in which he has been described, adding if he thinks fit his proper signature (s. 32(4)). In any event, it has been held that the proper signature of the payee or indorsee by itself is valid and sufficient to pass the property in the instrument.[19]

The regularity of an indorsement is a different thing from its validity. In *Arab Bank Ltd.* v. *Ross*[20] two promissory notes were indorsed by one of the partners of a firm but the word "Company" which formed part of the firm's name was omitted. The court held that although the partner's indorsements were valid to pass the title in the instruments to the bank, the failure to include the word "Company" in the indorsements made them irregular so as to give rise to doubt as to whether it was the indorsement of the named payees. The instruments were therefore not complete and regular on the face of them and so the bank could not

---

[19] *Arab Bank Ltd.* v. *Ross* [1952] 2 Q.B. 216 at p. 226.
[20] [1952] 2 Q.B. 216.

become holders in due course of them. The bank were nevertheless holders for value of the notes and succeeded on this basis.

Holder of a cheque

The holder of a cheque is the payee or indorsee who is in possession of it or the bearer thereof (s. 2). In both cases, possession is essential to constitute a person the holder of a cheque. However, the possessor of a cheque is not necessarily the holder of it. For example, if a cheque is in the hands of a thief he is the possessor of the cheque but does not fall within the definition of a holder. Again, the holder of a cheque may not necessarily be the owner of it, as for example, when a cheque is handed to a bank for collection. The bank, while in possession of the cheque, is the holder of it but it is not the owner. The holder of a cheque has certain rights and powers in relation to the indorsement and crossing of a cheque. Also, where a cheque has been lost before it is overdue—see section 36(3)—the person who was the holder of it may apply to the drawer to give him another cheque, giving security to the drawer if required to indemnify him in case the cheque alleged to have been lost is found again (s. 69). In such a situation, the drawer can be compelled to give a duplicate cheque. The necessity for the indemnity arises because the original cheque may be in the hands of a holder in due course. If this is the case, the drawer may be liable to such a holder and cannot escape liability by instructing his bank to stop payment of the original cheque. Generally, the holder of a cheque may negotiate it to another person or if he does not do so, may present it for payment to the bank on which it it drawn. If the cheque is an open one he may present it personally to the drawee bank and request payment in cash. The banker, if he has funds in his hands to do so, is bound to pay such a cheque. The holder will be asked to indorse the cheque but the banker has no obligation to ascertain that the indorsement is *bona fide*.

Holder in due course

The rights and powers of the holder of a cheque include the right to sue on the cheque in his own name (s. 38(1)). Where he is a holder in due course[21] he holds the cheque free from any defect of title of prior parties, as well as from mere personal defences available to prior parties among themselves and may enforce payment against all parties liable on the cheque (s. 38(2)). In *Arab Bank Ltd.* v. *Ross*[22] the difference between their respective rights was described as follows:

"The difference between the rights of a 'holder in due course' and those of a 'holder' is that a holder in due course may get a better title than the person from whom he took, whereas a holder gets no better

---

[21] See s. 29(1).
[22] [1952] 2 Q.B. 216 at p. 229.

title. In this regard a person who takes a bill which is irregular on the face of it is in the same position as a person who takes a bill which is overdue. He is a holder but not a holder in due course. He does not receive the bill on its own intrinsic credit. He takes it on the credit of the person who gives it to him . . . he can sue in his own name, but he takes it subject to the defects of title of prior parties: see section 38 of the Act."

In the first place, a holder in due course of a cheque must be a holder. If a prior signature on the cheque has been forged or is unauthorised, no one can thereafter become a holder because a forged or unauthorised signature is "wholly inoperative" and no right to retain the cheque or to give a discharge of it or to enforce payment of it against any party to the cheque can be acquired through or under that signature, unless the party against whom it is sought to retain or enforce payment of the cheque is precluded from setting up the forgery or want of authority (s. 24). However, an indorser is precluded from denying to a holder in due course the genuineness and regularity in all respects of the drawer's signature and all previous indorsements (s. 55(2)). An innocent transferee is therefore entitled to sue any indorser who became a party to the cheque subsequent to the forgery. Again, if any essential element of form is lacking in the cheque the transferee cannot be a holder in due course. Looking at the cheque, front and back, without the aid of outside evidence, it must be complete and regular in itself.[23] Also, the cheque must not be overdue. Since a cheque is a bill payable on demand, it is deemed to be overdue when it appears on the face of it to have been in circulation for an unreasonable length of time. What is an unreasonable length of time for the purpose is a question of fact (s. 36(3)). If a cheque has been dishonoured, the fact and reason for dishonour will usually appear on the face of it. A transferee taking such a cheque cannot be a holder in due course.

The holder must have taken the cheque for value. Value is defined as "valuable consideration" (s. 2)[24] but a cheque is valid in Scotland although given for no valuable consideration. The plea of non-onerosity is, however, relevant in certain circumstances.[25]

The cheque must have been negotiated before a holder can become a holder in due course. The payee of a cheque cannot be a holder in due course.[26] Further, the holder must have had no notice of any defect in the title of the person who negotiated it to him. The Act does not define "defect in title" but provides that the title of a person who negotiates a cheque is defective when he obtained the cheque by fraud, duress, or force and fear, or other unlawful means, or for an illegal consideration, or

---

[23] *Ibid.*, at p. 226.
[24] See s. 27(1).
[25] See Bell, *Prin.*, § 333. A cheque can be challenged for fraud, illegality or failure of the consideration and non-onerosity pleaded as evidence.
[26] *R. E. Jones Ltd.* v. *Waring & Gillow Ltd.* [1926] A.C. 670.

when he negotiates it in breach of faith, or under such circumstances as to amount to a fraud (s. 29(2)). The holder may have express notice of the particular facts. In *Midland Bank Ltd.* v. *Reckitt*[27] a solicitor held from a client a power of attorney entitling him to draw cheques on the client's account and to apply them for the purposes of the client. For his own purposes he fraudulently drew cheques, signing them as attorney on behalf of his client "Harold G. Reckitt by Terrington, his attorney". He paid them into his own account with a bank with whom he had an overdraft which he was being pressed to reduce. The court held that as the bank had from the form of the cheques notice that the money did not belong to their customer, they were negligent in making no inquiry as to the customer's authority to make these payments into his own account and that they were liable to repay the amount of the cheques to the solicitor's client.

Section 29(3) of the Act provides that a holder, whether for value or not, who derives his title to a cheque through a holder in due course and who is not himself a party to any fraud or illegality affecting it, has all the rights of that holder in due course as regards all parties to the cheque prior to that holder. This means that where a cheque which is affected by some fraud or illegality is negotiated to an innocent person who becomes a holder in due course, this person can negotiate the cheque to someone who has knowledge of the fraud or illegality although he is not a party to it himself. Under the circumstances, although the second transferee has knowledge of the irregularity and even if he has not given value for the cheque, he has all the rights of the original holder in due course as regards all parties prior to that holder.

Every holder of a cheque is *prima facie* deemed to be a holder in due course (s. 29) but if it is admitted or proved that a cheque is tainted with illegality, the holder in order to secure the privileges of a holder in due course must prove that he has given value for it in good faith (s. 30).[28] In other words, he must prove both that he has given value and that he had no notice or knowledge of any illegality. If his proof fails in any particular, he cannot recover.[29] It is competent to prove by parole evidence that a cheque was granted subject to certain conditions and a holder for value who takes such a cheque with notice of the conditions is not entitled to recover unless the conditions are implemented.[30]

Forged or unauthorised indorsement

A forged or unauthorised indorsement on a cheque payable to order operates not only to annul all rights and obligations of the indorsers and

---

[27] [1933] A.C. 1. All but two of the cheques were crossed and marked "Not negotiable". The bank were recognised as holders for value of these two cheques but the notice referred to defeated their right to the greater status of holders in due course.

[28] See s. 90.

[29] *Tyler* v. *Maxwell* (1892) 30 S.L.R. 583 at p. 584. See also *Pollok* v. *Burns* (1875) 2 R. 497; *Couston* v. *Miller* (1862) 24 D. 607.

[30] See s. 100 and *Semple* v. *Kyle* (1902) 4 F. 421.

indorsees subsequent to such indorsement but also to extinguish the debt due to any such indorsee by the indorser from whom he received the cheque (s. 24).[31] Each *bona fide* holder may, however, recover from his predecessor in title, until the author of the forged or unauthorised signature is reached.[32] A *bona fide* holder for value subsequent to the forged or unauthorised indorsement of a cheque payable to order cannot go beyond it so as to sue a party, whether as drawer or indorser, liable on the cheque prior to such indorsement.[33] Thus if A draws a cheque payable to B or order which is lost and falls into the hands of a dishonest person who then forges B's indorsement and transfers it for value, the holder for value has no recourse against A if payment of the cheque has been stopped. Nor is such a holder entitled even to retain the cheque.[34]

Presentment for payment

A cheque must be presented to the banker at his place of business within bank hours and on a business day by the holder or some person authorised by him to receive payment on his behalf (s. 45(3)). A bank is entitled to a reasonable time after its advertised closing time in which to pay a cheque.[35] A cheque payable at a branch bank must be presented there and if presented and paid at the head office or at another branch of the bank, the latter are not to be regarded as having paid the cheque as the banker of the drawer but rather as collecting agent for the payee.[36] Where authorised by agreement or the usage of trade, a cheque may be presented for payment to a bank through the post office (s. 45(8)) but the usage of bankers does not authorise presentment by post except by another bank.

Time for presentment

A cheque is said to be issued when it is delivered complete in form to a person taking it as a holder and must be presented for payment within a reasonable time of its issue (ss. 2 and 74(1)). In determining what is a reasonable time, regard has to be had to the nature of the cheque, the usage of trade and of bankers, and the facts of the particular case (s. 74(2)). As between the drawer and the payee, unless the drawer can prove actual loss as a result of delay in presentment, the holder may present it at any time within five years.[37] In other words, the drawer is liable on the cheque until the holder's right of action has prescribed and he is not discharged by mere delay, unless the delay has caused him damage and then only to the extent of the damage as provided by section 74(1). By virtue of section 45(2) the indorser of a cheque is discharged

---

[31] *Alderson* v. *Langdale* (1832) 3 B. & A. 660.
[32] *Macdonald* v. *Union Bank of Scotland* (1864) 2 M. 963.
[33] *Bobbett* v. *Pinkett* (1876) L.R. 1 Ex.D. 368; *Burchfield* v. *Moore* (1854) 23 L.J.Q.B. 261.
[34] *Johnson* v. *Windle* (1836) 3 Bing.N.C. 225.
[35] *Baines* v. *National Provincial Bank Ltd.* (1927) 96 L.J.K.B. 801.
[36] *Woodland* v. *Fear* (1857) 26 L.J.Q.B. 202; *Garnett* v. *McKewan* (1872) L.R. 8 Ex. 10.
[37] Prescription and Limitation (Scotland) Act 1973, s. 6 and Sched. 1, para. 1(e).

unless it is presented for payment within a reasonable time (after indorsement) as defined by that section.

At common law the time for presentment depends on whether or not the person who receives the cheque lives in the same place as the bank on which the cheque is drawn. However, this rule must now be considered to have been modified by the express statutory recognition of the usage of bankers so that the question of reasonable time must depend upon the reasonableness of the banking practice adopted. In addition, mercantile (as well as domestic) practice has to be looked at to ascertain what is a reasonable time within which to present a cheque for payment. Most banks return unpaid with the answer "Out of date" cheques which are dated more than six months prior to the date of presentment. Such cheques are regarded as "stale" as opposed to "overdue".

Overdue cheques

A cheque is deemed to be overdue when it appears on the face of it to have been in circulation for an unreasonable length of time (s. 36(3)). By this is meant such a length of time as ought to have excited suspicion in the mind of an ordinary careful holder.[38] Where a cheque which appears to have been in circulation for an unreasonable length of time is presented to a banker for payment he is entitled to take time to consult the drawer before paying it. Most banks refuse to pay a cheque six months old without special instructions from their customer but there is no general practice in the matter.[39]

Alterations on cheques

The alteration of a cheque in a material part, without the consent of all parties liable on it, renders such a cheque void, except as against a party who has himself made, authorised or consented to the alteration, and subsequent indorsers (s. 64(1)). Where a cheque has been materially altered but the alteration is not apparent, a holder in due course may avail himself of the cheque as if it had not been altered and may enforce payment of it according to its original tenor (s. 64(1)). Any alteration of the date or the sum payable is a material alteration (s. 64(2)).

Lost and stolen cheques

The finder of a cheque can be compelled to deliver it up to the true owner or where he has transferred it for value to another, to pay over the amount which he received for it. A holder in due course cannot be compelled either to deliver up the cheque or where he has transferred it, to account for the amount he has received. A holder for value if he has not acquired the status of a holder in due course (by reason, for example, of a

---

[38] See, for example, *Serrell* v. *Derbyshire Ry. Co.* (1850) 9 C.B. 811; *London and County Bank* v. *Groome* (1881) L.R. 8 Q.B.D. 288; *Griffiths* v. *Dalton* [1940] 2 K.B. 264.
[39] See Paget, *Law of Banking* (9th ed.) at p. 235.

prior indorsement having been forged) is bound to deliver up a lost cheque and if he has obtained payment of it, to account for the amount which he has received. Thus a crossed cheque drawn by A payable to B lost by or stolen from B and passed on to C as a *bona fide* holder with B's indorsement forged on it, still remains B's property as the true owner. However, A may refuse to allow his banker to debit his account with the amount if the cheque has been paid by the banker contrary to the direction expressed by the crossing or, if properly paid, he may recover the amount paid to C who has acquired no title to the cheque. The person who receives payment of a cheque to which he has no title is held in law to have received it for the true owner.[40] A banker who collects payment of such a cheque does not incur any liability to the true owner by reason only of having received payment.[41]

Paid cheques

When a cheque is paid the holder is bound to deliver it up to the banker paying it (s. 52(4)). In his hands it is *prima facie* evidence of the payment of the amount. A cheque on payment becomes the property of the customer who drew it but the banker who pays it is entitled to keep it as a voucher until his account with his customer is settled or until the customer's account is docqueted. Nevertheless, some banks in Scotland deliver paid cheques to their customers along with the relative statements of account but an exception to this practice may be made in the case of business customers where cheques issued for the payment of wages may be retained in the bank's hands for four months.[42] An unindorsed cheque which appears to have been paid by the banker on whom it is drawn is evidence of the receipt by the payee of the sum payable by the cheque.[43]

Cheques as payment

The giving and taking of a cheque may operate as a payment and extinction of the debt for which it was granted. To do so it must, however, reach the hands of the payee. A cheque which has been delivered to the payee in payment of a debt operates as a payment of the debt for which it was granted, subject to the condition that if on due presentment it is not paid—either because there are no funds[44] or because payment has been countermanded by the drawer[45]—the original debt revives. Although a cheque is a bill of exchange which is payable on demand, protest and summary diligence on an unpaid cheque are incompetent.[46] If a bill, promissory note or cheque is taken on account of a debt and nothing is said at the time, the legal effect of the transaction is that the original debt

[40] *Bobbett* v. *Pinkett* (1876) L.R. 1 Ex.D. 368; *Smith* v. *Union Bank of London* (1875) 1 Q.B.D. 31.
[41] Cheques Act 1957, s. 4.
[42] *Cf.* pp. 243 and 267.
[43] Cheques Act 1957, s. 3. See also *Charles* v. *Blackwell* (1877) 2 C.P.D. 151.
[44] *Caine* v. *Coulson* (1863) 1 H. & C. 764.
[45] *Cohen* v. *Hale* (1878) 3 Q.B.D. 371.
[46] *Glickman* v. *Linda*, 1950 S.L.T. 19.

remains but the remedy for it is suspended until the maturity of the instrument in the hands of the creditor.[47] If the cheque has reached the payee and been lost by or stolen from him and cashed before he has time or while he delays to give intimation of the loss or theft, the loss will fall on him and not on the drawer.[48]

A creditor is not bound to accept a cheque in payment of a debt as a cheque is not money nor is it legal tender and where a creditor receives his debtor's cheque but refuses to accept it as payment, he may apparently sue for the original debt while retaining the cheque.[49] Even when the creditor accepts a cheque as payment, he is held to have done so only on the implied condition that the cheque will be honoured when presented and if it is not so honoured the creditor's right to sue for the original debt is not impaired.[50] The mere receipt of a cheque drawn in conditional terms does not operate as a payment. The mere keeping of a cheque sent "in full of all demands" is not conclusive evidence from which satisfaction of an obligation is to be presumed in law; the question whether or not it has been kept upon the terms sent is one of fact in each particular case.[51]

If a person makes a payment in a manner which makes its appropriation extremely easy—as, for instance, by means of a cheque payable to bearer—it is his duty to ensure that it reaches the person for whom it was intended. The sending of an ordinary uncrossed cheque payable to bearer is not a remittance in the ordinary course of business. If for any reason it is misappropriated, the sender, if the misappropriation was made possible through his negligence or failure to take proper precautions, will not be allowed to plead against the payee that payment has been duly made and he may be called on to make good the amount of the cheque.[52]

Discharge of cheque

A cheque is discharged by payment in due course when the proceeds are applied to the credit of the holder (s. 59(1)).[53] "Payment in due course" means payment to the holder in good faith and without notice that his title to the cheque is defective. The holder is the payee or indorsee of a cheque who is in possession of it or the bearer thereof (s. 2). The paying banker is protected against the forged indorsement of order cheques by section 1 of the Cheques Act 1957. Payment in due course by a banker of an uncrossed bearer cheque to anyone presenting it to him discharges not only the banker but, if the cheque had reached the payee, the drawer also.[54]

---

[47] *Allen* v. *Royal Bank of Canada* (1925) 41 T.L.R. 625.
[48] *Charles* v. *Blackwell* (1877) 2 C.P.D. 151.
[49] *Stuart* v. *Cawse* (1859) 28 L.J.C.P. 193.
[50] *Cohen* v. *Hale* (1878) 3 Q.B.D. 371: approved in *Leggat Bros.* v. *Gray*, 1908 S.C. 67.
[51] *Day* v. *McLea* (1889) 22 Q.B.D. 610; *Gilbey Vintners Scotland Ltd.* v. *Perry*, 1978 S.L.T. (Sh.Ct.) 48 and cases cited therein.
[52] *Robb* v. *Gow Bros. & Gemmell* (1905) 8 F. 90.
[53] *Coats* v. *Union Bank of Scotland Ltd.*, 1929 S.C. (H.L.) 114.
[54] *Charles* v. *Blackwell* (1877) 2 C.P.D. 151.

CHAPTER 8

THE COLLECTING BANKER AND THE PAYING BANKER

Duties of the collecting banker

A banker is under a duty to his customer to see that cheques paid in for collection are presented for payment with reasonable diligence. The precise time allowed for presenting a cheque for payment is not stated in the Bills of Exchange Act 1882. Section 45(2) of that Act, dealing with a bill payable on demand, provides that it must be presented for payment within a reasonable time. Under the former common law rules when the cheque was drawn on a bank in the same place, the banker to whom it was handed for collection was obliged to present it the day after he received it. When the cheque was drawn on a bank in another place, it was sufficient if the banker either presented it or forwarded it on the day following receipt.[1] At the present time the banker's duty can be said to depend upon the current practice of bankers and the facts of the particular case if regard is paid to the terms of sections 45 and 74 of the 1882 Act. Current practice is to present cheques through the clearings, which have their own rules. It is now settled that the presenting bank's responsibility to its customer in respect of the collection of a cheque is discharged only when the cheque is physically delivered to the branch of the bank on which it is drawn for a decision whether it should be paid or not. The paying bank is regarded as being, from the time of receiving the cheque in the clearing until the time of presenting it at the drawee branch, a sub-agent of the presenting bank, which is itself the agent of the payee.[2] Failure to present a cheque timeously renders a banker liable to his customer for loss occasioned by the delay.[3] Cheques and similar instruments may be presented specially by the collecting banker to the bank office where they are payable, by messenger during business hours or by post. Such a special presentation is made to establish fate more quickly than can be done through the normal clearing system.[4] The collecting banker also has a duty to give prompt notice to his customer of any cheques which are returned to him dishonoured after presentment for payment. He should send written notice of dishonour to the customer on the same day as the

---

[1] *Alexander* v. *Burchfield* (1842) 7 Man. & G. 1061; *Forman* v. *Bank of England* (1902) 18 T.L.R. 339; *Hamilton Finance Co. Ltd.* v. *Coverley, Westray, Walbaum and Tossetti Ltd.* [1969] 1 Lloyd's Rep. 53 at p. 72; *Hare* v. *Henty* (1861) 10 C.B.(N.S.) 65; *Prideaux* v. *Criddle* (1869) L.R. 4 Q.B. 455; *Heywood* v. *Pickering* (1874) L.R. 9 Q.B. 428.
[2] *Barclays Bank PLC and Others* v. *Bank of England* [1985] 1 All E.R. 385.
[3] *Lubbock* v. *Tribe* (1838) 3 M. & W. 607; see also *Forman* v. *Bank of England, supra,* and *Yeoman Credit Ltd.* v. *Gregory* [1963] 1 All E.R. 245.
[4] See *Ringham* v. *Hackett, The Times,* 8 February 1980.

unpaid item is received by the bank.[5] Unless the bank wishes to make a claim against the drawer of the cheque as holder for value, the bank will debit the amount of the cheque to its customer's account and return the cheque to him forthwith.

Bank as holder for value

When a cheque is returned unpaid to the collecting bank it may not be able to debit the amount of the cheque to the customer's account because either he has no funds in his account or the bank does not wish to increase an existing overdraft. In such cases, the collecting bank may have the option of retaining possession of the cheque, debiting a suspense account and claiming as holder for value against the drawer of the cheque. To do so, it must give notice of dishonour where this is necessary. It is not usually necessary to give notice to the drawer of the cheque (s. 50(2)(c)). If the bank returns the cheque to its customer it will no longer be the holder of the cheque and its claim as holder for value will fail (s. 2).[6] By virtue of section 2 of the Cheques Act 1957 the bank will have the same rights as a holder even if the person who pays in the cheque does not indorse it, as will normally be the case. This will be true even if the cheque is paid in for the credit of an account other than the account of the payee.[7]

To be a holder for value the bank must have given valuable consideration (s. 27(1)). It will have done so if it allows a customer to draw his own cheques against an uncleared cheque.[8] Again, if the bank receives the cheque in reduction of an overdraft the bank becomes a holder for value.[9] Similarly, by virtue of section 27(3) of the 1882 Act where the holder of a cheque has a lien on it, arising either from contract or by implication of law, he is deemed to be a holder for value to the extent of the sum for which he has a lien. Since a bank has a lien on any cheques delivered into its possession by a customer where the customer is indebted to the bank the fact that the customer's account is overdrawn is sufficient in itself to enable the bank to exercise its lien. Again, the bank should not part with the cheque, otherwise the right of lien will be lost.[10] If a bank cashes a cheque for a customer, the cheque having been drawn in the customer's favour by a third party, the bank again becomes a holder for value. In such a situation, the customer should negotiate the cheque to the bank by indorsing it.

If the customer has no title or a defective title to the cheque, this will be fatal to the bank's claim as a holder for value since the claim can be defeated by defects of title of prior parties as well as by mere personal defences available to prior parties among themselves (s. 38(2)). If, how-

---

[5] See s. 49 of the 1882 Act; also *Lombard Banking Ltd.* v. *Central Garage and Engineering Ltd.* [1963] 1 Q.B. 220.

[6] *Cf.* s. 2; and see *Westminster Bank Ltd.* v. *Zang* [1966] A.C. 182.

[7] *Ibid.*

[8] *National Bank Ltd.* v. *Silke* [1891] 1 Q.B. 435; *Midland Bank Ltd.* v. *R. V. Harris Ltd.* [1963] 2 All E.R. 685.

[9] *McLean* v. *Clydesdale Bank* (1883) 11 R. (H.L.) 1.

[10] *Westminster Bank Ltd.* v. *Zang, supra,*.

ever, the bank can plead that it is a holder in due course, its claim cannot be defeated. To be a holder in due course, the bank must satisfy the requirements of section 29 and in many cases will be able to do so.[11] The bank will therefore have no need to rely on section 27(3).

Statutory protection

Where a cheque has been stolen or obtained by fraud the true owner of the cheque may have a valid claim against the bank which collected the proceeds of the cheque as well as against the thief or person committing the fraud. In England, the action against the collecting banker is based on the tort of conversion as it applies to negotiable instruments. At common law, the tort is one of strict liability in which the concept of fault plays no part.[12] It is against this risk that the collecting banker in England is protected by statute. As there is no Scottish equivalent of conversion it has been suggested that the English authorities should be treated with caution.[13] Nevertheless, it has been customary to refer to them when considering claims against the collecting banker in Scotland.

When a claim is made against a bank on the ground that it has collected the proceeds of a cheque for someone other than the true owner, the bank may set up the statutory defence made available by section 4 of the Cheques Act 1957. This defence is available to it although it is a holder in due course or a holder for value to the extent of its lien.[14] This section provides that where a banker in good faith and without negligence (a) receives payment for a customer of an instrument to which the section applies or (b) having credited a customer's account with the amount of such an instrument, receives payment for himself, and the customer has no title or a defective title to the instrument, the banker does not incur any liability to the true owner of the instrument by reason only of having received payment. Section 4(2) specifies that the section shall apply to (a) cheques, (b) any document issued by a customer of a banker which, though not a bill of exchange, is intended to enable a person to obtain payment from that banker of the sum mentioned in the document, (c) any document issued by a public officer which is intended to enable a person to obtain payment from the Paymaster General or the Queen's and Lord Treasurer's Remembrancer of the sum mentioned in the document but which is not a bill of exchange, and (d) any draft payable on demand drawn by a banker on himself, whether payable at the head office or some other office of his bank. Section 4(3) provides that a banker is not to be treated for the purposes of the section as having been negligent by reason only of his failure to concern himself with the absence of, or irregularity in, indorsement of an instrument.

---

[11] See, for example, *Midland Bank Ltd.* v. *R. V. Harris Ltd.* [1963] 2 All E.R. 685 and *Barclays Bank Ltd.* v. *Astley Industrial Trust Ltd.* [1970] 1 All E.R. 719.

[12] See *Marfani & Co. Ltd.* v. *Midland Bank Ltd.* [1968] 2 All E.R. 573 at p. 578.

[13] See "The Collecting Banker's Protection in Scots Law" (D. J. Cusine), 1978 J.R. 233.

[14] See *Barclays Bank Ltd.* v. *Astley Industrial Trust Ltd.*, *supra*.

"Without negligence"

In order to qualify for protection under section 4 of the 1957 Act a banker must act in good faith and without negligence. Section 90 of the 1882 Act provides that a thing is deemed to be done in good faith where it is in fact done honestly, whether it is done negligently or not. The same meaning is applied to these words in the 1957 Act by virtue of section 6(1) of the 1957 Act. A bank acts in good faith if its employees act honestly in regard to the collection of cheques and other instruments. If an employee knew that a customer had no title to a cheque, for example, the statutory protection would be lost. The onus is on the collecting banker to prove that he has not been negligent. Negligence is a question of fact and one determining factor is whether the paying-in of any given cheque, coupled with the circumstances antecedent and present, was so out of the ordinary course that it ought to have aroused doubts in the banker's mind and caused him to make inquiry.[15] If a standard is sought, it should be the standard to be derived from the "ordinary practice of bankers"[16] although a court is always entitled to examine current banking practice and to form its own opinion as to whether or not it does comply with the standard of care which a prudent banker should adopt.[17] A variant of the test for determining whether or not a collecting banker has been negligent was given in *Lloyds Bank Ltd.* v. *E. B. Savory and Co.*[18]:

"The standard by which the absence, or otherwise, of negligence is to be determined must in my opinion be ascertained by reference to the practice of reasonable men carrying on the business of bankers, and endeavouring to do so in such a manner as may be calculated to protect themselves and others against fraud."

The same case held that a failure to obtain a reference and make inquiry as to the prospective customer's standing may prevent the collecting banker from establishing his statutory defence.[19] However, a bank account has long since ceased to be thought of as a privilege granted only to the better-off and cases decided when the use by the general public of banking facilities was much less widespread may not be a reliable guide to what the duty of a careful banker is today.[20] In opening a current account, the traditional practice of obtaining references may still be followed but bankers now question the value of this system and consider they can establish identity, standing and creditworthiness using other sources of information.[21]

In cases where the customer does not have a good title to the cheque

---

[15] *Commissioners of Taxation* v. *English, Scottish and Australian Bank Ltd.* [1920] A.C. 683 at p. 688. See also *Thackwell* v. *Barclays Bank PLC* [1986] 1 All E.R. 677.

[16] *Ibid.*, at p. 689. See also *A. L. Underwood Ltd.* v. *Bank of Liverpool* [1924] 1 K.B. 775 at p. 793.

[17] *Marfani & Co. Ltd.* v. *Midland Bank Ltd.* [1968] 2 All E.R. 573.

[18] [1933] A.C. 201 at p. 221.

[19] *Ibid.*, at p. 231.

[20] *Marfani & Co. Ltd.* v. *Midland Bank Ltd.*, *supra* at p. 579.

[21] See also p. 8 on the measures which banks ought to take to prevent money laundering.

which the bank is being asked to collect, there may be circumstances surrounding the collection which should put the bank upon inquiry. For example, if the bank has from the form of the cheques notice that the money does not belong to their customer they are negligent if they make no inquiry as to the customer's authority to make these payments into his account.[22] Again, when a bank is asked by a customer to collect the proceeds of a cheque which was originally payable to a third party, there is a risk that the customer is not entitled to the cheque even although it appears to have been indorsed by the payee. In *Baker* v. *Barclays Bank Ltd.*[23] Devlin J., in dealing with the collection of third party cheques said:

"Of course, cheques are indorsed over to third parties, but usually for small amounts and only occasionally. When the bank manager sees it happening for large sums and quite regularly, I think he is put on enquiry."

If a cheque has been crossed "Account payee" bankers will not normally collect cheques with this crossing for someone other than the named payee.[24] Where a cheque is payable to the customer's employer the bank should be put upon inquiry since it has been held that when opening an account for a new customer, a bank should ascertain the name of the prospective customer's employer or, if the customer is a married woman, the name of her husband's employer; failure to take this precaution may amount to negligence if the customer subsequently pays into his account cheques which are either payable to his employer or drawn by his employer in favour of a third party.[25] It is however not thought that a bank is under an obligation "continually to keep itself up to date" as to the identity of a customer's employer.[26]

In *United Australia Ltd.* v. *Barclays Bank Ltd.*[27] it was stated that "every bank clerk sees the red light when a company's cheque is indorsed by a company's official into an account which is not the company's." Since it is the invariable practice for cheques payable to a limited company to be paid into the company's account it may amount to negligence on the part of the collecting bank if, in the absence of special circumstances, such cheques are credited to any account other than that of the company. In *A. L. Underwood Ltd.* v. *Bank of Liverpool*[28] a bank lost its statutory protection where it allowed a director of a limited company to

---

[22] See, for example, *Hannan's Lake View Central Ltd.* v. *Armstrong & Co.* (1900) 16 T.L.R. 236; *Morison* v. *London County and Westminster Bank Ltd.* [1914] 3 K.B. 356 and *Souchette Ltd.* v. *London County, Westminster and Parr's Bank Ltd.* (1920) 36 T.L.R. 195, in addition to the other cases cited in this section of the chapter.

[23] [1955] 2 All E.R. 571. See also *Nu-Stilo Footwear Ltd.* v. *Lloyds Bank Ltd., The Times,* 19 June 1956; 7 *Legal Decisions Affecting Bankers,* 121.

[24] *Bevan* v. *National Bank Ltd.* (1906) 23 T.L.R. 65.

[25] *Lloyds Bank Ltd.* v. *E. B. Savory & Co.* [1933] A.C. 201. However, see the comments on this case in *Marfani & Co. Ltd.* v. *Midland Bank Ltd.* [1968] 2 All E.R. 573 at p. 582.

[26] *Orbit Mining and Trading Co. Ltd.* v. *Westminster Bank Ltd.* [1963] 1 Q.B. 794 at pp. 824, 825.

[27] [1941] A.C. 1 at pp. 23, 24.

[28] [1924] 1 K.B. 775.

pay into his private account a cheque drawn in favour of the company even although the director held all the shares in the company with the exception of one. Where a cheque payable to a partnership is collected for the account of a partner the collecting banker should make inquiries to satisfy himself that the cheque has not been misappropriated by the partner who tenders it for the credit of his account.[29] Similarly, inquiries should be made if a cheque payable to an office-holder is to be collected for the account of a private individual.[30]

The question whether or not the state of the customer's account is a material fact to be looked at in considering whether or not a banker has been negligent in collecting a cheque is not an easy one to answer since little guidance can be derived from the decided cases.[31] The view among bankers is that sudden fluctuations in an account are not significant,[32] although the opening of an account with a small amount of cash soon followed by the paying-in of a cheque for a large amount may call for some explanation. Where the bank's own internal rules have not been followed in the collection of cheques, failure to comply with these rules is not conclusive evidence of negligence.[33]

Contributory negligence

If a collecting banker cannot rely on the protection of section 4 of the Cheques Act 1957 because he has not collected the cheque in question without negligence it is now the case that in proceedings for conversion in England the defence of contributory negligence is available.[34] Section 47 of the Banking Act 1979 provides that in any circumstances in which proof of absence of negligence on the part of a banker would be a defence in proceedings by reason of section 4 of the 1957 Act, a defence of contributory negligence shall also be available to the banker. Although this section was passed to eliminate a doubt which had arisen as to whether or not a banker who could not rely on section 4 could plead contributory negligence in an action against him for conversion, it is suggested that the defence will also be available to the collecting banker in Scotland.

The paying banker

Until the contractual relationship between a banker and his customer

---

[29] *Bevan* v. *National Bank Ltd.* (1906) 23 T.L.R. 65; *Smith and Baldwin Ltd.* v. *Barclays Bank Ltd.*, 5 *Legal Decisions Affecting Bankers*, 370; *Baker* v. *Barclays Bank Ltd.* [1955] 2 All E.R. 571.

[30] *Ross* v. *London County and Westminster Bank* [1919] 1 K.B. 678.

[31] In *Commissioners of Taxation* v. *English, Scottish and Australian Bank Ltd.* [1920] A.C. 683 and *Morison* v. *London County and Westminster Bank Ltd.* [1914] 3 K.B. 356 little or no weight was attached to the matter. In *Crumplin* v. *London Joint Stock Bank Ltd.* (1913) 109 L.T. 856 and *Motor Traders Guarantee Corporation Ltd.* v. *Midland Bank Ltd.* [1937] 4 All E.R. 90 the position was otherwise.

[32] Paget, *Law of Banking* (9th ed.), p. 345.

[33] *Motor Traders Guarantee Corporation Ltd.* v. *Midland Bank Ltd.* [1937] 4 All E.R. 90 at p. 96; see also *Orbit Mining and Trading Co. Ltd.* v. *Westminster Bank Ltd.* [1963] 1 Q.B. 794 and *Lumsden* v. *London Trustee Savings Bank* [1971] 1 Lloyd's Rep. 114.

[34] Law Reform (Contributory Negligence) Act 1945; *Lumsden* v. *London Trustee Savings Bank*, *supra.*

has been terminated the banker has an obligation to honour cheques drawn on him by his customer, provided that he has in his hands sufficient funds to meet them, either on current account or by way of an agreed overdraft limit.[35] The customer for his part undertakes to exercise reasonable care in executing his written orders so as not to mislead the banker or facilitate forgery.[36] The cheque itself must be regular and unambiguous in form.[37]

If the funds consist of uncleared effects, the banker has the right to refuse to pay cheques although he may establish a course of business to the effect that an uncleared balance may be drawn against. If a customer has two current accounts he cannot expect a cheque drawn on an account on which the balance is insufficient to be met, despite the fact that the combined balance is sufficient. The banker on the other hand may combine the accounts and pay it. If he does so, he can set the other balance off against the first to the extent to which this is necessary to keep the position regular.[38]

Where a banker has permitted his customer to overdraw his account with or without security, his having done so in the past does not preclude his refusing to continue to do so in the future. The banker may, without assigning any reason, intimate that he will not allow any further overdrafts on the account and may call upon the customer and his sureties (if any) to make immediate provision for the repayment of the debt.[39] Where a customer has been allowed to overdraw against security, the banker is under no obligation to continue facilities until the security is exhausted and where no special period has been stipulated for, he may at any time refuse to cash his customer's cheques and call for repayment. This rule is, however, modified to the extent that the banker must not act with undue harshness towards his customer, and if the customer has in the past been allowed to overdraw his account against security a banker is liable in damages if in similar circumstances with the same customer without reasonable notice,[40] he dishonours a cheque.[41] In Scotland, presentation of a cheque for a sum exceeding the credit balance in the customer's account operates as an intimated assignation of these funds which the payee can have paid to him if he gives up the cheque appropriately indorsed with a receipt and discharge.[42]

Duties of the paying banker

The duties of a banker as to crossed cheques are set out in section 79 of

---

[35] *London Joint Stock Bank Ltd.* v. *Macmillan and Arthur* [1918] A.C. 777; *Joachimson* v. *Swiss Bank Corporation* [1921] 3 K.B. 110.

[36] *London Joint Stock Bank Ltd.* v. *Macmillan and Arthur, supra.* See pp. 30 *et seq.*

[37] *Ibid.*; *Burnett* v. *Westminster Bank Ltd.* [1966] 1 Q.B. 742.

[38] See p. 24 (combining of accounts).

[39] *Johnston* v. *Commercial Bank of Scotland* (1858) 20 D. 790; *Ritchie* v. *Clydesdale Bank Ltd.* (1886) 13 R. 866; *Barnes* v. *Williams and Glyn's Bank Ltd.* (1981) Com.L.R. 205.

[40] *Johnston* v. *Commercial Bank of Scotland, supra*; *Smith* v. *Hughes* (1871) L.R. 6 Q.B. 597; *Buckingham & Co.* v. *London and Midland Bank* (1895) 12 T.L.R. 70.

[41] *Forman* v. *Bank of England* (1902) 18 T.L.R. 339.

[42] 1882 Act, s. 53(2).

the 1882 Act. Where a cheque is crossed generally, it should be presented to the banker on whom it is drawn by a banker and paid only to that banker. Similarly, where a cheque is crossed specially it should be presented by and paid only to the banker named in the crossing or to his agent for collection, being a banker. Where a cheque is crossed specially to more than one banker, except when crossed to an agent for collection being a banker, the banker on whom it is drawn should refuse payment. If the paying banker disregards these rules, he is liable to the true owner of the cheque for any loss which he may sustain owing to the cheque having been paid in disregard of the crossing (s. 79(2)). The paying banker however need not concern himself with the implications of the words "Not negotiable" in the crossing nor the words "Account payee", even if it appears that the cheque has been negotiated by the payee to a third party.[43]

If the cheque is an open one, i.e. uncrossed, it may be presented for payment in cash by the holder at the bank branch on which it is drawn and the banker must decide immediately whether or not to pay. Payment is irrevocable as soon as the money is placed on the counter.[44] Prior to payment, the payee or indorsee should be asked to indorse the cheque. The banker need only ask the person presenting the cheque to confirm that he is the payee or indorsee unless there is something about his appearance and demeanour which ought to put him on further inquiry.[45] Payment in cash should only be made during the bank's advertised hours of business or within a reasonable time after closing.[46]

When a cheque is presented to him for payment, the paying banker obviously has to satisfy himself that the signature or signatures on the cheque are genuine. If a signature has been forged, then no matter how expert the forgery, the banker has no mandate to debit his customer's account. The banker is presumed to know his customer's signature but the mere fact that he has honoured a cheque on which his customer's signature has been undetectably forged does not carry with it the implied representation to the payee that it is genuine.[47] The paying banker also has to look at the date on the cheque, for although an undated cheque is not invalid merely because the date is omitted, in practice such a cheque may be returned by the paying banker with the answer "Date required". Cheques presented more than six months after the date which they bear are usually returned unpaid with the answer "Out of date". Where a post-dated cheque is presented for payment it is returned with the answer "Post-dated". It is thought that in Scotland the presentment of such a cheque attaches funds.[48] If there is a discrepancy between the words and figures written on the cheque, the sum as expressed in words is the

[43] *Akrokerri Atlantic Mines Ltd.* v. *Economic Bank* [1904] 2 K.B. 465 at p. 472.
[44] *Chambers* v. *Miller* (1862) 13 C.B.N.S. 125.
[45] *Bank of England* v. *Vagliano Bros.* [1891] A.C. 107; *Auchteroni & Co.* v. *Midland Bank Ltd.* [1928] 2 K.B. 294.
[46] *Baines* v. *National Provincial Bank Ltd.* (1927) 96 L.J.K.B. 801.
[47] *National Westminster Bank Ltd.* v. *Barclays Bank International Ltd.* [1975] 1 Q.B. 654.
[48] Finlayson, *Law Lectures to Bankers* (1939), p. 54.

amount payable (s. 9(2)). In practice however such cheques are usually returned unpaid with the answer "Words and figures differ" unless the discrepancy is not large and it is the smaller amount which is claimed by the collecting bank. Any alteration to a cheque should be authenticated by the initials or signature of the drawer. If there is any doubt about the authenticity of an alteration, the paying banker should not pay the cheque until he has obtained confirmation from his customer that it is in order. If a cheque is paid with an unauthorised alteration, the paying banker cannot debit his customer's account since he does not have his customer's mandate to do so. He can however debit his customer's account with the amount of an altered cheque where the customer did not exercise reasonable care in drawing the cheque and so facilitated the alteration and the alteration was not apparent.[49]

Time for payment

In the case of a cheque presented through the clearing, the drawer has in practice until the close of business on the day when it reaches his branch to countermand payment, unless the bank presenting the cheque telephones for advice of fate earlier in the day. When a special presentation of a cheque is made by the collecting banker, it is thought that the paying banker can hold the cheque until the day after receipt before making payment (s. 49(12)). Nevertheless, in the case of a special presentation made by post, in practice the cheque is usually returned, if unpaid, at the close of the day on which it is received. However, the paying bank branch will normally be prepared to respond to a telephone inquiry as to fate received from the collecting banker even if this is made before the close of business hours on the day of receipt. Similarly, where presentation is made by a messenger, advice of fate is normally given at the time when the item is presented. Where the payee himself specially presents a cheque at the account holding branch there is no doubt that in the case of an open cheque he is entitled to an immediate answer in the form of payment since the cheque has been presented as required by section 45 of the 1882 Act. In the case of a crossed cheque it was thought that a payee could only present such a cheque through a banker. It is now considered that this is not the case.[50] In practice however each bank judges for itself whether or not to give an immediate answer on presentation, leaving payment to be made through banking channels to the payee's bank. In all cases, where the paying banker has answered that the cheque is paid his customer no longer has the right to countermand payment. Similarly, if a cheque is drawn by one customer of a branch and paid in for collection by another customer at the same branch, in practice the bank decides on the day when the cheque is presented whether to pay or return it. The drawer has until the close of business to stop payment but if the customer paying

---

[49] *London Joint Stock Bank Ltd.* v. *Macmillan and Arthur* [1918] A.C. 777.
[50] *Ringham* v. *Hackett, The Times*, 8 February 1980.

in the cheque asks whether it is paid and is told that it is, such payment is irrevocable and the drawer again effectively loses his right to countermand payment.[51]

Statutory protection of the paying banker

Section 59(1) of the 1882 Act provides that a cheque is discharged by payment in due course by or on behalf of the drawee. "Payment in due course" means payment made to the holder of a cheque in good faith and without notice that his title to the cheque is defective. To protect the banker who pays the cheque to someone other than the holder section 60 provides that when a banker pays a cheque in good faith and in the ordinary course of business it is not incumbent on him to show that the indorsement of the payee or any subsequent indorsement was made with the authority of the person whose indorsement it purports to be and the banker is deemed to have paid the cheque in due course although such indorsement has been forged or made without authority. In addition, section 80, which has to be read in conjunction with section 79, provides that where the banker on whom a crossed cheque is drawn, in good faith and without negligence, pays it, if crossed generally to a banker, and if crossed specially to the banker to whom it is crossed or his agent for collection being a banker, the banker paying the cheque is to be entitled to the same rights and be placed in the same position as if payment of the cheque had been made to the true owner. Unlike section 60, section 80 applies only to crossed cheques and in order to qualify for protection, payment by the banker must be made "without negligence." Although section 60 contains no such express provision, it has been suggested that a paying banker who has acted negligently would not be granted protection under section 60 on the basis that a banker who pays a cheque negligently is necessarily acting otherwise than "in the ordinary course of business."[52] Neither section can be relied on for protection if a cheque has been materially altered within the meaning of section 64 of the 1882 Act.[53] Section 19 of the Stamp Act 1853, which was left unrepealed by the 1882 Act, protects the paying banker in connection with drafts and orders which are not cheques or bills of exchange for the purposes of the 1882 Act and imposes on him no requirement for payment to be made in good faith or in the ordinary course of business.[54]

The protection which is given by section 19 of the Stamp Act 1853 and sections 60 and 80 of the 1882 Act is added to by section 1 of the Cheques Act 1957. This section is in the following terms:

"(1) Where a banker in good faith and in the ordinary course of business pays a cheque drawn on him which is not indorsed or is

---

[51] See, however, Paget, *Law of Banking* (9th ed.), pp. 244, 245.
[52] *Ibid.*, p. 363.
[53] *Slingsby* v. *District Bank Ltd.* [1932] 1 K.B. 544.
[54] *London City and Midland Bank Ltd.* v. *Gordon* [1903] A.C. 240. See also *Charles* v. *Blackwell* (1877) 36 L.T. 195.

irregularly indorsed, he does not, in doing so, incur any liability by reason only of the absence of, or irregularity in, indorsement, and he is deemed to have paid in due course.

(2) Where a banker in good faith and in the ordinary course of business pays any such instrument as the following, namely:

(a) a document issued by a customer of his which, though not a bill of exchange, is intended to enable a person to obtain payment from him of the sum mentioned in the document;

(b) a draft payable on demand by him on himself, whether payable at the head office or some other office of his bank;

he does not, in doing so, incur any liability by reason only of the absence of, or irregularity in, indorsement, and the payment discharges the instrument."

The result of the passing of the 1957 Act is that paying bankers no longer require cheques to be indorsed, save in the case of cheques cashed at the counter and combined cheque and receipt forms distinguished by "R", although the signature is now regarded as being evidence of receipt rather than a true indorsement.

Marking cheques

Bankers are occasionally asked to mark a cheque to the effect that the drawer has funds at his credit sufficient to meet it and that the cheque will be paid on presentation. The usual practice in Scotland is to mark on the cheque that it will be paid if presented within seven days of the date appearing on it. So far as Scotland is concerned, there appears to have been no decision as to the precise effect of such a marking but a banker having once committed himself by marking a cheque would not be likely to repudiate it. In England the marking of cheques as "good" as between banker and banker has been judicially recognised.[55] However, the marking by a banker of a cheque has been held not to be an acceptance within the meaning of the 1882 Act[56] and as a consequence, marking at the request of the customer does not render the banker liable to the payee or holder. Nevertheless, it is thought that where the marking clearly carries a representation to the payee or holder that the cheque will be paid, the bank would be personally barred from refusing payment.

Countermand of payment

The authority of a banker to pay a cheque drawn on him by his customer is determined by countermand of payment (s. 75(1)). One party to a joint account may countermand payment of a cheque issued by another joint account holder. Similarly, a partner of a firm or a director of a limited company has power to countermand payment of cheques issued

---

[55] *Goodwin* v. *Robarts* (1875) L.R. 10 Ex. 337 at p. 351.
[56] *Bank of Baroda Ltd.* v. *Punjab National Bank Ltd.* [1944] A.C. 716.

by another partner or director. The drawer's right to countermand payment lasts until the time when the cheque is paid within the terms of the banker/customer contract or until the time when the banker has either to pay or dishonour, whichever is the earlier. A cheque may be countermanded verbally but for obvious reasons the drawer should be asked to put his instruction in writing and this should be in unambiguous terms. On receipt of telephoned instructions, a banker is justified, should the cheque be presented before confirmation is received, in postponing payment pending inquiry.[57] The cheque may be returned with the answer "Payment countermanded by telephone and postponed pending confirmation." To be effective, the countermand must actually come to the notice of the bank and be unequivocally referable to the cheque in question. In *Hilton* v. *Westminster Bank*[58] a customer stopped payment of a post-dated cheque by telegram but gave the wrong number. The bank paid the cheque on presentation at or after its date and as a result dishonoured another cheque that was presented later. It was held that as the number of a cheque is the one certain item of identification the bank were entitled to assume that the number of the cheque mentioned in the telegram was that of the cheque intended to be stopped and as the instructions were not otherwise so clear as to render the bank liable for negligence, the action against them failed.

When the drawer of a cheque stops payment by giving notice only to the branch on which the cheque is drawn and the payee afterwards indorses it to another branch of the same bank who advance money on the cheque in good faith and without notice that payment of the cheque has been stopped, it has been held in England that the bank as holder for value is entitled to recover from the drawer.[59] In other words, branch banks are independent for this purpose and notice of countermand sent to one branch of the bank is not effective at another branch. If a bank by mistake overlooks a notice of countermand and pays a cheque in spite of it, it can recover the money from the payee as money paid under a mistake of fact, unless the payee has *bona fide* altered his position to his disadvantage as a result of the mistake and in ignorance of it.[60]

A cheque granted for valuable consideration cannot, in a question with a holder for value, be countermanded by the drawer[61] unless it has been drawn, for example, on condition that it will only be used on the occurrence of a certain event, which does not happen, or in payment of goods which have not been delivered.[62] Where the payee has paid the cheque in to his banker to reduce the amount of his overdraft, the banker becomes a holder for value who is entitled to sue the drawer if he has counter-

---

[57] *Curtice* v. *London, City & Midland Bank Ltd.* [1908] 2 K.B. 293.
[58] (1926) 136 L.T. 315.
[59] *London Provincial and South-Western Bank* v. *Buszard* (1918) 35 T.L.R. 142.
[60] See p. 137.
[61] *Watt's Trs.* v. *Pinkney* (1853) 16 D. 279.
[62] *Fortune* v. *Luke* (1831) 10 S. 115; *Agra & Masterman's Bank* v. *Leighton* (1866) L.R. 2 Ex. 56.

manded payment.[63] When payment has been countermanded the subsequent presentment of the cheque no longer operates as an intimated assignation of money in the hands of the paying banker since he is treated as having no funds available for payment (s. 75A).[64]

Death of customer

Section 75(2) of the 1882 Act provides that the duty and authority of a banker to pay cheques drawn on him are determined by notice of the customer's death. The death of the customer does not, of itself, operate as a revocation of the banker's authority and payment of a cheque by him subsequent to his customer's death but before he has had reasonable time to inform himself of the fact will be valid.[65] Where a cheque is issued by a customer but is not presented for payment until after his death, a banker with notice of the death will naturally decline to honour the cheque but it is thought, especially if there has been no undue delay in presentment, that in a question between the creditors of the deceased and the holder of the cheque, presentment would operate as a good transfer of funds in favour of the holder.[66]

Money paid by mistake

If a bank pays money by mistake it is, as a general rule, entitled to recover it and in Scotland the *condictio indebiti* applies. This term is used to denote an action having for its object the recovery of money paid under the mistaken belief that it was due.[67] It applies, for example, in cases where payments are made under a mistake in identity[68] or where the purchaser of goods has been directed to pay one party and by mistake pays another.[69] Repayment of money paid by mistake has always been regarded as an equitable claim, not to be sustained unless it appears that retention of the money would be inequitable.[70] In *Barclays Bank Ltd.* v. *W. J. Simms, Son and Cooke (Southern) Ltd.*[71] a housing association who were customers of the bank countermanded payment of a cheque on learning that the payee had gone into receivership. The bank overlooked the notice of countermand and paid the cheque. It was held that the bank could recover the money from the receiver as money paid under a mistake of fact unless the payee had changed its position in good faith or was deemed in law to have done so. On the facts, the money was held to

---

[63] *McLean* v. *Clydesdale Bank* (1883) 11 R. (H.L.) 1. Today such a case would be decided under s. 27(1)(b) of the 1882 Act. The valuable consideration would be constituted by the bank overdraft, this being an "antecedent debt or liability".

[64] Inserted in the 1882 Act by the Law Reform (Misc. Prov.) (Scotland) Act 1985, s. 11.

[65] See *Tate* v. *Hilbert* (1793) 2 Ves. 111.

[66] See *Bank of Scotland* v. *Reid and Others* (1886) 2 Sh.Ct.Rep. 376.

[67] Bell, *Prin.*, § 531.

[68] *Crédit Lyonnais* v. *Stevenson* (1901) 9 S.L.T. 93.

[69] *Kleinwort, Sons & Co.* v. *Dunlop Rubber Co.* (1907) 97 L.T. 263.

[70] Ersk., III, iii, 54. See also *Chase Manhattan Bank N.A.* v. *Israel-British Bank (London) Ltd.* [1981] 1 Ch. 105 (equitable remedy of tracing in English law).

[71] [1979] 3 All E.R. 522.

be recoverable and the way was cleared for the real dispute between the association and the receiver to be resolved on its merits. If a person has received a payment without negligence or misrepresentation on his part, and has been led to alter his position in reliance on that payment, especially if the claim for repetition has been unnecessarily delayed, the money cannot be recovered.[72]

It is clearly established that money paid by mistake may be recovered although the party who has paid it may have had the means of discovering the true facts.[73] English law goes further and holds that negligence in payment is no bar to such an action although in extreme cases it may be evidence that the payment was really well advised.[74] In Scotland however the authorities are not conclusive on this point[75] and on the question whether or not it is equitable that the money should be refunded, the negligence of the pursuer in paying or of the defender in receiving payment, may be material. In *National Westminster Bank Ltd.* v. *Barclays Bank International Ltd.*[76] a blank cheque form was stolen from a customer of the plaintiffs. It was made out for £8,000 and the signature of the customer was forged. The cheque was then given to a customer of the defendant bank in circumstances described by the judge as "reeking of suspicion" and he sent it to them for collection. The cheque was duly presented for payment and paid. In an action for recovery of the £8,000 as money paid under a mistake of fact, the defendant bank's customer contended that the plaintiffs were estopped from making the claim since, by honouring the cheque, the plaintiffs had represented that it was genuine and in reliance on that representation, he had acted to his detriment. It was held that the mere fact that a banker had honoured a cheque on which his customer's signature had been undetectably forged did not carry with it a representation by the banker to the payee that it was genuine. There was accordingly no foundation for an estoppel against the plaintiffs and no bar to their right to recover the money.

---

[72] *Dixon* v. *Monklands Canal Co.* (1831) 5 W. & S. 445; *Crédit Lyonnais* v. *Stevenson* (1901) 9 S.L.T. 93; *Holt* v. *Markham* [1923] 1 K.B. 504. The principle was also recognised in *Kleinwort, Sons & Co.* v. *Dunlop Rubber Co.* (1907) 97 L.T. 263.

[73] *Baird's Trs.* v. *Baird & Co.* (1877) 4 R. 1005.

[74] *Kelly* v. *Solari* (1841) 9 M. & W. 54; *Imperial Bank of Canada* v. *Bank of Hamilton* [1903] A.C. 49; *R. E. Jones Ltd.* v. *Waring & Gillow Ltd.* [1926] A.C. 670.

[75] See *Wilson & McLellan* v. *Sinclair* (1830) 4 W. & S. 398; *Youle* v. *Cochrane* (1868) 6 M. 427; *Balfour* v. *Smith & Logan* (1871) 4 R. 454.

[76] [1974] 3 All E.R. 834.

CHAPTER 9

PROMISSORY NOTES AND OTHER INSTRUMENTS

Promissory notes

Sections 83 to 89 of the Bills of Exchange Act 1882 deal with promissory notes. A promissory note is defined by section 83(1) as an unconditional promise in writing made by one person to another, signed by the maker, engaging to pay on demand, or at a fixed or determinable future time, a sum certain in money to or to the order of a specified person or to bearer. It is apparently valid although containing neither the name of a specified payee nor the words "to bearer" if, in fact, the document contains a promise to pay and is handed by one person to another.[1] An instrument in the form of a note payable to the maker's order is not a promissory note within the meaning of this section until it is indorsed by the maker (s. 83(2)). A note is not invalid by reason only that it contains also a pledge of collateral security with authority to sell or dispose of it (s. 83(3)) but a writing which contains a pledge of collateral security so expressed as to be of the nature of a bond or similar obligation with security would not be regarded as a promissory note. But while an instrument may not be valid as a note it may still be valid as an agreement.[2] The decided cases show that a document is a promissory note if it fulfils the following conditions: (a) it contains what is in substance a promise to pay, whatever language may be used to couch that promise, (b) the sum payable is a definite sum of money, (c) the writing does not purport to do substantially anything more than make such promise of payment, and (d) the writing is completely unilateral in the sense that it does not require the grantee or any third party to do anything so as to bring it into operation or make it effective.[3]

Essentials

The essentials of a promissory note are that it must be in writing. With the exception of the signature it may be printed, lithographed or engraved. It may be written and subscribed in pencil.[4] It must contain a promise although the word "promise" is not necessary nor need a promise be actually expressed if it be unequivocally implied. In addition, it must be delivered.

Documents in the following terms have been held to be promissory

---

[1] *Daun* v. *Sherwood* (1895) 11 T.L.R. 211 at p. 212.
[2] *Kirkwood* v. *Smith* [1896] 1 Q.B. 582.
[3] *McTaggart* v. *MacEachern's J.F.*, 1949 S.L.T. 363 at p. 365.
[4] *Geary* v. *Physic* (1826) 5 B. & C. 234.

notes. "I acknowledge to have this day received from you eighty pounds, which I shall pay when required."[5] "I hereby acknowledge that I have this day received from you £20, which I shall repay you when demanded."[6] "I acknowledge to be due you the sum of £10, which sum I promise to pay at any time when required."[7] "At fourteen days after the date I accept to pay A B or order the sum of £50 stg."[8] The following docquet written on the back of a cheque was held to be a promissory note: "2nd August 1887. Received from Catherine McCraw the sum of £104 sterling, and I agree to pay on demand".[9]

In the following cases the documents were held not to be promissory notes. "I hereby acknowledge that I have this day received from you £20 sterling for which I shall account."[10] "Received from Mr Thomas Watson the sum of Fifty Pounds on loan at the rate of five per cent."[11] "In consideration of your advancing to M & H £250 on their joint and several notes, I undertake to pay £250 on demand should their note not be met at maturity."[12] A letter in the following terms—"Borrowed from A £67 Pounds, July 1878, Paid back £5 Pounds, May 1885, Leaving a balance of £62 Pounds to pay still"—holograph of and signed by the grantor but neither dated nor stamped—was held to be neither a promissory note nor an agreement nor a receipt.[13]

Delivery

In order to make a promissory note complete, there must be an actual or constructive transfer of possession from the maker to the payee or bearer, pending which the note is incomplete and revocable (ss. 84 and 21(1)).[14] The transfer must be made by or with the authority of the maker.

Joint and several notes

A promissory note may be made by two or more makers and they may be liable thereon jointly or jointly and severally, according to its tenor (s. 85(1)). A note which runs "We promise to pay" or "I promise to pay" and is signed by two or more obligants, is in Scotland the joint and several obligation of all the persons who sign it (s. 85(2)),[15] any one of whom may be called upon by the creditor to pay the full amount for which the note is granted, though entitled to relief *pro rata* from his co-obligants. On the

---

[5] *Alexander* v. *Alexander* (1830) 8 S. 602.

[6] *Pirie's Reps.* v. *Smith's Exrs.* (1833) 11 S. 473.

[7] *McIntosh* v. *Stewart* (1830) 8 S. 739.

[8] *McKinney* v. *Van Heck & Co.* (1863) 1 M. 1115; see also *Vallance* v. *Forbes* (1879) 6 R. 1099; *Blyth* v. *Forbes* (1879) 6 R. 1102.

[9] *McCraw* v. *McCraw's Trs.* (1906) 13 S.L.T 757. See also *Macfarlane* v. *Johnstone* (1864) 2 M. 1210.

[10] *Pirie's Reps.* v. *Smith's Exrs.* (1833) 11 S. 473.

[11] *Watson* v. *Duncan* (1896) 4 S.L.T. 116.

[12] *Dickinson* v. *Bower* (1897) 14 T.L.R. 146.

[13] *Todd* v. *Wood* (1897) 24 R. 1104. See also *Lamberton* v. *Aiken* (1899) 2 F. 189, the cases cited in *McTaggart* v. *MacEachern's J.F.*, 1949 S.L.T. 363, *Dick* v. *Dick*, 1950 S.L.T. (Notes) 44 and *Dickie* v. *Singh*, 1974 S.L.T. (Notes) 3.

[14] See *Martini & Co.* v. *Steel & Craig* (1878) 6 R. 342.

[15] Bell, *Comm.*, I, 363. This is contrary to the general rule that a joint obligation is *pro rata*. See *Coats* v. *Union Bank of Scotland*, 1929 S.C. (H.L.) 114.

other hand, in a note which is signed by two or more obligants "jointly" each person so signing is liable only for his own share.

Presentment for payment

Although it is in general not necessary in order to charge the maker who in terms of his obligation is always liable without notice, presentment for payment is necessary in order to render the indorser of a note liable. When a note payable on demand has been indorsed it must be presented for payment within a reasonable time of the indorsement, otherwise the indorser is discharged (s. 86(1)). In determining what is a reasonable time, regard is had to the nature of the instrument, the usage of trade and the facts of the particular case (s. 86(1)). In one case a promissory note dated 24 February 1864 and payable on demand although payment was not contemplated by the maker at any immediate specific date, was not presented for payment until 14 December in the same year. It was held that as it appeared from the evidence that the note was intended to a certain extent to be a continuing security, the delay in presentation had been in the interest of all parties and that the holders of the note were entitled to recover on it.[16]

Where a note payable on demand is negotiated, it is not deemed to be overdue for the purpose of affecting the holder with defects of title of which he had no notice, by reason that it appears that a reasonable time for presenting it for payment has elapsed since its issue (s. 86(3)). So far as defects of title are concerned, the holder of a note, presentment of which has been unreasonably delayed, is in the same position as a holder of a bill in due course.

Where a promissory note is in the body of it made payable at a particular place, it must be presented for payment at that place in order to render the maker liable. In any other case presentment is not necessary to render the maker liable (s. 87(1)) although it is to render the indorser liable (s. 87(2)). There is no limit as to time imposed by the Act, and even where, to render the maker liable, the note must be presented at a particular place, it need not be so presented on the day when payment is due, presentment on a subsequent day being sufficient.[17] When a note is in the body of it made payable at a particular place, presentment at that place is necessary to render an indorser liable (s. 87(3)) but when a place of payment is indicated by way of memorandum only, presentment at that place is sufficient to render the indorser liable; but a presentment to the maker elsewhere, if sufficient in other respects, also suffices (s. 87(3)).

Liability of the maker and indorser

The position of the maker of a note corresponds to that of the acceptor of a bill. By making it he (1) engages that he will pay it according to its

---

[16] *Chartered Mercantile Bank of India, etc.* v. *Dickson* (1871) L.R. 3 P.C. 574.
[17] *Gordon* v. *Kerr* (1898) 25 R. 570.

tenor and (2) is precluded from denying to a holder in due course the existence of the payee and his then capacity to indorse (s. 88). The position of the first indorser of a note corresponds to that of a drawer of an accepted bill payable to drawer's order. It is considered doubtful whether the payee of a note can under any circumstances be the holder of it in due course.

Generally, the rules of law applicable to bills of exchange apply, with the necessary modifications, to promissory notes except those rules applicable to bills which relate to (1) presentment for acceptance, (2) acceptance, (3) acceptance *supra* protest and (4) bills in a set. Further, protest of a foreign note which is dishonoured is unnecessary (s. 89). A promissory note is exempt from stamp duty by virtue of section 32 of and Schedule 7 to the Finance Act 1970.

Bank notes

Bank notes are promissory notes issued by bankers, payable to bearer on demand, and pass from hand to hand by delivery.[18] "Bank notes," said Lord Mansfield in *Miller* v. *Race*,[19] "are not goods, not securities nor documents for debts,. . . They are as much money as guineas themselves are, or any other current coin that is used in common payments as money or cash." In Scotland the right to issue bank notes was formerly regarded as a common law right not confined to banks but extending to individuals whose power of issuing notes was limited only by their credit with the public and their ability to maintain their notes in circulation. The issue and circulation of bank notes in Scotland is now regulated by the Bank Notes (Scotland) Act 1845, the Currency and Bank Notes Act 1954 and the Coinage Act 1971 (as amended by the Currency Act 1983). Section 5 of the 1845 Act provided that all bank notes to be issued or re-issued in Scotland must be expressed to be for payment of a sum in pounds sterling without any fractional parts of a pound. Under section 29 of the Stamp Act 1891 no bank other than the Bank of England can issue a bank note for more than one hundred pounds. It is not lawful for any bank in Scotland to have in circulation on the average during a period of four weeks a greater amount of notes than the average of its authorised issue plus (1) the amount of the monthly average of gold and coin other than gold coin held by such bank at its head office or principal place of issue and one other approved office or branch and (2) Bank of England notes held by such bank or by the Bank of England earmarked for its behoof during the same period of four weeks (s. 6 of the 1845 Act).

Bank notes are exempt from the application of the short negative prescription[20] but there seems no reason for holding them exempt from the long negative prescription. The question has been raised but not

---

[18] Stamp Act 1854, s. 11 (explaining Bank Charter Act 1844, ss. 10, 11 and 28).
[19] (1758) 1 Burr. 452; Smith's *Leading Cases*, Vol. 1 (13th ed.), p. 524.
[20] Prescription and Limitation (Scotland) Act 1973, Sched. 1, para. 2(*b*).

decided whether bank notes may be poinded.[21] No *vitium reale* attaches to bank notes. Where bank notes have been stolen, it is well settled as an exception to the rule of restitution that they cannot be recovered by the owner from someone who has acquired them in *bona fide*, *i.e.* without notice that the previous holder was not a *bona fide* holder, in the course of trade. In such circumstances, property passes with possession.[22] The same rule applies to money in the form of coin.

Money orders and postal orders

These are instruments embodying instructions for the money deposited at one post office to be paid there or at another post office. Money orders issued by the Post Office were introduced in 1840 but are rarely seen today. If crossed either generally or specially they will be paid only to a bank but otherwise they do not come under the notice of the Bills of Exchange Act 1882. When paid into a bank account, the Post Office pays the collecting bank without examination and if it is found that payment ought not to have been made the Post Office may deduct the amount from subsequent collections made by the same bank in respect of money orders. The bank's only remedy is to debit its customer. Money orders are not negotiable and a banker paying a wrongful holder is liable in repetition to the true owner, whether the order is crossed or not.[23]

Postal orders were introduced in 1880 and are now governed by section 21(3) of the Post Office Act 1953 (as amended by the Post Office Act 1969) which protects bankers collecting postal orders by providing that any such banker shall not incur liability to anyone except the principal for whom he has collected the postal order by reason of having received payment or presented the order for payment. By arrangement with the Post Office payment of postal orders is made by them to bankers provided they bear the bank's crossing stamp. As with money orders, the Post Office has a right of recourse if it discovers an order ought not to have been paid. Postal orders are not negotiable. It follows that a bank should never cash either type of order for a stranger.

Dividend warrants

A dividend warrant represents a sum of money payable to a shareholder in respect of a dividend due to him on his holding in a company. The warrant, which is unconditional, is drawn on the company's bank and made payable to the shareholder or his mandatary. There is usually attached a memorandum addressed to the shareholder stating the amount of the dividend and the tax credit. This portion is retained by the shareholder as a voucher since it is accepted by the Inland Revenue as evidence of tax credit in respect of which the shareholder may

---

[21] *Alexander* v. *McLay* (1826) 4 S. 439.

[22] Bell, *Prin.*, § 528. See also *Gorebridge Co-operative Society* v. *Turnbull*, 1952 S.L.T. (Sh.Ct.) 91 and *Re Diplock, Diplock* v. *Wintle* [1948] 2 All E.R. 318 (English tracing order).

[23] *Fine Art Society* v. *Union Bank of Scotland* (1886) 17 Q.B.D. 705.

be entitled to claim payment or relief. Under section 95 of the Bills of Exchange Act 1882 the provisions of the Act as to crossed cheques apply to a warrant for payment of a dividend and a banker collecting a dividend warrant so crossed is entitled to the same statutory protection as for the collection of a crossed cheque. It has been held that this also applies to interest warrants.[24] The provision in section 97(3)(*d*) of the 1882 Act relating to payment on the signature of the first-named holder in respect of dividend warrants on joint holdings still subsists but has little practical importance since the Cheques Act 1957 abolished the necessity for indorsements on cheques in most cases. As most dividend warrants fall within the statutory definition of a cheque, then unless a warrant contains any condition inconsistent with this statutory definition, it is negotiable to the same extent as a cheque. A dividend warrant issued by a bank to its own shareholders does not satisfy this definition because the drawer and drawee are the same. Such warrants are bankers' drafts.

IOUs

An IOU is a writing, signed by the granter, containing the words "I owe you" or the letters "IOU". It must be holograph of the granter.[25] It need not be addressed to a specified person but the amount due must be stated. If a wrong date is inserted, this of itself will not invalidate the document. It requires no stamp. It is not a promissory note or bill since it contains neither a promise to pay nor a fixed date of payment. The addition of the words to an ordinary IOU "for value received" does not constitute the document a promissory note. Again, an IOU is not a receipt since it need not acknowledge the receipt of any money nor need its language necessarily imply the receipt of any money. It is not a bond, since it need contain no word of obligation though the law implies obligation from its terms. Lastly, it is not an agreement since it is unilateral.[26]

In *Bishop* v. *Bryce*[27] Lord Kinnear said that it was said that an IOU was a written document establishing a debt which could only be discharged by payment, and that payment could only be proved by writ or oath. He went on:

"But an IOU is nothing but an acknowledgment of debt. As long as it stands it is good against the granter to prove that he acknowledges a debt to the grantee. But it does not express the ground of debt or give any indication whatever of the kind of contract out of which the debt has arisen. It does not, therefore, follow that when an IOU is granted it is granted for a loan or in respect of any particular

[24] *Slingsby* v. *Westminster Bank (No. 1)* [1931] 1 K.B. 173.
[25] *Haldane* v. *Spiers* (1872) 10 M. 537 at p. 541.
[26] *Thiem's Trs.* v. *Collie* (1899) 1 F. 764 and cases there cited.
[27] 1910 S.C. 426 at p. 434, commenting on *Thiem's Trs.* v. *Collie, supra.* See also *McKenzie's Exrx.* v. *Morrison's Trs.*, 1930 S.L.T. 616 and *Black* v. *Gibb*, 1940 S.C. 24.

contract, and it does not follow that, to get rid of it, the granter of the IOU must prove payment of money."

The granter accordingly always has the right to demand restitution upon satisfaction of the obligation, whatever it may have been, in respect of which it was granted. The question whether in any case it is necessary to prove payment cannot be solved by anything which appears on the face of the IOU, and it depends entirely upon the circumstances under which it was granted and the intention with which it was given by one party to the other. The IOU is the result of some transaction, but the kind of transaction is not disclosed. In order, therefore, to determine the rights of the parties, if there is a difference between them on the facts, it is indispensable that there should be proof of these facts. It may now therefore be taken as the law on the subject that it is competent to prove by parole evidence facts and circumstances from which it may be inferred that the obligation in an IOU has been discharged and that it is no longer a living document of debt in the hands of the holder.

Interest, if not expressly stipulated for in the IOU, is exigible only from the date of citation in an action for payment of the principal sum.[28] An IOU is not a negotiable instrument. The property in it cannot, therefore, be transferred by indorsement and delivery. It may, however, be assigned and the assignee's right is completed by intimation to the debtor. The obligation is enforced by suing the debtor for the sum payable using the IOU as evidence of the amount due.[29] An IOU is only extinguished by the long negative prescription established by section 7 of the Prescription and Limitation (Scotland) Act 1973 if constituted or evidenced by a probative writ.[30]

Bankers' drafts

A banker's draft may be defined as any draft payable on demand drawn by a banker upon himself, whether payable at the head office or some other office of the bank. Such drafts do not fall within the definition of bills of exchange or cheques because both drawer and drawee are the same person but the holder of such an instrument may treat it at his option either as a bill of exchange or a promissory note.[31] When a request to issue a banker's draft is made by a customer the form of request should be signed by him or by someone duly authorised to act on his behalf.[32] A banker's draft can be crossed by virtue of section 5 of the Cheques Act 1957. A banker's draft drawn payable to bearer on demand would be an instrument analogous to a bank note and accordingly they are always drawn payable to order.

---

[28] *Winestone* v. *Wolifson*, 1954 S.L.T. 153.
[29] *Neilson's Tr.* v. *Neilson's Trs.* (1883) 11 R. 119.
[30] Sched. 1, para. 2(*c*). "Probative writ" is defined in para. 4(*b*).
[31] Bills of Exchange Act 1882, ss. 3(1) and (2), 5(2) and 73.
[32] See *Bank of Montreal* v. *Dominion Gresham Guarantee and Casualty Co. Ltd.* [1930] A.C. 659.

The duties of the collecting bank and the paying bank in relation to bankers' drafts are similar to those which govern the collection and payment of cheques. Although the same bank is both drawer and drawee, with the result that the instrument is not a cheque, the same provisions are expressly made applicable.[33] If a customer informs his bank that a draft which has been issued to him has been lost, the branch of the bank on which it is drawn should be notified immediately so that payment may be postponed until the title of the person presenting the draft has been investigated. If it turns out that he has a good title, the draft must be paid. Where the customer asks for a duplicate draft to be issued to him, this can be done provided that he indemnifies the bank against liability in the event of the lost draft being presented by someone who has obtained a good title to it.

Deposit receipts

A deposit receipt is an acknowledgment by a bank or other financial institution of the receipt of money which will be repaid in terms of the contract as evidenced by the receipt itself. The form of deposit receipt invariably contains a stipulation that the document must be delivered up indorsed by the depositor before any payment of principal or interest is made and this constitutes part of the contract between the bank and the depositor. Unless the receipt is so indorsed and delivered the bank may not be compelled to make payment except on its own terms but should the receipt be lost it is the usual practice to pay after the lapse of a reasonable time against a discharge and indemnity. Just how far a bank may insist on this has never been authoritatively settled in Scotland and the view has been expressed that as a deposit receipt is not a negotiable instrument the bank is not entitled to such an indemnity from the depositor.[34] In any event, the bank is certainly entitled to a formal discharge in respect of a payment made where the deposit receipt has been lost.

A deposit receipt is not in itself a negotiable instrument capable of being transferred by indorsement so as to confer on the indorsee by that fact alone a right to the property represented by the receipt. Possession of an indorsed deposit receipt implies no more than a mere mandate to uplift the money on behalf of the depositor.[35] There appears to be no doubt, however, that the debt represented by the receipt is transferable inasmuch as it is capable of being assigned. Accordingly an assignation written or indorsed on the receipt and formally intimated to the bank would be binding on them, subject to any right of set-off the bank might have against the original depositor.

---

[33] Cheques Act 1957, s. 4(2)(d); see also Commercial Banking Co. of Sydney v. Mann [1961] A.C. 1 at p. 7.
[34] Paget, Law of Banking (9th ed.), pp. 133, 134.
[35] Barstow v. Inglis & Hay (1857) 20 D. 230.

Discharge of deposit receipt

A deposit receipt granted in favour of A is discharged by the delivery of the receipt indorsed by A or, on A's death, by his executors, together with in the latter case exhibition of confirmation or probate and payment by the bank. A receipt in favour of A and B, payable to either or survivor, is, unless the bank is interpelled from paying—as, for example, by the lodging of an arrestment or by notice from either party—discharged by the indorsement of either A or B during their joint lives, or of the survivor on the death of one, or of the executors of the survivor on the death of both. A bank is not entitled in a question with, say, A, who produces the receipt indorsed by him to retain the sum in the receipt in security of a claim against B. This is the case whether or not the money belongs to B. In *Anderson* v. *North of Scotland Bank Ltd.*[36] A and B obtained a deposit receipt in their favour, payable to either or survivor. Later the issuing bank accepted B as an obligant in a cash credit bond on account of his brother C, relying on the security of the receipt which, they averred, belonged wholly to B. The bank having refused to make payment of the money to A although B consented to the payment, the court held that the bank could not by a course of dealing with one of the parties altogether destroy the rights of the other but was bound by its obligation to pay to either which it had undertaken by granting the deposit receipt. Even where A and B are husband and wife and a bank has made advances to A, it is not entitled to rely on a deposit receipt in the two names as security in the event of the husband's bankruptcy on the ground that although the money or some part of it may belong to the wife it has been inmixed with the funds of her husband.[37]

In the event of the debt represented by a deposit receipt in the joint names of A and B being arrested as belonging to A, the bank is not bound to pay to B because, for anything that appears on the face of the receipt, the money may belong wholly or partly to A and to pay it to B might defeat the rights of A's creditors. A deposit receipt is not a document of title and no inference can be drawn from the terms in which the money is deposited as to its true ownership.[38] In the event of payment being insisted on by the party to the receipt other than the person against whom the arrestment is used the bank should for its own protection raise an action of multiplepoinding and allow the court to determine to whom the money should be paid. Either party to a receipt issued payable to either or survivor may intimate to the bank that payment is not to be made without his indorsement and such an intimation must be given effect to even although the receipt is produced for payment bearing the other depositor's indorsement. Where a deposit receipt has been issued in favour of A and B it requires the indorsement of both or, on the death of one, of the survivor and the executors of the deceased, or, on the death of

---

[36] (1901) 4 F. 49.
[37] See p. 42.
[38] *Allan's Exr.* v. *Union Bank of Scotland Ltd.*, 1909 S.C. 206 and cases cited therein.

both, of their respective executors. In all cases where executors indorse, proof of their title to do so must be produced.

As a bank is accountable to the depositor, it is the duty of the bank to be satisfied as to the identity and *bona fides* of the person to whom repayment is made. In the event of payment to a wrongful holder, the bank is liable to the depositor unless it can show that he has been guilty of fraud or of such negligence that the responsibility for the wrongful payment rests with him.[39] In *Wood* v. *Clydesdale Bank Ltd.*[40] A lodged to his credit on deposit receipt with the bank the sum of £100 and afterwards went abroad, taking with him the deposit receipt. From there he wrote to the bank requesting them to pay to his brother £60 out of the £100 on presentation of the deposit receipt which he stated he had indorsed. At the same time A wrote to his brother enclosing the deposit receipt and also a letter addressed to the bank in similar terms to the letter sent direct to them. The letter to the bank was duly delivered but the letter to the brother was stolen in transit. A person pretending to be the brother presented the indorsed receipt at the bank and received payment of £60 and a new receipt in A's name for the balance of £40. In due course A raised an action against the bank and it was held that the bank was responsible to him for the sum which it had paid.

While payment in terms of its contract discharges the bank, the terms of a deposit receipt do not in any way determine the property in the money represented by it nor have they any testamentary operation or effect although they may have a bearing as indicating the intention of the depositor. In this connection questions often arise as to what constitutes *donatio mortis causa*, that is, a valid donation or gift of the money contained in a deposit receipt—to take effect at the depositor's death—but these do not directly concern the bank whose sole concern is to see that the money is repaid in terms of its contract. In *Dickson* v. *National Bank of Scotland Ltd.*[41] a sum forming part of a trust estate was deposited with a bank on a consignation receipt bearing that the money was received from the truster's executors and was to be repayable on the indorsement of a firm of solicitors who were the law agents in the trust. The firm was subsequently dissolved and some years afterwards B, one of the former partners, indorsed the receipt in the firm's name and uplifted and embezzled the money. In an action against the bank at the instance of the beneficiaries under the trust for payment of the sum deposited, it was held that as the uplifting of the deposit was necessary either to wind up the affairs of the partnership or to complete transactions begun but unfinished at the time of the dissolution within the meaning of section 38 of the Partnership Act 1890, B was entitled to adhibit the firm's signature and the bank was justified in paying over the money to him.

---

[39] *Forbes' Exr.* v. *Western Bank* (1854) 16 D. 807.
[40] 1914 S.C. 397.
[41] 1917 S.C. (H.L.) 50.

Consignation receipts

The principles just explained with reference to deposit receipts apply equally to ordinary consignation receipts as distinguished from receipts for judicial consignation. In the issuing of such receipts care should be taken to insert a clause providing for the manner in which the receipt is to be discharged and to whom the money is to be repaid. Such receipts are also usually issued on the basis that the bank has no responsibility for or concern with any statements made in the receipt apart from knowledge of the amount and conditions of discharge.

Judicial consignations

In Court of Session actions such consignations are regulated by the Court of Session Consignations (Scotland) Act 1895.[42] Where money is consigned by order of the court to await its orders, the practice is to pay on production and in terms of an extract or certified copy interlocutor. The interlocutor generally provides for payment on delivery of a certified copy and of the receipt indorsed by the Accountant of Court. If a bank is asked to issue a receipt acknowledging that money has been received to await the decision in a particular action the proper course is to provide in the receipt itself for the actual manner in which it is to be discharged, such as by the indorsement of certain named persons and delivery of the receipt. In the sheriff court such consignations are regulated by the Sheriff Courts Consignations (Scotland) Act 1893. The deposit receipt is issued in the name of the sheriff clerk and the discharge to the bank is delivery of the receipt indorsed by the sheriff clerk. A creditor in a standard security who cannot obtain a receipt or a discharge for a payment which he is required to make in terms of section 27(1) of the Conveyancing and Feudal Reform (Scotland) Act 1970 may consign the amount due, so far as ascertainable, in the sheriff court for the person having the best right thereto (s. 27(2) of the 1970 Act).

---

[42] See *Antrobus, Petr.* (1896) 23 R. 1032.

PART III

SECURITIES FOR ADVANCES

"Men lend their money to traders on mortgages or consignments of goods because they suspect their circumstances and they will not run the risk of their general credit" *Foxcroft* v. *Devonshire* (1760) 2 Burr. 931, *per* Lord Mansfield.

CHAPTER 10

HERITABLE SECURITIES

In Scotland prior to the passing of the Conveyancing and Feudal Reform (Scotland) Act 1970 there were three recognised methods of constituting a valid security over heritable property for sums advanced or intended to be advanced by a bank to a customer, namely (1) bond and disposition in security, (2) bond for cash credit and disposition in security and (3) disposition *ex facie* absolute, qualified by a back letter. As from 29 November 1970 a heritable security for a debt can only be constituted in the form of a standard security (s. 9(3)). Securities in the older forms are dealt with and enforced in accordance with the previous law (s. 31).

Standard security

The 1970 Act created a new form of heritable security known as a standard security. A standard security can only be granted over an interest in land and has to be in conformity with one of the forms prescribed in Schedule 2 to the Act. An "interest in land" means any interest in land which is capable of being owned or held as a separate interest and to which a title may be recorded in the Register of Sasines (s. 9(8)(*b*)). Included are salmon fishings, registrable leases and another standard security.

Section 11(2) of the Act provides that the standard conditions set out in Schedule 3, with such variations as have been agreed by the parties, will regulate every standard security. The standard conditions prescribed in the Schedule regulate (1) the maintenance, management and insurance of the security subjects by the debtor, (2) the rights and remedies of the creditor on failure or default by the debtor, (3) the exercise by the debtor of the right of redemption and (4) the expense of the preparation of the security and realisation of the security subjects. The right to vary the standard conditions by agreement is conferred by section 11(3) but the provisions of Schedule 3, so far as they relate to the powers of sale and foreclosure and to the exercise of these powers, may not be varied.

Section 13 of the Act provides that where the creditor in a duly recorded prior security has received notice of the creation of a subsequent security or of a subsequent assignation or conveyance, being a security, assignation or conveyance so recorded, the preference in ranking of the security of the prior creditor is restricted to cover (1) his existing advances, (2) future advances which he may be required to make under the security agreement, (3) interest present and future and (4) any expenses or outlays reasonably incurred by him in the exercise of any power contained in the security deed. His preference is restricted only when he has received notice and for this purpose the recording of the

153

deed creating the subsequent security or conveyance is not enough to constitute notice (s. 13(2)(*a*)). Accordingly, after notice to the bank of a second security or subsequent conveyance of the security subjects by the customer, the debt should be frozen at the date of notice, since where an account is continued without alteration or where no specific appropriation of fresh payments is made, such payments are credited to the earliest items on the debit side of the account and continue so to be credited until the balance secured under the first security is extinguished.[1]

Enforcement of standard security

The powers of the creditor derived from the heritable security are additional to the remedies available to him under the personal obligation contained in the standard security or in the separate bond (ss. 20(1) and 21(1)). Where the standard security or the bond includes a clause of consent to registration for execution, summary diligence on a charge of six days is competent. If such a clause has not been included, the personal obligation may nevertheless be pursued by ordinary action in court and diligence done upon an extract decree.

Calling-up notice

Where a creditor in a standard security intends to require the discharge of the debt secured and, failing that discharge, to exercise any power conferred by the security to sell the security subjects, or any other power which he may exercise upon failure to comply with a demand for payment, he may serve a calling-up notice (s. 19(1)). The calling-up notice should be in conformity with Form A of Schedule 6 to the Act. Where a standard security has been granted to secure a debt which fluctuates in amount, such as a bank overdraft, it is necessary to attach to each copy of the notice a certificate setting out the amount due as at the date of service of the notice. This certificate should be signed by the person authorised to do so in terms of the security deed.[2] An alteration in the amount due as a result of repayments or further advances made after the date of the notice will not invalidate it, since it will have been correct at the date of service.

Section 19 lists those persons on whom notice must be served. In this connection it is important to note that the creditor is obliged to serve a copy of the calling-up notice on any person against whom he wishes to preserve any right of recourse in respect of the debt (s. 19(5)). Accordingly, notice should be given to co-obligants, guarantors and the owners of all other property, heritable or moveable, over which security for the debt called up has been given. The period of notice mentioned in the calling-up notice (which will normally be two months) may be dispensed with or shortened by the person on whom it is served, with the consent of the creditors, if any, holding securities ranking *pari passu* with or postponed to the security held by the creditor serving the notice

---

[1] Ths is one effect of the rule in *Clayton's Case*. See also *Deeley* v. *Lloyds Bank* [1912] A.C. 756.
[2] See *Elswick Bay Shipping Co. Ltd.* v. *Royal Bank of Scotland Ltd.*, 1982 S.L.T. 62.

(s. 19(10)). A calling-up notice ceases to have effect for the purpose of a sale in the exercise of any power conferred by the security after five years (s. 19(11)).

Where the debtor is in default within the meaning of standard condition 9(1)(a), *i.e.* he has failed to comply with a calling-up notice, the creditor may exercise such of his rights under the security as he may consider appropriate (s. 20(1)). If the standard conditions have not been varied the creditor may exercise any of the remedies available to him under subparagraphs (2) to (7) of standard condition 10. He may (1) sell the security subjects; (2) enter into possession of them; (3) after he has entered into possession, exercise all the rights of the debtor in relation to the granting of leases or rights of occupancy of the security subjects and their management and maintenance; (4) effect repairs and such reconstruction, alteration and improvement as are required to maintain the market value of the subjects; and (5) apply for a decree of foreclosure.

Notice of default

Where the debtor is in default within the meaning of standard condition 9(1)(b), *i.e.* there has been a failure to comply with a requirement arising out of the security other than failure to pay the amount due after service of a calling-up notice, and the default is remediable, the creditor may serve a notice of default rather than a calling-up notice but the remedies are not mutually exclusive (s. 21(1)). The notice of default should be served on the debtor and, as the case may be, the proprietor where he is not the debtor (s. 21(2)). A copy of the notice of default need not be served on persons against whom the creditor wishes to preserve recourse (*cf.* s. 19(5)). Nevertheless, there will be some situations where a co-obligant or a guarantor should be advised of a failure on the part of the principal debtor for which he may become ultimately liable. The provisions as to the dispensing with or shortening the period of notice in relation to a calling-up notice apply also to a notice of default (s. 21(3)). A notice of default ceases to be authority for the exercise of the rights mentioned in section 23(2) five years from its date (s. 21(4)).

The rights which a creditor may exercise on a failure to comply with a notice of default fall into two categories. Rights which involve entering into possession of the security subjects (those contained in standard conditions 10(3), (4) and (5)) can be exercised only after an application to the sheriff court for a warrant to do what is necessary. Rights which do not require possession (those contained in standard conditions 10(2) and (6)) may be exercised upon failure to comply with a requirement in a notice of default without resort to the court.

Power of sale

The power of a creditor to sell the security subjects may be exercised where either a calling-up notice (s. 20(1) and (2)) or a notice of default (s. 23(1) and (2)) has been served and has not been complied with or where the proprietor of the security subjects is insolvent and the court has granted a warrant to the creditor to sell (s. 24(1)). The existence of other heritable securities does not prevent the creditor from selling the security subjects (s. 26). The creditor exercising his right to sell may do so either by private bargain or by exposure to sale. In either case, his duty is simply (1) to advertise the sale and (2) to take all reasonable steps to ensure that the price at which the security subjects are sold is the best that can be reasonably obtained (s. 25). He is not bound by the conditions as to advertisement which the Act imposes in sales under powers contained in a bond and disposition in security but if he in fact advertises in a similar manner, such advertisement would be difficult to challenge on the ground that it had been inadequate. The effect of a sale by the creditor of the security subjects followed by the recording of a disposition to the purchaser in implement of the sale disburdens the subjects of the standard security and all other heritable securities and diligences ranking *pari passu* with or postponed to that security (s. 26(1)).

Section 27(1) of the Act provides that the money which is received by the creditor from the sale is to be held by him in trust to be applied by him in payment, in the following order of priority, of (1) all expenses properly incurred by him in connection with the sale; (2) the whole amount due under any prior security to which the sale is not made subject; (3) the whole amount due under his standard security and in payment, in due proportion, of the whole amount due under any recorded security ranking *pari passu* with it; and (4) any amounts due under any securities with a ranking postponed to his security according to their ranking. Any residue of the money has to be paid to the person entitled to the security subjects at the time of sale or to any person authorised to give receipts for the proceeds of the sale. Provision is made for the residue to be consigned where the creditor cannot obtain a receipt or discharge for a payment which he is required to make in terms of section 27(1).

Right to enter into possession

Apart from his power of sale, a creditor has the statutory right to enter into possession under standard condition 10(3) where there has been default within the meaning of standard condition 9, *i.e.* there has been a failure to comply with a calling-up notice or some other requirement arising out of the security or the proprietor of the security subjects has become insolvent. If possession is to follow on from default arising out of the failure to comply with a requirement of the security (other than failure to comply with a demand for payment) or the insolvency of the proprietor, a warrant from the court to exercise the right to possession must be obtained (s. 24(1)). However, when a calling-up notice has not been complied with the creditor may exercise the right of entering into possession without the need of any action in court (s. 20(1)). Nevertheless, it is the usual practice for the creditor to raise an action of declarator of his right to enter into possession and where the defender is in personal occupation of the subjects a crave for ejection should also be included.

Alternatively, where there has been non-compliance with a calling-up notice, an action of ejection will be competent since the remedy in section 5 of the Heritable Securities (Scotland) Act 1894 is available. A creditor in possession is entitled to recover feu duties, ground annuals or rents, to let the subjects or grant leases and to manage, reconstruct or improve the subjects.

In terms of standard condition 10(6) where the debtor is in default the creditor is entitled to repair, reconstruct and improve the security subjects. The only work which can be done to the subjects however is such as can be considered reasonable for the maintenance of its market value. Other remedies available to the creditor are the right to poind the ground, *i.e.* to attach moveables on the subjects, the now little-used procedure of adjudication, and foreclosure.

Foreclosure

Where the creditor has exposed the security subjects to sale at a price not exceeding the amount due under his security and under any security ranking prior to or *pari passu* with it and has failed to find a purchaser or where, having failed, has succeeded in selling only a part of the subjects at a lesser price, he may apply to the court for a decree of foreclosure (s. 28(1)). The application can only be made after the lapse of a period of two months from the date of the first exposure to sale. The decree, if granted, will contain a declaration that following on the recording of the extract decree, any right to redeem that standard security has been extinguished and that the creditor has right to the security subjects or the unsold part of them (s. 28(5)). When the extract decree is recorded, the creditor will be vested in the subjects and they will be disburdened of the standard security and all securities and diligences postponed to it. The creditor in addition will have the same right as the debtor to redeem any security ranking prior to or *pari passu* with his own security (s. 28(6)).

Bond and disposition in security

This deed is in the form of a simple personal bond by the borrower to which is added for the creditor's further protection a conveyance in his favour of heritable subjects belonging either to the debtor himself or to some third party. It was the usual method of taking a security over heritage when the loan intended to be secured was advanced instantly and in one sum but could be made available as security for advances due or to become due on current account. A statutory form of bond and disposition in security was provided in section 118 of the Titles to Land Consolidation Act 1868. The creditor could charge the debtor under the personal obligation contained in the bond and proceed by summary diligence but this remedy is not available, save under special agreement, against purchasers of the property from the debtor. There is nothing to prevent a creditor from proceeding under both the personal obligation and the power of sale contained in the bond.

Realisation of security subjects

Sections 33 *et seq.* of the Conveyancing (Scotland) Act 1924 as amended by the 1970 Act set forth the manner in which this form of heritable security is to be realised and its provisions must be strictly followed. A notice calling up the bond must be given to the appropriate person and after the expiry of three months from its date or the expiry of such shorter period as may have been agreed to, the creditor, failing payment of the sum due to him, may advertise the subjects for sale by public roup or by private bargain for the best price that can be reasonably obtained (s. 35 of the 1970 Act). The requirements as to advertising and the time limits within which the sale must take place are set out in section 36 of the 1970 Act substituting a new section 38 in the 1924 Act. If the property is sold, the creditor executes in favour of the purchaser a disposition narrating the circumstances of the transaction. On receiving payment of the purchase price, the creditor, who is entitled to retain from the purchase price all expenses of the sale, must hold count and reckoning with the debtor or with any other party having an interest, and consign the surplus, if any, in bank. On any surplus being so consigned, the disposition by the creditor to the purchaser has the effect of completely disburdening the lands not only of the security and diligence of the creditor himself but of all subsequent securities and diligences.[3] If there is no surplus, the subjects are disburdened by recording in the appropriate Register of Sasines along with the disposition by the creditor to the purchaser, a certificate of no surplus by a solicitor or notary public (s. 42(1) of the 1924 Act). The creditor cannot bid at the sale[4] and in selling he must proceed with a due regard to the interests of postponed creditors.[5]

Provision is made by section 8 of the Heritable Securities (Scotland) Act 1894 as amended by section 39 of the 1970 Act for a heritable creditor to become proprietor of the security subjects if he has exposed them for sale and has failed to find a purchaser. As an alternative to selling, the creditor may also enter into possession of the subjects under a decree of maills and duties, which entitles him to collect the rents and to that end to sequestrate the tenant's effects.[6] He may also by a poinding of the ground attach the moveable effects on the ground belonging to the proprietor and also those of the tenants to the extent of the rents due by them. Where a creditor desires to enter into possession of security subjects and the proprietor is in personal occupation of them, such a proprietor is deemed to be an occupant without a title and the creditor may take proceedings to eject him in the same way in all respects as if he were such an occupant. This only applies, however, where the proprietor is in default with the punctual payment of interest under the security or in the due payment of principal after formal demand (s. 5 of the 1894 Act). A

---

[3] *Stewart* v. *Brown* (1882) 10 R. 192.
[4] *Maxwell* v. *Drummond's Trs.* (1823) 2 S. 122; *Stirling's Trs., Petrs.* (1865) 3 M. 851.
[5] See *Stewart* v. *Brown* (1882) 10 R. 192.
[6] *Railton* v. *Muirhead* (1834) 12 S. 757.

creditor in possession also has power to lease the security subjects (ss. 6 and 7 of the 1894 Act).

Bond for cash credit and disposition in security

To remedy the inconvenience caused by the fact that a simple bond and disposition in security was not available as a security for any sum of money advanced subsequent to the date of its recording (or in other words for fluctuating advances) it was provided by the Debts Securities (Scotland) Act 1856 that heritable securities could be given for cash accounts on condition that the principal sum and interest to become due under the bond be limited to a certain definite sum specified in the security, not exceeding the amount of principal and three years' interest at five per cent. While in terms of the 1856 Act the subjects conveyed in security can only be made available for the repayment of the specified amount of principal and interest, the personal obligation in the bond can be enforced for the repayment of whatever sum is due. The security subjects may be realised in the same manner as those conveyed in a bond and disposition in security. Letters of inhibition against a debtor do not affect advances made subsequent to the date of the inhibition on the security of a cash credit bond granted prior to their date[7] but despite this, doubt has been expressed as to the effect of the granting of a postponed security over the same subjects. The safer course to follow is not to continue to treat the bond as cover for future advances and to keep the account dormant and have it remain in existence for repayment purposes only.

Disposition ex facie absolute

This method of constituting a security over heritable property was more convenient than either of the two forms last described and was the most common method used prior to the introduction of the standard security. Using it, banks were able not only to make advances to an agreed amount to customers on the security of heritable property but also to make further advances beyond the amount originally agreed if requested. The disposition in favour of the creditor is in absolute terms ("for certain good causes, etc.") and is qualified by a back letter or a minute of agreement, where the nature of the transaction and the conditions entitling the proprietor to a reconveyance of his property are stated.

The right conveyed is an absolute right of property and imposes on the creditor the rights and responsibilities of a proprietor although the back letter usually provides for the borrower (or true owner) relieving him of any such liability. He is entitled to sell the subjects, to collect rents, to grant leases, to remove tenants and even to remove the owner himself from possession.[8] This form of security has the additional advantage of

---

[7] *Campbell's Tr.* v. *De Lisle's Exrs.* (1870) 9 M. 252.
[8] *Rankin* v. *Russell* (1868) 7 M. 126.

eliding prescription.[9] However, where an owner grants an *ex facie* absolute disposition in favour of a creditor and is allowed to continue in possession of and to manage the property, the right of the creditor does not deprive the owner of his title to dispose of the property in any way provided he does not prejudice the security of the creditor.[10] Where resort is had to a sale, the creditor must have due regard for the interests of the true owner.[11] The creditor's interest in the lands being nominally that of a feudal proprietor and not of a creditor, he is not entitled to use the diligence of poinding the ground. Although the disposition is recorded in the appropriate Register of Sasines the back letter is not. The effect of recording the back letter would be to render the security unavailable for any sum advanced subsequent to the date of recording.[12] The security conferred by an absolute disposition qualified by a back letter may be restricted in the same way as a standard security since by virtue of section 42 of the 1970 Act section 13 of the same Act applies to heritable securities constituted by *ex facie* absolute dispositions as it applies to standard securities.[13] It was competent to stipulate that the *ex facie* absolute disposition was to be a security for certain specified obligations and if this is clearly expressed the property cannot be held for any other debt.[14] The general practice, however, was to provide in the back letter that the borrower was to be entitled to demand a reconveyance only on payment of all sums due to the creditor.

A creditor holding an *ex facie* absolute disposition can never become the true owner of the security subjects by prescription or otherwise. Hence, even if the debtor becomes bankrupt and the creditor, after deducting from his claim the estimated value of his heritable security, ranks simply for the balance due to him, if any, he does not thereby acquire an absolute right to the property nor is the debtor's trustee to be held as having abandoned the debtor's reversionary interest in the security subjects. If the trustee is not to take over the property and the creditor wishes to retain it with a view to getting his debt repaid, his course is to have the trustee grant a disposition of the reversionary interest and the recording of this deed vests the creditor in the property absolutely. On the other hand, a creditor who holds a property in security under an *ex facie* absolute disposition and who finds himself, on the bankruptcy of the true owner, involved in onerous obligations of ownership may wish to denude himself of the property and its attendant burdens. In this situation, his remedy is to compel the true owner or his representatives—by action in court if necessary—to accept a reconveyance.[15]

---

[9] *Campbell's J.F.* v. *National Bank of Scotland*, 1944 S.C. 495.
[10] *Edinburgh Entertainments Ltd.* v. *Stevenson*, 1926 S.C. 363.
[11] *Shrub* v. *Clark* (1897) 5 S.L.T. 125.
[12] Bell, *Comm.*, I, 725.
[13] See p. 153.
[14] *Robertson* v. *Duff* (1840) 2 D. 279; *Nelson* v. *Gordon* (1874) 1 R. 1093.
[15] *Clydesdale Bank Ltd.* v. *McIntyre*, 1909 1 S.L.T. 501.

Heritable fixtures

It was customary in taking an *ex facie* absolute disposition to include in the conveyance not only the ground and buildings but also the whole machinery and plant of every description, both heritable and moveable, in or about the premises. Similarly, it is also considered advisable to insert a reference to fixtures and fittings in the description of the security subjects in a standard security. Neither a conveyance nor a standard security can cover moveable property and difficult questions may arise as to what fixtures and fittings are heritable and what moveable. The determination of such questions depends largely on the facts of each particular case.[16] "Fixtures" in this context means anything affixed to heritable property, that is, fastened to or connected with it, and not in mere juxtaposition. They are regarded by the law as heritable, being things which, although in their nature moveable, have become heritable in respect that they are so attached to the ground or to a building thereon that they cannot be removed without materially injuring or destroying their usefulness.[17] Such things are held to become the property of the owner of the ground on the principle that where two things are connected with each other the ownership of the principal thing draws after it that of its accessory. In deciding whether any structures, machinery, plant or additions are to be regarded as fixtures, there are two elements to be considered, firstly, their own character as more or less of the nature of fixtures and, secondly, the intention of the parties in making them or in consenting to their being made.[18] As regards the character and nature of the structures, the general rule is that the subject must be fixed in or to the ground or in or to something fixed in the ground. If something, however large, merely rests on the ground, it has not generally the character of a fixture[19] but things retained in position merely by their own weight may be so specially adapted to a building or their surroundings as to become fixtures.[20]

Deposit of title deeds

By the law of Scotland only such moveables as are by their nature intrinsically valuable or substantially serviceable and which would fetch a price in the open market, can be made the subjects of pledge and that only by delivery, actual or constructive. Title deeds have no intrinsic value[21] and cannot form the subject of a pledge by mere delivery so as to confer on the pledgee a title of possession to the subjects represented by them which is capable of competing with rights competent to the proprietor or a heritable creditor. Although title deeds cannot be retained in

---

[16] See generally on this subject *Brand's Trs.* v. *Brand's Trs.* (1876) 3 R. (H.L.) 16; Rankine on *Landownership* (4th ed.), pp. 116 *et seq.*
[17] *Jamieson* v. *Welsh* (1900) 3 F. 176.
[18] *Scottish Discount Co.* v. *Blin*, 1986 S.L.T. 123.
[19] See *Assessor for Glasgow* v. *R.N.V.R. Club (Scotland)*, 1974 S.L.T. 291.
[20] *Niven* v. *Pitcairn* (1823) 2 S. 290; *Christie* v. *Smith's Exr.*, 1949 S.C. 572.
[21] See s. 45 of the 1970 Act on the status of sasine extracts.

security of a loan,[22] banks occasionally ask, if only as a mark of good faith on the part of the borrower, for custody of these with a simple letter signed by the borrower agreeing to grant, if and when requested to do so, a formal security over the subjects referred to in the deeds.

In England a *prima facie* equitable mortgage is created over heritable (or real) property by a deposit of title deeds but where the deposit is accompanied by a written document, the terms of this document must be referred to in order to ascertain the exact nature of the charge. Title deeds may be deposited with a banker as an equitable security for the payment with interest of all money due by the mortgagor to the banker. As questions affecting heritable property are usually[23] decided in accordance with the law of the place where the property is situated, advances may competently be made in Scotland against the deposit of the title deeds of property situated in England.

---

[22] *Christie* v. *Ruxton* (1862) 24 D. 1182.
[23] See, however, *Studd* v. *Cook* (1882) 10 R. (H.L.) 53.

CHAPTER 11

SECURITIES OVER MOVEABLE PROPERTY

Moveable property is classified as either corporeal, *i.e.* things, the ownership of which is transferred by delivery, or incorporeal, *i.e.* things which are incapable of being transferred by delivery and require writing to effect their transfer. Household goods, stock in trade, etc., are examples of the former, while policies of assurance, share certificates, funds due under a contract and a vested interest in a trust estate are examples of the latter.

Corporeal moveables

Subject as aftermentioned, no security can be created over corporeal moveables unless the creditor or someone on his behalf obtains possession of them. A relaxation of this strict rule of law was introduced by the Agricultural Credits (Scotland) Act 1929 in cases where its provisions apply. A society formed in terms of Part II of the Act may charge its stock or merchandise to a bank as security for sums advanced to it in pursuance of the objects which it has been formed to carry out. The procedure under the Act is cumbersome and unsatisfactory and so far its provisions have been largely ignored. An exception to the rule has also been made in the case of a company incorporated in Scotland which may competently grant security by way of a floating charge over its assets by virtue of section 462 of the Companies Act 1985. Apart from these statutory provisions there is no procedure by which a security over corporeal moveable property can be obtained by a creditor so long as the debtor remains in possession of the property. A mere colourable contract of sale cannot create an effective security as, for example, where the pretended sale does not take immediate effect so as to give the ostensible purchaser the rights which a true contract of sale confers.[1]

Pledge

A contract of pledge is the means by which corporeal moveables which are not represented by documents of title are transferred in security. The debtor places in the hands of his creditor moveable property to remain with him in security of a debt or obligation, to be redelivered on payment or satisfaction.[2] In order to constitute a valid security it is necessary for the creditor or his agent to obtain actual or constructive delivery of the goods. Where a security is to be taken, it may be effected by the lender obtaining actual delivery or that constructive delivery which the law

---

[1] *Edmond* v. *Mowat* (1868) 7 M. 59: *Jones & Cos'. Tr.* v. *Allan* (1901) 4 F. 374. See also Sale of Goods Act 1979, s. 62(4).

[2] Pawn, a form of pledge, is regulated by the Consumer Credit Act 1974, ss. 114 to 122.

regards as equivalent to actual delivery. Actual delivery means giving actual possession by delivering the goods into the lender's warehouse, vehicle or vessel or into a warehouse where the lender is in the habit of storing goods, or in delivering to the lender the key of the place where the goods are stored.[3] Constructive delivery is effected by any of those acts which, although they do not give the purchaser the actual possession of the thing sold, have been held as equivalent in law to delivery. Intimating a delivery order to the custodier of goods[4] or transferring the goods in the custodier's books from the name of the borrower to that of the lender, are examples of constructive delivery. But while the owner of the goods retains them in his own possession or in a warehouse kept by a servant, no entry in his books will by itself operate as constructive delivery of these goods, even where the goods of others as well as of the borrower are kept in his store.[5]

. DELIVERY ORDER. The corporeal moveables which a banker most frequently deals with are goods belonging to his customer in the custody of a third person, the property in which he is prepared to transfer to the bank in security of his indebtedness. This is effected by means of a delivery order which is a document addressed to the warehousekeeper instructing the delivery of the goods to the bank or its order. It is usual for the warehousekeeper to acknowledge receipt of the order and to issue a fresh warehousekeeper's receipt. The contract of pledge is then complete. It does not affect the title of the bank as holders of a delivery order duly intimated that it appears from the transaction that a mere security was intended, because when a delivery order in absolute terms is presented to a warehousekeeper and given effect to by him in the warehouse books, a complete transfer of the goods from their previous owner to the bank as the holders of the delivery order takes place. The bank is put in possession of the goods to the same effect as if it had bought them and obtained actual delivery on a contract of sale. As holder of a delivery order, the bank is entitled to sell or otherwise dispose of the goods. By virtue of the fact, however, that the possession of the delivery order by the bank, accompanied by notification in the warehousekeeper's books, constitutes a transfer of the right of property in the goods to the bank, the bank is entitled to hold the goods represented by the delivery order in security of a general balance due by the original owner of the goods, even where the delivery order was given as a collateral security for a specific purpose.[6] In order that the bank's security may be effectively constituted, it is necessary that the goods intended to be pledged or delivered in security should be specifically ascertained and identified. In *Hayman & Son* v. *Thomson McLintock*[7] certain sacks of flour represented by a

[3] *West Lothian Oil Co.* v. *Mair* (1892) 20 R. 64.

[4] *Black* v. *Incorporation of Glasgow Bakers* (1867) 7 M. 622; *Vickers* v. *Hertz* (1871) 9 M. (H.L.) 65; *Distillers' Co.* v. *Russell's Tr.* (1889) 16 R. 479.

[5] *Anderson* v. *McCall* (1866) 4 M. 765; *Pochin & Co.* v. *Robinows & Marjoribanks* (1869) 7 M. 622, per Lord President Inglis at pp. 628, 629.

[6] *Hamilton* v. *Western Bank* (1856) 19 D. 152; *Hayman & Son* v. *Thomson McLintock*, 1907 S.C. 936.

[7] *Supra*.

delivery order were neither numbered nor marked nor put into receptacles nor specified in such a way as to distinguish them from other flour in the storekeeper's warehouse. It was held, in terms of section 16 of the Sale of Goods Act 1893 (which required that before the property, *i.e.* ownership, in any goods could pass to the vendor they must be ascertained or identified) that as the goods sold were unascertained no property in them had passed and no effectual right of security had been constituted by the delivery order.[8] Where a delivery order is taken by a bank in security of existing advances, there should be an express agreement to that effect entered into between the bank and its customer.[9] Indeed, it is desirable that there should be an agreement in all cases, in the form of a letter of pledge.

Three independent parties are necessary to constitute constructive delivery by means of a delivery order, namely, the granter, the person in whose favour it is granted, and the warehousekeeper or custodier of the goods. If the custodier is identified with the granter of the order, he ceases to be an independent third party and there cannot be constructive delivery by means of such a delivery order.[10] Mere possession of the delivery order is not sufficient to constitute constructive delivery. There must, over and above, be intimation to the warehousekeeper and the date of the intimation, not the date of the order, fixes the time of the change of ownership.[11] When the delivery order is indorsed to a third party, the indorsee to complete his right must intimate it to the warehousekeeper.

Bond and assignation in security

A direct security over corporeal moveables in the hands of a third party may competently be constituted by means of a bond and assignation in security. The bond is executed with reference to an inventory annexed to it of the goods assigned and the security is completed by intimation to the custodier of the goods and his acknowledgment.

Pledge by factor or agent

When a factor or agent is accredited with the ostensible ownership of goods, not merely by being entrusted with the bare custody of them, but by having documents put into his hands which *ex facie* confer upon him the character of owner, and which enable him to deceive those with whom he transacts, he may effectually pledge the property of his principal. This he may do by the transfer of the documents to a party making *bona fide* advances on the goods, the lender being entitled to rely on the

---

[8] *Cf.* Sale of Goods Act 1979, s. 16. See also *Price & Pierce Ltd.* v. *Bank of Scotland*, 1912 S.C. (H.L.) 19.

[9] See *Robertson* v. *Duff* (1840) 2 D. 279.

[10] *Anderson* v. *McCall* (1866) 4 M. 765; *Distillers' Co.* v. *Russell's Tr.* (1889) 16 R. 479; *Rhind's Tr.* v. *Robertson & Baxter* (1891) 18 R. 623.

[11] *Robertson & Baxter* v. *Inglis* (1898) 25 R. (H.L.) 70.

title with which the factor has been clothed and not being bound to make restitution without repayment of his advances.[12]

Incorporeal moveables

The Transmission of Moveable Property (Scotland) Act 1862 produced a simple and effective method of assigning a person's right in a personal bond or in a conveyance of moveable estate. The words "bond" and "conveyance" in the Act extend to and include personal bonds for payment or performance, bonds of caution, bonds of guarantee, bonds of relief, bonds and assignations in security of every kind, decrees of any court, policies of assurance of any assurance company or association in Scotland, whether held by parties resident in Scotland or elsewhere, protests of bills or of promissory notes, dispositions, assignations and other conveyances of moveable or personal property or effects, and also probative extracts of all such deeds from the books of any competent court. Moveable estate extends to and includes all personal debts and obligations and moveable or personal property or effects of every kind.

The Act provides that assigning a person's right may be done either by a separate writing or by an assignation indorsed on the bond or conveyance itself and forms are provided in the Schedules annexed to the Act. On such an assignation being duly completed and intimated to the debtor in the obligation, the assignee acquires the rights of the assignor, but until intimation there is no completed transfer to the assignee and in a competition an assignation first intimated will be preferred to one prior in date but subsequent in intimation.[13] An assignation is validly intimated (1) by a notary public delivering a copy of it certified as correct to the person or persons to whom intimation has to be made or (2) by the holder of such an assignation transmitting a certified copy by recorded delivery post to such person. In the first case a certificate by the notary public in the form set forth in Schedule C to the Act, and in the second case a written acknowledgment by the person to whom the copy has been transmitted by post of receipt of the copy, is sufficient evidence that intimation has been duly made.

In any competition among creditors the common debtor's private knowledge of the assignation cannot be pleaded by the assignee as an equivalent to intimation for such private knowledge does not amount to completion of the assignation and if it is not formally intimated, the assignee's right will be postponed to debts secured by arrestment or otherwise. Once intimated however, the assignee's right cannot be superseded by a subsequent arrestment.[14] Private knowledge of the assignation may, however, be a sufficient bar to the common debtor paying to the granter of the assignation. Registration of the assignation in the Books of

---

[12] *Pochin & Co.* v. *Robinows & Marjoribanks* (1869) 7 M. 622. See also the Factors Act 1889, s. 3.
[13] Stair, III, i, 6; Ersk., III, i, 10.
[14] *Executive Council for Glasgow* v. *T. Sutherland Henderson Ltd.*, 1955 S.L.T. (Sh.Ct.) 33.

Council and Session is not equivalent to intimation.[15] Where there are several debtors the assignation should be intimated to all of them and where the beneficial interest under a trust is assigned, the assignation should be intimated to all the acting trustees[16] although in one case it was decided that as a general rule an assignation of rights in a trust-estate is sufficiently intimated to trustees by intimation to their law agents.[17] In the case of trading firms, intimation should be made to each of the partners unless there is an appointed manager. Intimation to one who is *de facto* the managing partner is not sufficient.[18] In the case of a bank, intimation should be made to the bank at its head office. If the money is lying at a branch office it may also be expedient to intimate to the branch. In the case of companies incorporated under the Companies Acts, intimation should be left or sent by post in a recorded delivery letter addressed to the company at its registered office.[19] When the common debtor is furth of Scotland, the intimation must be made edictally.

Policies of life assurance

The mere possession by a creditor of a policy of assurance on the life of his debtor confers, in case of a contract entered into in Scotland, no right on the part of the creditor to the policy or to any claim arising under it. If in such circumstances the creditor pays the premiums, he is not entitled when a claim under the policy emerges to a preferential ranking in respect of such payments, these being regarded simply as cash advances to the assured for which the creditor is only entitled to an ordinary ranking.[20] Where a contract is entered into in England with a domiciled Englishman for a loan against a policy, although both the debtor and the insurance company are domiciled in Scotland, an equitable mortgage is created in favour of the creditor by the mere delivery of the policy and intimation of the fact to the insurance company.[21]

When a bank takes a policy in security, the assignation may be either *ex facie* absolute, *i.e.* for certain good and onerous causes, etc., or simply in security. The latter style is usually followed by the Scottish banks. The narrative clearly states for whose obligations the assignation is granted while in the case of an assignation for certain good and onerous causes, etc., the assignation requires to be qualified by an explanatory letter. The bank's right in either case is completed by sending a notice of intimation of assignation, in duplicate, to the assurance company who are usually asked to state whether they have received notice of any prior charge affecting the policy and whether they themselves have any claim thereon (for example, in respect of unpaid premiums). Any prior deeds relating to the policy should be delivered to the assignee (the bank) by the

---

[15] *Tod's Trs.* v. *Wilson* (1869) 7 M. 1100.
[16] But see *Jameson* v. *Sharp* (1887) 14 R. 643; Ersk., III, v, 5.
[17] *Browne's Trs.* v. *Anderson* (1901) 4 F. 195.
[18] *Hill* v. *Lindsay & Others* (1846) 8 D. 472.
[19] Companies Act 1985, s. 725.
[20] *Wylie's Exr.* v. *McJannet* (1901) 4 F. 195.
[21] *Scottish Provident Institution* v. *Cohen & Co.* (1888) 16 R. 112.

assignor. If the title to the policy is clear, the assignee's right is complete on the return of the duplicate notice of intimation bearing the assurance company's acknowledgment. It has been decided that an assignation of a life policy constituted a right in the assignee which was valid against the executor of the assignor although it had not been intimated to the assurance company prior to the assignor's death.[22] The date of the assurance company's acknowledgment and not that of the assignation regulates the priority of all claims in regard to the policy moneys.[23] Should the assignor be sequestrated before the assignation is intimated, his trustee may be able to establish a prior claim to the policy. This right of the permanent trustee requires no intimation as his act and warrant operates as a completed title in his favour as at the date of sequestration.[24]

POLICIES INVALIDATED. A contract of life assurance is a contract involving *uberrima fides, i.e.* entails the utmost good faith between the proposer and the assurance company. Accordingly, most if not all policies of assurance are issued subject to the condition that certain questions relative to the assured's habits of life, his health, his transactions with other companies, etc., put to and answered by him have been answered truthfully, and it is provided that false answers to any such questions may have the effect of invalidating the contract. The questions put must, however, be clear and unambiguous in their terms as the courts will not readily declare an answer to be false which may be only an innocent misinterpretation of an ambiguous question.[25] As a general rule, an answer is deemed to be true if true in the *bona fide* belief and to the best of the knowledge of the person making it.[26] The validity of a policy may, however, in certain circumstances depend on whether an answer was true in point of fact apart altogether from its truth in the *bona fide* knowledge and belief of the person making it.[27] This is important since an onerous assignee of a policy holds it subject to reduction on the same grounds as those on which it might have been challenged while still in the hands of the original grantee.[28]

Where a policy is effected by one person on the life of another, the person effecting the policy must have an insurable interest in the life of the person assured. A creditor has an insurable interest in the life of his debtor. A wife has an insurable interest in the life of her husband and vice versa. The insurable interest must, however, be pecuniary apart from the relationship.[29] The interest is presumed to the extent of the amount insured by the policy.[30] If, however, a creditor insures the same interest with several companies, he cannot recover in total more than the amount

---

[22] *Brownlee* v. *Robb*, 1907 S.C. 1302.
[23] *Campbell's Trs.* v. *Whyte* (1884) 11 R. 1078.
[24] Bankruptcy (Scotland) Act 1985, s. 31(4).
[25] *Fowkes* v. *Manchester and London Life Assurance Association* (1863) 3 B. & S. 917.
[26] *Life Association of Scotland* v. *Foster* (1873) 11 M. 351; *Scottish Equitable Life Assurance Society* v. *Buist* (1877) 4 R. 1076; (1878) 5 R. (H.L.) 64.
[27] *Standard Life Assurance Co.* v. *Weems* (1884) 11 R. (H.L.) 48.
[28] *Scottish Equitable Life Assurance Society* v. *Buist, supra.*
[29] See *Turnbull & Co.* v. *Scottish Provident Institution* (1896) 34 S.L.R. 146.
[30] *Griffiths* v. *Fleming* [1909] 1 K.B. 805.

of his insurable interest.[31] The original creditor under the policy may assign his claim to a third person and this person is entitled to recover under the policy to the extent of the insurable interest of the person from whom he took the policy. It is advisable in such circumstances to get the insurance company to indorse on the policy an admission of the insurable interest on the original creditor.

SALE OR SURRENDER OF POLICY. In the assignation, express power should be taken by the assignee to sell or surrender the policy at any time as no statutory authority exists in Scotland for the sale by a creditor at his own hand of any personal property belonging to his debtor, with the single exception of shares in ships.

MARRIED WOMEN'S POLICIES OF ASSURANCE (SCOTLAND) ACT 1880. A policy of assurance may be effected in trust for a spouse or children. A policy of assurance effected by any man or woman on his or her own life and expressed upon the face of it to be for the benefit of his or her spouse or children is deemed a trust for their benefit. Such a policy, immediately on being effected, vests in him or her and his or her legal representatives in trust for the purpose or purposes so expressed or in any trustee nominated in the policy or appointed by separate writing duly intimated to the assurance company, but in trust always as aforesaid. It is not otherwise subject to his or her control and does not form part of his or her estate and is not liable to the diligence of creditors and is not revocable as a donation or reducible on any ground of excess or insolvency. The receipt of the trustee for the sums secured by the policy is a sufficient and effectual discharge to the assurance company.[32] However, if it is proved that the policy was effected and the premiums paid with intent to defraud creditors or if the person upon whose life the policy is effected is made bankrupt within two years from the date of the policy, it is competent for the creditors to claim repayment of the premiums paid from the trustee of the policy out of the proceeds. Where a policy vests in trust by virtue of section 2 of the 1880 Act that trust constitutes a trust within the meaning of the Trusts (Scotland) Act 1921 and provided it is not at variance with the terms or purposes of the trust the trustees may *inter alia* surrender the policy.[33] In addition, a beneficiary may assign his or her interest in the policy in security or renounce that interest.[34] If a policy, although not taken out in terms of the 1880 Act, is assigned by the insured person to trustees for his wife and children and the assignation is intimated to the assurance company, the insured is not thereafter entitled, even with the consent of his wife, the trustees under the deed, and the children of the marriage, even if they have all attained majority, to assign the policy in security of advances to himself. The trustees might, however, be entitled

---

[31] *Simcock* v. *Scottish Imperial Insurance Co.* (1902) 10 S.L.T. 286.
[32] s. 2, as amended by s. 2 of the Married Women's Policies of Assurance (Scotland) (Amendment) Act 1980.
[33] s. 2 of the 1980 Act.
[34] s. 3 of the 1980 Act.

to surrender the policy or borrow money upon it for the purpose of the trust.[35]

Security over stocks and shares

Where advances are made by a bank against Government or other stocks or the shares of a company, the practice is to have these transferred into the name of the bank's nominee company and not into the name of the bank itself. The transfer must be duly registered in the books of the company as until registration the bank's title is not complete. A mere promise of security is not sufficient.[36] Where there is no agreement to hold securities so transferred for any specific debt or account, the bank is generally entitled to hold these in security of all sums due and to become due to them by their customer, and only on payment of these is the transferor entitled to a retransfer of the holdings. With the transfer is invariably taken a letter of pledge. Where the shares are transferred to and registered in name of the bank's nominee company, the bank renders itself liable as a contributory. For this reason it is not advisable to take a transfer of shares in a company which are not fully paid up or on which there is any other form of uncalled liability. If this is done, the bank will take from their customer a letter agreeing to relieve them of any liability. When such shares come to be retransferred the bank should see that the transfer is registered immediately. Delay in registering a transfer may result in the bank being placed on the list of contributories should the company go into liquidation. If the transferee delays registering the transfer, it is provided by section 183 of the Companies Act 1985 that a company shall on the application of the transferor of any share or interest in the company enter in its register of members the name of the transferee of such share or interest in the same manner and subject to the same conditions as if the application for such entry were made by the transferee.[37] It has been decided that in the absence of an express or an implied agreement to the contrary, it is the duty of a bank which has received specific shares in security of advances to retain and retransfer the identical shares to the borrower upon repayment of the loan.[38] Accordingly it is the practice of banks in accepting shares as security to provide that they are not bound to retransfer the identical shares. The pledger may with the consent of the bank dispose of shares pledged to the bank in security of advances. When he does so, and at his request a transfer is executed in favour of the purchaser and the bank receives from the pledger the purchase price in reduction *pro tanto* of his indebtedness, the bank is not, in a question with the purchaser, liable to make restitution of the price of the shares even if it should turn out that the sale has been induced by

---

[35] *Barras* v. *Scottish Widows' Fund, etc.* (1900) 2 F. 1094.
[36] *Bank of Scotland* v. *Liqr. of Hutchison Main & Co. Ltd.*, 1914 S.C. (H.L.) 1.
[37] *Symon's Case, Re Asiatic Banking Corporation* (1870) L.R. 5 Ch. 298.
[38] *Crerar* v. *Bank of Scotland*, 1922 S.C. (H.L.) 137.

fraud on the part of the pledger, so long as the bank is not a party to the fraudulent representations.[39]

STAMP DUTY ON TRANSFER. When stocks or shares are transferred to a bank's nominee company in security of advances the transfer is sufficiently stamped with a duty of 50p irrespective of the market value of the shares transferred. The consideration stated in the transfer is a nominal one, usually £1. The transfer must be stamped within 30 days of its date.

LODGMENT OF SHARE CERTIFICATES AS SECURITY. No security or right of property can be constituted or acquired in Scotland by the simple deposit of share certificates even if the deposit is accompanied by a letter from the registered owner binding himself to transfer the shares to the creditor whenever asked to do so. Similarly, the mere lodgment of a duly signed transfer of shares even if accompanied by the share certificate does not by itself confer any right of property in the shares. There must be an out-and-out transfer, duly registered.

FORGED TRANSFER OF SHARES. In sending a transfer for registration, a bank is held to warrant the genuineness of the documents and if there has been fraud or forgery it must bear any loss sustained by the true shareholder or the company whose shares have been transferred.[40] It is a safe general rule to have all deeds to be granted in favour of a bank or its nominee company signed in the presence of at least one of its own officials or an official of another bank.

Debentures

Advances against debentures are secured by the creditor obtaining from the holder a transfer or assignation of the debenture which requires to be intimated to the company which has issued it. Debentures issued by a company incorporated under the Companies Acts are mere personal obligations by a company for repayment of money advanced on loan and the holders are simply ordinary creditors of the company with no preferential rights over its assets in a liquidation. A special security may however be constituted in favour of debenture-holders by means of a conveyance of certain assets to trustees for their behoof, which vests the assets in the trustees and through them gives to the debenture-holders an effective security for repayment of their loans. The assets must be properly vested in the trustees before the debenture-holders can claim a preferential ranking over the ordinary creditors of the company. In *Clark* v. *West Calder Oil Co.*[41] a company limited by shares, in security of sums advanced on debentures, assigned to trustees for the debenture-holders certain leases of minerals of which the company were tenants, together with the moveables and plant on the ground. The assignations were duly intimated to the landlords but the assignees took no steps to enter into possession of the subjects. On the liquidation of the company it was held

---

[39] *Gibbs* v. *British Linen Co.* (1875) 4 R. 630.
[40] *Sheffield Corporation* v. *Barclay* [1905] A.C. 392. See also *Yeung* v. *Hong Kong and Shanghai Banking Corporation* [1980] 2 All E.R. 599.
[41] (1882) 9 R. 1017.

that as the assignation had not been followed by possession, the deben-ture-holders had no preference as regards the leasehold or moveable property over the ordinary trade creditors of the company.

There is no statutory form for the transfer of a debenture. In whatever form the transfer is made, the right of the creditor is not completed until intimation is given to the company which has issued it.

Bearer bonds

Bearer bonds are only occasionally seen in practice and when taken in security should be accompanied by a letter from the bearer stating the purposes for which they are lodged. If the bonds at the time of the constitution of the security are in the bank's possession for safe custody, the safe custody receipt should be delivered up. Delivery of the bonds accompanied by a relative explanatory letter is sufficient and no intima-tion to the issuing company is necessary except in the case of certain American share certificates which pass by delivery on being indorsed in blank by the holder. If however the holding is actually to be registered in the name of the bank, the usual intimation is necessary. In the letter pledging the securities, express power to sell should be taken for unless this is done a banker is not entitled to sell at his own hand but must apply to the court for authority.[42]

Letter of postponement

Banks may make advances to a customer on condition that certain prior loans made to him by third parties are postponed to the bank's claim. The legal effect of such a letter of postponement has not been determined in court but so long as the customer and the third party remain solvent it is thought that the third party could not enforce his claim in priority to that of the bank. In the event of the bankruptcy of the customer the third party would be entitled to rank on the estate of the customer but would be bound either to assign his claim to the bank or pay to the bank the dividend received by him so far as necessary to enable the bank to receive payment of its debt in full. A difficulty could arise in the event of the bankruptcy of the postponing creditor but it is thought that a letter in the appropriate terms coupled with a letter of acknowledgment from the debtor in receipt of the loan would give the bank the right to insist in their claim against a trustee in bankruptcy or liquidator.

Floating charge

In 1961 the floating charge was introduced into Scots law. It can cover all the property of the company which grants it—both heritable and moveable—but it is often taken by a creditor principally to secure movea-ble property as it is a means whereby a security can be obtained over such property without assignation or delivery. The original legislation was repealed and is now to be found in the Companies Act 1985. Any

---

[42] *Robertson's Tr.* v. *Royal Bank of Scotland* (1890) 18 R. 12.

incorporated company (whether a company within the meaning of the Act or not) can now grant a floating charge for the purpose of securing any debt or other obligation, including a cautionary obligation, and whether present or future (s. 462(1)). The charge may be over all or any part of the property (including uncalled capital) which from time to time is comprised in the company's property and undertaking. Until the company goes into liquidation or the appointment of a receiver the company is free to dispose of the property which is subject to the floating charge. On the occurrence of either of these events, however, the floating charge attaches to the property comprised in the company's property and undertaking as if it were a fixed security over that property for the debt or obligation to which it relates, together with any interest which is due (s. 463(1) and (2)). The interest secured includes interest which accrues after the commencement of the winding up or the appointment of a receiver until payment of the sum due under the charge is made (s. 463(4)).

When a floating charge crystallises and attaches to the property of the company it does so subject to the rights of any person who (1) has effectually executed diligence[43] on the property or (2) holds a fixed security or floating charge which ranks prior to it (s. 463(1)). In so far as the assets of the company available for the payment of general creditors are insufficient to meet the preferential payments provided for in section 175 of the Insolvency Act 1986 these preferential debts have priority over the claims of the holder of the floating charge and have to be paid out of any property comprised in the charge (Insolvency Act 1986, ss. 59(1) and 175(2)(b)).[44]

RANKING OF FLOATING CHARGES. The Act provides for the ranking of floating charges. A fixed security arising by operation of law ranks in priority to a floating charge (s. 464(2)). Subject to this provision, the instrument creating the floating charge may contain (1) provisions prohibiting or restricting the creation of any fixed security or any other floating charge having priority over or ranking *pari passu* with the floating charge; or (2) with the consent of the holder of any subsisting floating charge or fixed security which would be adversely affected, provisions regulating the order in which the floating charge shall rank with any other subsisting or future floating charges or fixed securities (s. 464(1)). Where a floating charge contains such prohibitive or restrictive provisions as are mentioned at (1) above, they are effective to confer priority on the floating charge over any fixed security or floating charge created after its date (s. 464(1A)). In the absence of any ranking provisions, a fixed security, the right to which has been constituted as a real right before a floating charge has crystallised, has priority over the floating charge. Otherwise, floating charges rank with one another according to the time of registration, floating charges which have been received by the

---

[43] See *Lord Advocate* v. *Royal Bank of Scotland Ltd.*, 1976 S.L.T. 130.
[44] For the grounds on which a floating charge may be declared invalid or avoided as an alienation or preference, see p. 227.

Registrar of Companies by the same postal delivery ranking equally with one another (s. 464(4)).

When the holder of a floating charge has received intimation in writing of the subsequent registration of another floating charge over the same property, the preference in ranking of the first-mentioned floating charge is restricted to security for the holder's present advances and future advances which he may be required to make under the instrument creating the floating charge, together with interest due on all such advances and any expenses or outlays which he may reasonably incur. In the case of a floating charge granted to secure a contingent liability, after intimation the preference in ranking is restricted to security for the maximum sum to which that contingent liability is capable of amounting (s. 464(5)). In the case of a bank making fluctuating advances to a company on current account, the account should be stopped when such intimation is received to avoid the prejudicial effect of the rule in *Clayton's Case*.

ALTERATION OF FLOATING CHARGES. The Act also contains provisions for the alteration of floating charges. An instrument of alteration must be executed by the company, the holder of the floating charge and the holder of any other charge, fixed or floating, which would be adversely affected by the alteration (s. 466(1)). Subsections (4) and (5) of section 466, which required the registration of any instrument altering a floating charge, were repealed by section 140(8) of the Companies Act 1989.[45]

ASSIGNATION OF FLOATING CHARGE. Although there is no statutory form for assigning a fixed security over incorporeal moveables, it has been established that a floating charge may be assigned by the holder. The assignation must be intimated to the company in writing and the company must enter the new creditor in its own register of charges, even although there is no provision for recording the change of creditor with the Registrar of Companies.[46]

Registration of floating charges

Sections 92 to 104 of the Companies Act 1989 amend the provisions of the 1985 Act by inserting in that Act (in place of sections 395 to 408 and 410 to 423) new provisions with respect to companies registered in Great Britain. Section 395 now states that the purpose of the provisions is to secure the registration of charges on a company's property and "charge" means any form of security interest (fixed or floating) over property and "property", in the context of what is the subject of a charge, includes future property. It is immaterial where the property subject to the charge is situated. Registration of a charge granted by a company registered in Scotland is made with the Registrar of Companies in Edinburgh. The charges requiring registration are (a) a charge on land or any interest in land; (b) a charge on goods or any interest in goods, other than a charge

---

[45] But see s. 401.
[46] *Libertas-Kommerz GmbH*, Appellants 1978 S.L.T. 222.

under which the chargee is entitled to possession either of the goods or of a document of title to them; (c) a charge on incorporeal moveable property of any of the following descriptions—(i) goodwill, (ii) intellectual property, (iii) book debts (whether of the company or assigned to the company), and (iv) uncalled share capital of the company; (d) a charge for securing an issue of debentures; or (e) a floating charge on the whole or part of the company's property (s. 396(1)). "Goods" means any corporeal moveable property other than money and "intellectual property" means (i) any patent, trademark, service mark, registered design, copyright or design right, or (ii) any licence under or in respect of any such right (s. 396(2)).

Not every charge created by a Scottish company is registrable. The list in section 396 does not include a fixed security over shares in another company[47] or over a life policy. It is doubtful whether a charge over a company's "book debts and other debts" covers a credit balance in the company's bank account which is normally designated as "cash at bank" and is not, as a matter of commercial practice, treated as a book debt.[48] Nevertheless, the Registrar of Companies will register charges in favour of a third party by a limited company customer of a bank over a credit balance held by that bank.

Registration in Scotland is necessary wherever the property charged is situated (s. 395(3)). In terms of section 398 it remains the duty of a company which creates a charge, or acquires property subject to a charge, to deliver the prescribed particulars to the Registrar within 21 days after the date of the creation of the charge or the date of the acquisition. Delivery of the prescribed particulars in the prescribed form is all that is required, even if registration is subsequently refused on the erroneous view that the charge is not registrable.[49] Registration may nevertheless be effected by any person interested in the charge. If there is a failure to deliver the prescribed particulars within the period of 21 days after the date of the charge's creation, the charge is void against (a) an administrator or liquidator of the company, and (b) any person who for value acquires an interest in or right over property subject to the charge, where either the beginning of the insolvency proceedings or the acquisition of that right or interest occurs after the creation of the charge (s. 399(1)). Where one of these events occurs on the same day as the charge is created it is to be presumed to have occurred after the charge is created unless the contrary is proved (s. 399(3)). However, where the prescribed particulars are delivered for registration after the end of the 21-day period section 399(1) does not apply in relation to the events described which occur after the particulars are delivered. But if, in such a case, the company is at the date of the delivery of the particulars unable to pay its debts (or becomes unable to do so in consequence of the particular

[47] *Scottish Homes Investment Co.*, 1968 S.C. 244.
[48] *Re Brightlife Ltd.* [1986] 3 All E.R. 673.
[49] *N.V. Slavenburg's Bank* v. *Intercontinental Natural Resources Ltd.* [1980] 1 All E.R. 955.

transaction) and insolvency proceedings begin before the end of the relevant period beginning with the date of delivery of the particulars, the charge is void as against an administrator or liquidator (s. 400(2)). For this purpose the "relevant period" is two years in the case of a floating charge created in favour of a person connected with the company, one year in the case of a floating charge created in favour of a person not so connected, and six months in any other case (s. 400(3)).

The time limit for registration is "within 21 days after" the date of creation of the charge (s. 398(1)). In the case of a floating charge the date of creation is the date of execution by the company creating the charge (s. 414(3)(*a*)). In the case of a fixed security, it is the date on which the right of the person entitled to the benefit of the security was constituted as a real right (s. 414(3)(*b*)). In the case of a heritable security, this is the date of recording or registration in the Sasine Register or Land Register as the case may be. In the case of a security over an incorporeal moveable right, the date of creation is the effective date of intimation.

Section 401 provides for further particulars of a charge, supplementing or varying the registered particulars, to be delivered to the Registrar for registration at any time. Section 402 sets out the effect of omissions and errors in registered particulars. Where such particulars are not complete and accurate, the charge is void, to the extent that rights have not been disclosed unless the court on the application of the chargee orders otherwise, as against an administrator or liquidator and any person who for value acquires an interest in the property subject to the charge (s. 402(2)). Where any of these events occurs at a time when the particulars are incomplete or inaccurate in a relevant respect, the court has power to order that the charge is effective if it is satisfied that the omission is not likely to have misled materially to his prejudice any unsecured creditor of the company or that no person became an unsecured creditor at a time when the registered particulars were incomplete or inaccurate (s. 402(4)). Similarly, the court may order that the charge is effective as against a person acquiring an interest in property subject to the charge if it is satisfied that he did not rely on the registered particulars when making the acquisition (s. 402(5)).

Further provision is made by section 404 with respect to the avoidance of charges. It provides that a charge which would otherwise be void by virtue of the foregoing provisions of the Act is not void as against a subsequent charge unless the relevant particulars of the subsequent charge are duly delivered for registration within 21 days after the date of its creation or before complete and accurate particulars of the earlier charge are duly delivered for registration. In other words, the first charge which would otherwise be void is not treated as void as against an unregistered second charge. Similarly, a charge is not void by virtue of the provisions of the Act as against a person acquiring an interest in property where the acquisition is expressly subject to the charge (s. 405).

Cash deposits

To create a security in favour of a third party over a credit balance in a bank account, assignation by the customer as creditor followed by intimation to the bank as debtor is required. In the case of a company incorporated under the Companies Acts on the basis that a bank balance may be a book debt, such a charge should be registered under section 395 of the 1985 Act.[50]

A customer may also place a sum of money in an account with a bank as security for sums and obligations due by him to the bank. To reinforce the bank's right of compensation or set-off and its right to combine accounts, the customer is usually asked to undertake not to withdraw the deposit so long as he is under an obligation to the bank and to give the bank the right, at any time without notice to him, to apply the sum in the account in reduction or extinction of his liabilities. It is suggested that since there can be no assignation and intimation, such an arrangement cannot create a security in distinction to making set-off or combination possible and if entered into between a bank and a limited company does not constitute a charge over a book debt of the company and registrable as such under section 395 of the Act.[51]

Charges on property of oversea company

Section 105 of the 1989 Act provides that the provisions in Schedule 15 thereto are to be inserted in Part XXIII of the 1985 Act and these are designed to secure the registration of charges over the assets of oversea companies.

---

[50] But see *Re Brightlife Ltd.* [1987] Ch. 200.
[51] *Re Charge Card Services Ltd.* [1986] 3 W.L.R. 697.

CHAPTER 12

SECURITIES OVER SHIPS AND AIRCRAFT

Ships

Under the Merchant Shipping Acts 1894 to 1988 the property in a ship is divided into 64 shares, and save as regards joint owners, or owners by transmission, not more than 64 persons can be registered at the same time as owners of any one ship (s. 5).[1] A share may be held by not more than five persons jointly, who, for the purposes of holding or conveying such share, constitute one person in law, though no one is entitled to be registered as the owner of a fractional part of a share in a ship. A ship or any share therein may be held by a company incorporated under the Companies Acts or under any Act of Parliament, and may be registered under such company's corporate name (s. 5).[2] A partnership cannot be registered as the owners of a ship or any share therein, the entry in the register requiring to be in name of the partners, or one or more of their number, individually. No notice of a trust, whether express, implied or constructive, can be entered in the register or received by the registrar (s. 56). Where trustees as such are vested in the property of a ship, or of any shares therein, their names must appear on the register simply as joint owners and not as trustees.

A registered ship, or a share in any such ship, may be made a security for the repayment of a loan or the discharge of any other obligation; and on production of the deed it will be recorded in the register kept at the ship's port of registry (s. 31(1)). The creditor's right is completed by the registration of the mortgage at the ship's port or registry, and the registrar is usually asked to furnish a transcript of registry showing that the ship is free of other incumbrances. The priority of mortgages is determined, not by their dates, but by the dates of their respective registrations, the registrar, on a mortgage being presented to him for registration, notifying the fact by a certificate indorsed on the mortgage, setting forth the day and hour of registration (s. 33). An unregistered mortgage is not invalid, but will be postponed to all those which are registered even although the registered mortgagees are aware of the charge. If a bank holding a first mortgage receives actual notice of a second mortgage, operations on the customer's account should be stopped, since the bank will have no priority over the other mortgage in respect of sums advanced after receipt of notice of its execution.[3] Any person, on payment of a fee, is entitled on

---

[1] References to sections are to sections of the 1894 Act unless otherwise stated.
[2] A mortgage over a ship by a company has to be registered as a charge under the Companies Act 1985, s. 396.
[3] *The Benwell Tower* (1895) 72 L.T. 644.

application to the registrar at a reasonable time during the hours of his official attendance to inspect the information contained in the register and obtain a certified copy of such information (s. 64).

The mere granting of a mortgage does not deprive the owner of his rights of ownership unless and until the mortgagee takes steps to realise under his security (s. 34).[4] Where the transferee is to become the owner of the ship or share, even if only in name, the transfer is effected by means of a bill of sale duly registered, but bankers should proceed with caution in a transaction of this nature, as by becoming the transferee under a bill of sale they may render themselves liable for risks incidental to shipowners.

Powers of mortgagee

A mortgagee cannot take possession until there has been default on the part of the mortgagor in payment or a breach of his duty in respect of the mortgage by his unlawfully impairing the subject of security. Apart from this, every registered mortgagee has power to sell the ship or share in respect of which he is registered, and to grant effectual receipts for the purchase money. Where two or more persons are registered in succession as mortgagees of the same ship or share, a subsequent mortgagee cannot, except under the authority of a competent court, sell such ship or share without the concurrence of every prior mortgagee (s. 35). A mortgagee who takes possession for the purpose of sale is bound to exercise that care and diligence which a prudent man would exercise in dealing with his own property. The mortgagee so selling holds any surplus that may emerge, after paying himself, as trustee for the owner and subsequent mortgagees according to their respective rights. The mortgagee has also the power to take possession of the ship and to draw the earnings, though to employ the ship in the exercise of this power he must act with prudence, and he is liable for necessary disbursements.[5] He is entitled to the freight if he enters on possession before it becomes payable, and he is further entitled to remain in possession until his debt is paid either by the mortgagor or from the ship's earnings. On payment of his loan he is bound to retransfer. The usual method of a mortgagee taking possession of a ship is to put a representative on board. When the ship is at sea, notice to the charterer to pay freight to the mortgagee is held equivalent to taking possession. A mortgagee may competently transfer his mortgage to another person and the transfer requires to be registered. There is a certain amount of risk in taking such a transfer, since, if the original mortgagor has paid the debt, or it has been satisfied in any other competent manner, even although a discharge has not been executed and registered, the mortgage is nevertheless at an end; and since the original mortgagee can confer no higher right than he himself possesses, any subsequent transfer becomes worthless.

---

[4] See *Laming & Co.* v. *Seater* (1889) 16 R. 828.
[5] *Haulland, Routh & Co.* v. *Thomson* (1864) 3 M. 313.

Insurance of mortgaged ship

The question of insurance is one of importance to bankers. In taking a mortgage over a ship, the bank should see that the policy of insurance on the ship is transferred to it, or that it is in its possession or under its control, for if this is not done and the ship is lost, even although fully insured by the owner, the bank has no preferable claim over the insurance money in respect of the mortgage, although it still has a personal claim against the mortgagor for the amount due. To obviate this risk, the bank should (1) have the policy transferred to it by getting its interest noted thereon by the insurers, (2) obtain delivery of the policy duly indorsed by the customer, with relative letter of hypothecation or (3) effect in its own name an insurance for the amount of its interest under the mortgage.[6] The bank may, in special circumstances, deem it expedient to insure special risks through clubs, or otherwise.

Discharge of mortgage

On production of a mortgage deed, with a receipt for the mortgage money duly signed and attested indorsed thereon, the registrar makes an entry in the register to the effect that the mortgage has been discharged whereupon the property (if any) which passed to the mortgagee vests in the person in whom, having regard to intervening acts and circumstances (if any), it would have vested, had the mortgage not been granted (s. 32).

Fishing vessels

Provision is made in Part II of the 1988 Act for the registration of British fishing vessels. For the purposes of registration the property in a fishing vessel is divided into 64 shares and not more than 64 persons shall be entitled to be registered at the same time as owners of any one vessel (s. 18). No person is entitled to be registered as the owner of any fractional part of a share in a vessel, but any number not exceeding five may be registered as joint owners of one vessel or of a share or shares therein.

Any vessel registered under Part II of the 1988 Act may be made security for the repayment of a loan or the discharge of any other obligation and rules—set out in Schedule 3 to that Act—similar to those in the case of ships apply in regard to granting and registration of mortgages, transfer and discharge thereof. In addition, there is provision for the interests of intending mortgagees to be recorded on the register, a procedure not available under Part I of the 1894 Act.

Bill of lading

A bill of lading is the written evidence of contract for the carriage and delivery of goods sent by sea. It contains an acknowledgment by the master of the ship, or others authorised by the owners to grant it, of the

---

[6] See *Tyne Dock Engineering Co.* v. *Royal Bank of Scotland*, 1974 S.L.T. 57.

shipment of certain goods or merchandise, subject usually to conditions therein specified as to the perils of the sea, etc., and an obligation to deliver them at the port of discharge to the consignor or his order, or to bearer, or to a named consignee, his order or assigns, upon payment of freight.[7] It is customary for three copies of the bill of lading to be signed, one of which is retained by the consignor of the goods, one forwarded to the consignee, and the other given to the master of the ship. The three parts constitute one contract like a bill of exchange, and they each usually contain a clause "the one of which being accomplished the others to stand void." Without delivery of one of the parts of the bill of lading the shipmaster is not bound to deliver his cargo. There is no difference in law between the different parts of the instrument in conveying a title to an indorsee.

Indorsement

Formerly by the custom of merchants, and now by section 1(4) of the Factors Act 1889 a bill of lading represents the goods for which the shipmaster has signed and the transference of the bill of lading transfers the ownership of the goods. A bill of lading may therefore be transferred by indorsement, and the indorsement and delivery thereof by the shipper or owner of the goods, or mercantile agent with the consent of the owner in possession thereof, transfers the property to the indorsee, who may in turn transfer his right to a subsequent indorsee. A bill of lading is not a negotiable instrument and the indorsement of a bill of lading differs in effect from that of a bill of exchange or promissory note. An indorsee of a bill of lading takes it subject to the same liabilities in respect of the goods as if the contract contained in the bill of lading had been made with himself.[8] The bill of lading only represents the goods, and the transfer of the symbol does not operate as more than a transfer of what is represented. If it be stolen from the consignee, or transferred without his authority, a subsequent *bona fide* transferee for value cannot compel delivery of the goods as against the shipper. In the hands of a *bona fide* indorsee for value however a bill of lading is equivalent to actual delivery of the goods thereby represented.[9] A bill of lading remains in force as a symbol of property until the goods have been delivered, but no longer, unless the goods have been wrongfully delivered.[10]

Bills of lading are frequently made use of as securities for advances, and the pledge of a bill of lading duly indorsed is as effectual as a pledge of the goods themselves, but the right conferred by such delivery depends upon the contract under which it is delivered. Accordingly, if one buys a cargo afloat, the indorsement and delivery of the bill of lading is equivalent to the delivery of the goods sold, and passes the property

[7] Bell, *Comm.*, I, 212.
[8] Bills of Lading Act 1855, s. 1; *Craig & Rose* v. *Delargy* (1879) 6 R. 1269; *Schuster* v. *McKellar* (1857) 26 L.J.Q.B. 281.
[9] *Rodocanachi, Sons & Co.* v. *Millburn Bros.* (1886) L.R. 18 Q.B.D. 67.
[10] *Pirie & Sons* v. *Warden* (1871) 9 M. 523; *Barber* v. *Meyerstein* (1870) L.R. 4 H.L. 317.

therein to the buyer. Similarly, if the goods are stored, the delivery of the bill of lading has the same effect in all respects, whether as a title of property or as a security, to the person to whom it has been indorsed or delivered, exactly as if the goods were on board ship. It is now settled that the question as to the effect of a bill of lading does not depend upon the arrival, or even the unloading, of the ship, and that a bill of lading must be taken to be an effective document of title representing the goods until these have been actually delivered to the person in right of the bill.[11] If the contract be one not of sale but of pledge then the delivery of the indorsed bill of lading completes the contract just as if the goods themselves had been deposited with the pledgee, but gives the pledgee no higher right to the goods than delivery of the subject of pledge gives him. The pledge of a bill of lading requires no intimation for when the vessel is at sea, parting with the bill of lading is parting with something which is the symbol of property and is, for the purpose of conveying a right and interest in the property, regarded as the property itself.[12]

There is a certain risk attending the giving of an advance against delivery of one part of a bill of lading, and the practice is to insist on delivery of the full set or a proper indemnity. Where the different parts of a bill of lading are acquired by different persons *bona fide* and for value, the person who first gets any one of the parts acquires the property.[13] The master of a ship is justified or excused in giving delivery of his cargo according to his contract to the person appearing to be the assignee of the bill of lading which is produced to him, although there has been in point of fact a prior indorsement for value of another part, provided he acts in good faith and without notice or knowledge of such prior indorsement. But where the master has notice or, it may be, even knowledge, of a prior indorsement, he must deliver to the first indorsee, and if he delivers to the wrong person it is at his own risk.[14] If he is in doubt as to whom he should deliver, the course is to raise an action of multiplepoinding and have the question judicially determined.

Trust letters

It is the practice when produce is returned to the customer for sale to take from him a trust letter acknowledging that the goods, or the bill of lading, are received by him as agent for the bank, and undertaking to hold the goods when received, and their proceeds when sold, in that capacity, the object being to preserve the right of the bank as secured creditors over the goods until sold, and the proceeds when sold until the debt due to the bank is paid. The validity of such letters has, in England, been challenged, but unsuccessfully.[15] There is always the risk, however, of the

---

[11] *Hayman & Sons* v. *Thomson McLintock*, 1907 S.C. 936 at p. 951.
[12] *North-Western Bank Ltd.* v. *Poynter, Son & Macdonalds* (1894) 21 R. 513; see also *Sewell* v. *Burdick* (1884) 10 App.Cas. 74; *Tool & Son* v. *Merchant Banking Co. of London Ltd.* (1883) 10 R. 1009.
[13] *Barber* v. *Meyerstein* (1870) L.R. 4 H.L. 317.
[14] *Glyn, Mills & Co.* v. *East and West India Dock Co.* (1882) 7 App.Cas. 591; *Sanders* v. *Maclean* (1883) 11 Q.B.D. 327.
[15] *Re David Allestair Ltd.* [1922] 2 Ch. 211.

customer, in fraud of the holder of a trust letter, pledging the documents to another lender and thereby defeating the rights of such holder.[16]

Conditional indorsement

Where the seller of goods draws on the buyer for the price and transmits the bill of exchange and bill of lading to the buyer together to secure acceptance, or payment, of the bill of exchange, the buyer is bound to return the bill of lading if he does not honour the bill of exchange, and if he wrongfully retains the bill of lading the property in the goods does not pass to him.[17] So when the indorsement and delivery of a bill of lading is made conditional on the acceptance of a bill of exchange, or the performance of a similar obligation, for the price of the goods shipped, the indorsee cannot retain the bill of lading and refuse to accept the bill of exchange or perform the obligation, and any transferee taking the bill of lading from him takes it subject to the condition imposed on the original indorsee.[18]

Holders for value

The value requisite to constitute a *bona fide* holder is the same as that required for a bill of exchange, so that an antecedent debt or liability is a good consideration.[19] The shipowner is not entitled to question the right of an indorsee on the ground that he does not possess more than one copy of the bill of lading. No action, therefore, lies against the shipmaster, or the owner of the goods or ship, in respect of delivery of the goods having been made in *bona fide* to an indorsee of a bill of lading, though it should afterwards turn out that there was a prior indorsee whose right was preferable.[20]

Liability of indorsee

The indorsee of a bill of lading is subject to the same liabilities in regard to the goods as was his indorser. The weight of this burden is diminished by the facts that as soon as the indorsee transfers the right of property he ceases to be under obligation to fulfil the duties imposed on the merchant under the bill of lading. It is of even less importance in the case of bankers and others who ordinarily hold bills of lading as security for advances. So long as the bill of lading is held by a banker by way of security solely, and so long as he does not proceed to take possession of the goods themselves, the property in the goods does not pass to him so as to make him liable under the Bills of Lading Act 1855 for the liabilities imposed upon the merchant.[21] Apart from the statute, but probably under it also, the

---

[16] *Lloyds Bank Ltd.* v. *Bank of America N.T. and S.A.* [1938] 2 K.B. 147; see also *Mercantile Bank of India* v. *Central Bank of India* [1938] 1 A.C. 287.

[17] Sale of Goods Act 1979, s. 19(3).

[18] *Shepherd* v. *Harrison* (1871) L.R. 5 H.L. 116.

[19] *Leask* v. *Scott* (1877) L.R. 2 Q.B.D. 376.

[20] *Glyn, Mills & Co.* v. *East and West India Dock Co.* (1882) 7 App.Cas. 591.

[21] *North-Western Bank Ltd.* v. *Poynter, Son & Macdonalds* (1894) 21 R. 513; *Sewell* v. *Burdick* (1884) 10 App.Cas. 74.

holder and indorsee of a bill of lading, whether he holds it merely by way of security or not, who applies for and takes delivery of the goods, renders himself liable to fulfil the obligations imposed on the merchant in the bill of lading.[22]

Aircraft

The Civil Aviation Act 1968 made provision for the mortgaging of aircraft and the Mortgaging of Aircraft Order 1972[23] was made in terms of section 16 of the Act. An aircraft registered in the United Kingdom together with any store of spare parts for that aircraft may be made security for a loan or other valuable consideration (Art. 3). Such a mortgage may be registered in the Register of Aircraft Mortgages kept by the Civil Aviation Authority (Art. 4). If the mortgage has been granted by an incorporated company registered in Scotland the charge should also be registered with the Registrar of Companies (Companies Act 1985, s. 396). A notice of intention to enter a mortgage, referred to as a priority notice, may also be entered in the register (Art. 5). A mortgage of an aircraft entered in the register has priority over any other mortgage of or charge on that aircraft apart from another mortgage entered in the register (Art. 14(1)). Where two or more mortgages of an aircraft are entered, these mortgages shall as between themselves have priority according to the times at which they were respectively entered in the register (Art. 14(2)) but where a priority notice has been entered and the contemplated mortgage is made and entered in the register within 14 days thereafter, that mortgage shall be deemed to have priority from the time when the priority notice was registered (Art. 14(2)(ii)). A registered mortgage however does not have any priority over any possessory lien in respect of work done on the aircraft (Art. 14(5)).

Article 19 of the Order provides that the provisions of Schedule 2 to the Order shall have effect for the purpose of its application to Scotland. As applied to Scotland, an aircraft mortgage is a security created in Scotland under Article 3 of the Order and requires to be constituted by a mortgage in the form specified in Part II of Schedule 2 (para. 2). It is thought that the words "a security created in Scotland" refer to the place of execution of the mortgage deed rather than the place where the aircraft is at the time of execution of the mortgage. A mortgage once registered under the Order has effect without any requirement that delivery of the aircraft be made to the mortgagee (para. 3).

Default

Where there has been default within the terms of para. 8 of Schedule 2 the mortgagee may sell the mortgaged aircraft but before doing so must give not less than 60 days' notice in writing to the mortgagor, the owner

---

[22] *Brandt* v. *Liverpool, Brazil and River Plate S.N. Co. Ltd.* [1924] 1 K.B. 575.
[23] S.I. 1972 No. 1268.

and every other registered mortgagee (para. 9(*a*)). On the expiry of the period of notice, which may be dispensed with or shortened by consent, the mortgagee may sell the aircraft provided he obtains the consent in writing of every other registered mortgagee (para. 9(*b*)). If such consent is not forthcoming the mortgagee may apply to the Court of Session for a warrant to sell the aircraft (para. 9(*c*)). In terms of para. 10, moneys received by a mortgagee from a sale have to be held by him in trust to be applied in making payments, in the following order of priority, of (1) his expenses; (2) the amount due under any prior mortgage; (3) the amount due under his own mortgage and any other mortgage ranking *pari passu* with it; (4) the amount due under any postponed mortgage; and (5) the amount due under any other mortgage where the holder has lodged with the mortgagee a claim in writing countersigned by the mortgagor. Any residue of the moneys has to be paid to the owner of the aircraft. Alternatively, where default has occurred the mortgagee may apply to the Court of Session for a warrant for possession of the aircraft (para. 11(1)). Subject to any conditions imposed by the court a warrant for possession empowers the applicant to enter into any premises and remove the aircraft from them (para. 11(3)). Once in possession, the mortgagee may manage the aircraft and receive all income accruing from its operations. Additionally, he can pay insurance premiums and generally meet the expenses of its management including the cost of repairs and replacement parts (para. 11(3)). A mortgagee in possession may at any time sell the mortgaged aircraft after giving not less than 30 days' notice in writing of his intention to do so to the mortgagor, the owner and every other registered mortgagee (para. 11(4)).

Form of security
The most comprehensive and effective form of security for a bank to take in relation to an aircraft is, in the case of a company incorporated under the Companies Acts, (1) a first fixed charge expressed as a charge on the aircraft and its engines and on all accessories, appliances and equipment at any time attached to or installed on the aircraft and its engines; (2) a first fixed charge on specific engines identified by make and serial number; and (3) a floating charge over (a) the stock of spare or replacement engines, accessories, parts or equipment of any kind which is sufficient for the use and maintenance of the aircraft, (b) all other spare or replacement parts which relate to or may be used in the aircraft and the engines and (c) any other engines belonging to the company which relate to or may be used in the aircraft.

"Aircraft" is not defined in the Order but given its purpose any security will continue to operate so long as the aircraft, looked at as a whole, remains identifiably the same despite alteration of its parts or constituents. However, difficulties may arise if an engine which is the unencumbered property of the mortgagor is substituted for an engine which was in the aircraft at the time of granting the security. The substitute engine will fall under the security while the removed engine (unless specifically charged) will cease to be subject to it. Again, if the mortgagor were to instal an engine which was not his property the mortgagee would acquire no rights in respect of that engine on the basis that the engine can be separated from the airframe without material damage and that there is no effective way of constituting a security in Scotland over such an engine taken by itself without delivery to the mortgagee.[24]

---

[24] *Cf.* Bell, *Prin.*, § 1279 and Ersk., II, i, 17. There is no new species and no change in property rights.

CHAPTER 13

CHAPTER 13

PERSONAL SECURITIES

Cautionary obligations

Cautionary obligations are of two kinds, proper and improper. In proper cautionary obligations, *e.g.* by way of a guarantee, there must be three parties—the principal debtor or obligant, the cautioner or surety, and the creditor—the obligation of the cautioner being expressly recognised as such on the face of the deed. In an improper cautionary obligation the cautioner is taken bound as co-obligant and debtor with the principal debtor, his rights as cautioner being renounced *quoad* the creditor but reserved *quoad* the principal debtor.

Nature and essentials

The obligation or engagement of a cautioner is a collateral one, meaning that in the event of the principal on whose behalf the obligation is undertaken failing to pay a debt or perform an act for which he is or may become liable, the cautioner will pay the debt or fulfil the obligation as the case may be. An undertaking, given not to the creditor but to the debtor in a contract, to keep him, *i.e.* the debtor, indemnified against any liability arising out of the contract, is not a cautionary obligation but a contract of indemnity. It is of the essence of a cautionary obligation that there should be someone, independent of the cautioner, primarily bound for payment of the debt or performance of the obligation and there can be no contract of caution if the principal obligation is in law a nullity. However, in obligations undertaken by a minor without the consent of his curator, while the primary obligation may not be enforceable against the minor as the principal obligant, the obligation may still be enforceable against the cautioner.[1] In England, there may be circumstances in which a guarantor for a minor may be liable for a loan to him on the basis that the cautioner's obligation falls to be treated as one of indemnity and the cautioner himself as a principal.[2]

Subject to the above qualification, a cautioner in Scotland has a right to avail himself of any defence in bar or reduction of payment competent to the principal debtor; and although *ex facie* of his obligation he may be bound for a larger sum, he cannot be compelled to pay more than is due by the principal debtor.[3] When the principal obligation comes to an end,

---

[1] See Bell, *Prin.*, § 251.
[2] *Wauthier* v. *Wilson* (1912) 28 T.L.R. 239. See, however, *Coutts & Co.* v. *Browne-Lecky and Others* [1946] 2 All E.R. 207.
[3] *Jackson* v. *McIver* (1875) 2 R. 882; see also *Duncan, Fox & Co.* v. *N. & S. Wales Bank* (1880) L.R. 6 App. Cas. 1

the liability of the cautioner automatically ceases.[4] A cautionary obligation may be nullified by the grantor being under a misapprehension as to the nature of the document signed by him. In *Carlisle and Cumberland Banking Co.* v. *Bragg*[5] a form of guarantee was entrusted by a bank to its customer who induced a party to sign it on the representation that the document was an insurance paper. The court held that there was a fundamental mistake on the part of the guarantor and that the guarantee was void. Again, a cautioner cannot be subjected to a liability greater than that to which he had previously agreed although it may be more strict.[6]

Constitution

The Mercantile Law Amendment (Scotland) Act 1856, section 6 provides that "from and after the passing of this Act all guarantees, securities, or cautionary obligations, made or granted by any person for any other person, and all representations and assurances as to the character, conduct, credit, ability, trade, or dealings of any person, made or granted to the effect, or for the purpose, of enabling such person to obtain credit, money, goods, or postponement of payment of debt or of any other obligation demandable from him, shall be in writing, and shall be subscribed by the person undertaking such guarantee, security or cautionary obligation, or making such representations and assurances, or by some person duly authorised by him or them, otherwise the same shall have no effect." Under these provisions it is immaterial that the person making the representations has in view some ulterior and improper purpose beyond inducing the party to whom they were made to give credit or money to a third party.[7] Every cautionary obligation must therefore be in writing and with the exception of those *in re mercatoria*, or those which although improbative have been perfected *rei interventu*,[8] must be holograph of the grantor or authenticated by witnesses. Cautionary obligations are strictly construed, and nothing is to be inferred which the terms of the obligations do not warrant. An offer of a guarantee in writing importing an understanding that such a guarantee would be given when required is a valid cautionary obligation, as is one offered contingently on the acceptance of an offer which is duly accepted on the strength of the offered guarantee.[9] A letter of comfort is not a guarantee.[10]

Misrepresentation

In entering into a cautionary obligation, good faith between a bank and

---

[4] *Commercial Bank of Tasmania* v. *Jones* [1893] A.C. 313 at p. 316; *Aitken's Trs.* v. *Bank of Scotland*, 1945 S.L.T. 84.
[5] [1911] 1 K.B. 489. But see also *The Royal Bank of Scotland plc* v. *Purvis*, 1990 S.L.T. 262.
[6] *Wylie & Lochhead* v. *Hornsby* (1889) 16 R. 907.
[7] *Clydesdale Bank Ltd.* v. *Paton* (1896) 23 R. (H.L.) 22 at p. 27.
[8] *Church of England Life Assurance Co.* v. *Wink* (1857) 19 D. 1079.
[9] *Wallace* v. *Gibson* (1895) 22 R. (H.L.) 56.
[10] *Kleinwort Benson Ltd.* v. *Malaysia Mining Corp. Bhd.* [1989] 1 All E.R. 785.

the proposed guarantor is necessary but a contract of guarantee is not a contract *uberrimae fidei* imposing the universal obligation to disclose which is present in contracts of insurance.[11] A bank is under no obligation to disclose voluntarily the affairs of its customer or the state of his account, it being the duty of the cautioner to make, through the customer, such inquiries as he considers necessary so as to inform himself regarding the various matters material to the obligation he is about to undertake.[12] It has been held, however, that disclosure would be a duty where what had taken place between the bank and the principal debtor was not naturally to be expected.[13] Again, it is not the bank's duty to explain to the cautioner the nature and effect of the document which he is to sign but if the banker takes it on himself to do so, he is under an obligation not to misstate the position.[14] It has been decided in England that if the proposed guarantor is also a customer of the bank and relies on its manager for advice about the transaction, this confidential relationship imposes on the bank a duty of fiduciary care, *i.e.* a duty to ensure that the guarantor has formed an independent and informed judgment on the proposed transaction before he commits himself. In some circumstances it may be the bank's duty to advise the guarantor to obtain independent advice.[15]

Mere silence on the part of the banker will not be regarded as a degree of concealment sufficient to afford grounds for the reduction of the deed.[16] On the other hand, a creditor may become bound to inquire and inform the cautioner of circumstances in the principal debtor's conduct such as may reasonably create a suspicion of fraud, for wilful ignorance is equivalent to knowledge.[17] If a bank chooses to disclose anything it must disclose the whole state of affairs between it and its customer, so far as material to the obligation about to be undertaken, and the court will protect a cautioner in the event of misrepresentation or undue concealment.[18] Subsequent knowledge gained by the creditor of matters materially affecting the cautioner and increasing his risk need not be communicated if the guarantee was valid at its inception.[19]

Since parole proof is generally incompetent to explain the terms of an executed deed, care should in every case be taken to see that any correspondence which passes between the bank and the cautioner or the customer does not qualify the terms of the written obligation. Where it

---

[11] Gloag and Irvine, *Rights in Security*, p. 706.

[12] *Young* v. *Clydesdale Bank Ltd.* (1889) 17 R. 231; *Royal Bank of Scotland Ltd.* v. *Greenshields*, 1914 S.C. 259; *Cooper* v. *National Provincial Bank* (1945) 62 T.L.R. 36.

[13] *Falconer* v. *North of Scotland Banking Co.* (1863) 1 M. 704; *Hamilton* v. *Watson* (1845) 4 Bell 67; cited with approval in *London General Omnibus Co. Ltd.* v. *Holloway* [1912] 2 K.B. 72 and *Lloyd's Bank Ltd.* v. *Harrison* (1925) 4 *Legal Decisions Affecting Bankers* 12.

[14] *Cornish* v. *Midland Bank plc* [1985] 3 All E.R. 513.

[15] *Lloyd's Bank Ltd.* v. *Bundy* [1974] 3 All E.R. 757; but see *National Westminster Bank PLC* v. *Morgan* [1985] 2 W.L.R. 588, and *Midland Bank plc* v. *Shephard* [1988] 3 All E.R. 17.

[16] *Young* v. *Clydesdale Bank Ltd.*, *supra.*

[17] Bell, *Prin.*, § 251.

[18] *Mackenzie* v. *Royal Bank of Canada* [1934] A.C. 468.

[19] However, the cautioner's liability for subsequent advances might be affected. See *Bank of Scotland* v. *Morrison*, 1911 1 S.L.T. 153.

can be proved that the negotiations have been conducted in circumstances which demonstrated that the obligation was obtained from the cautioner other than in the ordinary course of business the cautioner may be able to repudiate liability. In *Falconer* v. *North of Scotland Banking Co.*[20] a cautioner was induced to sign a guarantee as a result of representations made by the bank that there would be an immediate advance of money to the debtor when in fact this was not to be the case. Rather, credit was to be allowed for what was already owing as part of an arrangement under which the bank had agreed to accept a composition on its debt. On the cautioner afterwards repudiating liability, the court decided that he had been induced to sign in ignorance of the true nature of the transaction and since the bank was responsible for the misrepresentation he was not liable. Unless the wording of a guarantee specifies it as a condition precedent to the guarantor's liability that the creditor obtain collateral security, the guarantee will not be invalidated by failure to obtain such security.[21]

Where a person signs a guarantee to a bank for behoof of another, his signature is presumed to have been adhibited at the request of the debtor rather than the bank. To entitle a cautioner to repudiate liability, it is not sufficient for him to prove that he was led to draw certain erroneous inferences from his conversations with the bank manager; he must show that misleading statements were unequivocally made to him.[22] In *North of Scotland Bank Ltd.* v. *Mackenzie*[23] an averment that a guarantor was induced to sign a guarantee by misrepresentations made outwith the presence of the bank's representative by the principal debtor "acting as agent for and in the interest of the bank" was held insufficient to justify a proof to support the plea that the guarantor signed the guarantee under essential error due to the fault of the bank. If the cautioner proposes to consult his legal adviser, and the creditor actively dissuades him from doing so, then very little more might be required to warrant reduction of the obligation.[24]

Liability of cautioner

An obligation by several cautioners will not import a joint and several liability unless such a liability is clearly expressed. Where cautioners are so bound the creditor may call on any one of them for payment of the full amount due, and the party so paying is entitled as against his co-cautioners to recover from them their rateable proportion of the amount paid.[25] In the event of one of the cautioners being bankrupt, the others are liable for his share. When the principal is unable to pay and one of the

---

[20] (1863) 1 M. 704. See also *Hamilton* v. *Watson* (1845) 4 Bell 67.
[21] *T.S.B. Ltd.* v. *Gray* [1988] 1 All E.R. 108.
[22] *Bank of Scotland* v. *Dunnet*, 10 May 1893 (unreported).
[23] 1925 S.L.T. 236.
[24] *Sutherland* v. *Low & Co. Ltd.* (1901) 38 S.L.R. 710.
[25] See p. 202.

cautioners is bankrupt, it is competent for the creditor to rank on and recover a dividend from the bankrupt's estate on the full amount of his claim, whereas if a solvent cautioner is called on to pay and he does so in full, he can rank on the estate of the bankrupt cautioner only for his share of the amount which he has paid.[26] Where the creditor ranks on the estate of a bankrupt cautioner for the full amount of his debt, so long as the dividend received by him does not exceed the share which in ordinary course would fall to be paid by the bankrupt, the co-cautioners cannot be asked by the trustee to repay any part of the dividend received by the creditor on his claim as lodged.[27]

Firm as cautioner or co-obligant

A partner of a firm cannot bind the firm by signing the firm's name to an obligation such as is contained in a bond of caution or guarantee unless it can be shown that the granting of such an obligation is necessary and incidental to the conduct of the firm's business or provided for in the contract of co-partnery.[28] To render a firm liable for obligations outwith the scope of the partnership business, the signature of the firm must be adhibited to the contract or obligation by one of the partners along with the signatures of each individual partner. In obligations where a firm and partners are taken bound it is usual to add the obligation of the partners as individuals over and above their obligation as partners.[29] The dissolution of the firm terminates its existence as a separate legal entity and its liability as a cautioner for any future obligations. As the release of one cautioner without the consent of the other cautioners also frees them, the dissolution of the firm operates to free the partners unless the obligation specially provides that the liability of the individual partners is not to be affected by a dissolution of the firm. Where the obligation contains no such provision, the course to follow on the dissolution of a partnership is either to get the surviving or remaining partners of the firm to agree in writing to the continuance of the obligation or to have a new guarantee executed. Where a new partner is assumed into a firm, he is in a different position since he cannot be held liable under a deed to which he was not a party without express provision to that effect in the contract of co-partnery, or the adoption by the new firm of which he is a member of the liability under the old obligation.

Where the obligation is granted for behoof of a firm and a change takes place in its constitution as the result of the death or retiral of one or more of the partners or by the assumption of a new partner, the obligation of the cautioners is, in the absence of agreement to the contrary, cancelled as to future obligations. Where, however, as is usual, express provision is made for the obligation of the cautioners to continue and for them to

---

[26] Bell, *Comm.*, I, 371–372.
[27] Bell, *Comm.*, I, 373.
[28] *Fortune* v. *Young*, 1918 S.C. 1. See also Partnership Act 1890, s. 7.
[29] *Hamilton & Co.* v. *Freeth* (1889) 16 R. 102.

remain bound notwithstanding any change in the constitution of the firm, the agreement will receive effect and bind the cautioners for subsequent advances and obligations. It may however be preferable to take a fresh guarantee, particularly if there has been a change of name of the firm.

Commencement of obligation

No transactions in reliance on a cautionary obligation should be permitted until all the parties to it have signed and it has been delivered to the creditor as a completed deed. In one case a charge against a co-obligant under a cash credit bond was suspended on the ground that while the bond bore to be granted by four parties it was signed by only three of them.[30] Care should also be taken to see that all the obligants are alive at the date of delivery of the deed, since it has been held that if one of the parties should die before delivery, his executors are not responsible for any sum advanced, the implied mandate to deliver the deed having fallen with his death.[31] The result in such a situation would be that the surviving obligants, other than the principal debtor, would also be freed from the obligation. It is the duty of the creditor to see that the signatures of the cautioners are properly adhibited to the deed. If he does not do so and any one or more of the signatures should turn out to have been forged, the result would be to free not only the person whose signature was forged but also all the other cautioners.[32] The principal debtor would, of course, still remain bound.

Discharge of the cautioner

The creditor may stipulate that the relationship between them shall have incidents different from those of normal cautionary obligations and the cautioner may renounce in advance the usual equities and privileges of a cautioner.[33] In the absence of such a renunciation, generally if the creditor does anything which discharges the principal debtor or extinguishes his claim against him without the cautioner's consent, he thereby discharges the cautioner although it is competent for the creditor to agree with the principal debtor not to enforce his remedies against him and if he does so in a deed which at the same time reserves his rights against a cautioner, the cautioner is not discharged.[34] If the principal debtor discharges the debt by payment, the cautioner's obligation is extinguished. It must, however, be a valid payment and if a payment is accepted by a creditor in good faith but subsequently set aside as an unfair preference, and the money returned, this payment will not discharge a cautioner.[35] Again, to the general rule that a discharge of the principal

---

[30] *Paterson* v. *Bonar* (1844) 6 D. 987.
[31] *Life Association of Scotland* v. *Douglas* (1886) 13 R. 910.
[32] *Scottish Provincial Assurance Co.* v. *Pringle and Others* (1858) 20 D. 465; *James Graham & Co. (Timber) Ltd.* v. *Southgate-Sands and Others* [1985] 2 W.L.R. 1044.
[33] *Bank of Scotland* v. *MacLeod*, 1986 S.LT. 504.
[34] *Murray* v. *Lee* (1882) 9 R. 1040; see also *Muir* v. *Crawford* (1875) 2 R. (H.L.) 148.
[35] *Petty* v. *Cooke* (1871) L.R. 6 Q.B. 790; *cf. Roy's Trs.* v. *Stalker* (1850) 12 D. 722.

debtor frees the cautioner, an exception is made in the case of sequestration. Section 60 of the Bankruptcy (Scotland) Act 1985 provides that where a creditor has a co-obligant bound to him along with the debtor, the co-obligant is not freed or discharged by reason of the discharge of the debtor or by virtue of the creditor's voting or drawing a dividend, or assenting to or not opposing the debtor's discharge, or any composition (s. 60(1)). Where the creditor lodges a claim in the sequestration and a co-obligant of the debtor holds a security over any part of the debtor's estate, the co-obligant has to account to the permanent trustee so as to put the estate in the same position as it would have been in if the co-obligant had paid the creditor and himself claimed in the sequestration after deduction of the value of his security (s. 60(2)). A co-obligant who has paid the debtor's debt is entitled to obtain at his own expense from the creditor an assignation of it and thereafter to submit a claim in the sequestration, if otherwise legally entitled to do so (s. 60(3)). Except in the case of a sequestration, if the creditor agrees to accept a composition from his debtor in full discharge, as, for example, under a trust deed or offer of settlement, without the cautioner's consent, he thereby frees the cautioner. Before agreeing to any such arrangement, therefore, a creditor should first obtain the consent in writing of all the other parties bound for the debt. If this is not forthcoming he should add to his assent the following or similar words: "subject to the necessary consents being received", thus leaving him free to act as circumstances may dictate. If consent is refused and he desires to draw a dividend, then his receipt for the composition should expressly reserve in any discharge his rights against the other obligants, by the following or similar words: "without prejudice to my rights against A B and C D, which are hereby expressly reserved". This would, it is thought, enable him to recover payment of the balance from cautioners[36] but as a precaution any dividend or composition received should be credited to a suspense account until the position is clarified.

Discharge of co-cautioner

Section 9 of the Mercantile Law Amendment (Scotland) Act 1856 provides that where two or more parties become bound as cautioners for any debtor, any discharge granted by the creditor in such debt or obligation to any one of such cautioners without the consent of the other cautioners shall be deemed and taken to be a discharge granted to all the cautioners. Where a bank holds two or more guarantees from different persons, the one bearing no reference to the other, it is a question of circumstances whether the bank can competently release one of the guarantors without the consent of the others. The separate guarantors are not co-cautioners, there being no unity of obligation, but if one of the guarantors became bound in reliance on an agreement with the bank that he was a co-cautioner with other guarantors whose obligation was already

---

[36] *Smith* v. *Ogilvie* (1825) 1 W. & S. 315, affg. (1821) 1 S. 159.

held, or where the guarantees were granted at the same time and under some reciprocal arrangement, the bank could not release one of the guarantors without the consent of all the other guarantors otherwise all the guarantors would be discharged. To entitle a cautioner to claim his discharge in such circumstances, he must show an existing right to contribution from the cautioner so released which has been taken away, or injuriously affected, by the release.[37] Where a person enters into a bond as a cautioner for the performance by another of two separate and distinct obligations, a subsequent agreement made by the creditor without the cautioner's consent to vary one of the obligations, does not relieve the cautioner from his obligation as to the other.[38]

Essential alteration in position

Any essential alteration in the respective positions of the creditor and the principal debtor not assented to by the cautioner has the effect of freeing the cautioner. In *Bonar* v. *Macdonald*[39] three persons became cautioners for the conduct of a bank agent and in the bond the agent was taken bound to have no other business of any kind. The bank afterwards entered into an agreement with the agent whereby he became liable for one-fourth of the losses arising from discounts but this arrangement was not communicated to the cautioners. Losses having arisen from the misconduct of the bank agent, it was held that the cautioners were relieved by the mere fact of the agreement having been entered into. Similarly, in *Ellesmere Brewery Co.* v. *Cooper*[40] four persons, as cautioners for a principal debtor, executed a joint and several obligation in which the liability of two of them was limited to £50 each and that of the other two to £25 each. One of the two whose liability was limited to £50 signed it after the other three had executed the deed but added to his signature the words "£25 only". It was held that these words constituted a material alteration in the deed and that the first three cautioners, being unaware of the alteration, were discharged from their obligation; and further, that as the last signatory executed the deed only as a joint and several obligant, he also was not bound by it.

Giving time

An agreement on the part of the creditor with the principal debtor, without the cautioner's consent, to give time for the payment of the obligation has the same effect as the release of a cautioner by a change in the character of the obligation to which he has not assented. Mere forbearance on the part of the creditor to enforce payment from the principal debtor, or even an agreement not to sue him, provided the cautioner's right of recourse is not thereby impelled, will not have the

---

[37] *Morgan* v. *Smart* (1872) 10 M. 610; *Ward* v. *National Bank of New Zealand* (1883) 8 App. Cas. 755; *Union Bank of Scotland* v. *Taylor*, 1925 S.C. 835.
[38] *Harrison* v. *Seymour* (1866) L.R. 1 C.P. 518.
[39] (1850) 13 D. (H.L.) 37. See also *N. G. Napier Ltd.* v. *Crosbie*, 1964 S.L.T. 185.
[40] [1895] 1 Q.B. 75.

effect of freeing the cautioner. But if the creditor so ties his hands as to prevent him from enforcing his obligation at any time, should he wish to do so, the cautioner will be freed. Where a cautioner endeavoured to evade his obligation on the ground that the creditor had for two years delayed to enforce payment from the principal debtor, the court repelled his plea.[41] By taking bills of exchange from the principal debtor instead of seeking payment of the sum due, the creditor may be held to have given time to the principal debtor and thus to have freed the cautioner.[42] If it can be shown, however, that the taking of a bill is usual in the particular trade in which the principal debtor is engaged, and to which the cautioner's obligation extends, he will remain bound.[43]

Where two or more persons primarily indebted as principals subsequently agree that, as between themselves, one shall be a cautioner only, this one thereby acquires the rights of a cautioner as against all parties with notice of the change but this rule may be modified by circumstances. In *Rouse* v. *Bradford Banking Co. Ltd.*[44] a partner retired from a firm under a deed of dissolution whereby he assigned his interest in the business to the remaining partners on an agreement that they should pay the partnership debts and indemnify him against them, with a proviso that so long as he was thus kept indemnified, he should not be entitled to insist on the debts being discharged. Among the debts of the firm was an overdraft to a bank for £50,000. After the dissolution, the terms of which were communicated to the bank, a transaction was entered into between the new firm and the bank whereby the firm was allowed for a limited period to increase the overdraft to £53,000. It was held that under these circumstances there was no agreement on the part of the bank to give time to the new firm or to alter the relations between the parties, since the bank had as much power to enforce payment of the £53,000 during the limited period as they had formerly to enforce payment of the £50,000.

Extreme neglect

A cautioner will also be freed by extreme neglect on the part of a creditor to enforce his rights against the principal obligant, provided the cautioner can show that his position has been prejudiced. While mere delay in continuing legal proceedings will not relieve the cautioner,[45] extreme neglect of such proceedings on the part of the creditor (especially if proceedings have already been begun against the estate of the principal), may in certain circumstances have this effect.[46] But mere inactivity on the part of a creditor is not sufficient to discharge the cautioner unless there be such a degree of negligence as to imply connivance or fraud. There must, over and above mere neglect, be some

---

[41] *Fleming* v. *Wilson* (1823) 2 S. 336.
[42] *Richardson* v. *Harvey* (1853) 15 D. 628.
[43] *Stewart, Moir & Muir* v. *Brown* (1871) 9 M. 763.
[44] [1894] A.C. 586.
[45] Bell, *Prin.*, § 263.
[46] *Smith* v. *Wright* (1829) 8 S. 124; *Macfarlan* v. *Anstruther* (1870) 9 M. 117.

positive action by the creditor to the prejudice of the cautioner, or the omission of an act which it was his duty to perform, resulting in injury to the cautioner.[47] Examples are the omission to complete or take advantage of a security,[48] or undue neglect in negotiating a bill,[49] or allowing a debt to prescribe.[50]

In an ordinary cautionary obligation for the payment of money the creditor is not bound to give intimation to the cautioner that the principal debtor has not paid the sum or instalments thereof when due and prestable. That is a matter on which the cautioner should inform himself. There may however be exceptions to this general rule. For example, if during the currency of a continuing cautionary obligation, circumstances come to the knowledge of the creditor which materially affect the risk undertaken by the cautioner and which, had they existed when the obligation was undertaken, would probably have deterred the cautioner from entering into it, the creditor might very well be bound to communicate these circumstances to the cautioner.[51] There is no authority, however, for the view that it is the duty of a bank, whenever it becomes aware of any circumstance seriously affecting the credit of a customer, to communicate at once with anyone who has committed himself as a cautioner for the customer's obligations. It might be otherwise however if the bank subsequently gave fresh accommodation and thereby increased the cautioner's liability.[52]

Relinquishment of security

Where a creditor, without the cautioner's consent, relinquishes any security held by him over the estate of the principal debtor and the cautioner is thereby prejudiced, the cautioner will be discharged[53] since a cautioner has the right, on payment of the principal debt, to an assignation of any security the creditor may hold for it.[54] However, this right only extends to security granted by the debtor or by co-cautioners.[55]

Prescription

In place of the Acts which regulated the various prescriptive periods, including the septennial prescription of cautionary obligations, the Prescription and Limitation (Scotland) Act 1973 substituted a new negative prescriptive period of five years. Section 6 enacts, in substance, that if an obligation to which it relates has subsisted for a continuous period of five years and in that time the creditor has not made a demand for payment and the debtor has not acknowledged the existence of the debt,

---

[47] *Clapperton, Paton & Co.* v. *Anderson* (1881) 8 R. 1004.
[48] *Fleming* v. *Thomson* (1826) 2 W. & S. 277, revg. (1825) 4 S. 244; *Storie* v. *Carnie* (1830) 8 S. 853.
[49] *National Bank of Scotland* v. *Robertson* (1836) 14 S. 402.
[50] See also *Murray* v. *Lee* (1882) 9 R. 1040.
[51] *Britannia Steamship Insurance Association Ltd.* v. *Duff*, 1909 S.C. 1261.
[52] *Bank of Scotland* v. *Morrison*, 1911 1 S.L.T. 153.
[53] *Sligo* v. *Menzies* (1840) 2 D. 1478; *Wright's Trs.* v. *Hamilton* (1835) 13 S. 380.
[54] Bell, *Prin.*, § 255; *Sligo* v. *Menzies* (1840) 2 D. 1478.
[55] *Thow's Tr.* v. *Young*, 1910 S.C. 588.

it is then extinguished. This new provision does not merely alter the onus and mode of proof but extinguishes the obligation entirely. A cautionary obligation is included among the obligations affected by the prescriptive period of five years under section 6[56] and the appropriate date for the *terminus a quo* the prescriptive period runs is "the date when the obligation became enforceable."[57] If demand is a condition precedent to the obligation becoming prestable the obligation is not enforceable until the demand has been made. In *The Royal Bank of Scotland Ltd.* v. *Brown and Others*[58] a guarantee was granted in favour of the bank in 1955. The company on whose behalf it had been granted went into liquidation in 1969 and the bank made a claim in the liquidation on 1 September 1969. The bank wrote to the guarantors' executors (the guarantors being dead) on 27 May 1974 demanding payment of the sum due under the guarantee and eventually raised an action for payment on 23 May 1979. The defenders submitted that the *terminus a quo* was 1 September 1969. It was held that the words "on demand" which appeared in the guarantee made demand a condition precedent to the obligation being enforced by the bank and that the obligation only became enforceable on the date when a written demand was made for payment. The appropriate date for calculating when prescription began to run was 27 May 1974 and as the action had been raised within five years of this date, the liability remained enforceable.

Guarantees

In terms of section 6 of the Mercantile Law Amendment (Scotland) Act 1856 a guarantee must be in writing and subscribed by the grantor. So far as guarantees relating to mercantile transactions are concerned, the only solemnities necessary in their execution are that they should be in writing and subscribed by the granter or by someone duly authorised by him.[59] The creditor in such a guarantee should be named but it is not necessary that the guarantee should be addressed to any person specifically, provided the creditor is indicated with reasonable certainty.[60] The provisions of the statute only apply to guarantees in or connected with mercantile transactions. It has not been decided whether a guarantee to a bank falls within this category but consideration of a series of decisions terminating in *Johnston* v. *Grant*[61] relating to documents alleged to be guarantees *in re mercatoria* indicates that, while an improbative guarantee to a bank for future advances followed by *rei interventus* will be held to be binding, there is no satisfactory authority for the view either that an improbative guarantee for past advances, which by its nature is incapable

---

[56] See Sched. 1, paras. 1(*g*) and 2(*c*) of the Act.
[57] s. 6(3) of the Act.
[58] 1983 S.L.T. 122.
[59] See *B.O.C.M. Silcock Ltd.* v. *Hunter*, 1976 S.L.T. 217.
[60] *Clapperton, Paton & Co.* v. *Anderson* (1881) 8 R. 1004.
[61] (1844) 6 D. 875.

of support by *rei interventus*, or that such a guarantee for future advances unsupported by evidence of *rei interventus*, would be held binding. To set up *rei interventus* it is not necessary to prove the guarantor's knowledge of what followed his subscription although proof of such knowledge might be important as throwing a light on the facts following the granting of the guarantee. The principle of *rei interventus* in such a case is that the person signing the document has given it to the creditor to be used in the way and for the purpose intended and that if others have acted on the faith of it, he is not entitled to plead defects in point of form against those whom he has encouraged to rely on his signature. The fact that money has been advanced on the faith of a guarantee constitutes sufficient *rei interventus* to render it binding on the grantors.[62] In *National Bank of Scotland* v. *Campbell*[63] the bank agreed to make advances to A on his obtaining B's guarantee and a formal letter of guarantee, ending with the words "in witness whereof", was prepared by the bank and handed to A for execution by B. A obtained B's signature and afterwards got two persons to sign as witnesses who had neither seen B sign nor heard him acknowledge his signature. A returned the document to the bank with particulars of signing, including the names and designations of the witnesses, and the testing clause was completed by the bank who then advanced money to A on the faith of the guarantee. In an action by the bank against B under the guarantee, B pleaded that he was not bound as the deed was not witnessed. The above facts were admitted or proved, but it was held that B having signed the deed and delivered it to A, who was in this particular matter the bank's agent, had delivered it to the bank itself and that the bank having made advances on the faith of it, any imperfection in the obligation had been purged by *rei interventus*. There is however sometimes difficulty in distinguishing between a guarantee which, to be probative, must be in writing and a primary obligation which is capable of proof by parole evidence. Thus, where a person undertook to see that an account was paid, it was held that this was a primary and substituted obligation in which the guarantor was in effect the principal obligant.[64] A letter of comfort is not a guarantee.[65]

Construction and interpretation

It is a general rule that the obligation undertaken by a guarantor is to be construed in the narrowest sense which the words used will reasonably bear, that is, *contra proferentem*.[66] Nothing will be presumed which the terms of a guarantee do not expressly warrant and any limitation that may be imposed will be rigidly interpreted.[67] A guarantee is restricted to the person or persons to whom it is addressed[68] and the document alone must

---

[62] *Church of England Life Assurance Co.* v. *Wink* (1857) 19 D. 1079.
[63] (1892) 19 R. 885.
[64] *Morrison* v. *Harkness* (1870) 9 M. 35. See also *Milne* v. *Kidd* (1869) 8 M. 250.
[65] *Kleinwort Benson Ltd.* v. *Malaysia Mining Corp. Bhd.* [1989] 1 All E.R. 785.
[66] Gloag, *Contract* (2nd ed.), pp. 400 and 401; *Aitken's Trs.* v. *Bank of Scotland*, 1944 S.C. 270.
[67] *Harmer* v. *Gibb*, 1911 S.C. 1341; *Veitch* v. *National Bank of Scotland*, 1907 S.C. 554.
[68] Bell, *Comm.*, I, 374; *Bowie* v. *Watson* (1840) 2 D. 1061; *Raines* v. *Alexander* (1842) 4 D. 1167.

be looked to for its terms. A separate agreement between the creditor and the principal debtor, unless it forms part of the obligation, cannot be looked to for the interpretation of the terms of the obligation.[69] Any limitation in regard to time,[70] or the number of transactions or operations to take place on the faith of the guarantee, will receive effect. Where the cautioner's undertaking covers only liabilities of the principal debtor contracted within a limited time, the expiry of the period without there having occurred any default on the part of the principal debtor extinguishes the liability of the cautioner. The creditor, if he wishes to keep the cautioner undischarged, must demand payment from the debtor at or before that date, provided he is entitled to do so.[71] A cautioner domiciled in another E.C. State may be sued in Scotland if the accounts of the debtor are maintained in Scotland, since in accordance with ordinary banking practice the accounts are regarded as localised at the branch where they are kept and that is where payment has to be made by the debtor.[72]

Continuing guarantees

A continuing guarantee is one which relates to a contemplated course of dealing in the future and not to any one particular transaction. The guarantor, if there is nothing to the contrary expressed in his obligation, is presumed to have granted it, not on the faith of any specific conditions but rather to have had in view the general usage of trade. Where a person guarantees payment of all goods which may be furnished to a trader, or all sums that may become due to a banker, he leaves it to the principal debtor and the creditor to arrange the details of their transactions so long as these are in conformity with the ordinary custom of merchants and bankers respectively.[73] If the guarantee bears that the transactions or operations intended to be secured are to be on current account, or implies that such is the plain intention of the parties, it will be construed as a permanent and continuing guarantee.[74] A guarantee is usually, although not invariably, for a definite sum and under it the guarantor is liable not only for one dealing but for successive dealings, up to the amount of the guarantee.[75] Any words implying that a guarantee is applicable not to a series of transactions nor to a continuous course of dealing but only against loss in one transaction or advance, will receive effect. In *Scott* v. *Mitchell*[76] a letter in the following terms: "As you have become security to the Clydesdale Bank for £150 on account of J W, I hereby guarantee you against any loss by your doing so", was construed as a guarantee against

---

[69] *Nicholson* v. *Burt* (1882) 10 R. 121.
[70] *McLagan & Co.* v. *McFarlan*, 19 November 1813, F.C.; *Douglas* v. *Gordon*, 24 December 1814, F.C.
[71] Gloag and Irvine, *Rights in Security*, p. 845.
[72] *Bank of Scotland* v. *Seitz*, 1990 S.L.T. 584.
[73] *Bank of Scotland* v. *MacLeod*, 1988 S.L.T. 504.
[74] *Caledonian Banking Co.* v. *Kennedy's Trs.* (1870) 8 M. 862.
[75] *Ibid.*; *Stewart, Moir & Muir* v. *Brown* (1871) 9 M. 763.
[76] (1866) 4 M. 551. See also *Rennie* v. *Smith's Trs.* (1866) 4 M. 669.

loss on one advance of £150 and not as a continuing guarantee in security of advances on a fluctuating account. However, a letter guaranteeing an overdraft on a current account has been decided to be a continuing guarantee.[77]

Although a cautioner's power to withdraw from a guarantee depends on the terms of the guarantee in each case,[78] where his obligation is for a fixed period he cannot withdraw prior to the expiry of that period without meeting his obligation to the creditor.[79] In the case of a continuing guarantee the obligation of a cautioner remains prestable until recalled. In the absence of express provision[80] a continuing guarantee is revoked as to subsequent advances by notice of the death of the guarantor.[81] In all cases, however, no matter what the terms of the guarantee may be, if it is intended to hold the estate of a deceased guarantor liable for any sum due at the date of his death, a bank on receiving notice of the death should stop operations on the guaranteed account[82] and intimate the obligation to the representatives or their agents. Similarly, when a cautioner intimates his withdrawal from the obligation undertaken by him the account should be stopped. If payments-in continue to be made in either case, the rule in *Clayton's Case* will apply to the effect that these will reduce *pro tanto* the debt secured under the guarantee. In *Buchanan* v. *Main*[83] where five persons guaranteed the account of a limited company, two of the guarantors subsequently intimated to the bank their desire to withdraw from the guarantee. The bank then stopped the account, which was considerably overdrawn. Immediately thereafter the directors of the company made a call on the shareholders, payable at the bank, for the unpaid amount of their shares. The sums so received were placed to the credit of an account called "No. II call account", and this account was always kept in credit. Subsequently a third account was opened, upon which the ordinary operations of the company took place. On the company going into liquidation, a question was raised as to the amount due by the guarantors, who claimed that the call made upon the shares should have been applied to reduce the balance due on the guaranteed account, but it was held that the bank were not bound to apply the call money in extinction of the debtor balance due on the guaranteed account.

Discussion

Prior to the passing of the Mercantile Law Amendment (Scotland) Act 1856 it was necessary, before proceeding against a cautioner in a proper cautionary obligation, to discuss the principal debtor; that is, to take action against him for recovery of the amount due and follow it up with

[77] *Sir W. Forbes & Co.* v. *Dundas* (1830) 8 S. 865; see also *Houston's Exrs.* v. *Speirs* (1834) 12 S. 879.
[78] *Roughead* v. *White*, 1913 S.C. 162.
[79] Bell, *Prin.*, § 256; *Spence* v. *Brownlee* (1834) 13 S. 199.
[80] *Harris* v. *Fawcett* (1873) 8 Ch. App. 866; *Lloyds* v. *Harper* (1880) 16 Ch.D. 290.
[81] *Coulthart* v. *Clementson* (1879) 5 Q.B.D. 42.
[82] *London and County Banking Co.* v. *Terry* (1884) 25 Ch.D. 692.
[83] (1900) 3 F. 215; see also *Doig* v. *Lawrie* (1903) 5 F. 295.

legal diligence. It is no longer necessary to do so, and by virtue of section 8 of the Act a creditor may now proceed directly against the cautioner without having first constituted his debt against the principal obligant as soon as there has been default by him, such as non-payment following a demand for payment of a debt payable on demand or expiry of the date fixed for payment without payment being made.[84] Alternatively, he may, if he choose, include in the same action both the principal debtor and the cautioner, provided no stipulation is contained in the obligation that the principal debtor shall first be discussed before the cautioner is called on. It has, however, been decided that when a number of persons are alleged to be bound jointly and severally, no one of them can be separately sued for payment or performance of the whole debt or obligation till the debt or obligation has been constituted by writing or by decree; in other words, where the debt or obligation has not been so constituted, all of the co-obligants subject to the jurisdiction of the Scottish courts must be called in any action to enforce payment or performance.[85] Payment of the amount due may be made or performance of the obligation implemented by anyone and unless the creditor can give a satisfactory reason for his refusal he may not object to fulfilment by a stranger. A stranger so paying is entitled to an assignation of the debt, and of any security specially held therefor.[86] Where the obligation is one *ad factum praestandum, i.e.* for performance, the provisions of the 1856 Act do not apply and in such obligations it is still necessary to discuss the principal obligant before calling on the cautioner.

Effect of ultimate loss clause

In the form of guarantee taken by a bank provision is invariably made to allow the bank to exhaust the estate of the principal debtor, including any security pledged by him, and still call on the cautioners up to the full amount of their liability. This "ultimate loss" clause means that in the event of the bankruptcy of the borrower the bank may rank on his estate for the whole sum due, less the value of any security pledged by him, and after drawing a dividend or dividends from his estate, call on the cautioners to make good any deficiency up to the amount of their guarantee and interest thereon.[87] As there can be no double ranking on the same estate, the effect of this is to preclude the guarantors from participating in any benefits under the sequestration.[88] The legal principle on which this rule is based is that the guarantor guarantees the whole debt with the proviso that his liability is limited to a certain specified sum.[89] In addition, the guarantee usually provides that interest is exigible from the guarantor

---

[84] *Morrison* v. *Harkness* (1870) 9 M. 35; *Johannesburg Municipal Council* v. *Stewart & Co. Ltd.*, 1909 2 S.L.T. 313.

[85] *Neilson* v. *Wilson* (1890) 17 R. 608.

[86] *Rainnie* v. *Milne* (1822) 1 S. 377.

[87] *Ex p. National Provincial Bank of England Ltd.* [1896] 2 Q.B. 12; see also *Logan's Sequestration* (1908) 25 S.L.R. 160.

[88] See p. 242.

[89] *Houston's Exrs.* v. *Speirs* (1835) 13 S. 945; *Harvie's Trs.* v. *Bank of Scotland* (1885) 12 R. 1141.

as from the date when it was last applied to the account of the principal
debtor prior to the demand made on the cautioner. As a rule, no further
interest will be applied to the account of the principal debtor after the
date of bankruptcy.

When a guarantor pays up the amount of his guarantee before the
sequestration of the principal debtor, he is entitled to require from the
bank an assignation of the debt to the extent paid by him. He may then
rank on the principal debtor's estate in preference to the bank. In
Mackinnon's Trs. v. *Bank of Scotland*[90] a guarantor wishing to terminate
his liability paid to the bank the full amount for which he was liable. The
bank placed the money in a suspense account, wrote on the back of the
guarantee a receipt which contained a reservation of its rights to claim on
the estate of the principal debtor for the full amount of his indebtedness,
and delivered the guarantee to the guarantor. It was held that the fact that
the bank had written a reservation of its claim on the guarantee and that
the guarantor had obtained from the debtor the greater part of the money
with which he made the payment, did not prevent the trustee in the
sequestration of the debtor from rejecting the bank's claim to the extent
of the payment made by the guarantor. Any payment received from a
cautioner after the sequestration of the principal debtor should be credited to a suspense account to await the outcome of the sequestration after
which count and reckoning should be held by the bank with the cautioner
in respect of the sum paid by him.

Relief of cautioners

An important right which cautioners have is that of total relief against
the principal debtor for any sums paid by them under their obligations.[91]
This right of relief arises either on actual payment of the debt by the
cautioners, or on their being distressed for it by the creditor, or they may
at any time, unless there is an agreement to the contrary, insist upon
being relieved from their obligation.[92] Where they have actually paid the
debt, they are entitled to an assignation of it, and of any securities held
against it, to the effect of enabling them to take proceedings as though
they were the original creditors. Payment of part only of the debt confers
no right to demand an assignation, so that in the case of a cautioner who
has become bankrupt, payment of a dividend out of his estate to the
creditor on the whole debt confers on his trustee no right to call for an
assignation in his favour.[93] But where a cautioner undertakes payment of
sums periodically and has paid up all that was due at a particular time, he
is entitled to an assignation to the extent of the sums paid although his

---

[90] 1915 S.C. 411.
[91] The effectiveness of this right is limited in cases where an ultimate loss clause operates and the rule
against double ranking in bankruptcy comes into force. See *Bank of Scotland* v. *MacLeod*, 1986 S.L.T.
504.
[92] *Doig* v. *Lawrie* (1902) 5 F. 295.
[93] *Ewart* v. *Latta* (1865) 3 M. (H.L.) 36.

RELIEF OF CAUTIONERS

203

obligation may not have been wholly implemented.[94] When the cautioners are distressed for payment of the debt, they may at once insist on relief. Even before this, if the debtor is *vergens ad inopiam*, a court will, on equitable grounds,[95] sustain an action of relief although the cautioner's liability for the sum then due continues until settlement by the principal debtor or otherwise. If the principal obligant has assigned to the creditor certain securities, not given specially as against the debt for which the cautioners are responsible but held generally, and there are further sums due, the creditor will not be bound to assign such securities except on payment of his whole debt. Even then, the matter being one of equity, the creditor may refuse an assignation if it would conflict with some legitimate interest of his own.[96]

Relief of cautioners inter se

The principle on which the liability of cautioners *inter se* rests is that cautioners for the same principal and for the same engagement, even although bound by different instruments and for different amounts, have a common interest and a common burden; so that if one cautioner who is directly liable to the creditor pays such creditor, he can claim contribution from his co-cautioners whose obligation to the creditor he has discharged.[97] The rule applies only where the cautioners are bound jointly and severally, or substantially so even though in separate deeds.[98] Therefore, in a question among themselves, cautioners can always insist on mutual rateable relief,[99] but they are each bound to communicate the benefit of any deduction, as well as of any security over the estate of the principal debtor.[1] The right of relief among cautioners does not arise until one of them has paid more than his share.[2] Where one of the cautioners has paid up the whole debt due under the bond or guarantee he is entitled to an assignation thereof to the effect of enabling him to operate his right of relief against his co-cautioners and to the benefit of any securities granted to the creditor by his co-cautioners.[3] The measure of the cautioners' liability *inter se* was defined by the Court of Session in *Buchanan* v. *Main*[4] where five persons, jointly and severally, guaranteed payment of all sums for which a company might become liable to a bank. The company having gone into liquidation, the bank called on two of the cautioners to pay the balance due under the guarantee. They did so, and then brought an action against another of the guarantors for relief to the

---

[94] *Lowe* v. *Greig* (1825) 3 S. 543.
[95] *Kinloch* v. *McIntosh* (1822) 1 S. 491; *Spence* v. *Brownlee* (1834) 13 S. 199; *McPherson* v. *Wright* (1885) 12 R. 942.
[96] Bell, *Prin.*, § 557.
[97] *Ellesmere Brewery Co.* v. *Cooper* [1895] 1 Q.B. 75.
[98] *Morgan* v. *Smart* (1872) 10 M. 610.
[99] *Marshall & Co.* v. *Pennycook* (1908) 15 S.L.T. 96.
[1] *Steel* v. *Dixon* (1881) 17 Ch.D. 825; *Berridge* v. *Berridge* (1890) 44 Ch.D. 168.
[2] *Alston* v. *Denniston & Co.* (1828) 7 S. 112. See also *Davies* v. *Humphreys* (1840) 6 M. & W. 153; *Ex p. Snowdon* (1881) 17 Ch.D. 44.
[3] *Thow's Tr.* v. *Young*, 1910 S.C. 588.
[4] (1900) 3 F. 215.

extent of one-third of the sum they had paid. The pursuers averred, and led evidence to prove, that the two remaining guarantors were insolvent. The defender denied that the insolvency of either of the remaining guarantors had been proved, and pleaded that he was liable in relief only to the extent of a fifth of the sum paid by the pursuers; but the court held that whether the two remaining guarantors were insolvent or not, the pursuers were not bound to bear the whole risk of their insolvency and that the defender was liable in relief to the extent of one-third of the sum paid by the pursuers. The right of relief of cautioners *inter se* cannot be impaired or discharged by the creditor without discharging the co-cautioners.[5]

Pledge of a guarantee

Guarantees are not negotiable instruments and the hypothecation or pledge of the guarantee document itself creates no right or security over the funds or the guarantee in favour of the person in whose hands it is placed.[6] However, a written agreement amounting to a guarantee to pay a proportion of the loss arising out of the holding of an exhibition was held in one case to have been validly assigned to a bank.[7]

---

[5] Ersk., III, iii, 38; *Smith* v. *Ogilvie* (1825) 1 W. & S. 315, affg. (1821) 1 S. 159.
[6] *Robertson* v. *British Linen Bank* (1891) 18 R. 1225.
[7] *Lloyds Bank Ltd.* v. *Walker*, 1928 S.N. 7.

PART IV

DILIGENCE, INSOLVENCY AND BANKRUPTCY

"[A] notion that lending money to traders knowing them to be in dubious, tottering, or distressed circumstances, upon mortgages or liens, is fraudulent; and consequently the contract void in case a bankruptcy ensues, would throw all mercantile dealings into inextricable confusion" *Foxcroft* v. *Devonshire* (1760) 2 Burr. 931, *per* Lord Mansfield.

CHAPTER 14

DILIGENCE

The term "diligence" is here used to apply generally to the process of law by which the property, estate and effects of a debtor are attached for payment of debts due by him or in security of the payment of such debts.

Arrestment

Arrestment is the diligence used to attach money or moveable property (including an obligation to account) belonging or owed to the debtor in the hands of or under the control of a third party. Until completed by a furthcoming it is an inchoate or incomplete diligence. The party in whose hands an arrestment is lodged is called the arrestee, the person using the arrestment the arrester, and the party against whom the arrestment is used the common debtor. An arrestment in the hands of the debtor himself, or of his servant, or of anyone who is a mere custodier for him, or of his factor, is invalid.[1] Service of an arrestment on a bank should be made at its registered office or the schedule of arrestment should be delivered to an official at its head office. In all cases, notice by way of another schedule should be served on the branch where the account of the common debtor is kept to prevent money being paid away in ignorance of the arrestment. If an arrestment simply attempts to arrest a sum of money on deposit with a Scottish bank and the particular funds have been deposited furth of Scotland, the arrestment will fail since the debt cannot be recovered in Scotland.[2] But where the arrestment seeks to attach *inter alia* all debts, the debt which is attached is the obligation to account and to repay the deposit.[3] Where funds are arrested in the hands of trustees, the arrestment must be used in the hands of each person acting under the trust deed. Arrestments are preferable *inter se* according to their date of service,[4] the date of any decree of furthcoming being irrelevant for this purpose. The arrestee is entitled to exhibition of the warrant under which the arrestment is used but it is now sufficient if the messenger or sheriff officer has a duly certified copy of the summons or other writ in his hands at the time of service.[5]

---

[1] *Trowsdale's Trs.* v. *Forcett Ry. Co.* (1870) 9 M. 88.

[2] *J. Verrico & Co. Ltd.* v *Australian Mutual Provident Society*, 1972 S.L.T. (Sh.Ct.) 57.

[3] See *Rae* v. *Neilson* (1742) Mor. 716; and the opinion of Lord Kyllachy in *Dunn's Exr.* v. *The Canada Investment and Agency Co. Ltd.*, February 1898 (not reported) deciding that an arrestment in the hands of the officials at the head office of a Scottish bank was effectual to attach money at the bank's office in London.

[4] *Hertz* v. *Itzig* (1865) 3 M. 813.

[5] Rules of Court 1965, Rule 74(i).

Arrestment to found jurisdiction

Strictly speaking an arrestment *ad fundandam jurisdictionem* is a method of subjecting a foreigner to the jurisdiction of the Scottish courts in an action about to be raised against him rather than diligence. The arrestment proceeds on a warrant granted in either the sheriff court or Court of Session. The small size of the sum arrested is not an objection to the foundation of jurisdiction. In one case 46p was held enough.[6] The subject arrested must be one which can be arrested in execution and jurisdiction is not constituted by arresting plans and documents of no mercantile value in the hands of the common debtor's agent in Scotland.[7] The arrestment of a liability to account suffices unless it can be instantly verified that there is nothing due by the arrestee at the time of the arrestment.[8] In the case of an arrestment in the hands of a bank, a point for consideration is whether, after such an arrestment has been used, such a *nexus* has been placed on the money as to prevent the bank parting with it. It is now considered that there is no *nexus* over the subject arrested and a bank as arrestee is not interpelled from paying the money away to its customer.[9] It will be found in practice, however, that an arrestment to found jurisdiction is usually, if not invariably, followed by an arrestment on the dependence of an action, for the purpose of raising which the arrestment to found jurisdiction was used.

The use of this form of diligence is restricted by the Civil Jurisdiction and Judgments Act 1982. Where, as determined by the Act, the defender is domiciled in another contracting state and the subject-matter of the action is within the scope of the 1968 Convention (which covers all civil and commercial matters with some exceptions, which include insolvency proceedings) he cannot be made subject to the jurisdiction of the Scottish courts by means of an arrestment of property belonging to him in Scotland. Where he is domiciled in Scotland or any other part of the United Kingdom, arrestment can be used to found jurisdiction only where the action concerns the limited range of matters which are outwith the scope of the Convention and of Schedules 4 and 8 to the 1982 Act. If the action is outwith the scope of Schedule 8 and the defender is not domiciled in any contracting state, jurisdiction can be founded by the arrestment of moveable property belonging to him. In cases not covered by the Convention and Schedules 4 and 8 arrestment to found jurisdiction is always competent, provided the action is raised to obtain a decree for a sum of money.

Arrestment on the dependence of an action

Such an arrestment proceeds on a warrant to arrest contained in the summons or initial writ in the action. If the action is not served on the defender within 20 days after the date of the execution of the arrestment,

[6] *Ross* v. *Ross* (1878) 5 R. 1013; *Shaw* v. *Dow & Dobie* (1869) 7 M. 449.
[7] *Trowsdale's Trs.* v. *Forcett Ry. Co.* (1870) 9 M. 88.
[8] *Murray* v. *Wallace, Marrs & Co.*, 1914 S.C. 114.
[9] *Leggat Bros.* v. *Gray*, 1908 S.C. 67; *Fraser-Johnson Engineering Co.* v. *Jeffs*, 1920 S.C. 222.

or if the summons or petition is not called in court within 20 days thereafter, the arrestment fails.[10] By statute, it is not competent to arrest on the dependence of an action any earnings or pension.[11]

Arrestment in execution

This arrestment proceeds on an extract of a decree of any court; on a warrant endorsed on an extract from the Books of Council and Session of a duly recorded bond or obligation or on an extract registered protest of a bill of exchange or promissory note; or on a summary warrant for the recovery of local authority rates and community charges.

Where a creditor holds a liquid document of debt, such as a bond or bill not yet due, and can show that his debtor is *vergens ad inopiam* or *in meditatione fugae*, he may, on application to the court, obtain a warrant upon which arrestments can at once be used. It is essential to the granting of such a warrant that the creditor aver one or other of these facts.

The subjects of arrestment

These consist of the whole personal debts and moveables in the hands of a third party or of his servant, or of anyone who is a custodier for him, for which as debtor he is accountable to the common debtor. An "obligation to account" is what is attached by arrestment[12] and among the subjects liable to arrestment are a sum standing at the credit of a customer in bank on deposit receipt, current account or deposit account; a debtor's interest in a deceased's estate, provided his interest is to be paid to him in cash or other moveable subjects; assuming an obligation to account, a contingent debt, even if nothing turns out to be due by the arrestee to the common debtor[13]; the interest held by a debtor in an assurance policy payable at his death even if further premiums have to be paid before it falls due[14]; shares of a company registered in Scotland; the subject of a pending lawsuit; arrears of alimentary funds[15]; and ships. It appears that the diligence of arrestment may be used against the earnings of seamen other than fishermen to enforce payment of an ordinary debt.[16] Should a customer have pledged securities to a bank, an arrestment in the hands of the bank will attach any reversion thereon after allowing for the debt and interest at the date of serving the arrestment. In such a situation, any overdrawn current account should be stopped and another account opened for future transactions to avoid the adverse effect of the rule in *Clayton's Case*. It has been decided that an arrestment in the hands of a bank of funds belonging to A attaches money deposited in the name of

---

[10] Debtors (Scotland) Act 1838, s. 17; Sheriff Courts (Scotland) Act 1907, First Sched., Rule 112 (as amended by S.I. 1983 No. 747). For summary causes in the sheriff court, the period is 42 days: Act of Sederunt (Summary Cause Rules, Sheriff Court) 1976, Rule 47.

[11] Debtors (Scotland) Act 1987, s.46.

[12] Bell, *Comm.*, II, 63; *Agnew* v. *Norwest Construction Co.*, 1935 S.C. 771.

[13] *Boland* v. *White Cross Insurance Co. Ltd.*, 1926 S.C. 1066; *Park, Dobson & Co.* v. *Taylor*, 1929 S.C. 571.

[14] *Bankhardt's Trs.* v. *Scottish Amicable Society* (1871) 9 M. 443.

[15] *Muirhead* v. *Miller* (1877) 4 R. 1139.

[16] Debtors (Scotland) Act 1987, s. 73(3)(c) and Sched. 8.

"A in trust", the beneficiary not having been specified.[17] Similarly, it is considered that funds in an account designated, for example, "AB Client Account", are caught by an arrestment against AB.[18] If the account is in the name of "CD in trust for AB", the success of an arrestment against AB will depend on whether or not the trust established by the truster and common debtor (AB) is revocable or irrevocable. If the trust is in the latter category, it is impossible to arrest funds since someone other than the common debtor has an interest in the account. A common example is an account opened by a trustee under a trust deed for creditors. If the trust is revocable and exists solely for the purposes of the truster, the existence of the trust has to be disregarded and effect given to the arrestment.[19] If an arrestment is served on a bank after instructions have been accepted to transfer funds from the account of the common debtor to another customer's account at the same branch and the computer processes for doing so have been set in motion, it is considered that the funds are not caught by the arrestment.[20]

Subjects not liable to arrestment in execution include the reversion of heritable security granted to a bank; debts due on bills of exchange and the bills themselves[21]; goods or money specially appropriated; alimentary funds; the pay of serving members of the armed forces[22]; debts, the term of payment of which has not arrived or which are contingent, in the absence of a present obligation either to pay or to account, unless on the ground that the debtor is *vergens ad inopiam*[23]; and property left with a bank for safe custody where the bank has no right of lien.[24] The only diligences competent against earnings to enforce payment of an ordinary debt are an earnings arrestment and a conjoined arrestment order.[25]

Effect of arrestment

Except in the case of an arrestment to found jurisdiction, the purpose of arrestment, whether in security or in execution, is to attach such a sum in the hands of the arrestee as will pay the debt of the arrester—principal, interest and expenses. The sum attached by the arrestment and for which the arresting creditor may claim in competition with others, may be more than the sum mentioned in the schedule of arrestment if this is in the usual terms "£ more or less".[26] When funds are so arrested, the bank as arrestee has to be cautious about parting with any sum in excess of that specifically stated in the arrestment save on judicial authority or with the consent of

---

[17] *Union Bank of Scotland* v. *Mills* (1925) 42 S.L.R. 141.

[18] *Plunkett* v. *Barclays Bank Ltd.* [1936] 2 K.B. 107.

[19] *Rigby* v. *Fletcher* (1833) 11 S. 256; *Lindsay* v. *London and N.-W. Ry. Co.* (1860) 22 D. 571.

[20] *Momm* v. *Barclay's Bank International Ltd.* [1976] 3 All E.R. 588, distinguishing *Rekstin* v. *Severo Sibirsko etc. and Bank for Russian Trade Ltd.* [1933] 1 K.B. 47.

[21] Bell, *Comm.*, II, 68.

[22] Deductions may be made from the pay of members of the armed forces as provided for in the Armed Forces Act 1971, ss. 59 and 61.

[23] *Symington* v. *Symington* (1875) 3 R. 205; *Smith* v. *Cameron* (1879) 6 R. 1107.

[24] Graham Stewart, *Diligence*, pp. 107 to 109.

[25] Debtors (Scotland) Act 1987, s. 46(1)(*a*). See p. 212.

[26] Graham Stewart, *Diligence*, p. 134.

the arresting creditor, as the practical effect of these words is to prevent payment by the arrestee of whatever sums he holds. The common debtor's remedy is to apply for the arrestment to be loosed or restricted to a definite sum. If, however, the sum at credit exceeds substantially that in the arrestment a bank may be prepared, particularly if the customer is considered undoubted, to take the risk of holding as attached only sufficient to cover the arrestment plus an allowance for expenses, etc. In all cases where cheques are returned unpaid because of an arrestment these should be met in the order of their presentation if the funds attached or any part of them should later be freed from the arrestment. As a general rule, an arrestee does not owe a duty to the common debtor to invest funds attached by an arrestment.[27]

Loosing of an arrestment

An arrestment will be loosed by the court on caution being found that the funds will be made furthcoming to the arrester. Where the funds arrested are greater than the amount due to the arrester, the court will restrict the amount of the caution to be found; and where the arrestment can be shown to have been used oppressively, the court may recall it, without caution, and may even find the arrester liable in damages.[28]

Action of furthcoming

The *nexus* imposed by an arrestment does not of itself operate as a transfer of the money or other moveable property to the arrester nor does it entitle the bank, where an arrestment has been lodged in its hands, to pay over the funds arrested. To complete the right of the arrester and to make the arrestment effective, it is necessary for him either to raise an action of furthcoming citing both the arrestee and common debtor or to get from the common debtor a letter addressed to the arrestee consenting to the arrested funds, or sufficient of them to meet the arrester's claim, being paid over. Until an extract decree of furthcoming or such a letter is delivered to him, the arrestee cannot in safety part with the arrested subjects. It is the usual practice for a bank if it has any funds in its hands belonging or owing to the common debtor to disclose the amount of these to the arrester to enable a proper action of furthcoming to be raised. It should be noted that the bank's duty of confidentiality prevents it from disclosing details of its customer's affairs where the arrestment is on the dependence of an action since the customer's liability to the arrester has not been judicially determined.

The objects of an action of furthcoming involving a bank are (1) to ascertain the amount due by the bank to the common debtor, or, where other subjects, such as the reversionary right of the common debtor to an insurance policy or shares, have been attached, the present extent of these subjects; and (2) to have the bank as arrestee decerned to pay the

---

[27] *Glen Music Co. Ltd.* v. *Glasgow District Council*, 1983 S.L.T. (Sh.Ct.) 26.
[28] *Ritchie* v. *Maclachlan and Others* (1870) 8 M. 815.

attached funds or so much of them as will pay the common debtor's debt to the arrester, or, where other subjects have been arrested, to authorise a sale and payment out of the proceeds.[29] The bank does not require to enter an appearance in an action of furthcoming so long as the sum sued for is not in excess of the amount in its hands and, if that should not be the case, matters can usually be arranged by the pursuers' solicitor agreeing to restrict the claim. Delivery to the bank of an extract decree for payment protects the bank in paying over the arrested funds. Care should be taken to see that the summons of furthcoming asks for expenses only in the event of the bank entering an appearance. The expenses of the arrestment and the action of furthcoming may be recovered out of the subjects arrested.[30] Questions as to the validity of arrestments can only be tried in an action of furthcoming.[31] Accordingly, in such an action it is competent for the common debtor to prove that he is not the debtor of the arrester, in which case the action falls to be dismissed, and for the arrestee to prove (1) that he is not the debtor of the common debtor, (2) that he has a lien over the property arrested, (3) that the arrestment is informal or (4) that there are competing claims for the money. When there are competing claims, the proper course for the arrestee to adopt is to raise an action of multiplepoinding and allow the court to allocate the arrested subjects among the various claimants according to their respective rights and interests.

Prescription of arrestments

An arrestment in execution prescribes in three years from its date; arrestments on a future or contingent debt, or on the dependence of an action, prescribe in three years from the time the debt becomes due, the contingency is purified, or decree in the action is pronounced, unless during the said period of three years the arrestments are pursued and insisted on.[32] Arrestments may be renewed, but in any question of preference the date of the renewal, and not of the original arrestment, is the determining factor. Prescription may be interrupted by the arrester raising either an action of furthcoming or a multiplepoinding, or appearing in such a process raised by someone else within the prescriptive period.[33]

Diligence against earnings

Section 46 of the Debtors (Scotland) Act 1987 introduced a diligence known as an "earnings arrestment" to be used against the earnings of a

---

[29] *Lucas's Trs.* v. *Campbell* (1894) 21 R. 1096; see also *Stenhouse London* v. *Allwright*, 1972 S.C. 209.
[30] In the sheriff court, the position in ordinary causes is uncertain since the provisions of Rule 129 of the former Sheriff Court Rules are not found in the Rules as amended by S.I. 1983 No. 747. In summary causes, Rule 64 of the Act of Sederunt (Summary Cause Rules, Sheriff Court) 1976 applies.
[31] *Vincent* v. *Chalmers & Co.'s Tr.* (1877) 5 R. 43: *Barclay, Curle & Co. Ltd.* v. *Sir James Laing & Co. Ltd.*, 1908 S.C. 82.
[32] Debtors (Scotland) Act 1838, s. 22; *Jameson* v. *Sharp* (1887) 14 R. 64.
[33] *Jameson* v. *Sharp* (1887) 14 R. 64.

debtor in the hands of his employer to enforce the payment of an ordinary debt. The Act also made provision for an order to be known as a "conjoined arrestment order" to enforce the payment of two or more debts owed to different creditors against the same earnings. The effect of an earnings arrestment is to require the employer to deduct a sum calculated in accordance with section 49 of the Act from the debtor's net earnings and to pay the sum deducted to the creditor. The arrestment remains in effect until the debt has been paid, the debtor has ceased to be employed by the employer, or the arrestment has been recalled by the creditor (s. 47). For the purposes of the Act an "ordinary debt" means any debt other than current maintenance, and "earnings" means any sums payable to the debtor (a) as wages or salary or (b) as fees, bonuses, commission, etc., payable under a contract of service (s. 73). Generally speaking, a sum payable under a statutory pension scheme will not be treated as earnings (s. 73(3)). The debt recoverable by an earnings arrestment consists of (a) the debt and any expenses due under the decree or other document on which the arrestment proceeds; (b) any accrued interest on these sums; and (c) the expenses incurred in executing the earnings arrestment and the charge which preceded it. (An earnings arrestment is not competent unless a charge for payment has been served on the debtor and the period for payment specified in the charge has expired (s. 90(1)). Section 49 contains detailed provisions for calculating the sums to be deducted from net earnings by an employer following service of an earnings arrestment. While an earnings arrestment is in effect, another earnings arrestment against the earnings of the same debtor payable by the same employer is not competent (s. 59(1).

A creditor may apply to the sheriff for a conjoined arrestment order where there is an earnings arrestment already in effect and another creditor would be entitled, but for section 59 of the Act, to enforce his debt by executing an earnings arrestment (s. 60). The order, if made, has the effect of (a) recalling the existing earnings arrestment and (b) requiring the employer concerned to deduct a sum calculated in accordance with section 63 of the Act and to pay it as soon as reasonably practicable to the sheriff clerk (s. 60(3)). The amount recoverable under a conjoined arrestment order in respect of an ordinary debt consists of (a) the sum (including expenses) in the decree or other document; (b) any accrued interest on that sum; and (c) the expenses of any previous earnings arrestment and the charge which preceded it (s. 61). While a conjoined arrestment order is in effect it is not competent to execute any earnings arrestment or for the sheriff to grant any other conjoined arrestment order against the earnings of the same debtor payable by the same employer (s. 62). Sums paid to the sheriff clerk under section 60(3) are disbursed by him to the creditors whose debts are being enforced by the order in accordance with Schedule 3 to the Act (s. 64).

Poinding

Poinding is the ordinary diligence by which a creditor may attach, and thereafter sell for payment of his debt, moveable property belonging to and in the hands of the debtor. In general, any corporeal moveable property which is of commercial value may be poinded. The following items, no matter where they are situated, if reasonably required for use by the debtor or any member of his household are exempt from poinding—clothing; implements, tools of trade and books (whether for use in the practice of a profession or for training) but not exceeding in aggregate value £500; and medical aids and equipment. Toys and articles reasonably required for the care and upbringing of a child are also exempt. Similarly exempt, if they are at the time of the poinding in a dwelling-house and reasonably required for use therein, are a wide range of household goods including beds, household linen, furniture, food, lighting and heating appliances, curtains, floor coverings, cookers and cooking utensils, refrigerators and tools used for maintenance and repair.[34] It is also incompetent to poind horses or the implements used in husbandry during the season of agricultural labour if the debtor has other effects, although growing crops may be poinded.[35] It is also incompetent to poind goods of which the debtor is only joint owner[36] or in which he has only a qualified or temporary interest.[37] The fact that goods belonging to the debtor are in the creditor's possession does not prevent their being poinded.[38] The question has been raised, but not decided, whether bank notes or money in a person's pocket can be lawfully poinded.[39]

A poinding must be preceded by a charge for payment. Warrants to poind are contained in extract decrees of the Court of Session and sheriff court and deeds or protests registered in the Books of Council and Session, by virtue of which it is lawful on the expiry of the days of charge to poind the moveable effects of the debtor to an extent sufficient to cover the creditor's debt with interest and expenses. A summary warrant for the recovery of rates, community charge or taxes by poinding may also be obtained on application to the sheriff. The poinding must be reported within 14 days (or thereafter only on cause shown) to the sheriff, who grants warrant to sell the poinded articles by public auction at a specified time and place. A warrant sale cannot be held in a dwelling-house except with the consent of occupier (and the debtor if he is not the occupier). The manner of the publication of the sale is contained in the warrant and the sale must be carried out in terms of the Debtors (Scotland) Act 1987. A poinding is preferable to a prior arrestment.

---

[34] Debtors (Scotland) Act 1987, s. 16.
[35] *Elder* v. *Allen* (1833) 11 S. 902. See also Rankine, *Leases*, p. 705.
[36] *Fleming* v. *Twaddle* (1828) 7 S. 92.
[37] *Scott* v. *Pirie* (1837) 15 S. 916.
[38] *Lochhead* v. *Graham* (1883) 11 R. 201.
[39] *Alexander* v. *McLay* (1826) 4 S. 439.

Equalisation of diligence

Section 75(1)(*b*) of the Bankruptcy (Scotland) Act 1985 re-enacted certain provisions of the Bankruptcy (Scotland) Act 1913 repealed by that Act. Section 10 of the 1913 Act now appears as paragraph 24 in Part II of Schedule 7 to the 1985 Act. It provides that all arrestments and poindings which have been executed within 60 days prior to the constitution of the apparent insolvency of the debtor, or within four months thereafter, shall be ranked *pari passu* as if they had been executed on the same date. It does not apply in relation to an earnings arrestment.[40] Any arrestment which has been executed on the dependence of an action must be followed up without undue delay. Any creditor judicially producing in a process relative to the subject of such arrestment or poinding, such as a furthcoming or multiplepoinding, liquid grounds of debt, *i.e.* a probative writ, bond, bill or decree for payment, within the 60 days or four months referred to, is entitled to rank as if he had executed an arrestment or a poinding. Since sequestration is equivalent to an arrestment in execution and decree of furthcoming, an arrestment in execution and warrant of sale, and a completed poinding in favour of all creditors,[41] if sequestration occurs within 60 days before or four months after apparent insolvency, an arresting or poinding creditor within that period ranks *pari passu* with the other creditors.[42] In the event of the first or any subsequent arrester obtaining in the meantime a decree of furthcoming and recovering payment, or a poinding creditor carrying through a sale, he is accountable for the sum recovered to those who, by virtue of the foregoing provisions, are entitled to a *pari passu* ranking and he will be liable in an action at their instance for payment to them proportionately, after allowing out of the fund the expense of the diligence which he has used in such recovery.[43] Arrestments executed for attaching the same effects after the period of four months subsequent to the constitution of apparent insolvency do not compete with those within the previously mentioned periods prior or subsequent thereto, but may rank with each other on any reversion of the fund attached according to law and practice.

Poinding of the ground

This form of poinding is competent to a superior for his feu duties, to a heritable creditor, such as a creditor in a bond and disposition in security or in a standard security, and generally to all creditors in debts which constitute a real burden on land. The diligence is usually resorted to when, by miscalculation or emerging circumstances, the value of the heritable property is likely to prove inadequate to cover the heritable debt.[44] The theory on which a poinding of the ground proceeds is that the

---

[40] Debtors (Scotland) Act 1987, s. 67.
[41] Bankruptcy (Scotland) Act 1985, s. 37(1)(*b*).
[42] *Stewart* v. *Jarvie*, 1938 S.C. 309.
[43] *Gallacher* v. *Ballantine* (1876) 13 S.L.R. 496.
[44] See *Royal Bank of Scotland* v. *Bain* (1877) 4 R. 985.

creditor has a real right in the lands and by virtue of that right has a title to the moveables on the grounds as accessory thereto, so long as no alienation of them, voluntary or judicial, has taken place.[45]

In form, it is an action competent in either the Court of Session or sheriff court which contains no personal conclusion but only concludes for execution against moveables. The subjects attached by a poinding of the ground are all moveables situated on the ground at the date of service in the action and belonging to the proprietor of the lands.[46] He need not be the debtor if he is the proprietor of the lands over which the heritable security extends. Moveables belonging to tenants may be poinded in so far as the value does not exceed the rents due and unpaid,[47] but moveables belonging to a third party cannot be poinded, nor moveables that have been removed prior to the date of service in the action.[48] There is no equalisation of poindings on the ground of bankruptcy, as in ordinary poindings.

Inhibition

Inhibition has been defined as "a personal prohibition, prohibiting the party inhibited to contract any debt, or grant any deed by which any part of his lands may be alienated, or carried off, to the prejudice of the creditor inhibiting."[49] Inhibition may be used in security either of debts already due or of future debts. The diligence proceeds upon an extract decree or liquid document of debt, whether registered or unregistered, or upon the dependence of an action containing a conclusion for the payment of money alleged to be presently due, other than expenses.[50] Inhibition for a debt not yet due is competent only when the debtor is *vergens ad inopiam* and an averment to that effect is made.[51] If a notice is registered in the Register of Inhibitions and Adjudications before execution of the inhibition, and the inhibition and its execution are duly registered as aforesaid not later than 21 days after the date of the registration of the notice, such inhibition takes effect from the date when the notice was registered.[52]

When completed by registration, an inhibition strikes at all voluntary alienations of and all diligence done against the debtor's heritable estate for debts contracted subsequent (but not prior)[53] to the date of the inhibition.[54] An inhibition has no force or effect against any heritable property acquired by the person inhibited after the date of registration of the inhibition or of the previous notice, except such property as was at the

---

[45] *Thomson* v. *Scouler* (1882) 9 R. 430.
[46] *Urquhart* v. *Macleod's Tr.* (1883) 10 R. 991.
[47] *Brown* v. *Scott* (1859) 22 D. 273.
[48] *Lyons* v. *Anderson* (1880) 8 R. 24.
[49] Ersk., II, xi, 2.
[50] *Burns* v. *Burns* (1879) 7 R. 355.
[51] *Symington* v. *Symington* (1875) 3 R. 205.
[52] Titles to Land Consolidation Act 1868, s. 155.
[53] *Livingstone* v. *McFarlane* (1842) 5 D. 1.
[54] *Baird & Brown* v. *Stirrat's Tr.* (1872) 10 M. 414.

date of registration destined to the person inhibited by an indefeasible title.[55]

An inhibition strikes at any voluntary sale of heritable property. It has no effect on prior debt and where heritable security had been given for a cash credit bond before the inhibition was registered, advances made after it were not affected.[56] It similarly does not affect rights which are not due to any voluntary act of the debtor. Accordingly, it is no bar to the exercise of a power of sale conferred on a heritable creditor prior to the inhibition. But an inhibition subsequent in date to a bond and disposition in security will secure for the inhibitor a ranking on the free proceeds of sale preferential to that of ordinary creditors who have taken steps to secure their debts and also to that of other creditors who have sought to obtain a preference by, for example, arrestment, but whose preference postdates that of the inhibitor.[57] Similarly, a receiver appointed to a company which has granted a floating charge over its heritable property may take possession of and sell that property even although affected by an inhibition, provided the floating charge was granted prior to the date of registration of the inhibition.[58]

If the debtor is sequestrated, the act and warrant in favour of the trustee has the effect of an adjudication for the benefit of all creditors, including the inhibiting creditor.[59] In such cases the principle of ranking has been decided to be that as a first step all creditors should be ranked *pari passu* on the proceeds of the heritable estate; that the right to participate in that ranking of creditors whose debts were contracted anterior to the inhibition is not affected by the inhibition; and that the inhibitor is entitled, at the expense of the ranking awarded to posterior creditors, to the difference between an equal dividend to all and the dividend which he would have drawn had there been no debts contracted subsequent to the inhibition.[60] Accordingly, where a bank has lent money on current account to a customer who owns heritable property, the account should be stopped as soon as the bank learns of the inhibition to prevent the adverse effect of the rule in *Clayton's Case* which would result in an anterior debt being repaid by credits to the account and a posterior one created by further advances, since they would be regarded as debts contracted after the inhibition. If the debt is heritably secured by a standard security or by an *ex facie* absolute disposition, it is thought that the account should be stopped for the same reason, since the inhibiting creditor acquires a preferential claim over the debtor's reversionary right to the heritage.[61]

---

[55] Titles to Land Consolidation Act 1868, ss. 156 and 157; *Leeds Permanent Building Society* v. *Aitken, Malone & Mackay*, 1986 S.L.T. 338.

[56] *Campbell's Tr.* v. *De Lisle's Exrs.* (1870) 9 M. 252.

[57] *Bank of Scotland* v. *Lord Advocate and Others*, 1977 S.L.T. 24.

[58] Insolvency Act 1986, ss. 55, 60 and 61; *Armour and Mycroft, Petrs.*, 1983 S.L.T. 453.

[59] Bankruptcy (Scotland) Act 1985, s. 31(1)(b). See also Insolvency Act 1986, s. 185.

[60] Bell, *Comm.*, II, 408; *Baird & Brown* v. *Stirrat's Tr.* (1872) 10 M. 414; *Scottish Wagon Co.* v. *Hamilton* (1906) 13 S.L.T. 779.

[61] Graham Stewart, *Diligence*, p. 565.

The diligence of inhibition is personal to the party inhibited and strikes at him only. If he dies, his heir will not be affected by the inhibition unless it is renewed against him. The diligence confers no active right on the creditor using it and in order to obtain such a right he must follow up the inhibition with an adjudication. An inhibition followed by a decree of adjudication gives the inhibiting creditor an available preference over all the creditors whose debts were contracted subsequent to the registration of the inhibition. Creditors whose debts were incurred prior to the date of the inhibition are not prejudiced thereby, but if such creditors do not secure a *pari passu* ranking by adjudging within a year and a day of the inhibiting and adjudging creditor, the latter excludes them in virtue not of his inhibition but of his adjudication.

Inhibitions prescribe in five years and cannot be renewed to the effect of keeping them alive.[62]

Adjudication

Adjudication is the diligence by which land and other heritable subjects are attached in satisfaction of debt. The subjects which may be adjudged are any right to land, including not only feudal rights but all rights or interests affecting or connected with land, such as heritable bonds and real securities, and personal rights to land, stocks of any chartered body where the diligence of arrestment is excluded, and the like. In a competition between adjudgers, all adjudications prior to that first made effectual and all creditors who obtain a decree in an action of adjudication within a year and a day from the date of decree in the first effectual adjudication, rank *pari passu* with the first adjudger.[63] Sequestration is equivalent to a decree of adjudication of the heritable estates of the bankrupt and when the sequestration is dated within a year and a day of any effectual adjudication the estate is disposed of under the sequestration.[64] A winding-up order under the Companies Act 1985 has the same effect.[65] For these reasons, the adjudication procedure is now rarely resorted to by a creditor.[66]

Effect of sequestration on diligence

In terms of section 37 of the Bankruptcy (Scotland) Act 1985 sequestration, as from the date of the first deliverance, is equivalent to an arrestment in execution and decree of furthcoming, an arrestment in execution and warrant of sale, and a completed poinding in favour of the creditors (s. 37(1)(*b*)). No arrestment or poinding of the estate of the debtor executed within the period of 60 days before the date of sequestration and whether or not subsisting at that date, or on or after the date of

---

[62] Conveyancing (Scotland) Act 1924, s. 44(3).
[63] Diligence Act 1661, c. 62.
[64] Bankruptcy (Scotland) Act 1985, s. 37(1)(*a*).
[65] Companies Act 1985, s. 623(3).
[66] As to the meaning of "effectual" see Graham Stewart, *Diligence*, p. 638.

sequestration, is effectual to create a preference for the arrester or poinder. The estate so arrested or poinded, or the proceeds of sale, have to be handed over to the permanent trustee (s. 37(4)). An arrester or poinder who is deprived of the benefit of his diligence is entitled to payment, out of the arrested or poinded estate or the proceeds of sale, of the expenses incurred in obtaining the extract of the decree or other document on which the arrestment or poinding proceeded, in executing the arrestment or poinding, and in taking any further action in respect of the diligence (s. 37(5)). But while arrestments used within the 60 days are ineffectual to create a preference in favour of the arresting creditor, they are effectual to impose a *nexus* on the funds to the effect of prohibiting the arrestee from parting with them to the prejudice of the permanent trustee to whom they are transferred by the sequestration.[67]

Sequestration as from its date also has the effect of a decree of adjudication of the heritable estate of the debtor for payment of his debts which has been duly recorded in the Register of Inhibitions and Adjudications on that date in favour of the creditors (s. 37(1)(*a*)). No inhibition which takes effect within the period of 60 days before the date of sequestration is effectual to create a preference for the inhibitor and any right of challenge which would have vested in the inhibiting creditor vests at the date of sequestration in the permanent trustee as does any right of the inhibitor to seek payment for the discharge of the inhibition (s. 37(2)). However, the trustee is not entitled to receive any payment made to the inhibitor before the date of sequestration and section 37(2) does not affect the validity of anything done before that date in consideration of such a payment.

The section also provides that no poinding of the ground executed within the period of 60 days before the date of sequestration or on or after that date shall be effectual in a question with the permanent trustee, except for the interest on the debt of a secured creditor, being interest for the current half-yearly term and arrears of interest for one year immediately before the commencement of that term (s. 37(6)).

The foregoing provisions of section 37 apply to the estate of a deceased debtor if, within 12 months after his death, his estate has been sequestrated or it was absolutely insolvent at the date of death and a judicial factor has been appointed under section 11A of the Judicial Factors (Scotland) Act 1889 (s. 37(7)).

---

[67] *Mackenzie* v. *Campbell* (1894) 21 R. 904.

CHAPTER 15

INSOLVENCY

Insolvency

In the ordinary sense, this may be described as the condition of a person who is unable to pay his debts. In the law of bankruptcy, insolvency is looked at from two points of view. Practical insolvency consists in the present inability of a debtor to pay his debts as they fall due. In a question with the debtor himself, it is this state of insolvency which is considered and it is immaterial that if he were given time to realise his assets his estate would be adequate to meet all of his debts. Insolvency in the absolute sense signifies that a person's debts exceed his assets. In questions among creditors, there must in many cases be proof of absolute insolvency.[1] Insolvency, unlike bankruptcy, is not a status established by any public legal criterion but depends on the circumstances of each case. When a person becomes insolvent, he becomes in effect a trustee of his property for behoof of the general body of his creditors and any fraudulent alienation of his estate made to the prejudice of his creditors is reducible either at common law or under statute.[2] Further, a person who is insolvent, whether he is aware of it or not, is precluded as a general rule from parting with his assets to one particular creditor so as to give this creditor a preference over his other creditors. However, so long as he is not apparently insolvent—an expression introduced into the law of bankruptcy by section 7 of the Bankruptcy (Scotland) Act 1985 to describe those circumstances pointing to practical insolvency previously denoted by the term notour bankruptcy—it is not a breach of trust for an insolvent person who knows of his absolute insolvency to fulfil obligations which are due and prestable and the fact that the receiving creditor is aware of the insolvency is irrelevant.[3] The creditor's mere knowledge of the absolute or irretrievable insolvency of his debtor does not of itself demonstrate collusion. But cash payments, like other preferences, will, subject to certain exceptions, be set aside whenever the creditor not merely suspects that his debtor is insolvent but has definite knowledge that the debtor is immediately to become apparently insolvent and in that knowledge not only connives at but actively concerts with the debtor a plant for diverting to himself funds that truly belong to the general body of creditors.[4]

---

[1] Bell, *Comm.*, II, 152 to 154.
[2] At common law, a creditor can challenge such an alienation made by a limited company incorporated under statute: *Bank of Scotland, Petrs.*, 1988 S.L.T. 90.
[3] See *Nordic Travel Ltd.* v. *Scotprint Ltd.*, 1980 S.L.T. 189 and the authorities therein reviewed.
[4] *Jones' Tr.* v. *Jones* (1888) 15 R. 328.

Alienations reducible at common law

At common law, independently of such preferences as were struck at by the Bankruptcy Act 1621 (c. 18) and the Bankruptcy Act 1696 (c. 5)—now both repealed but with their respective purposes re-enacted in the Bankruptcy (Scotland) Act 1985—any preference granted by an insolvent debtor to a favoured creditor or any alienation by way of a gift[5] or a purchase at an exorbitant price[6] or the granting of any additional security or advantage whatever, by means of which the insolvent person prevented or defeated a fair division of his estate among his creditors, was reducible. Section 34 of the 1985 Act, which deals with gratuitous alienations, assumes the retention of the common law right to challenge such alienations at the instance of the debtor's creditors, posterior or anterior,[7] a permanent trustee, a trustee acting under a protected trust deed or a judicial factor (s. 34(7)). Cash payments are included among the alienations which may be challenged at common law.[8] The receiving creditor's fraud is not a necessary element in the challenge.[9] The fact that the debtor is himself aware of his own insolvency—which in this context means absolute insolvency—is necessary to reduce a transaction at common law.[10] Transactions in the ordinary course of business or in implement of prior obligations are not struck at. The alienation or preference sought to be reduced must be voluntary and to the prejudice of the insolvent debtor's creditors.[11]

Alienations reducible by statute

At common law, the onus of proof that the transaction was gratuitous and the debtor insolvent rests on the challenger. As such proof may be difficult, the reduction of gratuitous deeds will usually be based on section 34 of the 1985 Act. This applies to an alienation by a debtor whereby any of the debtor's property has been transferred to or any claim or right of the debtor has been discharged or renounced. The Bankruptcy Act 1621 was held to apply to all deeds by which property or obligations were transferred.[12] Deeds liable to challenge included conveyances,[13] assignations, contracts, obligations, bills, promissory notes, discharges and generally any deed whatever which might confer on the grantee a claim to property belonging to the debtor or enable him to claim as a creditor in competition with the true creditors of the grantor, or save him from a demand for payment of what he owed to the debtor.[14] Section 34

---

[5] Bell, *Comm.*, II, 184; *Wink* v. *Speirs* (1867) 6 M. 77; *Main* v. *Fleming's Trs.* (1881) 8 R. 880.
[6] *Abram Steamship Co. Ltd. (in liqn.)* v. *Abram*, 1925 S.L.T. 243.
[7] *Wink* v. *Speirs* (1867) 6 M. 77.
[8] *Dobie* v. *Mitchell* (1854) 17 D. 97.
[9] *North British Ry. Co.* v. *White* (1882) 20 S.L.R. 129 at p. 131; *Armour* v. *Learmonth*, 1972 S.L.T. 150.
[10] *McDougall's Tr.* v. *Ironside*, 1914 S.C. 186.
[11] *Main* v. *Fleming's Trs.* (1881) 8 R. 880.
[12] *Thomas* v. *Thomson* (1865) 3 R. 1170; *Obers* v. *Paton's Trs.* (1897) 24 R. 719.
[13] See *McManus's Tr.* v. *McManus*, 1978 S.L.T. 255; also 1979 S.L.T. (Notes) 71.
[14] Bell, *Comm.*, II, 174.

applies not only to deeds by which property or obligations are transferred but also to cash payments.

The alienation becomes challengeable if (1) the debtor's estate has been sequestrated (other than, in the case of a natural person, after his death); or (2) he has granted a trust deed which has become a protected trust deed[15]; or (3) he has died and within 12 months after his death, his estate has been sequestrated; or (4) he has died and within 12 months after his death a judicial factor has been appointed under s. 11A of the Judicial Factors (Scotland) Act 1889 to administer his estate and the estate was absolutely insolvent at the date of death (s. 34(2)(b)).

Further, if the alienation is to be challenged, where it has had the effect of favouring a person who is an associate of the debtor the day on which the alienation became completely effectual must be a day not earlier than five years before the date of sequestration, the granting of the trust deed or the debtor's death, as the case may be (s. 34(3)(a)). In the case of any other person, the day must be not earlier than two years before this date (s. 34(3)(b)).

For the purposes of the Act section 74 (as amended by regulation 11 of the Bankruptcy (Scotland) Regulations 1985) provides that a person is an "associate" of another person if that person is the individual's husband or wife, or is a relative, or the husband or wife of a relative, of the individual or of the individual's husband or wife. Subsection (4) defines who are to be classed as relatives of an individual. Similarly, a person is an associate of any person with whom he is in partnership, and of any person who is an associate of any person with whom he is in partnership. Conversely, a firm is an associate of any person who is a member of the firm. Further, a person is an associate of any person whom he employs or by whom he is employed. In this connection, a director or other officer of a company is treated as employed by that company.

If a challenge is brought under section 34 the court will grant decree of reduction or for such restoration of property to the debtor's estate or other redress as may be appropriate unless the person seeking to uphold the alienation establishes (1) that the debtor's assets immediately after the alienation or at any time thereafter were greater than his liabilities[16]; or (2) that the alienation was made for adequate consideration; or (3) that the alienation was a conventional or charitable gift which it was reasonable for the debtor to make (s. 34(4)).

An alienation will only be challengeable if the estate alienated was such that it might have been attached by the diligence of the debtor's creditors.[17] Again, to take an alienation outwith the scope of the Act any price paid must be just, that is, reasonably adequate to the value of the subject

---

[15] See para. 8 of Sched. 5 to the 1985 Act.

[16] *i.e.* he was not insolvent in the absolute sense. It is not clear whether or not contingent and prospective liabilities should be taken into account. See Bell, *Comm.*, II, 153 and 154 but contrast s. 123(2) of the Insolvency Act 1986.

[17] Bell, *Comm.*, I, 52 and II, 191; *Buchanan* v. *Carrick* (1838) 16 S. 358.

alienated.[18] It is however not necessary that the consideration be a payment in cash. Any deed granted for a genuine and adequate consideration is considered to be free from challenge under the statute. The consideration may take the form of value received in money or money's worth or the alienation may have been in implement of a prior specific obligation undertaken while solvent.[19] Again, a payment made to a debtor's future wife in consideration of their forthcoming marriage has been held to be free from challenge.[20]

Any successful challenge must be without prejudice to any right or interest acquired in good faith and for value from the transferee in the alienation (s. 34(4)).

Section 35 provides for the court making an order in certain circumstances for the recall of an order for the payment by the debtor of a capital sum on divorce where on the date of the making of the order the debtor was absolutely insolvent or was rendered so when he implemented the order.

Preferences reducible at common law

Any voluntary transactions which have the effect, directly or indirectly, of conferring a benefit on one creditor in preference to others are challengeable at common law on the ground of insolvency. Such transactions are struck at by the common law as a fraudulent interference with the rights of creditors *inter se*.[21] Transactions which may be challenged include a security given for a previously unsecured debt or an obligation to grant such a security[22] and action on the part of the debtor which facilitates a creditor's attempt to execute diligence or obtain a decree.[23] Once it has been proved that the transaction was entered into voluntarily by the debtor while he was conscious of his insolvency, fraud is presumed and it is unnecessary to prove collusion on the part of the favoured creditor.[24] Certain classes of transactions however cannot be challenged. These transactions are (1) transactions in the ordinary course of trade; (2) payments in cash of debts which are due and payable; and (3) *nova debita*.[25]

Preferences reducible by statute

Section 36 of the Act deals with unfair preferences and is applicable to a transaction entered into by a debtor which has the effect of creating a preference in favour of a creditor to the prejudice of the general body of

---

[18] *Hodge* v. *Morrison* (1883) 21 S.L.R. 40; *Tennant* v. *Miller* (1897) 4 S.L.T. 440.
[19] *Horne* v. *Hay* (1847) 9 D. 651; *Thomas* v. *Thomson* (1886) 5 M. 198; *Williamson* v. *Allan* (1882) 9 R. 859; *Pringle's Tr.* v. *Wright* (1903) 5 F. 522.
[20] *Armour* v. *Learmonth*, 1972 S.L.T. 150. See also *Robertson's Tr.* v. *Robertson* (1901) 3 F. 359.
[21] Bell, *Comm.*, II, 226.
[22] *McCowan* v. *Wright* (1853) 15 D. 494; *Thomas* v. *Thomson* (1866) 5 M. 198.
[23] *Lawrie's Tr.* v. *Beveridge* (1867) 6 M. 85.
[24] *McCowan* v. *Wright*, *supra* at p. 504; *Whatmough's Tr.* v. *British Linen Bank*, 1932 S.C. 525 at p. 543; see also *McDougall's Tr.* v. *Ironside*, 1914 S.C. 186.
[25] See p. 224.

creditors, being a preference created not earlier than six months immediately before (1) the date of sequestration of the debtor's estate (if, in the case of a natural person, this is a date within his lifetime); or (2) the granting by him of a trust deed which has become a protected trust deed; or (3) his death where, within 12 months after his death (a) his estate has been sequestrated, or (b) a judicial factor has been appointed under s. 11A of the Judicial Factors (Scotland) Act 1889 to administer his estate and his estate was absolutely insolvent at the date of death (s. 36(1)).

Every form of transaction by which a preference is conferred on a creditor, directly or indirectly can be challenged. It is not necessary that the transaction struck at should have been entered into in bad faith but only that the equality of the distribution of the debtor's estate among his creditors has been disturbed.[26] Transactions struck at in the past have included bills of exchange granted by the debtor within what was then the restricted period,[27] the conveyance of property in security of a prior debt,[28] an arrangement with a debtor to pay one of his creditors direct,[29] and the indorsement to a creditor of a cheque received by a firm from a third party.[30] However, a bank is entitled to discount a bill either by means of cash or giving credit.[31] The substitution for an existing security of another of equivalent value has been held not to be struck at.[32] It is also probably the case that when money is advanced on the faith of a specific security to be immediately granted, the 1985 Act will not apply even although the security is not completed until after an interval of time.[33] However, a security over heritable property granted in implement of a purely verbal agreement made outwith the six months' period will be open to challenge.[34]

Transactions in the ordinary course of trade or business

A transaction in the ordinary course of trade or business is not challengeable (s. 36(2)(a)). Such transactions include payments or other operations in the course of a current account between two merchants, or between a banker and his customer, whether made in cash or by the indorsement of bills.[35] In *Nordic Travel Ltd.* v. *Scotprint Ltd.*[36] tour operators placed an order with printers for travel brochures. The debt for the printing was due and payable at the time when payments were actually made by the tour operators and these payments were abnormal only in so far as by arrangement with the printers they were made

---

[26] *Renton and Gray's Tr.* v. *Dickison* (1880) 7 R. 951.

[27] *Blincow's Tr.* v. *Allan & Co.* (1828) 7 S. 124.

[28] *Stiven* v. *Scott & Simpson* (1871) 9 M. 923; *T.* v. *L.*, 1970 S.L.T. 243.

[29] *Newton & Son's Tr.* v. *Finlayson & Co.*, 1928 S.C. 637.

[30] *Raymond Harrison & Co.'s Tr.* v. *North West Securities Ltd.*, 1989 S.L.T. 718.

[31] *Blincow's Tr.* v. *Allan & Co.* (1828) 7 S. 124.

[32] *Roy's Tr.* v. *Colville and Drysdale* (1903) 5 F. 769.

[33] *Cowdenbeath Coal Co.* v. *Clydesdale Bank Ltd.* (1895) 22 R. 682 at p. 689; see also Bell, *Comm.*, II, 211; *Taylor* v. *Farrie* (1855) 17 D. 639; *Price & Pierce* v. *Bank of Scotland*, 1912 S.C. (H.L.) 19.

[34] *Barclay* v. *Cuthill*, 1961 S.L.T. (Notes) 62; see also *T.* v. *L.*, 1970 S.L.T. 243.

[35] *Stewart* v. *Sir William Forbes & Co.* (1791) Mor. 1142; *Sievwright* v. *Hay & Co.*, 1913 S.C. 509; *McLaren's Tr.* v. *National Bank of Scotland* (1897) 24 R. 920.

[36] 1980 S.L.T. 189. Cf. *Re F. P. & C. H. Mathews Ltd.* [1982] 1 All E.R. 338.

subsequent to the due date as and when cash was available. When the brochures were ordered the tour operators were insolvent to the knowledge of the printers. All of the payments were made within the period of six months prior to the commencement of the winding up of the tour operators' company. It was held (1) that it was not a breach of trust for an insolvent person who knows of his absolute insolvency to fulfil obligations which are due and prestable, and the fact that the receiving creditor was aware of the insolvency was irrelevant; (2) that the creditor's mere knowledge of the absolute or irretrievable insolvency of his debtor at the time of payment did not of itself demonstrate collusion; and (3) that the circumstances of the case did not disclose that the transaction was unusual as a matter of business and therefore out of the ordinary course of business.

Cash payments

A payment in cash for a debt which when it was paid had become payable is not challengeable unless the transaction was collusive with the purpose of prejudicing the general body of creditors (s. 36(2)(b)). Collusion means more than a creditor's mere knowledge of the absolute or even irretrievable insolvency of his debtor at the time of payment. In this context it refers to participation by a creditor, whose co-operation is necessary to achieve the result, in some device or transaction designed particularly to confer upon him a preference which would itself be unfair.[37] Certain equivalents to cash payments have been recognised. These include the debtor's cheque on his own banker and in the absence of fraud or collusion, a cheque drawn by a third party in favour of a debtor, even when it represents the realisation of assets belonging to the debtor and which is used to liquidate the debtor's bank overdraft, is a payment in cash.[38] However, a cheque drawn by a third party in favour of a debtor and indorsed by him to a creditor within the statutory period in payment of a debt already due has been held to be struck at as being neither a payment in cash nor a transaction in the ordinary course of the debtor's particular business.[39] Similarly, in *Anderson's Tr.* v. *Somerville & Co. Ltd.*[40] where in payment of an unsecured debt of the debtor his law agents indorsed to one of his creditors a cheque in their favour which they had received in payment of the price of property belonging to the debtor, it was held that the transaction was not a cash payment in the ordinary course of business but an assignation and therefore null and void. In England, it has been held to be a fraudulent preference and a breach of fiduciary duty on the part of a company director where, at a time when company A owed money to company B but both were insolvent, he instructed company A to transfer money to company B (whose bank

---

[37] *Nordic Travel Ltd.* v. *Scotprint Ltd.*, *supra* at p. 198.
[38] *Whatmough's Tr.* v. *British Linen Bank*, 1934 S.C. (H.L.) 51.
[39] *Carter* v. *Johnstone* (1886) 13 R. 698. See *Scott's Trs.* v. *Low & Co.* (1902) 4 F. 562; *Raymond Harrison & Co.'s Tr.* v. *North West Securities Ltd.*, 1989 S.L.T. 718.
[40] (1899) 1 F. 90. See also *Newton & Son's Tr.* v. *Finlayson & Co.*, 1928 S.C. 637.

account was overdrawn) and the effect was to reduce his liability under a personal guarantee given to the bank to secure company B's overdraft.[41]

Nova debita

A transaction whereby parties undertake reciprocal obligations (whether the performance by the parties of their respective obligations occurs at the same time or at different times) is not challengeable unless the transaction was collusive with the purpose of prejudicing the general body of creditors (s. 36(2)(c)). Nova debita have previously been defined as reciprocal obligations, the one undertaken by the debtor being undertaken in respect of some consideration received from another party at the same time or within a very short period of time thereafter.[42] For example, where cash was advanced or goods transferred, and a simultaneous undertaking given to grant a specific security for the advance, the security was allowed to be completed within the statutory period,[43] but the obligation to grant the security had to be "instantly and absolutely enforceable."[44] It is thought that the same considerations will apply to nova debita as now defined. If so, a security granted by the debtor outwith the statutory period, the completion of which does not require any further action on his part, is unchallengeable even although the creditor may have done something to complete the security within the statutory period.[45] Again, although a security may have been granted within this period, if no advances are made against the security until after its completion it is unchallengeable.[46] But where money is advanced not on the faith of a present or instant security but on the undertaking of the debtor, if so desired by the creditor, to grant the security and such security is completed within the period, the transaction will be set aside.[47] A security which is substituted for an already existing security in consideration of a loan granted in respect of the prior security not being called up is not struck at by the Act[48] but a conveyance of property which is made in fulfilment of a promise to give security for a past loan is challengeable.[49] In *Craig's Trs.* v. *Macdonald and Fraser*[50] where a farmer who had received an unsecured advance of £200 from a firm of auctioneers employed them within 60 days of his bankruptcy to carry through his displenishing sale, at the same time giving them an ante-dated receipt for the £200 as a payment "towards my displenishing sale", it was held that

---

[41] *Liqr. of West Mercia Safetywear Ltd.* v. *Dodd* (1988) 4 B.C.C. 30.
[42] *Cowdenbeath Coal Co.* v. *Clydesdale Bank Ltd.* (1895) 22 R. 682.
[43] Bell, *Comm.*, II, 211; *Bank of Scotland* v. *Stewart & Ross*, 7 February 1811, F.C.
[44] *per* L.P. Inglis in *Stiven* v. *Scott & Simpson* (1871) 9 M. 923 at p. 933.
[45] See, for example, *Taylor* v. *Farrie* (1855) 17 D. 639; *Lindsay* v. *Adamson & Ronaldson* (1880) 7 R. 1036; *Scottish Provident Institution* v. *Cohen & Co.* (1888) 16 R. 112.
[46] *Robertson's Tr.* v. *Union Bank of Scotland*, 1917 S.C. 549; *Price & Pierce* v. *Bank of Scotland*, 1912 S.C.(H.L.) 19 (affg. 1910 S.C. 1095).
[47] *Barclay* v. *Cuthill*, 1961 S.L.T. (Notes) 62; *T.* v. *L.*, 1970 S.L.T. 243. See also *Jones & Co.'s Tr.* v. *Allan* (1901) 4 F. 374.
[48] *Roy's Tr.* v. *Colville and Drysdale* (1903) S.F. 769.
[49] *Hill's Trs.* v. *McGregor* (1901) 8 S.L.T. 387.
[50] (1902) 4 F. 1132.

the transaction was struck at and that the auctioneers were not entitled to retain £200 out of the sum realised at the sale.

Effect of challenge

A transaction to which the Act applies is challengeable by (1) any creditor who is a creditor by virtue of a debt incurred on or before the date of sequestration, the granting of the protected trust deed or the debtor's death, as the case may be; or (2) the permanent trustee, the trustee acting under a protected trust deed, or the judicial factor, as the case may be (s. 36(4)(*b*)). If the challenge is successful, the court will grant decree of reduction or for such restoration of property to the debtor's estate or other redress as may be appropriate, provided that this can be done without prejudice to any right or interest acquired in good faith and for value from the creditor in whose favour the preference was created (s. 36(5)). In the case of gratuitous alienations, section 242 of the Insolvency Act 1986 provides that an alienation by a company is challengeable by any creditor or the liquidator following a winding up or by the administrator where an administration order has been made on substantially the same grounds as apply in a sequestration, substituting for the date of sequestration the commencement of the winding up or the making of the administration order (s. 242(3)). Similarly, section 36 of the Bankruptcy (Scotland) Act 1985 (unfair preferences) has its counterpart in section 243 of the Insolvency Act 1986.

Floating charge

A floating charge can now be challenged as a gratuitous alienation or fraudulent preference. Additionally section 245 of the Insolvency Act 1986 lays down statutory grounds for the avoidance of certain floating charges. These are charges created at a "relevant time". In the case of a charge in favour of a person connected with the company, this is any time in the period of two years ending with the commencement date, defined in subsection (5) as the date of the presentation of the petition for an administration order or commencement of the winding up, as the case may be (s. 245(3)(*a*)). In the case of a charge in favour of any other person, the relevant period is reduced to 12 months but the charge cannot be challenged unless the company was unable to pay its debts within the meaning of section 123 of the Act at the time when the charge was created (or became unable to do so in consequence of the transaction in question) (s. 245(4)). A charge which is created at a relevant time is invalid except to the extent of the aggregate of the value of so much of the consideration for the creation of the charge as consists of (i) money paid, or goods and services supplied, to the company and (ii) the discharge or reduction of any debt of the company at the same time as, or after, the creation of the charge, together with a specified amount of interest (s. 245(2)). In the case of money the exception is available only for money actually paid to the company and not for payments made to third parties for its benefit. It is not available to secure existing debts although it may protect a charge to secure money advanced to the company on condition that it is used to meet certain debts of the company.[51] A bank advancing money to a company on overdraft and which takes a floating charge by way of security is entitled on the basis of the rule in *Clayton's Case* to apply sums paid in by the company to extinguish the oldest outstanding debits in the first place. Advances made by way of debits to the account after the creation of the charge will be regarded as money paid within the terms of the exception.[52] The payment of money may include the honouring of cheques by a bank.[53]

---

[51] *Libertas-Kommerz GmbH* v. *Johnson*, 1977 S.C. 191.
[52] *Yeovil Glove Co. Ltd.* [1965] Ch. 148.
[53] *Ibid.*, at p. 178.

CHAPTER 16

SEQUESTRATION

Sequestration has been defined as "a judicial process for rendering litigious the whole estate of a bankrupt in order that no part of it may be carried away by a single creditor for his own benefit, but that the whole may be vested in a trustee, to be administered by him and distributed among the various creditors in accordance with certain fixed legal rules of distribution".[1] Sequestration is now governed by the Bankruptcy (Scotland) Act 1985.[2]

Administration

The functions of the Accountant in Bankruptcy include the supervision of persons connected with sequestrations and the maintenance of a list of interim trustees and a register of insolvencies (s. 1). This register is available for inspection by members of the public (s. 1(5)(a)). An interim trustee has to be appointed in every sequestration. He must be a qualified insolvency practitioner (s. 2(2)). His general functions are to safeguard the debtor's estate and administer the sequestration process pending the appointment of a permanent trustee, and to ascertain the reasons for the debtor's insolvency and the extent of his assets and liabilities (s. 2(1)). He is appointed by the court either on or, in some circumstances, before sequestration is awarded (s. 13(1)), and he is not entitled to decline to accept appointment (s. 13(6)). In every sequestration there must also be appointed a permanent trustee whose general functions are the recovery and management of the debtor's estate, its distribution among his creditors, the ascertainment of the reasons for his insolvency and the state of his assets and liabilities. Provision is made for the election of commissioners in any sequestration other than one to which Schedule 2 to the Act applies (s. 4).

Petitions for sequestration

Sequestration of the estate of a debtor is made on the petition of (1) the debtor, with the concurrence of a qualified creditor; (2) a qualified creditor, if the debtor is apparently insolvent; or (3) the trustee acting under a trust deed (s. 5(2)). The estate of a deceased debtor may be sequestrated on the petition of (1) an executor or a person entitled to be appointed as executor on the estate; (2) a qualified creditor; or (3) the trustee acting under a trust deed.

---

[1] *Sinclair* v. *Edinburgh Parish Council*, 1909 S.C. 1353 at p. 1359.
[2] The Act applies to all sequestrations in which the petition is presented on or after 1 April 1986. See the Bankruptcy (Scotland) Regulations 1985 (S.I. 1985 No. 1925). Any defect in procedure can be cured under the provisions of s. 63. In this chapter, references to sections are to sections of the Act.

In the Act "qualified creditor" means a creditor who is a creditor of the debtor in respect of a liquid or illiquid debt (other than a contingent or future debt), whether secured or unsecured, which amounts to not less than £750 or such sum as may be prescribed (s. 5(4)). If, before sequestration has been awarded, a petitioning or concurring creditor withdraws his petition, any creditor who is a qualified creditor is entitled to be sisted in his place (s. 5(8)).

Sequestration may also competently be awarded in the case of (1) a trust, in respect of debts incurred by it; (2) a partnership; (3) a body corporate or an unincorporated body; and (4) a limited partnership[3] (s. 6(1)). It is not however competent to sequestrate the estate of a company registered under the Companies Act 1985 or under the former Companies Acts (s. 6(2)(a)).

Apparent insolvency

This is a new expression introduced into the law of bankruptcy by section 7 of the Act in place of notour bankruptcy. A debtor's apparent insolvency is constituted whenever his estate is sequestrated or he is adjudged bankrupt in England or Wales or Northern Ireland; or he gives written notice to his creditors that he has ceased to pay his debts in the ordinary course of business. It is also constituted if any of the following circumstances occur: (1) he grants a trust deed; (2) the days of charge of a duly executed charge for payment of a debt expire without payment; (3) 14 days elapse without payment following a poinding of any of his moveable property by virtue of a summary warrant for the recovery of rates or taxes; (4) a decree of adjudication is granted, either for payment or in security; (5) his effects are sold under a sequestration for rent; or (6) a receiving order is made in England or Wales (s. 7(1)(c)). However, it is open to the debtor to show that at the time when any of these circumstances occurred, he was able and willing to pay his debts as they became due.[4] Additionally, it is constituted if a creditor serves on the debtor by an officer of court a demand in the prescribed form for a debt of not less than £750 requiring him either to pay or find security for it and within three weeks after the date of service the debtor has neither complied with the demand nor intimated to the creditor that he denies that the debt is immediately payable (s. 7(1)(d)).[5] Where the debtor is already apparently insolvent, his apparent insolvency may be constituted again.[6]

While a petition for sequestration may be presented at any time by the debtor or by a trustee acting under a trust deed, where the petition is presented by a creditor, the apparent insolvency founded on in the petition must have been constituted within the previous four months (s. 8(1)).[7] In the case of a deceased debtor, the petition may be presented

---

[3] See the Bankruptcy (Scotland) Regulations 1985, reg. 12.
[4] See *Scottish Milk Marketing Board* v. *Wood*, 1936 S.C. 604.
[5] See the Bankruptcy (Scotland) Regulations 1985, reg. 5 and Sched., Form 1.
[6] *Balfour* v. *Pedie* (1841) 3 D. 612.
[7] See *Burgh of Millport, Petrs.*, 1974 S.L.T. (Notes) 23.

(1) at any time by an executor or a trustee acting under a trust deed; or (2) by a creditor at any time where the apparent insolvency of the debtor was constituted within four months before his death, but in any other case (whether or not apparent insolvency has been constituted) not earlier than six months after his death (s. 8(3)).

Jurisdiction

The Court of Session has jurisdiction if the debtor had an established place of business in Scotland, or was habitually resident there, at any time in the year immediately preceding the date of presentation of the petition (or the date of death in the case of a deceased debtor) (s. 9(1) and (5)). In the case of an entity which may be sequestrated by virtue of section 6 of the Act, the Court of Session has jurisdiction if the entity either had an established place of business in Scotland at any time in the year immediately preceding the date of presentation of the petition, or was constituted or formed under Scots law and at any time carried on business in Scotland (s. 9(2)). The court also has jurisdiction in the case of the partner of a firm, whether or not it has jurisdiction under section 9(1), if a petition has been presented for the sequestration of the firm of which he is or was a partner and the process of that sequestration is still current (s. 9(3)). Proceedings may also be initiated in the sheriff court, "the sheriffdom" being substituted for "Scotland" wherever it appears in section 9 (s. 9(4)).

The oath

The oath which must accompany every petition by a creditor for sequestration has to be in the form prescribed by the Act (s. 11(1)).[8] In addition, every creditor must produce a voucher which constitutes *prima facie* evidence of the debt and such evidence as is available to show the apparent insolvency of the debtor (s. 11(5)).

For sums due on an overdrawn current account it has been held that the proper vouchers, in addition to the account, are the last signed docquet and the cheques or bills paid by the bank[9] but it is considered that it would be sufficient to have the account, including the copy docquet, certified in terms of the Civil Evidence (Scotland) Act 1988. Again, it has been held that an account which has not been docqueted is not sufficiently vouched when it begins with a balance, either on the creditor or debtor side,[10] and that in all such cases it must go back to the first transaction. However, the current practice of the Scottish banks is to dispense with docquets except in special circumstances and to deliver to customers, with or without paid cheques, periodic statements of account and a copy of the last statement is usually accepted as sufficient evidence of the debt.

---

[8] See the Bankruptcy (Scotland) Regulations 1985, reg. 5 and Sched., Form 2. See also *Younger & Son Ltd., Petrs.*, 1926 S.L.T. 238.
[9] *Millar* v. *Romanes*, 1912 2 S.L.T. 209.
[10] *Low* v. *Baxter* (1851) 13 D. 1349.

Award of sequestration

Where the petition is presented by the debtor himself, the court must award sequestration unless cause is shown why it cannot be awarded (s. 12(1)). In the case of a petition presented by a creditor or a trustee under a trust deed, the court must award sequestration after proper citation has been made of the debtor in terms of section 12(2) unless (1) cause is shown why sequestration cannot be awarded; or (2) the debtor forthwith pays or produces written evidence of payment or gives sufficient security for payment not only of the debt in respect of which he became apparently insolvent but also any other debt due by him to the petitioning and any other concurring creditor (s. 12(3)).[11] For the purposes of the Act, the date of sequestration is the date on which sequestration is awarded in the case of a petition presented by the debtor and in the case of a petition presented by a creditor or a trustee under a trust deed, the date on which the court grants warrant for citation under section 12(2) (s. 12(4)).

Provision is made for the Court of Session to remit a sequestration to the sheriff court (s. 15(1)) or to transfer it from one sheriff court to another (s. 15(2)). If an award of sequestration is refused by the court, the petitioning creditor may appeal against the order within 14 days (s. 15(3)) but an award, if granted, is not subject to review otherwise than by recall under sections 16 and 17 of the Act. A non-entitled spouse within the meaning of section 6 of the Matrimonial Homes (Family Protection) (Scotland) Act 1981 may petition for the recall of a sequestration on the ground that the petition for sequestration was intended to defeat his or her occupancy rights (s. 41). The right to bring an action of reduction of an award of sequestration is not affected (s. 15(4)) but a reduction will only be granted in exceptional circumstances.[12]

Immediately after the date of sequestration, the court is required to send a certified copy of the relevant court order to the Keeper of the Register of Inhibitions and Adjudications for recording (s. 14(1)(a)). This provision applies to the order of the court awarding sequestration, if the petition has been presented by the debtor, and the order of the court granting warrant for citation under section 12(2) in the case of a petition by a creditor or trustee under a trust deed (s. 14(5)). Recording of a notice under section 14 has the effect, as from the date of sequestration, of an inhibition and of a citation in an adjudication of the debtor's heritable estate at the instance of his creditors (s. 14(2)). The effect of such a notice prescribes after three years unless the permanent trustee renews its effect by recording a memorandum in the same register (s. 14(4)).

Interim preservation of estate

The interim trustee appointed under section 13 is entitled to give

---

[11] *Stuart & Stuart* v. *MacLeod* (1891) 19 R. 223; *Bank of Scotland* v. *Mackay*, 1991 S.L.T. 163.
[12] *Central Motor Engineering Co. and Others* v. *Galbraith*, 1918 S.C. 755.

directions to the debtor in connection with the management of his estate and in exercising the functions conferred on him by section 2(1)(a) of the Act, he may *inter alia* (1) require the debtor to deliver to him any money or valuables or any documents relating to the debtor's financial affairs; (2) require him to deliver up any perishable goods and then arrange for their disposal; (3) prepare a valuation of any property belonging to the debtor; (4) require the debtor to implement any transaction which he has entered into; and (5) close down the debtor's business (s. 18(2)). On application to the court, the trustee may be granted power to carry on any business of the debtor and borrow money in so far as it is necessary for him to do so to safeguard the debtor's estate (s. 18(3)(a)). The court may also make other appropriate orders to safeguard the debtor's estate (s. 18(3)(b) and (c)).

The debtor is required by section 19 to deliver to the interim trustee a list of his assets and liabilities. The interim trustee then has a duty to prepare a preliminary statement of the debtor's affairs and to indicate whether, in his opinion, the debtor's assets are unlikely to be sufficient to pay any dividend whatsoever in respect of the debts listed in paragraphs (e) to (h) of section 51(1) (s. 20(1)). In connection with these duties the interim trustee may apply to the sheriff for an order requiring the debtor or any other person to appear before the sheriff in private for examination (s. 20(4)).

Statutory meeting

The interim trustee must call a meeting of the creditors, referred to in the Act as "the statutory meeting", to be held within 28 days after the date of the award of sequestration (s. 21(1)). Not less than seven days' notice of this statutory meeting has to be given to every creditor known to him (s. 21(2)). The notice, which also must be given to the Accountant in Bankruptcy, should invite creditors to submit claims and at the same time inform them of the interim trustee's duties under section 23(3) and (5).

Voting at the statutory meeting

In order to vote at the statutory meeting, a creditor requires to submit a claim in the prescribed form accompanied by a voucher which constitutes prima facie evidence of the debt (s. 22(1) and (2)). An acknowledgment dated after sequestration has been awarded is not admissible to vouch a claim incurred prior to sequestration.[13] A reference to the bankrupt's oath in support of the creditor's claim is also incompetent.[14] The amount which a creditor is entitled to claim is determined by the provisions of Schedule 1 to the Act (s. 22(9)). In a straightforward case this is the principal amount of his debt plus any interest due as at the date of sequestration (para. 1(1)). A claim cannot be made for a debt which depends on a contingency (para. 3(1)) but the permanent trustee or, if

---

[13] *Carmichael's Tr.* v. *Carmichael*, 1929 S.L.T. 230.
[14] *Adam* v. *McLachlan* (1847) 9 D. 560; *Thomson* v. *Duncan* (1855) 17 D. 1081.

there is none, the sheriff may put a value on the debt in so far as it is contingent and the creditor is then entitled to claim that amount (para. 3(2)). In the case of a secured debt, a creditor must deduct the value of any security held by him[15] unless he surrenders that security for the benefit of the estate, in which case he is not required to make a deduction (para. 5(1)). "Security" in this context includes any right of lien, retention or preference (s. 73(1)). A creditor is, however, entitled to vote in respect of the full amount of his debt, without deduction, in any question relating to the disposal or management of any part of the estate held by him in security.[16] A value of some kind must be placed on whatever security is held over the estate of the bankrupt. A nominal value will suffice or the creditor may even value it at nil.[17] The advantage of specifying a nominal value is that it can readily be adjusted from time to time before payment of a dividend but the permanent trustee may require a secured creditor to discharge his security on payment of the value specified by the creditor. The creditor may then claim only in respect of the balance of his debt (para. 5(2)). A promissory note granted by the bankrupt is not a security[18] although an arrestment[19] or an inhibition[20] may be. Where the creditor holds securities specifically appropriated for separate debts, these must be valued as against the particular debt to which they refer.[21] Where the creditor holds a security given to him by a third party this should be specified for the information of the trustee but does not require to be valued or deducted.

Where a creditor claims in respect of a debt of a partnership against the estate of one of its partners, he is required to estimate the value of either (1) the debt to the creditor from the firm's estate where that estate has not been sequestrated, or (2) the creditor's claim against that estate where it has been sequestrated. He must then deduct that value from his claim against the partner's estate and restrict his claim to the remaining balance (para. 6). Where the firm has been dissolved before the sequestration of the partner, the date for the valuation of the estate of the firm for this purpose is the date of the firm's dissolution.[22]

A security granted by a person independent of the debtor does not require to be deducted; nor does a security granted by one of the partners of a firm for the firm's indebtedness, although in ranking on the partner's individual estate it is necessary that it be deducted. The Act does not derogate from the common law rules relating to the valuation of claims by or involving co-obligants so that for voting purposes, as well as for

---

[15] *University of Glasgow* v. *Yuill's Tr.* (1882) 9 R. 643; *Clydesdale Bank Ltd.* v. *Liqr. of James Allan, Senior & Son Ltd.*, 1926 S.C. 235.
[16] *Addison & Sons* v. *Crabb* (1853) 25 Sc.Jur. 270.
[17] *Gibson* v. *Greig* (1853) 16 D. 233.
[18] *Boro*, 1 June 1811, F.C.
[19] *Dow* v. *Union Bank* (1875) 2 R. 459.
[20] *Hay* v. *Durham* (1850) 12 D. 676.
[21] *Smith* v. *Borthwick* (1849) 11 D. 517.
[22] *Clydesdale Bank Ltd.* v. *Morison's Tr.*, 1983 S.L.T. 42.

ranking purposes, claims against or securities held from co-obligants can be disregarded.[23]

At the commencement of the statutory meeting the chairman is the interim trustee but the creditors may elect one of their number as chairman in his place. If no one is elected, he remains the chairman (s. 23(1)(a) and (b)). After considering any representations made by the creditors about the debtor's list of assets and liabilities he must indicate whether, in his opinion, the debtor's assets are unlikely to be sufficient to pay any dividend in respect of the debts listed in paragraphs (e) to (h) of section 51(1) (s. 23(3)(b) and (c)). If, in his opinion, the debtor's assets are unlikely to be sufficient he must forthwith make a report of the proceedings at the statutory meeting to the sheriff who then appoints him as the permanent trustee (s. 23(4)). When such an appointment is made the provisions of the Act apply subject to the provisions of Schedule 2. In particular, section 53 is amended to provide that where the debtor's estate is insufficient to meet the outlays and remuneration of the interim trustee and the permanent trustee any shortfall has to be met by the Accountant in Bankruptcy provided that no dividend has been paid to creditors in the sequestration (para. 9).

Election of permanent trustee

Where section 23(4) does not apply, section 24 makes provision for the election by the creditors at the statutory meeting of the permanent trustee. Only one trustee can be appointed at one time. The debtor, a person who is not qualified to act as an insolvency practitioner, a person who holds an interest opposed to the general interests of the creditors, and a person who resides outwith the jurisdiction of the Court of Session are not eligible for election (s. 24(2)). Postponed creditors and creditors whose debts have been acquired after the date of sequestration are not entitled to vote (s. 24(3)). Associates of the debtor can vote but their claims should be closely scrutinised.[24] If no permanent trustee is elected, the interim trustee must report the proceedings to the sheriff who then appoints him as the permanent trustee (s. 24(4)). In this event, the sequestration is once again subject to the provisions of Schedule 2 (s. 24(5)). On the election of the permanent trustee, the interim trustee must report the proceedings at the statutory meeting to the sheriff (s. 25(1)(a)). Provided there is no objection under section 25(1)(b) the sheriff forthwith declares the elected person to be the permanent trustee and after his election has been confirmed he is issued with an act and warrant (s. 25(2)). The decision of the sheriff in declaring and confirming the election of the trustee or in deciding any objection to the appointment is final (s. 25(5)). Where the interim trustee does not himself become the permanent trustee he is obliged to hand over to the permanent trustee everything in his possession which relates to the sequestration. He

---

[23] *University of Glasgow* v. *Yuill's Tr.* (1882) 9 R. 643 at p. 650.
[24] *Anderson* v. *Guild* (1852) 14 D. 866; *Walker's Trs.* v. *Walker* (1883) 10 R. 699.

thereupon ceases to act (s. 26(1)) and can obtain his discharge pursuant to section 27. The permanent trustee may subsequently resign office or be removed from office in the circumstances provided for in sections 28 and 29 respectively.

Commissioners

At the statutory meeting or any subsequent meeting of creditors, the creditors may elect not more than five of their number to be commissioners in the sequestration (s. 30(1)). Neither the debtor nor a person who holds an interest opposed to the general interests of the creditors is eligible for election as a commissioner, nor is a person who is an associate of the debtor or of the permanent trustee (s. 30(2)). A commissioner may resign office at any time (s. 30(3)). Meetings of the commissioners are governed by the provision of Part III of Schedule 6 to the Act (s. 66). Commissioners are not personally liable for damage occasioned to the estate by the trustee acting on their advice,[25] but they are liable if it can be shown that through their wrongful actings anyone has suffered damage.[26]

Vesting of estate in permanent trustee

The whole estate of the debtor vests as at the date of sequestration in the permanent trustee for the benefit of the creditors. It does so by virtue of the act and warrant issued on confirmation of the permanent trustee's appointment (s. 31(1)). In relation to heritable estate in Scotland, the act and warrant has the same effect as if a decree of adjudication in implement of sale, as well as a decree of adjudication for payment and in security of debt, subject to no legal reversion, had been pronounced in favour of the permanent trustee (s. 31(1)(b)). If the debtor occupies heritable property he is reduced to the position of a squatter in that property without any title to remain there.[27] However, the powers of the permanent trustee in relation to the debtor's family or matrimonial home are circumscribed by the provisions of sections 40 and 41.[28] The act and warrant deprives a prior inhibition of any legal effect but there is reserved to the inhibiting creditor any effect which such an inhibition has on ranking (s. 31(2)). Moveable property vests in the permanent trustee by virtue of the act and warrant as if at the date of sequestration the permanent trustee had taken delivery or possession of the property or had intimated its assignation to him, as the case may be (s. 31(4)). Any non-vested contingent interest, such as a *spes successionis* under a will or a right under a deed of an irrevocable nature, also vests in the permanent trustee (s. 31(5)). While a claim for compensation for personal injuries is personal to the injured party, after proceedings have commenced the claim vests in the permanent trustee.[29] Property which is exempted from

---

[25] *Wilson* v. *Alexander* (1803) Mor. 13968.
[26] *McTaggart* v. *Watson* (1835) 1 S. & McL. 553.
[27] *White* v. *Stevenson*, 1956 S.C. 84.
[28] See p. 237.
[29] *Watson* v. *Thompson*, 1990 S.L.T. 374.

poinding for the purpose of protecting the debtor and his family[30] and property held on trust by the debtor for another[31] do not vest in the permanent trustee (s. 33(1)). If the debtor has paid money held by him in trust into an account which is not earmarked with reference to the trust and also keeps private money of his own in the same account, the court will, if possible, separate the trust funds from the private money.[32]

Any income received by the debtor after the date of sequestration, other than income arising from the estate vested in the permanent trustee, belongs to the debtor (s. 32(1)). However, the sheriff, on the application of the permanent trustee, may determine a suitable amount to allow for the maintenance of the debtor and his family and order any excess income to be paid to the permanent trustee (s. 32(2)).[33] Any estate which is acquired by the debtor after the date of sequestration vests in the permanent trustee (s. 32(6)). Any person who holds such estate is obliged to deliver it to the permanent trustee but if he has in good faith and without knowledge of the sequestration conveyed the estate to the debtor or to someone else on the instructions of the debtor, he incurs no liability to the permanent trustee except to account for any proceeds of the conveyance which are in his hands. Further, any person acquiring any right in the estate in good faith and for value is protected (s. 32(6)). In a question with the permanent trustee, no one can effectively deal with the debtor in relation to the estate which has vested in him (s. 32(8)). However, subsection (8) does not apply where he can establish (1) that the permanent trustee has abandoned the property, authorised the dealing or is personally barred from challenging it; or (2) that the dealing is (i) the performance of an obligation undertaken before the date of sequestration; (ii) the purchase from the debtor of goods for which he has given value to the debtor or is willing to give value to the permanent trustee; or (iii) a banking transaction in the ordinary course of business between a banker and the debtor (s. 32(9)). It is essential however that the person dealing with the debtor was unaware of the sequestration at the time when he dealt and had no reason to believe that the debtor's estate had been sequestrated or was the subject of sequestration proceedings (s. 32(9)(*b*)). Where a bank teller dealt with a debtor, unaware of his sequestration, the fact that the bank's head office had knowledge of it meant that the transaction was not protected.[34]

Debtor's family home

Before the permanent trustee can dispose of the debtor's family home in a case where it is occupied by the debtor's spouse or former spouse, he requires to obtain his or her consent, whether or not it is also occupied by

---

[30] See p. 209.

[31] *Heritable Reversionary Co.* v. *Millar* (1892) 19 R. (H.L.) 43; *Bank of Scotland* v. *Hutchison, Main & Co.*, 1914 S.C. (H.L.) 1.

[32] *Macadam* v. *Martin's Tr.* (1872) 11 M. 33; *Smith* v. *Liqr. of James Birrell Ltd.*, 1968 S.L.T. 174.

[33] *Caldwell* v. *Hamilton*, 1919 S.C. (H.L.) 100.

[34] *Minhas's Tr.* v. *Bank of Scotland*, 1990 S.L.T. 23.

the debtor. In any other case where the family home is occupied by the debtor with a child of the family, the consent of the debtor must be obtained (s. 40(1)(*a*) and (4)(*c*)). Where such consent cannot be obtained the permanent trustee must obtain instead the authority of the court (s. 40(1)(*b*)). In considering the matter the court has to have regard to the needs and financial resources of the debtor's spouse or former spouse and of any child of the family, the interests of the creditors and the length of time for which the family home was used as a residence (s. 40(2)).[35] It may refuse or postpone the granting of the application for up to 12 months.

Debtor's matrimonial home

If a debtor's estate includes a matrimonial home as distinct from a family home and immediately before the date of issue of the act and warrant the debtor had a non-entitled spouse, the permanent trustee must inform the non-entitled spouse, within 14 days of learning of his/her existence and place of residence, of the fact that sequestration of the debtor's estate has been awarded and of the right to petition for its recall under section 16 of the Act (s. 41(1)(*a*)). Where a petition is presented to the Court of Session by the non-entitled spouse within 40 days of the date of the act and warrant or 10 weeks from the date of sequestration, the court may either recall the sequestration or make such order as it thinks appropriate to protect the occupancy rights of the non-entitled spouse if it is satisfied that the purpose of the petition for sequestration was wholly or mainly to defeat these rights (s. 41(1)(*b*)).

Management and realisation of estate

As soon as he has been confirmed in office, the permanent trustee takes possession of the debtor's estate (s. 38(1)). He is entitled to delivery of any title deeds or other documents belonging to the debtor notwithstanding that a right of lien is claimed by the person holding them. If the holder delivers them, he will still have a preference over the estate if he in fact has a valid right of lien (s. 38(4)).[36] The permanent trustee has a duty to consult with the commissioners, or with the Accountant in Bankruptcy if there are none, concerning the recovery, management and realisation of the estate. In addition, he is bound to comply with any directions given to him by the creditors, the court, or the Accountant in Bankruptcy (s. 39(1)) except that he may sell perishable goods on his own initiative if he considers that the directions which he has been given would adversely affect the sale (s. 39(6)). He is entitled to carry on any business of the debtor or create a security over any part of the estate if he considers that it would be beneficial to do so (s. 39(2)) but these acts require the consent of the commissioners, if any, the creditors or the court. With consent he may also engage in litigation but if he does so he renders himself per-

---

[35] See *Salmon's Tr.* v. *Salmon*, 1989 S.L.T. (Sh.Ct.) 49.
[36] *Skinner* v. *Henderson* (1865) 3 M. 867; *Miln's Factor* v. *Spence's Trs.*, 1927 S.L.T. 425.

sonally liable to the opposite party for any expenses to which the latter may be found entitled.[37] Any sale of the debtor's estate may be by either public sale or private bargain (s. 39(3)). If he intends to sell any part of the debtor's heritable estate over which a heritable security has been created, he may sell that part only with the concurrence of the heritable creditor unless he sells at a sufficiently high price to discharge the security (s. 39(4)(a)). Provided there is no undue delay in proceeding with the sale, a heritable creditor cannot take steps to enforce his security after the permanent trustee has intimated that he intends to sell; conversely, the permanent trustee cannot proceed to a sale after a heritable creditor has intimated his intention to sell (s. 39(4)(b)). The permanent trustee has power to adopt any contract entered into by the debtor before the date of sequestration if he considers that it would be beneficial to do so, except where he is precluded from doing so by the express or implied terms of the contract (s. 42(1)). Alternatively, he may refuse to adopt any such contract (s. 42(2)). All money which he receives must be deposited by him in a bank or other financial institution although he is entitled to retain in his hands up to £200 (s. 43).

Supplies by utilities

In cases where the debtor has been supplied with gas, electricity, water or telephone services and either sequestration has been awarded or he has granted a trust deed, the interim trustee, the permanent trustee or the trustee acting under the trust deed, as the case may be, may request that the supplies be continued for the purposes of any business which was carried on by the debtor. If such a request is made, the supplier may make it a condition of making further supplies that the trustee personally guarantees the payment for these supplies but he cannot insist that any outstanding charges in respect of a supply given to the debtor before sequestration or the signing of the trust deed are paid (s. 70(2)).

Examination of debtor

The permanent trustee can request the debtor, the debtor's spouse or any other person to appear before him and supply him with information about the debtor's affairs (s. 44(1)). If necessary, he can ask the sheriff to make an order requiring any such person to appear before him for private examination (s. 44(2)). In addition, he may apply to the sheriff for an order for the public examination of the debtor or of any person who can give information about the debtor's affairs (s. 45(1)(a)). If requested by the Accountant in Bankruptcy or the commissioners (if any) or one-quarter in value of the creditors, the permanent trustee must make such an application (s. 45(1)(b)). In either case the examination must be held not less than eight weeks before the end of the first accounting period. On cause shown such an application may be made by the permanent trustee at any time (s. 45(1)). If a public examination is ordered it must take place

---

[37] *Cowie* v. *Muirden* (1893) 20 R. (H.L.) 81.

before the sheriff in open court.[38] Notice that a public examination is to
be held must be given (s. 45(3)). At the examination the permanent
trustee or a solicitor or counsel acting on his behalf and, in the case of a
public examination, any creditor may take part in the questioning. In
addition, the debtor may question any other person being examined
(s. 47(2)). Questions directed to the investigation of the merits of a
particular creditor's claim are incompetent.[39]

Adjudication of claims

A creditor who wishes to obtain an adjudication as to his entitlement
either to vote at a meeting of creditors other than the statutory meeting or
to a dividend out of the debtor's estate in respect of any accounting
period, must submit a claim to the permanent trustee at or before the
meeting or not later than eight weeks before the end of the accounting
period in question (s. 48(1)). A claim submitted by a creditor and
accepted by the interim trustee for the purpose of voting at the statutory
meeting, or accepted by the permanent trustee for the purpose of voting
at any other meeting or of drawing a dividend, is available for voting at
every meeting and for both the first dividend and any subsequent dividend (s. 48(2)). A creditor may submit a further claim for a different
amount but a secured creditor cannot specify a different value for his
security after the permanent trustee has required him to discharge,
convey or assign it under para. 5(2) of Schedule 1 (s. 48(4)). The permanent trustee accepts or rejects the claims of creditors according to the
provisions of section 49. A creditor who has had his claim accepted is
entitled to vote and to draw a dividend subject to the provisions of section
50. Once the trustee has issued his deliverance ranking a claim for a
particular dividend, he cannot afterwards alter it on the grounds that he
has discovered the claim to be bad.[40] This does not, however, prevent his
rejecting the claim, in whole or in part, as regards any subsequent
dividends.[41]

Claims on partnership estates

In the case of a firm consisting of more than one partner, the creditors
of the firm are entitled to rank on the partnership estate to the entire
exclusion of the private creditors of the partners, and also to rank equally
with the private creditors on the individual estates of the partners, after
deducting the amount of the dividend to which they are entitled from the
firm's estate.[42] Where one person carries on business under a firm name,
no distinction is made on his bankruptcy between his private and trade

---

[38] *Paxton* v. *H.M. Advocate*, 1984 S.L.T. 367.
[39] *Deloitte & Co.* v. *Baillie's Tr.* (1877) 5 R. 143.
[40] *Hamilton* v. *Kerr* (1830) 9 S. 40.
[41] *De Tastet* v. *McQueen* (1825) 4 S. 241; *Houston* v. *Duncan* (1841) 4 D. 80; *Adam & Kirk* v.
Tunnock's Tr. (1866) 5 M. 40.
[42] Bell, *Comm.*, II, 550; *Lusk* v. *Elder* (1873) 5 D. 1279; *Clydesdale Bank Ltd.* v. *Morison's Tr.*, 1983
S.L.T. 42.

creditors who rank equally on the funds available for division.[43] Similarly, where two or more persons are associated in carrying on the same or a similar business, but under different firm names, the whole estates of the firms are aggregated and divided among the creditors of the different firms without distinction. A different rule would apply if there was "real and perceptible distinction of trade and establishment" between the firms and in such a case the creditors of the respective firms would rank on the separate estates.[44]

Claims on estates of co-obligants

In claims for ranking, as for voting, where a creditor holds an obligant bound with, but liable in relief to, the debtor, he does not require to value and deduct the obligation of such party in ranking on the debtor's estate. The creditor is entitled to rank and draw a dividend for the full sum due to him. Where the creditor holds several obligants bound for the same debt and they are all sequestrated he is entitled to rank on each of the estates for the full amount due to him. He is however entitled to receive 100p in the £, but no more, on the total amount of his claim. He need not deduct payments or recoveries made after sequestration, except for the proceeds of a security over the estate of the debtor held by him before bankruptcy.[45] But in claiming on the estate of one obligant, the creditor must deduct the amount of a dividend previously received from the sequestrated estate of another obligant.[46]

Bills of exchange

Where a creditor claims on a number of bills held by him, the surplus on one bill cannot be applied towards the deficit on another.[47] Where ordinary trade bills are lodged in security of a debt and the principal obligant is sequestrated, the creditor is entitled to rank on his estate for the full amount of his debt without deduction and thereafter to call upon the other parties to the bills to make good the deficiency. In the event of all the parties being sequestrated, the creditor is entitled, to enable him to get full payment of his debt with interest, to rank on their several estates for the full amount appearing on the face of the bills, irrespective of the actual amount of his debt. If, however, in this way he gets more than the sum due to him, he requires to hold the surplus as trustee for the party from whom he received the bills.[48] In the case of a customer indorsing and delivering bills to a bank for the limited purpose of collection, the bills remain the property of the customer but are subject to the bank's right of lien. In the event of the sequestration of the customer, the obligations

---

[43] Reid v. Chalmers (1828) 6 S. 1120; Cullen v. Macfarlane (1842) 4 D. 1522.
[44] Commercial Bank of Scotland v. Tod's Tr. (1895) 33 S.L.R. 161 at p. 162.
[45] Royal Bank of Scotland v. Commercial Bank of Scotland (1881) 8 R. 805 at p. 817.
[46] Royal Bank of Scotland v. Commercial Bank of Scotland, supra.
[47] Patten v. Royal Bank of Scotland (1853) 15 D. 617.
[48] Black v. Melrose (1840) 2 D. 706; see also Jackson v. McIver (1875) 2 R. 882.

under the bills must be valued and deducted for the purposes of a ranking.[49]

Double ranking

It is a general rule of bankruptcy law that the same debt cannot be ranked for twice on the same estate.[50] If a creditor claims on the principal debtor's estate, a cautioner (as, for example, in a bank guarantee) who has paid the difference between the amount received by the creditor by way of a dividend on his ranking and the amount guaranteed, cannot also rank on the principal debtor's estate for the sum paid by him.[51] However, although a cautioner is not entitled to rank on the bankrupt's general estate for his loss as cautioner, if the cautioner holds a lien over any special fund or any security belonging to the debtor, his right to indemnity therefrom will not be affected by the prior ranking of the creditor on the general estate.[52]

Order of priority in distribution of estate

The permanent trustee must distribute the funds to meet the following debts and in the following order: (1) the outlays and remuneration of the interim trustee; (2) his own outlays and remuneration; (3) where the debtor is deceased, his deathbed and funeral expenses; (4) the expenses of the petitioning creditor; (5) preferred debts (as afterwards defined and excluding any interest which has accrued to the date of sequestration); (6) ordinary debts, i.e. debts which are neither secured nor otherwise mentioned; (7) interest on the preferred debts and the ordinary debts after the date of sequestration; and (8) any postponed debt within the meaning of section 51(3) (s. 51(1)). Any debt falling within any of categories (3) to (8) has the same priority as any other debt in the same category and where the funds of the estate are inadequate to enable all the debts within a category to be paid in full, they abate in equal proportions (s. 51(4)).

Preferred debts

These are the debts listed in Part I of Schedule 3 and are as follows:
  (1) Sums due to the Inland Revenue on account of deductions of income tax from wages, etc., paid to the debtor's employees (pay as you earn) during the period of 12 months before the relevant date (para. 1(1)). Sums due in respect of deductions which the debtor was required to make in relation to sub-contractors in the construction industry are also preferred (para. 1(2)).
  (2) Value added tax which is referable to the period of six months before the relevant date and other taxes and duties due to

---

[49] *Clydesdale Bank Ltd.* v. *Liqr. of James Allan, Senior & Son Ltd.*, 1926 S.L.T. 204.
[50] *Mackinnon* v. *Monkhouse* (1881) 9 R. 393.
[51] *Harvie's Trs.* v. *Bank of Scotland* (1885) 12 R. 1141.
[52] Bell, *Comm.*, I, 347 and 348; *Jamieson* v. *Forrest* (1875) 2 R. 700.

Customs and Excise at the relevant date and which became due within the previous 12 months (para. 2(1)).

(3) Sums due in respect of certain social security contributions due from the debtor in the period of 12 months before the relevant date (para. 3) and contributions to occupational pension schemes (para. 4).

(4) Remuneration owed by the debtor to an employee of his not exceeding the prescribed amount (currently £800) and which was payable during the period of four months before the relevant date (para. 5(1)). Any amount not exceeding the prescribed amount which is owed in respect of money advanced by a third party, such as a bank, for the purpose of payment of this remuneration (which if it had not been paid would have been a preferred debt) is entitled to a preference (para. 5(2)).[53] For the purposes of paragraph 5 remuneration includes wages and salary as well as accrued holiday remuneration and certain other payments due under employment protection legislation (para. 9(1) and (2)).

The "relevant date" means the date of sequestration (or the date of death in the case of a deceased debtor) (para. 7).

Accounting periods

The permanent trustee is obliged to make up accounts of his intromissions in respect of periods of 26 weeks, the first period commencing with the date of sequestration (s. 52(1)). If he is able to do so, he must pay a dividend out of the estate to the creditors in respect of each accounting period (s. 52(3)). He may pay the preferred debts and the debts which rank prior to these debts (other than his own remuneration) at any time (s. 52(4)) and may postpone or accelerate the payment of a dividend (s. 52(5) and (6)). Within two weeks after the end of an accounting period the permanent trustee may submit to the commissioners, or to the Accountant in Bankruptcy if there are none, an account of his intromissions, a scheme of division and a claim for his outlays and remuneration (s. 53(1)). The basis for fixing the amount of his remuneration may be a commission calculated by reference to the value of the debtor's estate which has been realised, but in any event it must take into account the work which it was reasonable for him to have undertaken and the extent of his responsibilities (s. 53(4)).

Discharge of debtor

Subject to the provisions of section 54, a debtor is automatically entitled to be discharged on the expiry of three years from the date of sequestration (s. 54(1)). However, not later than three months before the end of this period the permanent trustee or any creditor may apply to the

---

[53] Wages accounts can now be operated by banks for businesses run by firms and individuals as well as limited companies. See p. 267.

sheriff for a deferment of the debtor's discharge (s. 54(3)). A hearing is held and after considering any representations made by the applicant, the debtor or any creditor in relation to the declaration required of the debtor under section 54(4) and the report made by the permanent trustee or the Accountant in Bankruptcy pursuant to section 54(5) the sheriff either makes an order deferring the discharge for a period not exceeding two years or dismisses the application (s. 54(6)). Where the discharge is deferred, a certified copy of the order has to be registered in the Register of Inhibitions and Adjudications (s. 54(7)). A debtor whose discharge has been deferred may at any time thereafter, provided he lodges in court a declaration as to the matters mentioned in section 54(4), again petition for his discharge and the same procedure is followed (s. 54(8)). A discharge under section 54 operates so as to discharge the debtor within the United Kingdom of all debts and obligations for which he was liable at the date of sequestration, other than the liabilities and obligations mentioned in section 55(2) (s. 55(1)).

Discharge on composition

The provisions of Schedule 4 take effect when an offer of composition is made by or on behalf of the debtor (s. 56). At any time after the act and warrant has been issued to the permanent trustee, an offer of composition, which must specify the security to be provided for its implementation, may be made to the permanent trustee (paras. 1 and 2). The commissioners, or the Accountant in Bankruptcy if there are none, if it is considered that the offer, if implemented, would secure payment of a dividend of at least 25p in the £ in respect of the ordinary debts and that the security is satisfactory, must recommend that the offer be placed before the creditors (para. 3). The permanent trustee is then obliged to publish in the *Edinburgh Gazette* a notice stating that an offer has been made and inviting the creditors to accept or reject it (para. 4). The offer is considered to be accepted if a majority in number and not less than two-thirds in value of the creditors accept it (para. 5(1)). The permanent trustee must then submit to the sheriff confirmation of the acceptance of the offer and a declaration by the debtor as to the matters mentioned in section 54(4). At a subsequent hearing the sheriff either satisfies himself that the offer is reasonable and approves it or refuses to do so (para. 8). After the procedure under paragraphs 9 and 10 has been complied with, the sheriff makes an order discharging the debtor and the permanent trustee (para. 11). Such an order discharges the permanent trustee from all liability (other than any liability arising from fraud) to the creditors and to the debtor (para. 12). The order which discharges the debtor has the effect of reinvesting him in his estate and discharging him of all debts for which he was liable at the date of sequestration (para. 16). The debtor may make no more than two offers of composition in the course of a sequestration (para. 15).

Discharge of permanent trustee

After the final division of the debtor's estate has been made, the permanent trustee is required to deposit unclaimed dividends in an appropriate bank or institution. Thereafter, he may apply to the Accountant in Bankruptcy for a certificate of discharge (s. 57(1)), at the same time sending notice of his application to the debtor and the creditors (s. 57(2)). After considering any representations made to him, the Accountant in Bankruptcy may either grant or refuse the certificate (s. 57(3)). The grant of the certificate has the effect of discharging the permanent trustee from all liability (other than liability arising from fraud) to the creditors and to the debtor in respect of anything done by him in exercising his functions under the Act. Any dividend which remains unclaimed for more than seven years from the date of deposit is paid to the Secretary of State (s. 58).

Extortionate credit transactions

If the debtor has been provided with credit and his estate is sequestrated, the court may, on the application of the permanent trustee, if the transaction is or was extortionate and was not entered into more than three years before the date of sequestration, vary its terms (s. 61(1) and (2)). A transaction is extortionate if, having regard to the risk accepted by the creditor, its terms were such as to require grossly exorbitant payments to be made[54] or it otherwise grossly contravened ordinary principles of fair dealing; and it is presumed to be extortionate unless proved not to have been (s. 61(3)). If the court finds that the transaction is extortionate, it may set it aside or otherwise vary its terms; it may also require payment to the permanent trustee of any sums paid by the debtor by virtue of the transaction and the surrender to him of any property held in security (s. 61(4)). Any money or property acquired by the permanent trustee under this section vests in him (s. 61(5)).

The power given to the permanent trustee to seek an order in respect of an extortionate credit bargain is exercisable concurrently with any powers exercisable in relation to the same transaction as a gratuitous alienation (s. 34) or unfair preference (s. 36) but neither the permanent trustee nor an undischarged debtor can make an application under section 139(1)(a) of the Consumer Credit Act 1974 to reopen an extortionate credit agreement (s. 61(6)).

General offences by debtor

At common law any contract giving one creditor an unjust preference in the form of a payment in excess of his proper share of the debtor's estate is a *pactum illicitum*[55]; the creditor cannot enforce payment but the

---

[54] *A. Ketley Ltd.* v. *Scott* [1981] I.C.R. 241.
[55] *Thomas* v. *Waddell* (1869) 7 M. 558; *Farmer's Mart.* v. *Milne*, 1914 S.C. (H.L.) 84.

debtor may recover what he has paid.[56] Additionally, the 1985 Act by virtue of the provisions of section 67 makes certain conduct of the debtor during the period commencing one year immediately before the date of sequestration and ending with his discharge (see s. 67(11)) criminal. Such conduct includes the making of a false statement in relation to his assets or his financial affairs to any creditor or to any person concerned in the administration of his estate, unless he can show that he neither knew nor had reason to believe that his statement was false (s. 67(1)). In addition, any person who conceals or removes from Scotland any part of the debtor's estate or any document relating to it is guilty of an offence unless the debtor or the other person involved can show that there was no intent to prejudice the creditors (s. 67(2)). Similarly, the falsification of any documents relating to the debtor's affairs is an offence unless there was no intention to mislead (s. 67(4)). A person who is absolutely insolvent and transfers anything to another person for an inadequate consideration or grants any unfair preference to any of his creditors is guilty of an offence unless he can show that there was no intention to prejudice creditors (s. 67(6)). Collusion and secrecy are not material.[57] A debtor who is engaged in business is guilty of an offence if at any time in the period of one year ending with the date of sequestration he disposes of, otherwise than in the ordinary course of business, any property which he has obtained on credit and has not paid for unless he shows no intention to prejudice his creditors (s. 67(7)). A person in business is also guilty of an offence if at any time in the period of two years ending with the date of sequestration he has failed to keep such records as are necessary to give a fair view of the state of his business affairs unless he shows that the failure was neither reckless nor dishonest (s. 67(8)). However, he is not guilty if at the date of sequestration his unsecured liabilities did not exceed the prescribed amount (currently £20,000).

It is an offence for an undischarged bankrupt to obtain credit to the currently prescribed extent of £250 or more without informing the creditor that he was an undischarged bankrupt (s. 67(9)). The debtor is also required to take every practicable step, and in particular to execute any document, which may be necessary to enable the permanent trustee to carry out his duties (s. 64(1)) and failure to comply with an order of the sheriff in this regard is an offence (s. 64(3)).

---

[56] *Macfarlane* v. *Nicoll* (1864) 3 M. 237.
[57] *Pendreigh's Tr.* v. *McLaren & Co.* (1871) 9 M.(H.L.) 49; *Thomas* v. *Sandeman* (1872) 11 M. 81.

CHAPTER 17

EXTRA-JUDICIAL SETTLEMENTS WITH CREDITORS

Voluntary trust deeds

The estates of insolvent debtors may be realised and divided among their creditors under a private trust deed without resort to the judicial process of sequestration. Where all the creditors are agreeable, this course is in some respects preferable to sequestration. It is less expensive and allows the trustee more freedom of action in realising the debtor's estate. Trust deeds are allowed to operate without formal regulation except in several minor respects and can obtain a number of statutory advantages by becoming protected trust deeds in the manner provided in Schedule 5 to the Bankruptcy (Scotland) Act 1985.

Constitution of trust

The trust is usually constituted by a deed granted by the debtor which sets forth the purposes of the trust and conveys his whole estate and effects, heritable and moveable, to a trustee for behoof of his creditors. Such a deed creates a unilateral trust. To provide against the possibility of the trust lapsing through the death of the named trustee, it is usual to make the conveyance to the trustee and his executors and assignees, or to two or more trustees in succession. If this is not done and the trustee dies, the creditors require to take proceedings in court for the appointment of a new trustee. The deed must, in order to be effectual, be executed in regular form and delivered. To make the trust estate secure against diligence by non-acceding creditors or creditors to whom the debtor may have subsequently become indebted the trustee's title to the various subjects conveyed to him must be completed by the appropriate methods.[1] When this has been done, nothing is left with the debtor which can be attached by diligence.[2] It is advisable to provide in the deed that the trustee shall act with the advice of a committee of the creditors.

Protected trust deed

A voluntary trust deed granted by a debtor whereby his estate is conveyed to a trustee for the benefit of his creditors generally is the definition of a trust deed for the purposes of the Bankruptcy (Scotland) Act 1985 (s. 5(2)(c)). Provided that the trustee is qualified to act as a permanent trustee in a sequestration, he may, as soon as the trust deed has been delivered to him, both publish in the *Edinburgh Gazette* and

---

[1] Bell, *Comm.*, II, 386.
[2] *Gibson* v. *Wilson* (1841) 3 D. 974.

send to every creditor a notice stating that the trust deed has been granted and inviting creditors to accede to it within four weeks (Bankruptcy (Scotland) Act 1985, Sched. 5, para. 5(*a*) and (*b*)). If within this period a majority in number and not less than two-thirds in value of the creditors accede to the trust deed and the trustee has it registered with the Accountant in Bankruptcy, the trust deed becomes a protected trust deed (para. 8). A creditor who has not acceded has then no higher right to recover his debt than an acceding creditor and in addition the debtor loses his right to petition for sequestration (para. 6). Nevertheless, a qualified creditor who has not acceded may present a petition for sequestration not later than six weeks after the date of publication of the *Gazette* notice. The court may then award sequestration if it considers that to do so would be in the best interests of the creditors (para. 7(1)(*a*) and (2)). In addition, such a creditor may petition at any time provided that the apparent insolvency founded on in the petition was constituted within four months before the petition was presented. The petition on this occasion must contain an averment that the provision for distribution of the estate under the trust deed is likely to be unduly prejudicial to the creditors and sequestration will be awarded if the court is satisfied that the averment is correct (para. 7(1)(*b*) and (3)). An additional advantage offered to a protected trust deed is that the trustee may challenge gratuitous alienations (1985 Act, s. 34(7)) and unfair preferences (1985 Act, s. 36(6)).

General effect of trust deed

On the question whether it is competent for creditors to arrest in the hands of the trustee acting under the trust deed, it has been held that the general effect of a trust deed is that provided it has been granted by a debtor for the benefit of his creditors generally, and contains no extraordinary clauses, it is irrevocable by the grantor and available to bind non-acceding as well as acceding creditors if the estate is reduced into the possession of the trustee and the debtor is not sequestrated thereafter. The trustee does not represent the debtor but the creditors in their just proportions and all preferences by arrestment are excluded.[3] The effect is that no one creditor can by diligence against the trustee create a preference over the other creditors so as to draw more than his fair share of the trust estate[4] but apart from this, the conditions contained in the trust deed are ineffectual against non-acceding creditors. A trust deed is no longer considered to be a deed in the nature of a security for prior debts and as such liable to be reduced as an unfair preference.[5] A provision in the deed for the debtor's discharge is not a condition of such an extraordinary character as to render it invalid[6] but such a provision will

---

[3] *Nicolson* v. *Johnstone* (1872) 11 M. 179; *Henderson* v. *Henderson's Tr.* (1882) 10 R. 185; *Lamb's Tr.* v. *Reid* (1883) 11 R. 76.

[4] *McDougall* v. *Stevenson* (1834) 13 S. 55.

[5] This is the effect of the repeal of the Bankruptcy Act 1696 (c. 5) and s. 36 of the Bankruptcy (Scotland) Act 1985.

[6] *Henderson* v. *Henderson's Tr.* (1882) 10 R. 185.

not bind non-acceding creditors to the effect of discharging their claims against the debtor. Those creditors who were creditors of the debtor at the date of the granting of the trust deed are the only creditors entitled to any advantage under it.[7] Creditors whose debts are incurred subsequently have no claim against the trustee unless there is a reversion.[8] The trustee may from time to time record a notice in the Register of Inhibitions and Adjudications. This has the same effect as letters of inhibition registered against the debtor.[9] The trust may at any time be superseded by sequestration and when this happens the estate vests in the permanent trustee under the sequestration.[10]

Accession of creditors to trust deed

To make the trust effectual it is invariably devised in the form of a mutual contract consisting of a trust deed on the part of the debtor and accession to it on the part of the creditors. As a trust deed is a voluntary agreement, it follows that no creditor is bound by its terms unless it has become a protected trust deed or he has otherwise specially assented to it. Such assent may be proved either by writing or by oath, or, in some cases, even by parole evidence. Where no deed has been signed and proof of accession depends on facts and circumstances, a distinction has been recognised between its effect (1) as excluding creditors from carrying out diligence and (2) as binding them to any extraordinary conditions of the trust.[11] Where the creditor's assent is proved by writing or by oath, he is bound by all the conditions of the deed.[12] Where his consent is sought to be established from his actings, the most explicit proof is required before the creditor can be bound by the terms of the trust deed. It has been held that instructions to accede to a trust deed, given by a creditor to his agent, coupled with the fact that the agent had attended a meeting of the creditors and concurred in their measures, were sufficient to bind the creditor to the terms of the deed.[13] Lodging a claim is not sufficient to infer accession so as to bar a creditor from a preference[14] and while a creditor's accession to the terms of the trust deed cannot be implied from the fact of his having attended a meeting of creditors where common measures were resolved on without his having dissented, yet such conduct, if it induces the other creditors and the debtor to rely on his concurrence, will bar him from pursuing separate diligence.[15] In whatever way a creditor's accession is sought to be established, such accession

---

[7] Bell, *Comm.*, II, 387.
[8] *Marianski* v. *Wiseman* (1871) 9 M. 673.
[9] Bankruptcy (Scotland) Act 1985, Sched. 5, para. 2.
[10] *Jopp* v. *Hay* (1844) 7 D. 206; *Kyd* v. *Waterson* (1880) 7 R. 884. See also *Munro* v. *Rothfield*, 1920 S.C.(H.L.) 165.
[11] Bell, *Comm.*, II, 393 to 395.
[12] *Gibson* v. *McDonald* (1824) 3 S. 263.
[13] *Wilson* v. *McVicar* (1762) Mor. 1214; *Lea* v. *Landale* (1828) 6 S. 350.
[14] *Athya* v. *Clydesdale Bank* (1881) 18 S.L.R. 287; *Kyd* v. *Waterson* (1880) 7 R. 884.
[15] *Herriot* v. *Farquharson* (1766) Mor. 12404. (A fuller report is given in a footnote to Bell, *Comm.*, II, 394.)

implies (a) that perfect equality of division among the creditors according to their rights will be observed, and (b) that all creditors will accede, because, the contract being mutual, all must be bound or none.[16] An acceding creditor cannot resile and proceed to do diligence against the estate from the mere fact that certain creditors who have not acceded are doing nothing.[17] Should the creditor hold a cautioner for the debt, the consent of the latter should be obtained before acceding to, or accepting the provisions of, the trust deed.

Rights and liabilities of parties

Notwithstanding the trust deed, the radical right of property remains with the debtor,[18] who is entitled to any reversion there may be after the purposes of the trust have been satisfied and can compel the trustee to hold just count and reckoning with him.[19] He is entitled to see that the trustee is carrying out the purposes of the trust and is not impairing his reversionary interest. He can call upon the trustee to denude on his paying the creditors. If the trust deed is not a protected trust deed, he has a right to apply for sequestration provided he can obtain the necessary concurrence.[20] Should the trustee die, resign or become otherwise incapacitated from acting, the debtor has a right to appear and object to any new trustee, on the ground that he is not a fit and proper person for the office. He is entitled to a complete discharge, if this has been stipulated for and agreed to; but if there has been no such stipulation and the creditors do not voluntarily grant him a discharge, he remains liable for the debts under deduction of the dividends paid.

Having once acceded to the trust deed the creditors cannot pursue separate diligence against the estate. They have power, in the event of malversation on the part of the trustee, or on his non-acceptance of office, death or resignation, to have a successor appointed. They may, if they have power in the deed, nominate a new trustee. They are entitled to see that the estate is realised and divided among them according to their several rights and interests. They can take proceedings for the setting aside of preferences struck at by sections 34 and 36 of the Bankruptcy (Scotland) Act 1985 or at common law.[21] They can concur in a petition for sequestration. Where disputes arise among the creditors as to the division of an estate after it has been realised, very urgent cause must be shown to make an action of multiplepoinding competent. In such circumstances the proper course for acceding creditors is to raise a direct action against the trustee for their respective dividends, and for non-acceding creditors to have the estate sequestrated.[22]

---

[16] Bell, *Comm.*, II, 395.
[17] Bell, *Comm.*, II, 390.
[18] *McMillan* v. *Campbell* (1831) 9 S. 551; affd. (1833) 7 W. & S. 441; *Barbour* v. *Bell* (1831) 9 S. 334.
[19] *Ritchie* v. *McIntosh* (1881) 8 R. 747.
[20] *Thomson* v. *Broom* (1827) 5 S. 468; *Salaman* v. *Rosslyn's Trs.* (1900) 3 F. 298.
[21] Bankruptcy (Scotland) Act 1985, ss. 34(1)(*a*) and (7), and 36(4)(*a*) and (*b*).
[22] *Kyd* v. *Waterson* (1880) 7 R. 884.

The trustee has a right to take whatever action may be necessary for the realisation of the estate,[23] and in due course he will rank the creditors and pay them a dividend on their claims according to their respective rights and interests.[24] He cannot exceed the powers conferred on him by the trust deed. He may enter into obligations and bind the trust estate, so far as necessary, for the due fulfilment of his office. He cannot delegate his authority but he may appoint a factor. He has a lien over the estate for his outlays and expenses,[25] and for his remuneration as provided for in the trust deed. The Bankruptcy (Scotland) Act 1985 makes provision for the audit of the accounts of a trustee under a voluntary trust deed and for the fixing of his remuneration.[26] Moneys coming into the hands of the trustee should be lodged in bank in his official name.[27] He has a right on the termination of the trust, should he be unable to get his discharge from the creditors, to call them all in an action of multiplepoinding and exoneration in order to enforce it.[28] He cannot raise an action to reduce unfair preferences unless specially authorised by the creditors and has no title to do so unless an acceding creditor assigns to him his title to sue.[29] Where the debtor's estate has been sequestrated during the subsistence of the trust deed, the trustee under it must hand over the estate to the permanent trustee under the sequestration, upon payment of his outlays, expenses and remuneration.[30]

Claims and ranking

It is not necessary for creditors to lodge sworn affidavits in support of their claims under a trust deed, and a simple statement of claim is usually accepted as sufficient. Such a claim interrupts prescription.[31] Where, however, a formal affidavit and claim is called for, the forms appropriate to sequestrations may be altered to suit the requirements of the case. An important feature in ranking on trust deeds is that, apart from special stipulations inserted in the trust deed and agreed to by the creditors, the ranking of creditors is not regulated by the rules of sequestration but by common law. Accordingly, unless the trust deed otherwise provides, creditors holding securities over the debtor's estate have a right to be ranked for the full amount of their debts without deducting the value of such securities. Where there is a sufficiency of assets, the creditors are entitled to payment of interest on their claims, and in computing the amount due are entitled to attribute former dividends towards extinction of accrued interest in the first place.[32] In most trust deeds, however, it will

---

[23] *Ker* v. *Graham's Tr.* (1827) 6 S. 270.
[24] *Mansfield* v. *Burnet* (1843) 6 D. 146; *Globe Insurance Co.* v. *Scott's Tr.* (1849) 11 D. 618; affd. (1850) 7 Bell 296.
[25] *Thomson* v. *Tough's Tr.* (1880) 7 R. 1035; but see *Mess* v. *Sime's Tr.* (1898) 1 F. (H.L.) 22.
[26] See s. 59 and Sched. 5, para. 1.
[27] *Mansfield* v. *Burnet* (1843) 6 D. 146.
[28] *Kyd* v. *Waterson* (1880) 7 R. 884.
[29] Bankruptcy (Scotland) Act 1985, s. 36(4).
[30] *Thomson* v. *Tough's Tr.* (1880) 7 R. 1035; *Dall* v. *Drummond* (1870) 8 M. 1006.
[31] Bankruptcy (Scotland) Act 1985, Sched. 5, para. 3.
[32] See Goudy, *Bankruptcy*, p. 484.

be found that special provision is made for the insolvent's debts, preferred and ordinary, being ranked according to the principles of the bankruptcy statute, as if the estate had been sequestrated.[33] A non-acceding creditor is not bound to accede to the trust deed as a condition of his drawing a dividend. He is entitled to his rateable share of the debtor's funds, and should he not be paid, he has a direct action against the trustee for recovery thereof.[34] Nothing more can be enforced from a non-acceding creditor than a simple receipt for the money paid, and should the debtor be afterwards in a position to pay, the creditor has a right of action against him for the balance, provided of course, the debt has not been prescribed. Where a creditor does not wish to accede to a trust deed, he need simply intimate his claim to the trustee. This entitles him to receive a dividend along with the other creditors and does not bind him to the terms of the trust deed.

Composition contracts

Occasionally it may be to the advantage of creditors to allow a debtor to retain possession of his estate and to continue to carry on his business, if only for a limited period, but for the creditors' behoof. Instead of his divesting himself of his estate, therefore, in any of the ways already explained, an extra-judicial composition contract may be entered into under which the debtor is allowed such time as the creditors think proper for the payment of their debts or the acceptance by them of a composition.

Creditors not bound to accede

A creditor cannot be compelled to accept a composition nor can he be bound by any composition arrangement unless he has specially consented thereto.[35]

Effect

The contract is a mutual one and as the estate of an insolvent debtor is the common property of all his creditors, such a contract, unless it provides otherwise, implies (1) that all the creditors will be treated with equality[36]; (2) that no undue preference is being granted by the debtor to any of the creditors; and (3) that they all concur in the arrangement.[37] Following the rule of all consensual contracts, if a material part of the contract is not fulfilled, creditors who have previously agreed to its terms are entitled to resile; and they are also entitled to do so if the debtor has made any wilful misrepresentation or concealment as to the true state of his affairs which it was material the creditors should know.[38]

---

[33] Bankruptcy (Scotland) Act 1985, Sched. 5, para. 4.
[34] *Ogilvie* v. *Taylor* (1887) 14 R. 399.
[35] *Montgomerie* v. *Boswell* (1841) 4 D. 332.
[36] *Ironside* v. *Wilson* (1871) 9 S.L.R. 73; *Macfarlane* v. *Nicoll* (1864) 3 M. 237.
[37] Bell, *Comm.*, II, 400.
[38] *Baillie* v. *Young* (1837) 15 S. 893.

Method of carrying out

The composition contract usually provides for the debtor, or someone on his behalf, offering a sum in settlement of his debts under certain specified conditions, which include a stipulation for the debtor's discharge on the composition being met in full. If the composition is to be paid by instalments a cautioner may be imported for payment of instalments other than the first which usually falls to be paid on acceptance of the composition arrangement by the creditors. Unlike a composition under a sequestration, if the agreed-on composition is not paid when it falls due, the original debt revives,[39] and should such failure be in respect of the second or any subsequent instalment, the creditor is entitled to proceed for his whole debt, under deduction only of the payments received, unless at the time of agreeing to the composition he finally discharged the debtor.[40] In that event he can only proceed for the amount of his composition less any instalment paid. If the composition is not paid when due, the creditor is not bound to accept it afterwards.[41]

Illegal preferences

It is illegal for the debtor secretly to come under an obligation to give one of his creditors a preference as a condition of that creditor's accession to the composition arrangement and payment cannot be exacted by the party to whom the preference has been given. It is not necessary that the preference should be given directly as an inducement to grant a discharge. What the law forbids is any latent violation of that equality which the bankrupt is bound to observe towards all his creditors while he remains undischarged. Even an understanding, though never reduced to a legal contract, to give a creditor a special benefit has been held to vitiate a discharge.[42] Proceedings for the setting aside of the preference may be taken by (1) the debtor himself; (2) the permanent trustee on the sequestrated estate of the debtor or the trustee acting under a protected trust deed,[43] where sequestration has been awarded or the trust deed granted subsequent to the date of the preference[44]; (3) any creditor whose debt was incurred prior to sequestration or the granting of the protected trust deed or (4) the cautioner for the payment of the composition.[45] A voluntary payment after discharge is not subject to reduction.[46] The above general rules apply also to cautioners under composition contracts.[47]

---

[39] Bell, *Comm.* II, 400; *Horsefall* v. *Virtue* (1826) 5 S. 36.

[40] *Graham* v. *Cuthbertson* (1828) 7 S. 152.

[41] *Woods, Parker & Co.* v. *Ainslie* (1860) 22 D. 723.

[42] *Bank of Scotland* v. *Foulds* (1870) 42 Sc.Jur. 557.

[43] *Arrol* v. *Montgomery* (1826) 4 S. 499.

[44] *Macfarlane* v. *Nicoll* (1864) 3 M. 237.

[45] *Arrol* v. *Montgomery* (1826) 4 S. 499.

[46] *Macfarlane* v. *Nicoll* (1864) 3 M. 237; *Ironside* v. *Wilson* (1871) 9 S.L.R. 73.

[47] *Scott* v. *Campbell* (1834) 12 S. 447; *Thomson* v. *Craig and Latta* (1863) 1 M. 913.

CHAPTER 18

RECEIVERSHIP AND ADMINISTRATION

The holder of a floating charge created by a Scottish company may appoint a receiver of the property of the company covered by the charge in terms of the Insolvency Act 1986. Additionally, the Act makes provision for the appointment of an administrator in circumstances where the appointment of a receiver is not appropriate.[1]

Circumstances justifying the appointment of a receiver

The holder of a floating charge created by a company which the Court of Session has jurisdiction to wind up has power to appoint a receiver (s. 51(1)) or to apply to the court for such an appointment (s. 51(2)). The circumstances justifying the appointment are as follows:

(1) a receiver may be appointed by the holder of the floating charge on the occurrence of any event which, by the provisions of the instrument creating the charge, entitles the holder to make the appointment and, in so far as the instrument does not otherwise provide, on the occurrence of any of the following events—

(a) the expiry of a period of 21 days after the making of a demand for payment of the whole or any part of the principal sum secured by the charge, without payment having been made;

(b) the expiry of a period of two months during the whole of which interest due and payable under the charge has been in arrears;

(c) the making of an order or the passing of a resolution to wind up the company; and

(d) the appointment of a receiver by virtue of any other floating charge created by the company (s. 52(1)).

(2) a receiver may be appointed by the court on the occurrence of any of the foregoing events apart from (d) or where the court, on the application of the holder of the charge, pronounces itself satisfied that the position of the holder of the charge is likely to be prejudiced if no such appointment is made (s. 52(2)(a)).

The instrument of charge is usually drawn to provide for the appointment of a receiver by the holder of the charge if a request for the appointment is made by the company. Such a request should be preceded by a resolution of the directors resolving that such a request be made. If the instrument empowers the holder to appoint a receiver immediately in

---

[1] In this chapter, references to sections are to sections of the Insolvency Act 1986 unless otherwise stated.

the event of a failure to comply with a demand for payment, the appointment may be made in as short a time as one hour later.[2] If the demand notice requires to be signed by one of a group of specified officials, a notice signed in any other manner would not be a valid basis for making the appointment.[3]

Method of appointment

Where the holder of the charge appoints a receiver directly by virtue of the powers in the charge or under section 52 he does so by means of a validly executed instrument of appointment (s. 53(1)). If the holder requires to apply to the court for the appointment of a receiver, the court's interlocutor is equivalent to the deed of appointment. After execution of the deed, the holder must deliver an appropriately certified copy to the Registrar of Companies within seven days of its execution (s. 53(1)). In the case of an appointment by the court, a copy, certified by the clerk of court, of the interlocutor must be delivered to the Registrar within the same period or such longer period as the court may allow (s. 54(3)). Failure to register the appointment of a receiver involves no penalty other than a possible default fine (ss. 53(2) and 54(3)).

To be effective, the appointment must be accepted by the person appointed before the end of the business day following the day on which he received the deed and his appointment is deemed to be made at the time at which he received the deed, as evidenced by a written docquet by him (s. 53(6)). In the case of a court appointment, the effective date of appointment of a receiver is the date of the court's interlocutor (s. 54(5)). Where the appointment is discovered to be invalid, the court may order the holder of the charge to indemnify the person appointed against any liability arising out of the invalidity (s. 63(2)). When a receiver has been appointed, the directors' power to deal with the property comprised in the charge is circumscribed.[4] However, a statement of affairs has to be submitted to the receiver within the period specified in section 66 and the obligation to provide this statement rests with the persons specified in section 66(3) included among whom are the directors. The charge crystallises and attaches to the property then subject to it as if it were a fixed security (ss. 53(7) and 54(6)). If the floating charge covers the whole assets of the company, present and future, while the charge is in force, assets acquired or re-acquired by the company after the appointment of the receiver will be property subject to the charge in terms of sections 53(7) and 54(6).[5]

Powers of the receiver

The powers of the receiver in relation to the property of the company

---

[2] *R. A. Cripps & Son Ltd.* v. *Wickenden* [1973] 2 All E.R. 606.
[3] *Elswick Bay Shipping Co. Ltd.* v. *The Royal Bank of Scotland Ltd.*, 1982 S.L.T. 62.
[4] *Imperial Hotel (Aberdeen) Ltd.* v. *Vaux Breweries Ltd.*, 1978 S.L.T. 113. *Shanks* v. *Central Regional Council*, 1986 S.L.T. 410.
[5] *Ross* v. *Taylor*, 1985 S.L.T. 387.

which is attached by the floating charge are extensive and are specified in section 55 of and Schedule 2 to the Act. They include power to take possession of, collect and get in the property from the company or a liquidator or any other person and for that purpose to take such proceedings as may seem to him expedient; power to borrow money and grant security over the property; power to do all things, including the carrying out of works, necessary for the realisation of the property of the company; and power to carry on the business of the company. In addition, the court is empowered to give directions to a receiver in respect of any matter relating to his functions on the application of either the floating charge holder or the receiver himself (s. 63(1)). A person dealing with a receiver in good faith and for value need not inquire whether the receiver is acting within his powers (s. 55(4)). A receiver appointed under the law of Scotland may exercise his powers in the other parts of Great Britain so far as their exercise is not inconsistent with the law applicable there (s. 72). It has been held that in terms of section 473(4) of the Companies Act 1985 a company alone remains debtor and creditor in relation to obligations under a contract entered into by it prior to receivership and that a receiver takes its assets as they are, subject to any rights which others may have in respect of them including the right to set-off.[6]

In terms of section 55(3) the receiver's powers are subject to the rights of any person who has effectually executed diligence on any part of the property of the company prior to his appointment, and to the rights of any person who holds a fixed security or floating charge having priority over or ranking *pari passu* with the floating charge by virtue of which he has been appointed. "Effectually executed diligence" in this section should be construed as similar in meaning to the expression as found in section 185 of the Act in the case of liquidation. An arrestment which has not been completed by a decree of furthcoming is not an "effectual diligence."[7] A receiver cannot exercise his powers in relation to property subject to a floating charge which is also subject to a restraint order made under section 8 of the Criminal Justice (Scotland) Act 1987 before his appointment.[8]

Retention of title

The receiver takes the property of the company subject to the charge *tantum et tale* as it belonged to the company. Under sections 17 and 19 of the Sale of Goods Act 1979 where there is a contract for the sale of specific goods or goods are subsequently appropriated to the contract, the seller may reserve the property or right of disposal of the goods until certain conditions are fulfilled. Accordingly, retention of title is a contractual provision and title (*i.e.* ownership and property of goods) may be

---

[6] *Myles J. Callaghan Ltd.* v. *City of Glasgow D.C.*, 1988 S.L.T. 227.
[7] *Lord Advocate* v. *Royal Bank of Scotland*, 1976 S.L.T. 130.
[8] Criminal Justice (Scotland) Act 1987, s. 36.

retained by a seller until he is actually paid, notwithstanding the fact that the goods have been physically delivered into the possession of the company. The use of such clauses can prejudice secured creditors by removing assets from the property covered by a floating charge and they have become more common following the decision in the *Romalpa* case[9] and give rise to complex legal problems as each type of clause has to be construed to ascertain the precise nature of the right reserved.[10] If the right of property is reserved and the goods remain unprocessed in the hands of the company or a receiver, they belong to the seller until paid for and the court will order them to be delivered up.[11] Such a retention of title provision in a contract of sale does not constitute the creation of a charge and does not require to be registered under section 396 of the Companies Act 1985.[12] Where the goods have become converted or inmixed with the company's own property or money has become inmixed so that the property or money has become indistinguishable, the seller must rank as an ordinary creditor.[13] However, if it can be established that the company, having bought and sold goods in their original state, does in fact hold identifiable proceeds of sale in trust for the original seller, the latter can recover these proceeds from a receiver.[14]

Duties of the receiver

The nature and extent of the receiver's duties to the various interested parties (the company, the holder of the charge and other creditors) are not spelled out in the Act. It has been held that whether the receiver is appointed before or after the commencement of a liquidation, his rights take precedence over the rights of the liquidator and he is entitled to take control of the property of the company by virtue of section 55 and that on his appointment he becomes primarily liable for the payment of the secured and preferential creditors.[15] Although he can be said to have duties other than the duty to satisfy the debt of the floating charge holder, the receiver has no power to pay ordinary creditors. He has however a duty to notify all creditors of his appointment (s. 65(1)) and to send a copy of the report which he makes to the floating charge holder pursuant to section 67 to all creditors. He must also summon a meeting of creditors to consider the terms of this report unless the court otherwise directs. This meeting has power to establish a committee which can require the receiver to furnish such information about the carrying out by him of his functions as it may reasonably require (s. 68). In England, it has been

---

[9] *Aluminium Industrie Vaassen B.V.* v. *Romalpa Aluminium Ltd.* [1976] 1 W.L.R. 677.

[10] See *Re Bond Worth Ltd.* [1979] 3 All E.R. 919; *Borden (U.K.) Ltd.* v. *Scottish Timber Products Ltd.* [1979] 3 All E.R. 961 and other cases referred to in this paragraph.

[11] *Aluminium Industrie Vaassen B.V.* v. *Romalpa Aluminium Ltd.*, *supra*; *Clough Mills* v. *Martin* [1984] 3 All E.R. 982; *Armour and Anor.* v. *Thyssen Edelstahlwerke A.G.*, 1990 S.L.T. 891.

[12] *Clough Mills Ltd.* v. *Martin*, *supra*.

[13] Bell, *Prin.*, § 1298.

[14] *Smith and Ors.* v. *Liqr. of James Birrell Ltd.*, 1968 S.L.T. 174; *Tay Valley Joinery Ltd.* v. *C. F. Financial Services Ltd.*, 1987 S.L.T. 207.

[15] *Manley, Petr.*, 1985 S.L.T. 42.

held that when realising assets the duty of the receiver to sell them at the best price reasonably obtainable in the circumstances is owed not only to the floating charge holder but also to a guarantor of the floating charge holder's debt.[16]

Agency and liability of receiver for contracts

A receiver is the agent of the company in relation to the property attached by the charge (s. 57(1)). The floating charge holder is not responsible for the receiver's actings unless he interferes so as to take away some of the receiver's discretion.[17] The receiver is personally liable on contracts entered into by him, unless the contract otherwise provides,[18] and on contracts of employment adopted by him (s. 57(2)) but he is entitled to be indemnified out of the property in respect of which he was appointed (s. 57(3)). A receiver does not by virtue only of his appointment incur personal liability on contracts entered into before his appointment which continue in force thereafter (s. 57(4)). The court will not however order a receiver to perform such a contract where he has no means of doing so. In such circumstances the remedy of the other party is in damages only.[19]

Priority of payments

Where a receiver is appointed and the company is not at the time of the appointment in the course of being wound up, claims which would have ranked as preferential debts in a winding up by virtue of section 386 of and Schedule 6 to the Act must be paid out of any assets in his hands in priority to the claims of the holder of the floating charge (s. 59(1)). It is necessary however that such claims be intimated to the receiver within six months after he has advertised for them (s. 59(2)). The periods of time mentioned in the relevant provisions of the Act are reckoned in the case of a receivership from the date of the appointment of the receiver under section 53(6) or 54(5) (s. 387(4)). The same considerations apply to the operation by a bank of a separate wages account in a receivership as apply in a liquidation.[20]

In addition to the preferential creditors who are entitled to payment under section 59, the claims of the holder of the floating charge are postponed to the claims of certain other creditors. These are (a) the holder of any prior or *pari passu* ranking fixed security over the property subject to the floating charge; (b) persons who have effectually executed diligence on any part of the property of the company which is subject to the charge; (c) creditors in respect of all liabilities, charges and expenses

---

[16] *Standard Chartered Bank Ltd.* v. *Walker* [1982] 1 W.L.R. 1410. See also *Lord Advocate* v. *Maritime Fruit Carrier Co. Ltd.*, 1983 S.L.T. 357 at p. 359 and *Forth and Clyde Construction Co. Ltd.* v. *Trinity Timber & Plywood Co. Ltd.*, 1984 S.L.T. 94.

[17] *Standard Chartered Bank Ltd.* v. *Walker, supra.*

[18] *Hill Samuel & Co. Ltd.* v. *Laing*, 1989 S.L.T. 760.

[19] *Macleod* v. *Alexander Sutherland Ltd.*, 1977 S.L.T. (Notes) 44.

[20] See p. 267.

incurred by the receiver; and (d) the receiver in respect of his liabilities, expenses and remuneration (s. 60(1)).

The remuneration to be paid to the receiver is determined by agreement between the receiver and the holder of the charge (s. 58(1)). If the amount of his remuneration is disputed by either the receiver, the holder of any charge, the company or its liquidator an application may be made to the Auditor of the Court of Session to have it fixed (s. 58(2)).

After the provisions of sections 60(1) and 61 have been satisfied, any balance of moneys remaining falls to be paid to any other receiver, the holder of a fixed security over property subject to the floating charge and the company or its liquidator, as the case may be (s. 60(2)). If there is any dispute or the receiver cannot get a proper receipt or discharge, he must consign the amount in question in a Scottish bank in name of the Accountant of Court (s. 60(3)).

Disposal of property

If the receiver wishes to dispose of property which is subject to any security or burden or encumbrance in favour of a creditor ranking prior to, *pari passu* with or postponed to the floating charge, or property affected or attached by effectual diligence, and he is unable to obtain the consent of such creditor, he may apply to the court for authority to sell or dispose of the property free of any such security, interest, burden, encumbrance or diligence (s. 61(1)). The court may authorise the sale on such terms or conditions as it thinks fit.[21] Where there is a fixed security over the property in question, the court must have regard to the terms of section 61(3).

Resignation of receiver

A receiver appointed by deed of appointment may on application by the holder of the floating charge be removed from office by the court on cause shown or he may resign by giving notice to the person by whom he was appointed (s. 62(1)). If one month after the receiver has been removed or has ceased to act, no other receiver has been appointed by the holder of the same charge, the charge refloats (s. 62(6)). The property then ceases to be attached by the charge.

Administrator

An application for the appointment of an administrator to assume the management of a company may be made either by the company or by a creditor (s. 9).[22] Notice must be given to any floating charge holder who is entitled to appoint an administrative receiver whether or not such a

---

[21] See, for example, *Forth and Clyde Construction Co. Ltd.* v. *Trinity Timber & Plywood Co. Ltd.*, 1984 S.L.T. 94 and *Armour and Mycroft, Petrs.*, 1983 S.L.T. 453.

[22] An authorised institution within the meaning of the Banking Act 1987 is subject to the provisions of Pt. II of the Act. See s. 422 and the Banks (Administrative Proceedings) Order (S.I. 1989 No. 1276).

receiver has been appointed (s. 9(2)). (An administrative receiver is a receiver appointed under section 51 of the Act where the whole or substantially the whole of the company's property is attached by the charge (s. 251).) In making the application it is necessary to show that the company cannot pay its debts (see s. 123) and that the appointment would be likely to achieve (1) the survival of the company as a going concern; (2) the approval of a voluntary arrangement under Part I; (3) the sanctioning of a compromise or arrangement under section 425 of the Companies Act 1985; or (4) a more advantageous realisation of its assets than would be effected in a winding up (s. 8(3)).

An administration order will not be made after the company has gone into liquidation (s. 4(4)(*a*)). Where there is a receiver, the petition will be dismissed unless the floating charge holder consents to the making of the order or the court is satisfied that if an administration order were made, the charge would be avoided under section 245 of the Act or challengeable under section 242 or 243 of the Act or at common law (s. 9(3)). From the date of the presentation of the petition for the order until it is either made or dismissed, the rights of creditors in relation to the company are restricted. No resolution may be passed or order made for the winding up of the company, no security (as defined in section 248(*b*)(ii)) over the company's property may be enforced, goods subject to hire-purchase and retention of title[23] agreements may not be repossessed without the leave of the court and no other proceedings and no execution of diligence may be commenced or continued against the company or its property without the leave of the court (s. 10(1) and (5)). However, a creditor is not prevented from petitioning for the winding up of the company or appointing a receiver and a receiver (whenever appointed) may carry out his functions (s. 10(2)). As soon as an administration order has been made, any petition for winding up shall be dismissed and any receiver must vacate office (s. 11(1)). During the period while the administration order is in force, the company cannot be wound up and no receiver can be appointed, without the leave of the court, no security can be enforced, no goods can be repossessed under any hire-purchase or retention of title agreement and no legal proceedings or diligence can be commenced (s. 11(3)). The order must specify the purpose or purposes for whose achievement it is made (s. 8(1)).

Powers and duties of an administrator

The administrator's general duties are to manage the business of the company in accordance with any directions given by the court until such time as proposals have been approved under section 24 of the Act (s. 17(2)). He may do whatever is necessary for the management of the company's business and without prejudice to the generality of this power

---

[23] "Hire-purchase agreement" includes a chattel-leasing agreement (as defined in s. 251) and a retention-of-title agreement (Insolvency Act 1986, s. 10(4)).

he has the powers listed in Schedule 1 to the Act (s. 14(1)). In particular, he has power to borrow money and power to carry on the business of the company and to deal with the disposal of its assets and in exercising his powers he is deemed to be the agent of the company (s. 14(5)). He may dispose of property subject to a floating charge as if it were not subject to the security (s. 15(1) and (3)). However, the floating charge holder enjoys the same priority in respect of property representing the property disposed of as he would have had in respect of the property subject to his security (s. 15(4)). With the leave of the court, an administrator has power to compel the disposal of property subject to a security or hire-purchase agreement[24] and the court will authorise the disposal if it is satisfied that it will promote one or more of the purposes mentioned in section 8(3) of the Act and specified in the administration order (s. 15(2)). The net proceeds of such a disposal must be applied towards discharging the sums secured by the security or payable under the hire-purchase agreement (s. 15(5)). The administrator may at any time apply to the court for the administration order to be varied so as to specify an additional purpose (s. 18(1)).

Approval of the administrator's proposals

The administrator must within three months of his appointment prepare a statement of his proposals for achieving the purpose or purposes specified in the order. This must be circulated to creditors and laid before a meeting of creditors summoned for the purpose (s. 23(1)). This meeting will decide whether or not to approve the proposals (s. 24(1)). If they are approved but with modifications, these must be agreed to by the administrator (s. 24(2)). The decision of the meeting must be reported to the court and if the proposals have not been approved the court may discharge the administration order and make such other order as it thinks fit (s. 24(5)). If the administrator's proposals have been approved by the meeting, then he is obliged to proceed with them (s. 17(2)(b)). Any substantial revision of the approved proposals must in turn be approved under section 25 of the Act.

Rights of creditors

A meeting of creditors must be summoned by the administrator if requested by one-tenth in value of the creditors or directed by the court (s. 17(3)). The meeting of creditors summoned under section 23 of the Act may appoint a committee to exercise the functions conferred on it by the Act (s. 26(1)). This committee may at any time require the administrator to attend before it and provide it with such information about the progress of the administration as it may reasonably require (s. 26(2)). Any substantial revision of the administrator's proposals requires approval at a meeting of the company's creditors summoned for

---

[24] See Insolvency Act 1986, s. 15(9).

the purpose (s. 25(2)). If the creditors decide that they wish the administration order to be discharged or varied, the administrator must apply to the court (s. 18(2)(b)). At any time when an administration order is in force a creditor or member of the company who considers that its affairs are being managed by the administrator in a manner which is unfairly prejudicial to his interests may apply to the court for relief in respect of the matters complained of (s. 27(1)).

Termination of appointment of administrator

The administrator must apply to the court for the administration order to be discharged when he considers that the purpose or each of the purposes specified in the order either has been achieved or is incapable of achievement (s. 18(2)). Alternatively, he must do so when required by a meeting of creditors (s. 18(2)(b)). The administrator may at any time be removed by the court or may resign his office (s. 19(1)).

Voluntary arrangements

Part I of the Act makes provision for a liquidator or administrator to make a proposal for a composition in respect of the company's debts or a scheme of arrangement of its affairs. The directors of the company may do likewise where the company is not being wound up and there is no administration order in force. Such a proposal must provide for a qualified insolvency practitioner to act as trustee to supervise its implementation (s. 1). Where the person nominated is not the liquidator or administrator, he must report to the court whether or not he considers meetings of the company and of its creditors should be summoned to consider the proposal (s. 2). If the nominee is the liquidator or administrator, he must summon such meetings (s. 3(2)). These meetings have power to approve the proposed composition or scheme (with or without modifications) but the rights of secured and preferential creditors cannot be adversely affected without their consent (s. 4(1), (3) and (4)). If each meeting approves the proposal, it binds every person who had notice and was entitled to vote at that meeting of creditors (s. 5(2)). The court may then give such directions in relation to the winding up or administration as it thinks appropriate for facilitating the approved composition or scheme (s. 5(3)). An application may nevertheless be made to the court by a member, creditor, liquidator or administrator as the case may be to challenge these decisions if the proposal is thought to be unfairly prejudicial to the interests of creditors, members or contributors (s. 6(1) and (2)). The approved composition or scheme, where it takes effect, is implemented by a supervisor (s. 7(2)) and power is given to him to apply to the court for the winding up of the company or for an administration order (s. 7(4)).

CHAPTER 19

LIQUIDATION

A company incorporated under the Companies Acts does not cease to exist until formally dissolved. The estates of a company cannot be sequestrated under the Bankruptcy (Scotland) Act 1985[1] but under Part I of the Insolvency Act 1986[2] it can make a proposal for a composition in satisfaction of its debts or a scheme of arrangement of its affairs.[3] Winding up, or liquidation, is a necessary preliminary to the dissolution of a company and generally takes one of the following forms—(1) winding up by the court; (2) members' voluntary winding up; or (3) creditor's voluntary winding up (s. 73). The provisions of the Act with respect to winding up apply, unless a contrary intention is expressed, to a winding up in any of these forms (s. 73(2)).

Winding up by the court

In the circumstances laid down in the Act, a petition may be presented to the court for a compulsory winding-up order. The Court of Session has jurisdiction to wind up any company registered in Scotland (s. 120(1)) and where the paid-up share capital does not exceed £120,000 the sheriff court of the sheriffdom where its registered office is situated has concurrent jurisdiction (s. 120(3)). For this purpose the registered office means the place which has longest been the company's registered office during the six months preceding the presentation of the petition (s. 120(4)). The Scottish courts have jurisdiction to wind up companies formed and registered under Part I or Part XXII of the Companies Act 1985, and unregistered companies as defined in section 220 of the Act. Section 122 provides that the court may order a company to be wound up if *inter alia* (1) the company has by special resolution resolved to be wound up by the court; (2) the company does not commence its business within a year of incorporation, or suspends its business for a whole year; (3) the number of members is reduced, in the case of a private company, below two, or, in the case of any other company, seven; (4) the company is unable to pay its debts; (5) the court is of the opinion that it is just and equitable that the company should be wound up; or (6) the court is satisfied that the security of a creditor entitled to the benefit of a floating charge is in jeopardy.

Most petitions for a compulsory winding-up order are based on the company's inability to pay its debts. Under section 123(1) of the Act a

---

[1] Bankruptcy (Scotland) Act 1985, s. 6(2)(*a*). Its estates may be sequestrated and a judicial factor appointed at common law: *Patrick Frazer, Petr.*, 1971 S.L.T. 146.

[2] In this chapter, references to sections are to sections of the Insolvency Act 1986 unless stated otherwise.

[3] It cannot however grant a trust deed for behoof of its creditors: *London Joint City and Midland Bank Ltd.* v. *Herbert Dickinson* (1922) W.N. 13.

company is deemed to be unable to pay its debts "if a creditor, by assignment or otherwise, to whom the company is indebted in a sum exceeding £750 then due has served on the company, by leaving it at the registered office of the company, a demand in the prescribed form under his hand requiring the company to pay the sum so due and the company has for three weeks[4] thereafter neglected to pay the sum or to secure or compound for it to the reasonable satisfaction of the creditor." Section 123(1) is not available to a creditor whose claim is contingent or prospective,[5] or disputed on substantial grounds[6] and a winding-up petition is not the proper means of enforcing a debt which is disputed.[7] A Scottish company is in addition deemed to be unable to pay its debts if the induciae of a charge for payment on an extract decree, or an extract registered bond, or an extract registered protest have expired without payment being made (s. 123(1)(c)). A company is also deemed to be unable to pay its debts if it is proved to the satisfaction of the court that the company is unable to pay its debts as they fall due (s. 123(1)(e)) or that its liabilities, including its contingent and prospective liabilities, exceed its assets (s. 123(2)). Petitions based on the "just and equitable" grounds provided for by section 122(1)(g) are most frequently made by shareholders complaining that the management of the company is being conducted in a manner harmful to their interests but the courts are entitled to exercise their discretion in examining other grounds. If the dispute among the shareholders cannot be settled and a deadlock results, a winding-up order will be granted.[8]

Commencement of winding up

A winding up by the court is deemed to commence at the time the petition is presented to the court (s. 129(2)) unless a resolution for voluntary winding up has already been passed in which case it is deemed to commence at the time of the passing of the resolution (s. 129(1)). The court has power to appoint a provisional liquidator at any time after the presentation of the petition until an official liquidator is appointed (s. 135(1)) and the petition should contain an application for such an appointment, if desired. It is almost invariable practice to apply for the appointment of a provisional liquidator on presentation of the petition and he is entitled to carry out such functions as the court may confer on him (s. 135(4)). When a winding-up order is made by the court, a liquidator has to be appointed at the same time (s. 138). A liquidator appointed under s. 138 is referred to an interim liquidator (s. 138(1)). Section 138(3) provides that the interim liquidator must summon separate meetings of creditors and contributories but he need not summon a

---

[4] For computation of time, see *Neil McLeod & Sons Ltd., Petrs.*, 1967 S.L.T. 46.

[5] *Stonegate Securities Ltd.* v. *Gregory* [1980] 1 All E.R. 241.

[6] *Re Lympne Investments Ltd.* [1972] 2 All E.R. 385.

[7] *W. & J. C. Pollok* v. *Gaeta Pioneer Mining Co.*, 1907 S.C. 182; *Stonegate Securities Ltd.* v. *Gregory* [1980] 1 All E.R. 241.

[8] *Pirie* v. *Stewart* (1904) 12 S.L.T. 129; *Baird* v. *Lees*, 1923 S.L.T. 749.

meeting of contributors if the winding-up order was on the ground of inability to pay debts. The purpose of the meeting (or meetings) is to choose a liquidator in place of the interim liquidator. If no one is chosen, the court must appoint the interim liquidator or some other person to be the liquidator (s. 138(5)). To be entitled to vote, a creditor must produce his oath or notice of claim.[9] If the creditors and contributories nominate different persons, the creditors' nominee is preferred but any contributory or creditor of the company may apply to the court for an order appointing some other person (s. 139(4)). If the winding-up order is made immediately on the discharge of an administration order, the administrator may be appointed liquidator (s. 140(1)). The meeting of creditors summoned under section 138 of the Act (and the meeting of contributories if one has been summoned) may establish a liquidation committee to exercise the functions conferred on it by the Act (s. 142(1)). This committee has the powers and duties referred to in section 142(6) of the Act.

Duties of the liquidator

The functions of the liquidator of a company being wound up by the court are to secure that the assets of the company are got in, realised and distributed to the company's creditors (s. 143(1)). Subject to general rules, he has the same powers as a trustee on a bankrupt estate (s. 169(2)). The powers which he may exercise in performing his duties are listed in Schedule 4. Certain powers may be exercised without the sanction of the court or the committee of creditors while other powers require such sanction. If he disposes of any property of the company to a person connected with the company or employs a solicitor to assist him, such an exercise of his powers must be notified to the committee of creditors, if one has been formed (s. 167(2)). He may apply to the court for an early dissolution of the company in terms of section 204 of the Act if it appears to him that the realisable assets of the company are insufficient to cover the expenses of winding up.

Voluntary winding up

The majority of liquidations are voluntary and are initiated by resolution of the members. Section 84 provides that a company may be wound up voluntarily (1) by an ordinary resolution passed at the time when in terms of its articles the company is to be dissolved or on the occurrence of an event in respect of which similar provision has been made; (2) if the company resolves by special resolution that it be wound up; or (3) if the company resolves by extraordinary resolution that it cannot by reason of its liabilities continue its business and that it is advisable to wind up. All

---

[9] Rules dealing with this and other matters connected with the insolvency or winding up of companies have been made pursuant to the Act: Insolvency (Scotland) Rules 1986.

voluntary liquidations commence on the date of the resolution to wind up (s. 86).

Members' voluntary winding up

A winding up is a members' voluntary winding up if a declaration of solvency is filed under section 89. This is a statutory declaration by a majority of the directors to the effect that having made a full inquiry into the affairs of the company they have formed the opinion that the company will be able to pay its debts in full within a period not exceeding 12 months after the commencement of a winding up (s. 89(1)). The declaration has no effect unless it is made within the five weeks immediately preceding the date of the resolution or on that day but before the passing of the resolution (s. 89(2)(a)). The absence of such a declaration results in the liquidation being a creditors' voluntary winding up, regardless of the financial position of the company (s. 90). Criminal penalties attach to the making of a declaration of solvency without reasonable grounds and if there is a failure to pay or provide for the company's debts in full within the period stated it is presumed, until the contrary is shown, that the directors did not have reasonable grounds for their opinion (s. 89(4)). If the liquidator forms the opinion that the company will not be able to pay its debts in full within the stated period he must call a meeting of creditors and submit a statement of assets and liabilities to it (s. 95). As from the date of this meeting, the Act has effect as if the directors' declaration under section 89 had not been made and the meetings of the creditors and the company at which it was resolved to wind up were the meetings which must precede a creditors' voluntary winding up. The winding up then becomes a creditors' voluntary winding up (s. 96).

Striking off

As an alternative to a members' voluntary liquidation and to avoid the expense of such procedure, if the company is not carrying on business or in operation it is possible for an official or the solicitor acting for the company to ask the Registrar of Companies to initiate proceedings under section 652 of the Companies Act 1985 to strike the company off the register. The Registrar in turn may initiate such proceedings in the circumstances set out in the section.

Creditors' voluntary winding up

In a creditors' voluntary winding up the company must call a meeting of creditors for a day not later than the fourteenth day following the meeting of the company at which the resolution to wind up is to be proposed (s. 98(1)(a)). A liquidator nominated by the company before the creditors' meeting is held may not exercise except with the sanction of the court the powers conferred on a liquidator by section 165 during the period before the meeting is held, but he may nevertheless take any steps necessary to protect the assets of the company (s. 166(2)). At least seven days' notice of the meeting must be given to creditors (s. 98(1)(*b*)). The purposes of the meeting of creditors are to consider a statement of affairs which the directors are bound to submit (s. 99(1)), to decide whether to nominate a liquidator of the creditors' choice (s. 100(1)) and to appoint, if so desired, a committee of not more than five persons to exercise the functions conferred on it by the Acts (s. 101). If the creditors nominate a different person he is appointed in preference to the members' nominee, subject to the right of any director, member or creditor to apply to the court within seven days to resolve the dispute (s. 100(3)). A voluntary liquidator has the powers and duties specified in section 165.

Preferential creditors

The expenses of any voluntary winding up are paid in priority to all preferential and unsecured debts (s. 115 and s. 175(2)(*a*)). The order of preference is normally (1) expenses of realisation, (2) the liquidator's other expenses, (3) the liquidator's remuneration and (4) the petitioning creditor's expenses. Corporation tax on chargeable gains arising from the realisation of assets falls to be treated as a disbursement of the liquidator and not part of the cost of realisation.[10] Section 175 provides that in a winding up the preferential debts listed in Schedule 6 to the Act shall be paid in priority to all other debts. They rank equally among themselves after the expenses of the winding up and must be paid in full unless the assets are insufficient to meet them, in which case they abate in equal proportions. If the assets available to general creditors are insufficient to meet them, they are paid out of any property subject to a floating charge which would otherwise secure the claims of the holder of that charge (s. 175(2)(*b*)). The preferential debts listed in Schedule 6 are the same *mutatis mutandis* as those listed in Schedule 3 to the Bankruptcy (Scotland) Act 1985.[11] The relevant date in each case is (1) the date of the making of the administration order where the company is wound up immediately upon the discharge of that order; or (2) the date of the appointment of a provisional liquidator or making of a winding-up order where the company is being wound up by the court; or (3) the date of the passing of the resolution for winding up (s. 387). A bank can obtain the maximum benefit under paragraph 11 of Schedule 6 (which gives a preferential status to sums owed in respect of money advanced for employees' remuneration) by opening a separate "wages account" out of which advances are made for the payment of wages. If this is done, the danger of the reduction of its preferential claim by payments-in by virtue of the operation of the rule in *Clayton's Case* can be largely avoided. A separate account is not however essential provided the facts are otherwise clear and indeed the bank need not show either that the money was

---

[10] *Re Mesco Properties Ltd.* [1980] 1 All E.R. 117. In effect, if the realisation of an asset subject to a fixed or floating charge is left in the hands of a liquidator, any tax liability resulting from the sale has to be met out of the proceeds in priority to the claims of the charge holders.

[11] See p. 243.

advanced pursuant to an agreement or with the intention to become a preferential creditor.[12] If the company's operative account is maintained in credit, the interdependence of this account and the wages account may have the result that the bank cannot be said to have made advances for wages and to have a preferential claim.[13] On the other hand, if the bank holds security for its lending to the company it is entitled, on realising the security, to appropriate the proceeds in payment first of all the non-preferential part of the company's indebtedness.[14]

Effect of a winding-up order

A winding-up order operates for the benefit of all creditors (s. 130(4)). The company remains vested in its assets but the liquidator administers them.[15] The powers of the directors cease on the granting of a winding-up order but only to the extent that these pass to the liquidator. They retain, for example, power to appeal against the winding-up order itself or to seek recall of the liquidator's appointment. Any disposition of property after the commencement of a winding-up by the court is void unless otherwise ordered by the court (s. 127). Sums credited to the company's bank account and payments to third parties debited to that account are, in principle, dispositions of property and as such are invalid under section 127 unless sanctioned by the court.[16]

Effect on diligence

Diligence within 60 days of winding up is struck at by section 185 which applies the provisions of section 37(1) to (6) and section 39(3), (4), (7) and (8) of the Bankruptcy (Scotland) Act 1985 in the winding up.[17] For the purpose of this section, the commencement of the winding up in the case of a winding up by the court is the day on which the winding-up order is made (s. 185(3)).

Special manager

A liquidator or provisional liquidator may apply under section 177 of the Act for the appointment of a special manager of the business or property of the company where it appears to him that the nature of this business or property or the interests of the company's creditors, contributories or members generally require the appointment of another person to manage the business or property. A special manager can be given such powers as may be entrusted to him by the court (s. 177(3)).

---

[12] *Re Primrose (Builders) Ltd.* [1950] 2 All E.R. 334; *Re Rampgill Mill Ltd.* [1967] 1 All E.R. 56.
[13] *Re E. J. Morel (1934) Ltd.* [1961] 1 All E.R. 796.
[14] *Re William Hall (Contractors) Ltd.* [1967] 2 All E.R. 1150.
[15] See *Bank of Scotland* v. *Hutchison Main & Co.*, 1913 S.C. 255; *Smith* v. *Lord Advocate*, 1978 S.C. 259.
[16] *Re Gray's Inn Construction Co. Ltd.* [1980] 1 All E.R. 814. See p. 39.
[17] *Commercial Aluminium Windows Ltd.* v. *Cumbernauld Development Corp.*, 1987 S.L.T. (Sh.Ct.) 91.

Extortionate credit transactions

An office holder—meaning in this context a liquidator or administrator (s. 238(1))—may apply to the court to set aside any credit transaction entered into by the company in the period of three years prior to the liquidation or making of the administration order if it was extortionate, that is to say, if its terms were such as to require grossly exorbitant payments to be made or it otherwise grossly contravened ordinary principles of fair dealing (s. 244). Unless the contrary is proved, it is presumed that the transaction was extortionate and the court may set it aside or vary its terms. The same transaction may be challenged concurrently under section 242 of the Act as a gratuitous alienation.

Public utilities

An office holder may also request to be given supplies of gas, electricity, water and telecommunication services by the appropriate utility and while the supplier may insist that the office holder personally guarantees payment for such supplies he cannot demand as a condition of the supply that outstanding charges for supplies given to the company before the relevant date are paid (s. 233). For the purposes of this provision, "the relevant date" is the date of liquidation, the making of the administration order, the appointment of the receiver or provisional liquidator or the approval of the composition or scheme by the meetings summoned under section 4 of the Act, whichever is applicable (s. 233(4)).

Responsibility for fraudulent and wrongful trading

If in the course of a winding up it appears that the business of the company has been carried on with intent to defraud[18] the creditors of the company or any other person or for any fraudulent purpose, the court may declare that any persons who are knowingly parties to the carrying on of the business in this manner shall be personally liable, without any limitation of liability, for all or any of the debts or other liabilities of the company as the court may direct (s. 213(1) and (2)). Such persons are also criminally liable (s. 458 of the Companies Act 1985). If the company carried on trading and incurred debts dishonestly, an intent to defraud is established on proof of an intention dishonestly to prejudice creditors in receiving payment of their debts. Dishonesty and intent to defraud can be found if the company obtained credit when there was no good reason for the directors to think that funds would become available to pay the debt when it became due or shortly thereafter. It is no longer necessary to prove that the directors knew at the time at which the debts were incurred that there was no reasonable prospect of the creditors ever receiving payment of their debts.[19] A single transaction may amount to carrying on

---

[18] See *Rossleigh* v. *Carlaw*, 1986 S.L.T. 204.
[19] *R.* v. *Grantham* [1984] 2 W.L.R. 815.

business.[20] Where a company is in financial difficulties and is accepting money in advance for goods and services the "proper and honourable" thing for the company to do is to pay the money into a separate trust account as soon as doubts appear as to the company's ability to fulfil its future obligations.[21]

Section 214 of the Act (which operates without prejudice to section 213) empowers the court to declare a person who is or has been a director of a company to be liable to make a contribution to the company's assets where the company has gone into insolvent liquidation and at some time in the past when he was a director that person knew or ought to have concluded that there was no reasonable prospect of the company avoiding insolvent liquidation (s. 214(1) and (2)). He can however avoid such a declaration being made (assuming the other circumstances apply) if he satisfies the court that he took every step with a view to minimising the potential loss to the company's creditors he ought to have taken (s. 214(3)). The action required to be taken by a director in these matters is the action which ought to have been taken by a reasonably diligent person having both the general knowledge, skill and experience reasonably to be expected of a person carrying out the same functions in relation to the company and the general knowledge, skill and experience that he in fact has (s. 214(4)). Section 10 of the Company Directors (Disqualification) Act 1986 provides that a declaration under section 214 may be accompanied by a disqualification order under section 6 of that Act.

Disqualification of company directors

Section 6 of the Company Directors (Disqualification) Act 1986 provides that where the court is satisfied that a person is or has been a director of an insolvent company and that his conduct has made him unfit to be concerned in the management of a company, it must make a disqualification order against such a person. The period of disqualification must be not less than two years and the application for the order must be made within two years of the company becoming insolvent by the Secretary of State in the public interest (ss. 6(4) and 7(2)). A company becomes insolvent for the purposes of these sections when it goes into liquidation and its assets are insufficient to pay its debts and other liabilities; an administration order is made; or a receiver is appointed (under section 51 of the Insolvency Act 1986) (s. 6(2)). "Director" includes a shadow director within the meaning of section 741(2) of the Companies Act 1985 for the purposes of these sections and sections 8 and 9 of the Act and section 214 of the Insolvency Act 1986.[22] The matters to be referred to by the court in considering the application are those

---

[20] *Re Gerald Cooper Chemicals Ltd.* [1978] 2 All E.R. 49.

[21] *Re Kayford Ltd.* [1975] 1 All E.R. 604, *per* Megarry J. at p. 607.

[22] If a company implements recommendations made by its bank, the bank may be rendered a shadow director of the company if the directors were accustomed to act in accordance with its directions: *Re a Company No. 005009 of 1987* (1988) 4 B.C.C. 424.

mentioned in Schedule 1 to the Act and they include any breach of fiduciary duty by the director in relation to the company, the extent of his responsibility for the failure of the company to comply with the requirements of the Companies Act 1985 in relation to company records and, where the company has become insolvent, the extent of his responsibility for the causes of the insolvency and any failure to supply goods and services which have been paid for (in whole or in part) (s. 9(1)). A person involved in the management of a company in contravention of a disqualification order becomes personally liable for such debts of the company as are incurred at the time of his involvement (s. 15). Additionally, a person who was a director (or shadow director) of a company at any time in the period of 12 months prior to the company's insolvent liquidation may not for the next five years, except with the leave of the court or in such circumstances as may be prescribed, be a director or concerned in the management of any company or business which has the same or a similar name to any name which the company in liquidation had at any time in the same period (Insolvency Act 1986, s. 216(1) and (2)). A person who contravenes section 216 becomes personally liable for the relevant debts of the company (s. 217). Section 212 of the Insolvency Act 1986 provides a summary remedy against delinquent directors and others who have misapplied property of the company or been guilty of any breach of duty in relation to the company by empowering the court to compel repayment or compensation when an application is made to it for this purpose.

INDEX

273